Social Psychology
of Culture

PRINCIPLES OF SOCIAL PSYCHOLOGY

Series Editor

ARIE W. KRUGLANSKI, *University of Maryland at College Park*

Principles of Social Psychology is a new generation of social psychology textbooks, which aims to reflect the dynamic growth of the field, integrating diverse disciplinary perspectives on an increasingly global scale. The basic commitment of the series is twofold: to articulate the principles and explanatory mechanisms underlying a variety of social behavior; and to relate them to real-world phenomena and concerns. Therefore, the emphasis is on broad principles and dynamic processes that synthesize large bodies of empirical research, rather than on descriptive reviews of such research.

Each volume in the series will demonstrate the explanatory power of social psychology as a discipline. It will intellectually stimulate students by delving beyond the surface to identify underlying mechanisms of individual and social behavior, and relating them to genuine problems and issues besetting contemporary society. This series provides an opportunity to engage in the broader societal dialogue about social psychological issues—thereby taking its message beyond the laboratory and into the real world.

Published

Social Psychology of Culture, Chiu & Hong

Forthcoming

Psychology of Emotion, Niedenthal, Krauth-Gruber, & Ric

Principles of Attitudes and Persuasion, Albarracin

Conflict and Negotiation, De Dreu

Social Psychology of Culture

*Chi-Yue CHIU and
Ying-Yi HONG*

Routledge
Taylor & Francis Group
New York   London

Published in 2006 by Psychology Press

This edition published 2013 by Routledge

Routledge   Routledge
Taylor & Francis Group   Taylor & Francis Group
711 Third Avenue   27 Church Road, Hove
New York, NY 10017   East Sussex BN3 2FA

●●●●●●●●●●●●●●●●●●●●●●●●●●● ●●●●●●●● ●●●●●●●●●●●●●●●● ●●

Typeset by Macmillan India, Bangalore, India

Library of Congress Cataloging-in-Publication Data
      Chiu, Chi-yue, 1963–
      Social psychology of culture / Chi-yue Chiu & Ying-yi Hong.
              p. cm. – (Principles of social psychology)
      Includes bibliographical references and index.
      ISBN-13: 978-1-84169-085-8 (hardcover : alk. paper)
      ISBN-10: 1-84169-085-6 (hardcover : alk. paper)
      ISBN-13: 978-1-84169-086-5 (pbk. : alk. paper)
      ISBN-10: 1-84169-086-4 (pbk. : alk. paper) 1. Social psychology. 2. Culture. I. Hong, Ying-yi, 1964– II. Title. III. Series.
      HM1033.C55 2006
      306.01–dc22   2006001229

ISBN13: 978-1-84169-085-8 (hbk)
ISBN13: 978-1-84169-086-5 (pbk)

ISBN10: 1-84169-085-6 (hbk)
ISBN10: 1-84169-086-4 (pbk)

Dedication

To Harry Triandis, Richard Nisbett, Hazel Markus, and Shinobu Kitayama, four living icons of the social psychology of culture.

Harry Triandis

Richard Nisbett

Hazel Markus

Shinobu Kitayama

Contents

About the Authors

Chi-yue CHIU is Professor of Psychology at the University of Illinois, Urbana-Champaign. He received his Ph.D. from Columbia University (New York) in 1994. He had taught in the Department of Psychology at the University of Hong Kong for eight years before he moved to the University of Illinois in 2002. His current research projects focus on the social psychology of culture, group processes, and language and cognition.

Ying-yi HONG is Professor of Psychology at the University of Illinois, Urbana-Champaign. She received her Ph.D. from Columbia University in 1994 and taught at the Hong Kong University of Science and Technology from 1994 to 2002. She received the Otto Klineberg Intercultural and International Relations Award in 2001, and the Young Investigator Award (conferred by the International Society of Self and Identity) in 2004. Her main research interests include culture and cognition, and self and identity.

Preface

Social psychology of culture is a rapidly expanding research enterprise. This field would not exist but for the contributions of Harry Triandis, Richard Nisbett, Hazel Markus, and Shinobu Kitayama. Their works have inspired much of the research reviewed in this book. It is our greatest pleasure and honor to be able to dedicate this book to these four living icons of psychology and culture.

The study of psychology and culture is a truly international enterprise; its major contributors come from different countries and from different ethnic backgrounds. Their research presents colorful pictures of the ethos of their cultural heritage, and gives voices to diverse populations across the globe. The biographical sketches featured in this book highlight the cultural diversity of researchers in the field. They also illustrate how a researcher's cultural experiences could importantly transform their views of human individuality and sociality, and bring insightful theoretical perspectives to the field. We are indebted to the generous contributions from Verónica Benet-Martínez, Donnel Briley, Dov Cohen, Michele Gelfand, Emi Kashima, Yoshi Kashima, Jenny Kurman, Loraine Lau-Gesk, Darrin Lehman, Kwok Leung, Taka Masuda, Rudy Mendoza-Denton, Peggy Miller, Michael Morris, Ara Norenzayan, Daphna Oyserman, Sharon Shavitt, Mark Suh, Toshio Yamagishi, Kuang-Hui Yeh, and Ying Zhu. These contributions add luster to our book.

With the presence of diverse and sometimes conflicting perspectives, it is a challenge to find a way to present a coherent and convincing story of culture, mind, and behaviors to our readers. We seek to construct a narrative that reflects the complexity and excitement of the field, and at the same time tells the stories of how individuals situated in an increasingly globalized world are socialized into various cultural heritages, express these heritages in their thoughts, feelings, and behaviors, and use these heritages as behavioral guides and materials for constructing cultural identities. Our theoretical perspective has the dynamic flavor of the works of our mentors at Columbia University. We are proud to be the intellectual descendants of Carol Dweck, Robert Krauss, Tory Higgins, and Walter Mischel, but we take full responsibility for the injustice our unpolished ideas might have done to the richness and sophistication of our mentors' theoretical systems.

We hope this book will inspire researchers in the field to expand the research agenda in the social psychology of culture. Much research in the field has focused on cultural differences in thoughts, feelings, and behaviors. Cross-cultural comparisons have increased our awareness of the cultural relativity of thoughts and behaviors. Yet, no psychological accounts of culture and no cultural accounts of psychology are complete without a complementary analysis of cultural processes. The expanded agenda advocated in this book includes new items such as evolutionary, social, and psychological functions of culture, how individuals apply cultural knowledge in concrete situations, how cultures are reproduced and transformed, how cultures interact, and how individuals negotiate cultural identities in multicultural contexts.

We are fortunate to be participating members in this field. As our research proceeds, we gain a better understanding of the intricate relations of society, culture, and psychology. Many ideas presented in this book are original and represent our current understanding of the cultural nature of psychology and the psychological aspects of culture. Some of these ideas originated in our collaborations with David Ho, Eric Knowles, Ivy Yee-man Lau, Veronica Benet-Martinez, Tanya Menon, and Michael Morris. A discussion with Robert Wyer inspired the development of the knowledge perspective presented in the second part of the book, and he deserves full credit for this innovative framework.

Finally, we would like to acknowledge the contributions of our former and current students for leading the way in the intellectual explorations presented in this book. They are Melody Chao, Jing (Julie) Chen, Ho-ying (Jeanne) Fu, Wai-man (Grace) Ip, Sau-lai Lee, Ka-yee (Angela) Leung, Qiong Li, Sun No, Kim-pong (Kevin) Tam, Vivienne Tao, Yuk-yue (Jennifer) Tong, Ching (Catherine) Wan, and Rosanna Y. Wong.

Chi-yue Chiu
Ying-yi Hong

What Is Culture? 1

Culture in the News

At about 11:20 a.m. on Tuesday April 20, 1999, two boys named Eric Harris and Dylan Klebold armed themselves with guns and homemade bombs. The boys entered Columbine High School in Littleton, Colorado. In the next few minutes, they killed 13 people and wounded at least 24 others, before turning their weapons on themselves. Later, it was discovered that these boys were fond of violent video games.

In response to the Colorado school massacre, Hillary Rodham Clinton, the First Lady of the time, said, "When our culture romanticizes and glorifies violence on TV, in the movies, on the Internet, in songs, and where there are video games that you win based on how many people you kill, our children become desensitized to violence and lose their empathy for fellow human beings."

On the other side of the political fence, Republican leaders also called for a national dialogue on youth culture to inform the nation about modern culture and its impact on youth (*Boston Herald*, April 28, 1999).

Both Democrats and Republicans viewed youth culture, the culture of video games, or the culture of violence as the first cause of the Colorado shootings.

*****

On December 2, 2001, energy giant Enron, which had grown into one of the United States' largest companies in just a little over 15 years, filed for bankruptcy protection in New York. This is the largest bankruptcy and one of the most shocking failures in American corporate history. Enron's rapid growth was based on artificially inflated profits and dubious accounting practices.

The *Wall Street Journal* ran an article on August 28, 2002 with this headline: "Enron executives created culture of stretching limits." According to this article, Enron's corporate culture is the prime mover of the company's success as well as its dramatic demise: "It was a characteristic gesture inside Enron, where the prevailing corporate culture was to push everything to the limits: business practices, laws, and personal behavior … This culture drove Enron to dizzying growth, as the company remade itself from a strong energy business to a futuristic trader and financier. Eventually it led Enron to collapse under the weight of mindbogglingly complex financial dodges" (p. C4).

*****

Edward Rothstein, a *New York Times* columnist, began his article entitled "In a word, culture means anything, bad as well as good" with the following observation on public discourse:

> What led to the horrendous behavior of the convicted policemen in the Abner Louima case? What caused the killings of high school students in Littleton, Colo.? Why did welfare often fail to change the underclass into the working poor? Why has Microsoft been so ruthless? And why do so many American students perform so poorly on standardized tests?
>
> Culture.
>
> A culture of police conduct; a culture of racism; a culture of violence; a culture of video games; a culture of poverty; a culture of corporate aggression; a culture of permissiveness; a culture of capitalism; a culture of multiculturalism.
>
> (Rothstein, June 12, 1999, *New York Times*, p. B1)

To Rothstein, this roster suggests that on the one hand, the word *culture* has been denatured to the point of meaninglessness. On the other hand, culture has been invoked to explain almost every phenomenon in contemporary American societies. To him, culture appears to be at once everything and nothing. It is a villain at large, a con artist that must be subverted, unmasked, and contested.

In academic discussion, culture also appears to be an elusive concept that is given a tremendous amount of authority over people's acts and thoughts. *Culture* derives its original meaning from Latin: from *cultura*, which referred to the cultivation of the soil. In Latin, *cultura* also acquired a secondary meaning: cultivation of the soul (Barnard, 1968). In the Western history of ideas, the proliferation of meanings of *culture* has led a 20th century writer to complain that any attempt to encompass its meaning in words "is like trying to seize the air in the hand, when one finds that it is everywhere except within one's grasp" (Lowell, 1934, p. 115). In a classic review of the concept, anthropologists Kroeber and Kluckhohn (1952) brought more than 160 definitions to light.

In spite of the lack of consensus on the meaning of culture in the social sciences, researchers insist that culture has an enormous influence on almost every facet of people's life, ranging from personal tastes to manners, beliefs, values, worldviews, and actions. Indeed, Kroeber and Kluckhohn (1952) compared culture to the concepts of gravity in physics and disease in medicine.

For culture to be a useful explanatory construct in the behavioral sciences, we must first unveil its identity. For decades, anthropologists and psychologists have contested the meaning of culture. To grasp the meaning of this elusive concept, they have debated numerous definitional issues. Two of these issues are of primary concern in the present chapter. First, what does culture consist of? Second, what are the characteristics of culture? Intense discussions on these issues have helped to clarify the nature of culture. From different researchers' attempts to address these issues, the reader will begin to see the face of culture, or at least part of it, unmasked.

The Concept of Culture in Historical Context

Like other concepts in social sciences, the concept of *culture* has a history of its own. The term *culture* has different meanings in different intellectual traditions and in different historical periods. To situate the meaning of culture in historical contexts, before we consider any definition of culture, we will briefly review how *culture* was conceptualized in the writings of the early and contemporary anthropologists.

The English term *culture* came into use during the Age of Exploration and Colonization in the 15th century, when many countries of Western Europe began sending explorers around the world to look for new sources of wealth. As noted, *culture* is derived from the Latin word, *cultura*, which is connected to the practice of nurturing domesticated plants in gardens. In the 19th century, upper-class Europeans used the term *culture* to refer to the refined tastes, intellectual training, and mannerisms associated with the upper classes. During the same period, influenced by Charles Darwin's influential theory of biological evolution, British social philosopher Herbert Spencer proposed a theory of cultural evolution. According to Spencer, human societies developed over time, advancing toward perfection. Through the process of cultural evolution, stronger and more advanced races and civilizations replaced weaker races and societies. In the late 19th century, American anthropologist Lewis Henry Morgan posited that all aspects of culture (including family structure, marriage, kinship categories, forms of government, technology, strategies of food production) changed as societies evolved. In other words, various aspects of culture were tightly woven together and interrelated. Like his contemporaries, Morgan believed that Europeans were the biologically advanced people. The notion of cultural evolution had provided an intellectual justification for European nations' attempts to dominate the world through colonization. As Said (1991) observed, 19th century scholars considered the Orient as a vast region including most of Asia and the Middle East. The Orient was considered to be a cohesive whole, and a prototypic Oriental was depicted as feminine, weak, and yet strangely dangerous. The stereotypic image of the Oriental was liberally applied to justify European domination of the inferior races in the Middle East and the Far East.

In the early 20th century, American anthropologist Franz Boas revolutionized the study of culture by emphasizing the uniqueness of all cultures. According to Boas, the culture of any society must be understood as the result of the society's unique history, and not as a stage in the evolution of societies. At about the same time, French sociologist Emile Durkheim advanced a functional perspective. He emphasized the adaptive value of culture, and analyzed how elements of culture served to keep the society functioning. Between the 1930s and 1960s, some American anthropologists, including Alfred Kroeber, Julian Steward, Leslie White, and Marvin Harris, viewed culture as the result of human adaptation to the natural environment and changing technology. Their research focused on how ecological, economic, and technological factors shaped people's beliefs and thinking style.

Starting from the 1960s, students of culture shifted their attention away from the universal logic that underlies the development of human cultures.

Inspired by the work of American anthropologist Clifford Geertz and others, researchers turned their interest to ethnographic analysis of the way a human group assigns specific meanings to objects, behaviors, and emotions.[1]

In short, there are four major intellectual traditions in the study of culture: theories of cultural evolution, ecological theories, functional theories, and ethnographic theories. As these traditions evolve, they have undergone major changes. For example, the early ethnocentric bias is no longer evident in contemporary cultural evolution theories. It is not hard to discern the influence of these intellectual traditions in contemporary research. For example, Dov Cohen and his colleagues have examined how confronting the problem of self-protection in the lawless Old South fostered the development of a culture of honor, which shapes the development of legal institutions in the southern states of the United States, as well as the emotional and behavioral responses of American Southerners (Cohen, 1996, 1998; see Chapter 7). Richard Nisbett and his colleagues have demonstrated pronounced differences in the thinking style of East Asians and European Americans. Such differences, according to Nisbett (2003), are related to differences in the ecological environment in East Asia and North America (see Chapter 5).

Some psychologists have adopted a functional approach to culture. Their research has illustrated how culture may serve important evolutionary, cognitive, and social functions (Schaller & Crandall, 2004). Other psychologists have focused on how culture provides a shared frame of reference for making sense of reality (Markus & Kitayama, 1991). The perspective of culture as shared meanings or knowledge raises the question of how cultural knowledge is applied in specific contexts, an issue that has attracted tremendous research interest in the social psychology of culture.

Categories of Culture

One way to define culture is to determine what culture consists of. What constitutes culture depends on how culture is conceptualized. If culture develops from a human group's adaptive response to the natural environment, the economy, and technology, an important component of culture is the *material culture* (Harris, 1964). Material culture consists of all material

---

1. The discussion on the concept of culture in historical context is based on materials retrieved from the MSN Encarta Online Encyclopedia (http://encarta.msn.com/encyclopedia_761561730_2/Culture.html) on May 8, 2005.

artifacts produced by human beings, including strategies of food production, the economic system, and technology. If culture is developed to maintain basic social functions in a human group, the *social culture*, which consists of all social institutions and shared rules of social conduct, should be an important part of culture (Keesing, 1974). Finally, if culture is a system of meanings, it should consist of shared beliefs, values, and ideas, which give rise to a unique way of thinking about the world (Geertz, 1973; Goodenough, 1961; Schneider, 1968). This body of shared knowledge constitutes the *subjective culture* (see Figure 1.1).

Material Culture

Material culture includes among other things the methods by which people exchange and share goods or services, and technology. Contemporary capitalist societies have organized markets for almost every kind of commodities. People in smaller societies exchange goods through systems of barter and reciprocal sharing. Some cultures use fairly simple technologies for work. For example, horticultural groups use plant materials such as tree bark to make clothing. By comparison, much of the material culture in large modern societies consists of mass-produced industrial goods, such as home

(a)

(c)

(b)

FIGURE 1.1. Symbols of material culture (a), social culture (b), and symbolic culture (c) in traditional China: (a) Replicas of bronze vessels and other artifacts from ancient China; (b) Entrance to one of the three major colleges that prepared candidates for civil examinations; (c) A statue of Confucius, whose ideas have greatly influenced China's intellectual tradition.

entertainment systems and computers. In countries throughout Africa, many people build houses of sun-dried mud brick and thatch, whereas high-strength steel and glass furnish the giant skyscrapers in cosmopolitan urban cities in North America and Western Europe. The aspect of material culture that has received most research attention is the strategy of subsistence or the methods by which people in a society obtain and produce food.

Subsistence Strategy

Societies differ in the primary strategies of subsistence.[2] In most modern societies, *agriculture* is the major strategy of food production. Agriculture may take the form of small-scale peasant farming, plantation agriculture, and large-scale mechanized grain farming. People in industrial and commerce-based countries are generally familiar with large-scale food production made possible by expensive machinery, great quantities of chemical fertilizers and pesticides, and genetic engineering. In developing societies, beasts of burden (e.g., oxen or horses) instead of machines are used to do heavy labor. Agriculture is a cost-effective method of food production, which can produce quantities of food vast enough to release labor for non-food-producing activities. The surplus workers become specialists in other jobs, producing goods or providing services that other people need. These specialists settle in urban centers, which have become the heart of cultural innovations, the arts, and learning.

Agriculture is not the only strategy of subsistence in the world. The oldest human subsistence strategy is *foraging*. Before the introduction of agriculture around 10,000 years ago, all humans subsisted through foraging. Even today, some peoples in the tropical rain forests in Southeast Asia (e.g., the Penan hunter-gatherers of Borneo, East Malaysia) live as foragers or hunter-gatherers. They collect plants and hunt wild animals from the forests for subsistence. Some ecology anthropologists believe that these peoples have been subsisting in their forest habitats for millennia. Only recently have these peoples come into contact with sources of domesticated plants and animals (see Headland & Bailey, 1991).

Foragers live in groups of 25–30 individuals. Because of the small group size, interactions between people in a forager society are face-to-face. Because people have few possessions and the resources needed for daily living can be obtained from the environment, status distinction is not salient in forager societies.

---

2. The discussion on major strategies of subsistence is based on materials retrieved from Dennis O'Neil's website "Patterns of subsistence" (http://anthro.palomar.edu/subsistence/default.htm) on May 8, 2005.

Oftentimes, several families in a forager group are organized into a band, a relatively egalitarian social organization without central leadership. Most foragers live in camps, where food is consumed and important ceremonies are carried out. Through reciprocal food sharing, a common practice in a forager group, close social bonds are formed.

In Central and South America, Southeast Asia, and Africa, some human groups (e.g., the Yanomamo of South America, the Tsembaga of highland New Guinea) practice *horticulture* for subsistence. They work on small plots of land without draft animals, plows, or irrigation. They use simple tools to raise domesticated plants in a garden and tend to small, domesticated animals, such as pigs or chickens.

Horticulturists live in semipermanent settlements of between thirty and several hundred persons. Many horticulturists practice shifting cultivation. They prepare a field using the slash-and-burn method of gardening. This involves cutting down the natural vegetation of a field, burning the vegetation, using the potash as a fertilizer, and planting their crops in the burned area. A field remains in use until its soil nutrients are depleted. Then a new field is cleared and planted, and the old field is left fallow. During the fallow period, soil nutrients build up in the old field. Once the old field is fertile enough for cultivation, it is cleared and burned again. In horticultural societies, there is division of labor between men and women. Men are generally responsible for hunting, for tasks requiring much physical strength in the field, and for village business, such as negotiations with outside communities. Women are generally responsible for most agricultural work, domestic chores, and food preparation and distribution.

Another major subsistence strategy is *pastoralism*. Pastoralists rely on animal husbandry, the raising and breeding of animals such as horses, cattle, sheep, goats, and camels, to provide for their subsistence needs. Pastoralists live in areas such as semiarid plains that are not well suited for agriculture but are ideal for grazing. They migrate with their herds on the plains. Some pastoralists, like the Navajo in the North American Midwest and the Hottentots of southern Africa, follow the regular migratory patterns of their herd, usually between cool-summer and warm-winter grazing areas. Other pastoralists, like the Yukagir in northeastern Siberia, Scythians of southern Russia, the Mongols, and the Huns, just follow the irregular migratory patterns of their herd and do not move between fixed locations throughout the year.

Contrary to popular belief, pastoralists seldom kill their animals for food. Instead, animals are milked and a host of products are produced, including butter and cheese. Animals are killed mostly for ritual celebrations. On these occasions, meat is shared to solidify social bonds between pastoralists and to set up a pattern of reciprocity that ties the community together through mutual obligations.

The family is the primary group in a pastoralist society. A family is grouped together with other families into camps, based on ancestral lineage. Within the family, men make major decisions, own and care for the animals, and are responsible for agricultural production. Women take care of domestic duties such as child rearing, producing items used in the home, and other chores.

Aggression plays a large part in the lives of pastoralists. First, most pastoral groups rely heavily on the goods and services produced by farmers, merchants, and city dwellers. Conflict over such resources between the pastoral groups and the settled peoples can result in open hostility, raids, and warfare. Second, men in pastoral groups acquire prestige through bravery and military prowess. The braver a man can prove himself to be, the more prestige he will enjoy from his peers. Third, as we will elaborate later (in Chapter 7), men are expected to react with force to insults on themselves and their families in order to protect their honor and also that of their family (Cohen, 1996, 1998) (see Figure 1.2).

Social Culture

Social culture refers to the shared rules of social behaviors as well as formal and informal social institutions, such as family, marriage, and gender roles. Two examples of social culture are kinship terms and power distance.

Kinship Terms

The American kinship system is organized along three attributes: (1) female or male; (2) generations; and (3) lineal or colineal relation. For example, *father* is a man of the older generation from the direct family line (of lineal relation), and *niece* is a female of the younger generation from the collateral family line (of colineal relation). Other American kinship terms such as *mother* (female, older generation, lineal), *brother* (male, same generation,

FIGURE 1.2. Natural physical constraints of a region determine the dominant subsistence strategy there. However, technological advances may overcome these physical constraints. The construction of the Hoover Dam has created many acres of arable land, and Las Vegas, a major tourist city in the US, was built with modern technology in the middle of a desert.

lineal), *aunt* (female, older generation, colineal), and *cousin* (male or female, same generation, colineal) can be organized into one of the categories formed by crossing the three attributes. Americans have the same kinship terms for relatives from the mother's side (the matrilineal line) and those from the father's side (the patrilineal line). For example, the mother's brother and the father's brother are both referred to as *uncle*.

Not all cultures organize kinship terms in the same way. In some societies, different kinship terms are used to distinguish relatives from the male line and those from the female line. For example, in some peasant villages in Turkey, father (*baba*), father's brother (*emme*), and mother's brother (*dayi*) each get a separate term, and so is the case for mother (*anne*), mother's sister (*hala*), and father's sister (*amme*). In addition, there are four kinship terms for cousins, which refer to children of father's brother (*emme usaki*), children of mother's brother (*dayi usaki*), children of father's sister (*amme usaki*), and children of mother's sister (*amme usaki*), respectively.

In these societies, there is often a tradition of patrilocal practices. After marriage, the wife goes to live with the husband's family. In Turkish peasant villages, married women are placed under the authority of their mothers-in-law. They are generally confined to the inner room and not allowed to see men other than those of the household. The centrality of patrilineal ties in the village serves to justify the unequal distribution of power between men and women in the household. Although daughters have inheritance rights under Turkish law and Islamic traditions, in the villages, most property passes from the father to the sons along a patrilineal line. When the head of the household dies, his land and other property is divided equally among the sons.

In Turkish peasant villages, the patrilineages are the primary units of collective organization. Domestic units with the same patrilineal ancestor are organized into larger social units, called *kabile*. Households in the same *kabile* are usually located close to one another. Patrilineal ties, reinforced by neighborly contacts, make the *kabile* the center of collective activities (Schwimmer, 1995–2003).

Power Distance

In every society, some categories of people (e.g., boss, parents, teachers) enjoy higher social status than other categories of people (e.g., employees, children, students). There are shared rules that regulate the interactions between the high status groups and the low status groups in the society. Geert Hofstede (2001) has conducted extensive surveys of power relations in 50 countries and 3 regions. In some countries, such as Malaysia, Mexico, and the Philippines, less powerful members of organizations tend to expect and accept unequal distribution of power in the organizations. According to Hofstede, these countries have relatively large *power distance*. By contrast, in countries like Austria, New Zealand, and Sweden, people expect and prefer more or less equal distribution of power in organizations and institutions. These countries have small power distance. Of the 50 countries and 3 regions included in Hofstede's cross-national survey, the United States ranks 38 on the power distance index, and has relatively small power distance.

The power distance of a country is very telling of the pattern of social interactions in the country. In countries with small power distance, people in all strata of the society have equal rights, and people value and respect individuality. In the workplace, power and authority are decentralized, and the salary range from top to bottom is narrow. The ideal boss is a resourceful democratic leader, who consults the subordinates before making major decisions. In the family, parents treat children as equals. In school, teachers are facilitators of learning and students are expected to initiate the learning activities.

In sharp contrast, in countries with large power distance, people in power enjoy many privileges, resources and wealth are not equally distributed, and people respect authority. In the workplace, power and authority are centralized, subordinates are expected to take orders, and there is a wide salary range from top to bottom. The ideal boss is a benevolent autocratic paternal figure who makes major decisions with the benefits of the subordinates in mind. In the family, children are expected to be obedient to and respect their parents. In school, teachers are regarded as experts and expected to take all the initiatives in class.

Subjective Culture

Subjective culture refers to the set of ideas or knowledge that is shared in a human group. It consists of widely held beliefs, cultural values, and shared behavioral scripts. Subjective culture provides individuals in the group with a shared way of thinking about the self and the world, or a common frame of reference for making sense of reality. Not every piece of knowledge in the group belongs to the group's subjective culture. Every member in a social group has some private, personal experiences that are not shared by others. Such autobiographical knowledge is not part of the group's subjective culture. For example, what you had for breakfast yesterday is unlikely to be part of the subjective culture in your group, because other members of your group do not have this knowledge. Some autobiographical information will be incorporated into the subjective culture if enough people in the group know about it. For example, the biography of Abraham Lincoln is widely known in North America, and so is that of Elvis Presley. Such biographical knowledge does not reside in the memory of a single individual. Instead, it lives in the collective memory of many Americans. As such, it is part of the American subjective culture.

When a piece of knowledge is widely distributed in a group, one or both of the following will happen. First, most people in the group will realize that this piece of knowledge is shared, because this piece of knowledge is frequently used in daily communication and widely represented in social institutions and practices. For example, most American people expect that the vast majority of Americans would know that human rights is the moral foundation of American democracy, because American people celebrate the triumph of human rights on many important occasions (e.g., Independence Day). In addition, the concept of human rights is carried in many American social practices, and is frequently mentioned in public discourse. When most people in the group know that other group members share a piece of knowledge, it becomes a *subjective norm* (Ajzen & Fishbein, 1980) or a social expectation.

In every society, subjective norms or social expectations play an important role in regulating social behaviors. For example, in the United States, most men know that beating their wife is a socially disapproved behavior. Due to the presence of this subjective norm, domestic violence against women in American families is not as prevalent as it is in some other societies. In India, beliefs about women's rights are not widely shared, and normative sanction against domestic violence against women is weak. According to a survey conducted by the International Institute for Population Studies, 56% of Indian women believed that wife beating is justified in certain circumstances. On February 19, 2001, the BBC reported that at least 20% of married women in India between the ages of 15 and 49 had been subjected to domestic violence, many of them on a continual basis. Every 6 hours somewhere in India a young married woman is burnt alive, beaten to death, or driven to commit suicide. The triggering events of wife beating varied from going out without the husband's permission, to neglecting the house or children, to cooking a bad meal (http://news.bbc.co.uk/2/hi/south_asia/1178714.stm).

Second, people may attach personal significance to knowledge that is widely shared in the group. They may subscribe to the shared beliefs, identify with the shared values, and willingly follow the socially approved course of actions. The process through which elements of the subjective culture are internalized is often referred to as *enculturation*. Some members of a society may identify with the internalized subjective culture. Some may believe that their culture is superior to other cultures. The belief in the superiority of one's own cultural group leads to a sense of cultural pride or *collective self-esteem*, but is also the root of *ethnocentrism*.

Ethnocentrism may arise when people use their own cultural experiences as an anchor to evaluate the elements of other cultures. When people use the manner in which other cultures are similar or dissimilar to their own culture as the basis for judging other cultures, they may see the elements of their own culture as normal, moral, and desirable, and the elements of cultures that differ from their own culture as abnormal, immoral, or undesirable. An example of ethnocentrism in American societies is known as American exceptionalism, or the belief that because American values are superior to other cultures' values, it is legitimate for America to impose American values on other cultures.

Once the subjective culture is internalized, it follows the individual. When people move from one society to another, they bring their internalized culture with them. If they move to a society with a culture very different from the one in their hometown, they may experience *culture shock*, the feelings of confusion and anxiety upon being exposed to an unfamiliar cultural environment (see Figure 1.3).

Religion and Secularism

Two examples of subjective culture are *religion* and *secularism*. In some countries, traditional religious beliefs are widely shared. People in these countries believe that God is important in life, and that religious training is important in child rearing. In other countries, secular beliefs are widely shared. People in these countries believe in science and logic. They have

(a)   (b)

FIGURE 1.3. A sidewalk food stall in a night market in downtown Beijing serving (a) deep-fried scorpions, and (b) other insects. Many American tourists are shocked when they see these items on the trays, though these Chinese delicacies are not in Chinese people's regular diet.

faith in their ability to control the natural world, foster economic growth, and make technological progress. In a large-scale international value survey, political scientists Ronald Inglehart and Wayne Baker (2000) found that adherence to traditional religion versus secularism distinguishes several major clusters of countries. The most religious countries are Latin American countries (e.g., Mexico), Muslim countries (e.g., Jordan), and sub-Saharan African countries (e.g., Tanzania), whereas countries with the strongest secular beliefs are the Confucian countries (e.g., Japan), Northern European countries (e.g., Sweden), and countries in the former Soviet bloc (Russia).

Individualism–Collectivism

Individualism and collectivism is the most heavily researched dimension of subjective culture in social psychology. The essence of individualism is the belief that the self is a self-contained independent entity (Markus & Kitayama, 1991). An individualist's self-identity is built on a set of stable and distinctive personal beliefs, attitudes, preferences, and values (Triandis, 1989). Personal goals are the primary drivers of an individualist's actions. Central to collectivism is the belief that the self is interdependent with some ingroup (e.g., family, clan, tribe). From the perspective of a collectivist, people's social roles and positions in the relational network define their self-identities (Trafimow, Triandis, & Goto, 1991; Triandis, McCusker, & Hui, 1990). There is more communal sharing of material and nonmaterial resources in collectivist societies. In social interactions, collectivists attend to the effects of one's own actions or decisions on others, other people's thoughts and feelings, others' views of the self, interpersonal duties, and role expectations (Hui & Triandis, 1986).

In Geert Hofstede's (2001) international surveys, Sweden, the Netherlands, and the United States were identified as individualist countries, whereas China, Japan, and West Africa were identified as collectivist countries. It is easy to recognize the differences that exist between individualist countries and those that exist between collectivist countries. For example, people in Sweden want to be self-reliant but do not wish to "stick out." By contrast, individual competition is emphasized in the United States (Triandis, 1995). While Japanese collectivism is characterized by a strong preference to work in groups, Chinese collectivism is characterized by a heavy emphasis on obligations to family members (Oyserman, Coon, & Kemmelmeier, 2002). As some researchers have pointed out, individualism refers to a constellation of beliefs and so does collectivism (Ho & Chiu, 1994), and both individualism and collectivism can take different forms in different societies (Triandis, 1995).

Integration

In summary, as represented in Figure 1.4, culture has several layers. In response to the ecology, human beings develop different subsistence strategies, technology, and other aspects of material culture. To coordinate social activities in collective living, various aspects of social culture are invented. Finally, aspects of subjective culture are constructed to give meanings to people's experiences in their collective life.

The material, social, and subjective strata of culture are interconnected. Some aspects of material culture may facilitate the development of certain aspects of social culture, which in turn reinforce certain aspects of subjective culture. For example, the practice of nonindustrial agriculture in Chinese rural villages (material culture) leads to the development of patrilineal family relations (social culture), which in turn reinforce the value of filial obligations, or obligations of the sons to the father and the grandfather (subjective culture, Yeh & Bedford, 2003, see Chapter 2).

In return, the subjective culture may legitimize and strengthen the social and material culture. For example, Protestant ethics and secularism fueled the development of capitalism in the Northern European states (Inglehart & Baker, 2000). The beliefs in liberty and human rights form the ideological foundation of American political institutions. In summary, the material, social, and subjective components of cultures are interconnected. To understand a culture, it is necessary to study all three components, and to understand how they interact with each other (Markus & Kitayama, 1994; Triandis, 1980).

The Holy Cow

The special status of the cow in India provides a good illustration of the interconnectedness of material, social, and subjective culture. Traveling on Indian roads, it is not uncommon to find cows hanging around on busy roads, and herds at traffic lights. For these serene creatures, the exhaust

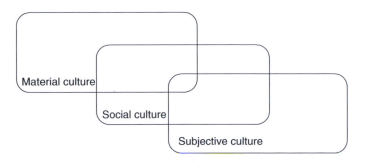

Material culture

Social culture

Subjective culture

FIGURE 1.4. Overlapping layers of culture.

fumes from the motor vehicles discourage flies, while the toxic fumes get them high. Thus, cows have good reasons to wander on busy roads. However, why are they let loose to begin with? In India, all animals are sacred, but why is the cow holier than other animals?

In India's ancient economy, when money had not come into vogue in the countryside, the number of cows a family possessed was the major measure of wealth. Cows became the legal tender, and were proudly presented as dowry at weddings. In addition, cow's milk was the main source of nourishment, and cow dung was converted into fuels. Thus, the cow, with its special roles in ancient Indian material culture, earned its holy status.

The holy cow was made holier with thousands of tales in Indian mythology (an element of symbolic culture) extolling the importance of the cow. For example, one tale describes how the gods rewarded a barren king with a son, because the king took care of a cow and risked his life to save it from a tiger. Social customs (an element of social culture) were evolved to protect the cow's special status. In the Hindu tradition, when a cow dies in an Indian home, the homeowner has to undertake a pilgrimage to all the holy cities of India to atone for the sin. Therefore, instead of letting their aging or sickened cow die in their house and then be hassled by the redemption customs, letting it loose on the streets is deemed an agreeable and economical option. Once the cows are out on the streets, they hardly starve, as every time a meal is cooked in a Hindu household, the first *roti* (unleavened bread) is reserved for a cow (Chopra, 2000).

Definition of Culture

Having a definition is useful for organizing the extant literature and guiding research practices in a discipline. However, culture is complex, dynamic, and fluid. No single definition of culture can fully capture the richness of the concept. In addition, a definition of culture that is most useful to a social psychologist may not be as useful to other social scientists. The definition of culture we propose in this section should therefore be treated as a hypothetical construct we developed to organize the extant research literature and research practices in the social psychology of culture (see Braumann, 1999; Rohner, 1984).

We begin the construction of a definition of culture by considering a set of generalizations that have emerged in the foregoing discussion. First, culture is a collective phenomenon. It consists of a set of shared meanings, which provides a common frame of reference for a human group to make sense of reality, coordinate their activities in collective living, and adapt to the external environment (C. Chiu & Chen, 2004; Hong & Chiu, 2001; Y. Kashima, 2000a; Shore, 1996, 2002; Sperber, 1996, see Chapter 4). Shared knowledge gives rise to shared meanings, which are carried in the shared physical environment (such as the spatial layout of a rural village, the subsistence economy), social institutions (e.g., schools, family, the workplace), social practices (e.g., division of labor), the language, conversation scripts, and other media (e.g., religious scriptures, cultural icons, folklores, idioms). Indeed, the research literature is richly furnished with excellent illustrations of how cultural knowledge is instantiated in a variety of media, including popular songs (Rothbaum & Tsang, 1998; Rothbaum & Xu, 1995), language (E. Kashima & Kashima, 1998; Y. Kashima & Kashima, 2003), news media (Hallahan, Lee, & Herzog, 1997; F. Lee, Hallahan, & Herzog, 1996; T. Menon, Morris, Chiu, & Hong, 1999; Morris & Peng, 1994), proverbs (Ho & Chiu, 1994), advertisements (Han & Shavitt, 1994; H. Kim & Markus, 1999), consumption symbols (Aaker, Benet-Martinez, & Garolera, 2001), and law and social policies (Cohen, 1996). These media are external carriers of culture. Instantiation of cultural meanings in external media is a necessary condition for transmission of culture; it ensures that shared meanings in the culture can be transmitted effectively to other people and to the newer generations.

Meet the Researcher: Yoshi Kashima

"In this globalizing world today, we now have the unprecedented opportunity to imagine the whole world as one community with great diversity, and yet at the same time, face a potentially devastating risk of divided humanity. A challenging, and fascinating, question is how we can steer ourselves in this treacherous water and pass our traditions on to the next generation."

Yoshi Kashima is an Associate Professor at the University of Melbourne, Australia. After completing a law degree at the University of Tokyo, he went to the University of California, Santa Cruz, for his B.A. in psychology, and completed his Ph.D. at the University of Illinois, Urbana-Champaign. He taught at the University of Queensland and La Trobe University, both in Australia, before he moved to the current position.

Second, every individual in a human group has acquired *a portion of* the shared knowledge, but no single individual in the group has the command of all shared knowledge in the culture (Y. Kashima, 2000a; Keesing, 1974).

Individuals apply the packet of cultural knowledge at their disposal to organize their experiences and to guide their life practices. A major research goal in social psychology is to explain the mental and social life of an individual in the cultural context. Achieving this goal entails identification of the knowledge that is widely shared in a human group. It also entails description of how individuals in the group mentally represent cultural knowledge, how they react to such knowledge emotionally and behaviorally, how they apply cultural knowledge, and how they transmit cultural knowledge to other group members. Based on these generalizations, we define culture as a network of shared knowledge that is produced, distributed, and reproduced among a collection of interconnected individuals (see Keesing, 1974; Rohner, 1984). We will discuss the components of this definition presently.

Shared Knowledge

As mentioned, cultural knowledge is *shared* knowledge, and not personal knowledge. Cultural knowledge is broadly represented in various external carriers of culture. In its broadest sense, knowledge includes learned habits of thinking, feeling, and interacting with people. As anthropologist F. Barth (2002) puts it, knowledge includes "all the ways of understanding that we use to make up our experienced, grasped reality" (p. 1). Although our definition of culture seems to focus on knowledge, cultural knowledge encompasses all shared behavioral expectations, and behavioral scripts, and is therefore intimately related to behaviors.

Network of Shared Knowledge

Culture consists of a coalescence of loosely organized shared knowledge. Some ideas in a culture are integrated coherently, while others are only loosely connected to each other (C. Chiu & Chen, 2004; Gabora, 1997). Disparate systems of beliefs can be found in the same society. For example, in many countries, economic development has led to increased popularity of secular values (the belief in progress, science, and logic). However, these secular values do not replace the broad traditional heritage of these societies. The influence of Protestantism is still strong in Northern Europe (Inglehart & Baker, 2000), as is the influence of Confucianism in some East Asian countries (K. Yang, 2003).

Production of Shared Meanings

People are not passive recipients of cultural influence. They are active agents who strive to adapt to their physical environment, and to live a productive and a harmonious life with other members in their group. To achieve these goals, they collaborate with other members in their group to create culture. In this sense, culture is both a product and a signature of human agency. An important research goal in the social psychology of culture is to understand how individuals in a human group collaborate to construct and perpetuate a shared reality.

Distribution of Shared Meanings

As mentioned, every individual has some, but probably nobody has perfect, knowledge of his or her culture. In addition, some knowledge is more widely shared in a society than is other knowledge. For example, almost every American knows that the national capital of the United States is Washington, DC. Few Americans know the first enclosed shopping mall in the United States was built in Edina, Minnesota.

The fact that at least some cultural knowledge is not perfectly shared in a society leaves room for *cultural diversity* within the group. This is an important point because in contemporary psychological studies of culture, the term *culture* is often used synonymously with a demarcated population (e.g., the Japanese, the Koreans; Friedman, 1994). In this usage, American culture refers to what Americans believe in, what they value, and how they behave, and Japanese culture is what Japanese people think, feel, and do. This practice has raised serious concerns in both anthropology and psychology. Critics are concerned that the practice of equating culture with a demarcated population may lead researchers to become insensitive to cultural diversity within the population. For example, in anthropology, Appadurai (1996) maintains that the concept of culture as a demarcated group "appears to privilege the sort of sharing, agreeing, and bounding that fly in the face of the facts of unequal knowledge and the differential prestige of lifestyles, and to discourage attention to the worldviews and agency of those who are marginalized or dominated" (p. 12). In psychology, Bandura (2002) insists, "cultures are diverse and dynamic social systems not static monoliths" (p. 275).

Treating culture synonymously with a demarcated population also reinforces the tendency to attribute global cultural traits or essences to a demarcated population. For example, Japanese are often described in psychological research as being interdependent or collectivist. This broad generalization may lead to the erroneous perception that all Japanese are interdependent or collectivist, and that Japanese think and behave in an interdependent or collectivist manner in all situations (Gjerde & Onishi, 2000). Such perceptions tend to reinforce national stereotypes. As Friedman (1994) points out, "Where difference can be attributed to demarcated populations we have culture or cultures. From here it is easy enough to convert difference into essence" (p. 207).

Our definition of culture acknowledges the fact that certain knowledge is more widely distributed in some populations than in other populations. For example, ideas that constitute collectivism are more widely shared among Japanese than among European Americans, and also more extensively represented in Japanese institutions, public media and practices than in American ones. However, we also acknowledge that some Japanese are less collectivist than others, and that in Japan, collectivism is more widely distributed in some domains than in others (Oyserman et al., 2002). Furthermore, a Japanese individual who applies collectivist ideas to guide their actions in a particular situation may not do so when the situation changes (Takano & Osaka, 1999, see Chapter 2).

Reproduction of Shared Meanings

Culture is to society what memory is to individuals (Kluckhohn, 1954). Culture consists of what people believe has worked well and is worth transmitting to the next generation. Through intergenerational transmission, culture is reproduced.

Some cultural ideas have been reproduced successfully through numerous generations. For example, the democratic values in contemporary American societies were passed down from the country's founding fathers. In Christian countries, children of many generations have read similar stories from the Testaments. In the West, Socrates' (469–399 BC) ideas have had a huge impact throughout the history of Western thought. In the Far East, the ideas of Confucius, who lived in China in 551–479 BC, continue to have important influence in many East Asian countries.

Culture is reproduced, but not always faithfully. Some cultural ideas are transformed as they are reproduced. For example, although the God in both the Testaments is the same God, God has the image of a punitive disciplinarian in the Old Testament, and the image of a forgiving guardian in the New Testament. Sometimes, several cultural ideas are merged when they are reproduced. Confucianism in the Han Dynasty (202 BC–AD 220) was a fusion of Confucius' ideas with those of the legalists. Confucianism in the Ming Dynasty (AD 1368–1644) was a fusion of Confucius' teachings with Taoism and Buddhism. Some elements of culture change quickly (e.g., means of electronic communication, such as electronic mails, electronic chat-rooms), but other elements do not change for a long time (e.g., writing from left to right). However, most cultural ideas and practices will change and evolve when there is a drastic change in the mode of economic production, technology, and social–political environment.

Changes may involve elaboration and proliferation of an idea or practice, or displacement of it. For example, in the 11th century, there was a revival of long-distance trade in Europe. When professional merchants halted their journeys, they congregated in crude trading communities, which soon grew into bustling towns. To facilitate exchange of commodities, professional merchants organized annual international fairs in France's Champagne region. With the rise of capitalism in Europe, international fairs spread to other parts of the continent, and became highly elaborate (Fremantle, 1965). In May 1851, London hosted the Great Exhibition at the Crystal Palace in Hyde Park. The Great Exhibition was designed to display industrial products of all nations. The opening ceremony was attended by the Royal Family, the Archbishop of Canterbury, and a vast assemblage of British and foreign dignitaries (Burchell, 1966).

In contrast, other practices that also emerged in 11th century France were displaced. As long-distance traders banded together in caravans to assure their safety en route, merchant guilds evolved. Soon, merchant guilds began to dominate and regulate the commerce in trading towns. To ensure equal opportunity for all members, the guild forbade a member to keep longer trading hours than other members, employ more apprentices, or pay better wages. The guild also prohibited its members to charge more than others for the same goods or service, or engage in usury. These practices went against the growing capitalist spirit and were gradually abandoned in Europe (Fremantle, 1965).

Culture change also occurs when economic, technological, and political changes bring ideas from different cultures into contact. Colonialism in the 19th century had brought European cultures to over 80% of the land outside Europe, and globalization in recent decades has increased both the scope and the intensity of intercultural contacts (see Chapter 11).

A Collection of Interconnected Individuals

Lincoln's concept of government applies equally well to culture. By its nature, culture is of people, for people, and by people. To begin with, culture emerges in social life and gives meanings to social life. Sometimes consciously and often not, people collaborate to produce, maintain, and reproduce culture. They do so to ensure that as a collective, the group can adapt to the environment and lead a harmonious and productive social life. Culture does not exist without people. However, the mere presence of individuals is not enough to create culture. Culture emerges because there is a need to coordinate the activities of interdependent individuals. Interdependence in human societies is a *sine qua non* for culture. As such, culture is a social psychological phenomenon.

Organization of the Book

We begin this chapter with a quote from *New York Times* columnist Edward Rothstein. As Rothstein pointed out, *culture* has been applied to "explain" a wide range of phenomena in human societies *after the fact*. Because *culture* is an elusive concept in much of everyday usage, *culture* seems to explain everything and nothing. To render culture a useful scientific construct, social scientists need to give it some specific meanings.

In the current chapter, we offer a working definition of culture. According to this definition, culture consists of a loosely organized network of knowledge produced and reproduced by a collection of interdependent people (Braumann, 1999). Some researchers are interested in identifying the specific knowledge shared by people in a particular population. Some researchers are interested in identifying the similarities and differences between major world cultures. Both groups of researchers are interested in the *contents* or *substance* of culture. Other researchers are interested in culture as a *process*. They are interested in the reciprocal influence of culture and psychology. Some researchers have studied how people produce and reproduce culture. Some have examined how culture influences the way people think, feel, and act. Finally, some researchers are interested in the interactions of different cultures, and the psychological implications of such interactions. Depending on their research focus, researchers may adopt different analytical and methodological strategies in their research. In Chapter 2, we will review two major strategies that have been employed to *describe* different aspects of culture. In the remaining chapters of the book, we will examine the different approaches that have been proposed to *explain* culture.

As mentioned, culture grows out of the need to coordinate the activities of interdependent individuals. Human beings lead a social life, as do many other animals. Yet, although other primates may possess some forms of culture, only human beings are capable of producing complex cultures (e.g., language, art, religion). What are the species-specific abilities that have supported the evolution of human cultures? If culture consists of shared knowledge, evolution of culture must be supported by species-specific abilities to learn, accumulate, share, and coordinate knowledge. In Chapter 3, we will discuss the biological and cognitive processes that support the evolution of culture.

We have emphasized the adaptive functions of culture. In Chapter 4, we will review how culture serves evolutionary functions, and how culture facilitates adaptation to the physical environment and coordination of social activities. We will also discuss how culture provides a frame of reference to make sense of the reality, a vehicle to manage existential terror, as well as symbolic materials for constructing self-identities.

As people apply culture to achieve their goals, their cognitions, feelings, and actions respond to the exigencies of culture. In Chapters 5–7, we will discuss cultural differences in different kinds of knowledge representations, and their associated psychological phenomena. If these three chapters give the impression that people are captive recipients of cultural influence, the subsequent chapters will correct this impression. In the subsequent chapters, we will describe how people organize and apply cultural knowledge to make sense of reality (Chapter 8), how they reproduce culture (Chapter 9), and how they use cultural knowledge as a resource to manage the changing demands of their cognitive and social environment (Chapter 10).

In Chapter 11, we shift our focus to intercultural psychology. We will discuss the psychological ramifications of colonization, political transition, migration, multiculturalism, and globalization. We will address the following questions: When cultures meet, how do people navigate between cultures? How do people negotiate their cultural identity in a multicultural environment?

Finally, in Chapter 12, we will discuss several conceptual and methodological issues in the social psychology of culture. Do universal principles of social behavior exist? Can they be compared directly? How can cultural processes be studied? Satisfactory resolution of these issues will foster the advancement of the field.

What is Social about Social Psychology of Culture?

To reveal the many facets of culture, we need to rely on research findings from disciplines outside social psychology. However, our theoretical approach to culture is primarily social psychological. We treat culture as a set of social psychological processes, and our goal is to understand the mental and social life of an individual in a cultural context. It is important to emphasize that we do *not* intend to show that cultural processes are just like other psychological processes social psychologists study. Instead, we believe that studying culture from a social psychological point of view can offer valuable materials for reflection, and a refreshing perspective for constructing a social psychological discourse. Carlson (1984) has challenged social psychologists to answer the following hard question: What is social about social psychology? Indeed, American social psychology has been criticized for its methodological individualism, or the belief that all social phenomena, including functioning of all social institutions, should be understood in terms of individual psychology (Popper, 1966). Some critics (e.g., Sampson, 1977) even suggested that American social psychology is just an expression of American individualism.

G. H. Mead (1934/1962) believed that the goal of social psychology is "to explain the conduct of the individual in terms of the organized conduct of the social group, rather than to account for the organized conduct of the social group in terms of the separate individuals belonging to it" (p. 7; see also Bruner, 1990; Moscovici, 1988; Vygotsky, 1978). Focusing on collective processes at the expense of individual processes may compromise the prospect of achieving thorough understanding of the psychology of individuals-in-society. Nonetheless, Mead's emphasis on holistic social psychology is a good reminder of the need to correct the biases ensuing from methodological individualism in American social psychology (C. Chiu & Chen, 2004).

To answer Carlson's hard question, we believe that the cultural dimension is what makes human cognition and action social. Culture exists in the mind of the individual. However, what matters most in the social psychology of culture is the individual's representation of shared meanings, and of the generalized others in the culture (Ho & Chiu, 1998). Culture is also a collective phenomenon. Studying the reciprocal influence of culture and psychology is a step toward reaching the goal George Herbert Mead set for social psychologists. In short, we envision that a social psychology of culture will provide a model for constructing social psychological theories of human cognition and action that are both culturally sensitive and culturally relevant.

Strategies for Describing Culture  2

Culture in the News ... and Fairy Tales

Here is the well-known Cinderella story ...

Once upon a time in Europe, a baby girl, who would be known to the world simply as Cinderella, was born. Cinderella's mother passed away when she was little. Her father took for his second wife an evil and jealous woman. Young Cinderella grew up with her stepmother and two step-sisters, and with the vile household tasks her stepmother had given her. Her only friends were some little mice. Because the young girl sat by the cinders to warm herself every day, she was nicknamed "Cinderella."

One day, all the women in the land were invited to a grand ball at the palace. The stepsisters dressed up for the ball and left Cinderella at home, alone and in tears. However, Cinderella's fairy godmother appeared and turned Cinderella into a stunning beauty. With magic, a pumpkin was turned into a handsome coach, mice into prancing horses, and Cinderella's rags into an exquisite dress. Cinderella, glamorously dressed, put on a pair of glittering glass slippers the fairy gave her, entered and enchanted everybody in the ballroom. She danced all evening with the prince, and forgot the time and that the fairy's magic would be gone by midnight. When the clock struck 12, Cinderella left the palace in a rush, leaving one of her glass slippers on the steps. Next day, the Prince sent a messenger to find the lady who could fit into the glass slipper. None of the women in the land except Cinderella could fit into it. Cinderella took out the other glass slipper, and wore it. Then, her fairy godmother changed Cinderella's rags into a magnificent dress. Her marriage with the Prince turned our humble Cinderella into glamorous royalty. The royal couple lived happily ever after.

Now enters the glamorous Princess Diana, Cinderella of the modern time …

Once upon a time in England, a baby girl, who would be known to the world simply as Diana, was born to the family of Lord Althorp. When the little girl was 8, her parents were divorced. She lived with her father, her brother, and two sisters. Six years later, when Diana's father inherited the title of Earl Spencer from his own father, she became Lady Diana Spencer.

Young Lady Diana was recognized for her commitment to service. She nurtured young children in a kindergarten until her royal romance enchanted the world. When Diana was 20, Prince Charles, heir to the Royal Crown, asked for her hand. On their wedding day, when the royal couple exchanged their vows at St Paul's Cathedral, the fresh beauty and innocence of Princess Diana charmed the world. The glittering wedding turned a humble, shy, and unpretentious beauty into England's most glamorous royalty.

Before anybody could find the words to announce a live-happily-ever-after ending, this most spectacular royal romance in modern history began to disintegrate into a royal nightmare, until a fatal blow mercilessly dashed everything into pieces. The death of the ill-fated princess released an out-pouring of emotions worldwide, as the newsmakers had it in their stories.

Describing Cultural Variations

You have read the synopses of the two stories, one about a real person, Diana, and one about a fictitious character in a fairy tale, Cinderella. The similarities of the two stories are striking. Is Diana not Cinderella in real life? Most people do not know much of Diana's real life, and the public will never know some parts of it. The most widely circulated stories about Diana are the stories covered in the news and written in the tabloids. These stories, like the fairy tale of Cinderella, are cultural constructions. The Diana in these stories is the princess meant to be known and be remembered.

The resemblance of the image of Diana and that of Cinderella is not a coincidence. In fact, Diana's image was designed to resemble that of Cinderella. At Diana's death, CNN set up an interactive website for Diana (http://edition.cnn.com/WORLD/9708/diana/). In the website, the romance between Diana and Prince Charles is described as "the fairy tale romance," and the wedding as "a glittering storybook wedding," and "a fairy tale in the making." The breakup is characterized as a disintegrated "fairy tale union." In short, Cinderella's tale and Diana's story share a similar storyboard. Diana is meant to be a modern-day Cinderella.

Cinderella is a recurrent motif in many cultural representations. It is found in Billy Wilder's 1954 film *Sabrina*, in which Audrey Hepburn played the humble chauffeur's daughter Sabrina, who later turned into a glamorous lady and the wife of Linus, a millionaire played by Humphrey Bogart. Forty-one years later, *Sabrina* hit the big screen again, this time with Julia Ormond as Sabrina and Harrison Ford as Linus. The same Cinderella motif was found in Wayne Wang's 2002 movie, *Maid in Manhattan*. In the film, Marisa Ventura (Jennifer Lopez) was a struggling single mother who worked as chambermaid in a swanky Manhattan hotel. When senatorial candidate Christopher Marshall (Ralph Fiennes) mistook her for a wealthy socialite, an enchanting romance developed between them. Finally, the maid married the senatorial candidate.

The image of Diana has been constantly renewed. The image of a shy Lady Spencer has over the years been turned into a fairy tale princess, a glamorous modern royal, a trapped victim, and the queen of people's hearts. Even the image of Cinderella in the Western world is not static. The earlier Cinderella was self-reliant, devoted to family and ancestors, and willing to make her own future. Cinderella did not earn her reputation as a simpering, whimpering wishing-only kind of woman until the later twentieth century (Northrup, 2000).

Cinderella is also a universal story told in many ways around the world. There are more than 1500 versions of the Cinderella story that have been written in different countries and cultures. In a Russian retelling of the Cinderella story, after Vasilisa's father died, her stepmother and stepsisters mistreated her. She was sent to serve a witch. The witch gave Vasilisa a series of impossible tasks to perform. With the help of a magical doll, Vasilisa pleased the witch, who sent her home with a magical light. With it, Vasilisa destroyed her stepmother and stepsisters. Then, she came to live with an elderly woman, and learned to spin and weave. The tsar was impressed by an exquisite piece of cloth she made, and asked for her hand in marriage.

In a Jewish Cinderella tale, Raisel was a granddaughter of a learned scholar. After her grandfather died, Raisel moved from her Polish village to a large city, where she worked in the kitchen of a rabbi. At the night of the Purim ball, she fed an old woman who granted her three wishes in return for Raisel's kindness. Raisel attended the ball, told the rabbi's son a riddle, and won his heart.

Vasilisa is by no means a simpering and whimpering woman. She is brave and competent. She has a strong will, and is not somebody to be messed with. Unlike Vasilisa, Raisel is intellectual, witty, and kind to the poor. These different cultural images of Cinderella may reflect cultural differences in how woman's image is constructed and romanticized.

The Cinderella stories raise a number of fascinating research questions. Do differences in the way the Cinderella story is told around the world reflect cultural differences? If so, how can we describe and characterize these differences? Why has Cinderella become a universal phenomenon? How do we explain the emergence of the different cultural versions of the Cinderella story? How do we explain the evolution of the Cinderella story in a society?

The Cinderella phenomenon is just one of the many cultural phenomena that interest social psychologists. Social psychologists have taken different routes to describe and explain cultural phenomena. In the current chapter, we introduce two major social-psychological approaches to describing culture. Each descriptive approach holds a different view of culture. Although some proponents of each approach insist that their approach offers the most faithful representation of culture, we submit that the divergent images of culture taken from the two perspectives complement each other and form a more complete picture.

The Global Approach

Evidently, cultures differ, but how? Do cultures differ in degree or in kind? Should social psychologists try to understand a culture by comparing it to other cultures? Or should they seek understanding of a culture through studying how its attendant normative meanings are socially and historically constituted?

Social psychologists who believe that cultures differ in degree have attempted to identify basic dimensions of cultures, and to compare world cultures on these dimensions (see Ronen & Shenkar, 1985). These dimensions, often referred to as *pan-cultural dimensions*, are like latitudes and longitudes in geography. Together they form a coordinate system. World cultures can be described in terms of their positions in this coordinate system. In Chapter 1, we introduce the dimensions of power distance and individualism–collectivism. Both are pan-cultural dimensions identified in previous research (Hofstede, 1991; Triandis, 1995). Using latitudes and lon-gitudes, we can place Buenos Aires, Argentina at 34s36, 58w27, New York City at 40n43, 74w0, Singapore at 1n16, 103e51, Sydney, Australia at 33s52, 151e13, and Tokyo at 35n42, 139e46. The coordinate system formed by pan-cultural dimensions is less precise than the one formed by latitudes and lon-gitudes. Still, based on international survey data (Hofstede, 1980), researchers can place countries in the power distance (PDI)–individualism (IDV) coordinate system. For example, as illustrated in Figure 2.1, we can place Argentina at 49 PDI, 46IDV, Australia at 36PDI, 90IDV, Japan at 54 PDI, 46IDV, Singapore at 74PDI, 20IDV, and the United States at 40PDI, 91IDV. Knowing a country's latitude, it is possible to infer its meteorological char-acteristics. For example, based on the latitudes of the above five cities, Singapore, being close to the Equator, is expected to have warmer climate than the other four cities. Likewise, knowing a country's coordinates on the pan-cultural dimensions, it is possible to infer the country's cultural ten-dencies. Based on the five countries' positions on the power distance dimen-sion, it is reasonable to expect more uneven distribution of power and status in Singapore than in Australia and the United States. It is also reasonable to infer from Figure 2.1 that Australian and North American cultures are sim-ilar in terms of individualism and power distance, whereas Singaporean culture is different from Australian culture in these two respects.

This approach to describing cultures is often referred to as the *cross-cultural* or *etic* approach. Because the term *cross-cultural psychology* is some-times used liberally to refer to all comparative research of culture, to avoid

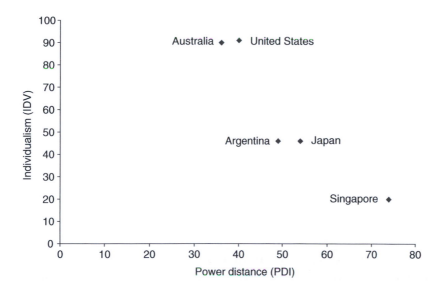

FIGURE 2.1. A cultural map of five nations.

confusion, we will not use this term here. The term etic is derived from *phonetics*, a branch of linguistics that involves scientific study of speech sounds. Etic refers to the use of preestablished categories or concepts for organizing and interpreting cultural data. In phonetics, sounds are transformed into sine waves, and preestablished parameters of the sine waves (e.g., amplitude, fundamental frequency) define the sounds. Researchers often pit the etic approach against the *emic* approach. Emic is derived from *phonemics*, another branch of linguistics that involves classification and analysis of the phonemes (the smallest units of speech sounds) of a language. Emic refers to the use of categories or concepts recognized within the culture being studied to interpret and organize data (U. Kim, Park, & Park, 2000; Sham, 2002; K. Yang, 2000). Both etic and emic have acquired mixed connotations in the literature. Because most etic categories (including individualism, power distance) are derived from concepts that originated in Western cultural traditions (e.g., Puritan Protestantism, individualism, male dominance, private property, and capitalism), the etic categories have been criticized for their Occidental biases (Gergen, Gulerce, Lock, & Misra, 1996; Hogan & Emler, 1978; Jahoda, 1979; Sampson, 1977, 1978). For example, some Asian researchers reject the use of etic categories to understand Asian behaviors because such etic categories tend to impose Western interpretations and their attendant values on Asian behaviors (K. Yang, 2000). On the other hand, the emic approach has been criticized for promoting intellectual provincialism and extreme cultural relativism, or the belief that all concepts, including what is good or bad, what is true or false, vary from culture to culture (see Ho, 1988, 1998; Triandis, 2000).

To avoid the mixed connotations attached to etic and emic, we will refer to the comparative approach described above as the *global* approach, as opposed to the *focal* approach we will discuss later. The word *global* captures the research objectives, methodology, and research findings in this approach. First, researchers who adopt this approach aim to measure and quantify cultures around the globe. Their goal is to construct a map of cultures, using the pan-cultural dimensions they identify in their international surveys. Second, to identify dimensions of cultures, researchers typically conduct surveys of values and beliefs throughout the world. They have respondents from tens of nations or regions who fill out the same value or belief survey. Next, for each nation or region, the mean of its respondents' responses to each survey item is computed, and a profile of values or beliefs is constructed. Using a variety of statistical scaling techniques, several common dimensions are derived. Finally, because the culture of each nation or region is summarized in terms of its positions on a handful of dimensions, only a global image of the culture with relatively low resolution is revealed.

The global approach has generated a great deal of excitement in the social psychology of culture. Because it allows researchers to measure and quantify cultures, it has elevated the scientific stature of cultural research. Research following this approach has generated useful data for constructing small-scale maps of cultures, as well as a high level of optimism that we can characterize major world cultures using a small set of cultural dimensions. However, this approach has a major limitation. The telescopic lens this approach uses to look at culture is not crafted for the purpose of revealing the fine texture of a culture.

Major Dimensions of Culture

The contributions of the global approach become obvious when we look at a few specific research examples. Between late 1973 and the end of 1978, Geert Hofstede collected survey data from 60,000 employees of the International Business Machines (IBM) Corporation in the US Headquarters and its subsidiaries in 65 countries (or regions). The survey consists of 32 items, measuring a wide range of work-related values. Relative to other countries, some countries had higher average scores on some items and lower average scores on others. When the country means were analyzed using factor analysis (a statistical technique), three major dimensions of culture emerged. These three dimensions explained about half of the cross-national variations in the responses to the 32 value items.

Countries with high scores on the first dimension (e.g., New Zealand, Denmark, USA) valued individualism (vs. collectivism) and a small (vs. large) power distance. Although countries adhering to individualism tended to prefer a small power distance, and countries adhering to collectivism tended to prefer a large power distance, Hofstede separated power distance from individualism–collectivism because they are conceptually distinct dimensions. Individualism–collectivism and power distance are two widely researched dimensions in psychology (see Chapter 1 for discussion on these dimensions).

Countries with higher scores on the second dimension (e.g., Japan, Austria, Venezuela) placed heavier emphasis on masculine (vs. feminine) values, such as recognition, challenge, and achievement. Finally, countries with higher scores on the third dimension (e.g., Greece, Portugal, Peru) had stronger preference for certainty (over uncertainty). They also had greater desire for clear company rules, precision, and punctuality.

Shalom Schwartz (1992, 1994; see also Schwartz & Bilsky, 1987) analyzed the relative importance of 56 values to respondents from 31 countries (regions), and found that these values can be organized into seven major clusters: conservatism, affective autonomy, intellectual autonomy, hierarchy, mastery, egalitarian commitment, and harmony. Figure 2.2 shows the five countries or regions with the highest scores on each cluster of values.

Inglehart (1997; Inglehart & Baker, 2000) analyzed the 1990–1993 World Survey data and derived two major dimensions of cultures. The sample in this data set consisted of 60,000 respondents from 43 countries. The first dimension is traditional authority vs. secular–rational authority. The traditional worldview upholds the importance of obedience to traditional authority (including religious authority), and adherence to family and communal obligations. In contrast, the secular–rational worldview emphasizes legitimate, rational–legal authority, economic accumulation, and individual achievement. The second dimension contrasts survival values (e.g., hard work, self-denial) with well-being values (e.g., quality of life, emancipation of women and sexual minorities, self-expression).

Dimension	Countries with highest scores on the dimension
Individualism	USA, Australia, Great Britain, Canada, Netherlands
Collectivism	Venezuela, Colombia, Pakistan, Peru, Taiwan
Large Power Distance	Philippines, Mexico, Venezuela, India, Singapore
Small Power Distance	Austria, Israel, Denmark, New Zealand, Israel
Masculinity	Japan, Austria, Venezuela, Italy, Switzerland
Femininity	Sweden, Norway, Netherlands, Denmark, Finland
Strong Uncertainty Avoidance	Greece, Portugal, Belgium, Japan, Peru
Weak Uncertainty Avoidance	Singapore, Denmark, Sweden, Hong Kong, Ireland
Conservatism	Malaysia, Bulgaria, Singapore, Poland, Taiwan
Affective Autonomy	France, Switzerland, Germany, Denmark, New Zealand
Intellectual Autonomy	Switzerland, France, Slovenia, Spain, Germany
Hierarchy	China, Thailand, Turkey, Zimbabwe, Bulgaria
Mastery	China, Zimbabwe, Greece, Malaysia, Mexico, USA
Egalitarian Commitment	Portugal, Italy, Spain, Denmark, France
Harmony	Slovenia, Mexico, Estonia, Finland, Spain
Traditional Authority	Nigeria, Brazil, South Africa, Chile, Northern Ireland
Secular–Rational Authority	China, Russia, East Germany, West Germany, Estonia
Survival Values	Russia, Bulgaria, Latvia, India, Lithuania
Well-Being Values	Sweden, Netherlands, Denmark, Finland, Norway
Dynamic Externality	Pakistan, Malaysia, Indonesia, Iran, Nigeria
Societal Cynicism	Pakistan, Georgia, Estonia, Thailand, Taiwan

FIGURE 2.2 Countries or regions with the highest scores on major cultural dimensions.

Hofstede, Schwartz, and Inglehart attempted to summarize cross-national variations in values with a handful of global value dimensions. However, culture consists of other symbolic elements as well. Recently, Kwok Leung and his colleagues (K. Leung & Bond, 2004; K. Leung et al., 2002) used beliefs instead of values to identify cultural dimensions. Respondents from 42 countries (regions) completed a 60-item survey, which covers a wide range of beliefs. From their data, Leung derived two major dimensions of cultures. *Dynamic externality,* the first dimension, consists of a constellation of beliefs, including reward for application, religiosity, fate control, and social complexity. Compared to other countries, countries with high scores on this dimension (e.g., Pakistan, Malaysia, Indonesia) place greater emphasis on effort, while at the same time they are more prepared to acknowledge the complexity of social life and the power of external forces (e.g., fate, supernatural forces). *Societal cynicism,* the second dimension, refers to a generalized negative view of human nature. Countries with high scores on this dimension (e.g., Pakistan, Georgia, Estonia) believe more strongly than other countries that human nature is easily corrupted by power and that social institutions cannot be trusted. These countries are also more likely to disregard ethical means for achieving an end.

Meet the Researcher: Kwok Leung

"My interest in culture was probably sparked by attending to a high school in Hong Kong that was modeled upon British public schools. I had a few Western teachers, and they seemed different from other Chinese teachers and people I knew. My personal experiences echo a well-known social psychological finding: Positive contact improves inter-cultural relations. Enthusiastic attitudes toward other cultures and a pluralistic view of the world are promoted by benign, pleasant intercultural contact that is free from the yoke of bigoted stereotypes. Unfortunately, the prerequisites for the positive effects of intercultural contact to emerge are hard to come by in real life, and many inter-cultural relations are anything but harmonious and satisfying. My belief is that cross-cultural psychological research is crucial to identifying processes and mechanisms that facilitate different cultures not only to co-exist peacefully, but also to work together synergistically to overcome severe challenges that threaten the entire human race."

Kwok Leung grew up in Hong Kong, and received his Ph.D. from the University of Illinois at Urbana-Champaign. He is Professor of Management at City University of Hong Kong.

The global approach offers a relatively parsimonious language to describe national cultures. For example, based on the data in Figure 2.2, compared to other national cultures, the national culture of Denmark is feminine, is committed to egalitarian values and well being, prefers a small power distance, and has high tolerance of uncertainty. Likewise, we can characterize the national culture of Singapore as a conservative culture that prefers a large power distance, and has high tolerance of uncertainty.

Interpreting Global Dimensions of Culture

The position of a particular national culture on a certain cultural dimension should be understood with reference to that nation's history, social–economic development, as well as intellectual–religious traditions. For example, preindustrial nations are likely to emphasize traditional authority and survival values, whereas industrialized nations are likely to emphasize rational–secular authority, and postindustrial nations (North European Protestant nations, such as Norway and Sweden) are likely to emphasize well-being values (Inglehart, 1997; Inglehart & Baker, 2000). Many Catholic nations (Belgium, Peru, Portugal) and Greece have low tolerance of uncertainty, probably because both Catholicism and the Greek Orthodox religion believe in one God, one Christ, and one Mother of God (Hofstede, 1991).

The foregoing analysis implies that as a nation's social–economic situations and predominant intellectual–religious traditions change, its position on the pertinent cultural dimensions will shift as well. For example, Japan, Taiwan, Hong Kong, Singapore, and South Korea have experienced rapid industrialization since the 1970s, and industrialization is often accompanied by an ascent of secular–rational authority and a decline of traditional authority (see Jackson, 2002). Thus, national cultures do not occupy fixed positions on these dimensions. Instead, global cultural dimensions are useful conceptual tools for describing the predominant values and beliefs in a culture, *and* for tracking how cultures change over time, as a result of social and economic changes (Triandis, 2004).

It is also important to note that global dimensions of national cultures cannot be directly applied to characterize individual psychology in a particular culture. Values or beliefs are variably distributed in a national group. Take individualism and collectivism as two opposing constellations of values as an example. The horizontal line in "Panel a" of Figure 2.3 represents different degrees of adherence to individualism or collectivism. When we move from left to right along the line, the extent of adherence to collectivism increases, and the extent of adherence to individualism decreases. In societies situated near the collectivism end of the

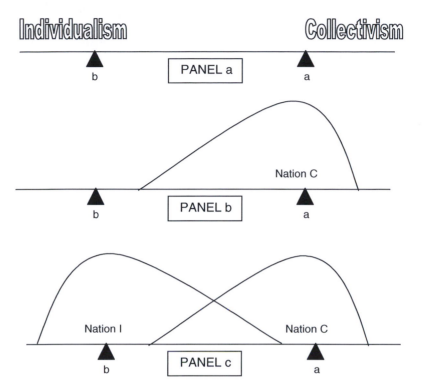

FIGURE 2.3. Illustration of within-culture variation in individualism–collectivism.

continuum (point a), we would expect to find a *greater tendency* for individuals to define the self in terms of their group memberships and their relationships with others (Bochner, 1994; Markus & Kitayama, 1991, 2003a; Triandis, 1989), to give priority to the goals and the needs of their in-groups (Schwartz, 1992; Triandis, 1990), and to follow social norms (Triandis, 1996). Likewise, when we move along the line from right to left, the extent of adherence to individualism increases, and the extent of adherence to collectivism decreases. In societies situated near the individualism end of the continuum (point b), we would expect to find a *greater tendency* for people to view the self as being independent of the groups (Markus & Kitayama, 1991, 2003a; Triandis, 1989), to give more weight to personal attitudes as determinants of their social behavior (Triandis, 1996), and to give priority to their personal goals and needs (Schwartz, 1992; Triandis, 1990).

In "Panel b" of Figure 2.3, we display the distribution curves of a hypothetical nation (Nation C) on the individualism–collectivism dimension. The vertical axis represents the number of people in a particular nation who adhere to a particular degree of individualism or collectivism.

In this hypothetical nation, only a few people adhere to individualism more than they do to collectivism, and a lot of people adhere more strongly to collectivism than they do to individualism. In this nation, collectivism is more widely distributed (popular) than individualism. Point a indicates the mean (or average) of the extent of individualism–collectivism of all the individuals in this nation. We may characterize this nation as a collectivist nation. "Panel c" of Figure 2.3 depicts the distribution of individualism and collectivism in a relatively individualist nation (Nation I), together with the distribution of individualism and collectivism in Nation C.

Although Nation C is more collectivist and less individualist than Nation I, there is substantial overlap in the two distributions. In both nations, some individuals adhere more strongly to individualism than to collectivism. These people are referred to as *idiocentrics* or individuals who adhere strongly to individualist values. Likewise, in both nations, some individuals adhere more strongly to collectivism than to individualism, and they are known as *allocentrics*. There are more idiocentrics and fewer allocentrics in individualist nations than in collectivist nations, but every nation houses some idiocentrics and some allocentrics (Triandis, Leung, Villareal, & Clack, 1985).

Both cultural characteristics (individualism–collectivism) and personal characteristics are important for predicting behaviors. Collectivist values are widely distributed and instituted in formal and informal practices in a collectivist nation. Despite this, idiocentrics in a collectivist society may be motivated to express their individuality and personal distinctiveness, resulting in many creative behavioral expressions of individuality in a collectivist society. For example, Japan is a collectivist nation, and expressions of individuality have generated a constant stream of creativity in Japanese paintings and literature. Indeed, it is not difficult to find fairly extreme expressions of individuality inside a collectivist society, and some of these expressions may be seen as deviant behaviors from the perspective of the mainstream culture. For example, the emergence of a "dark" youth subculture in contemporary Japan has started to attract attention in the nation. Members of this subculture have an extraordinary taste for pathological and medical things. They embrace the spirits of sicknesses and death in music and fashion, and express their enthusiasm for such dark spirits in behaviors. Some of them would carry small models of wooden coffins or blacken the area around their eyes with makeup to suggest a death mask. Some proudly announce that they have slashed their wrists by posting photos of their bloodied wrists on the Internet, and exchange information with their peers on what illnesses they have been diagnosed with, and what medications they have been prescribed.

Similarly, in an individualist nation, individualist values are widely distributed and instituted in formal and informal practices. Despite this, allocentrics in individualist nations may join groups, form congregations, organize unions, and initiate collective actions to change the society for the collective good. However, pathological collective behaviors have also been recorded in the history of some individualist nations. One extreme example of such pathological collective behaviors is mass suicide. Members of the Solar Temple, a religious sect, believe that ritualized suicides would lead to rebirth on a planet called Sirius. In 1994, 48 Solar Temple members committed mass suicide in Switzerland. In 1995, 16 Solar Temple members were found dead in a burned house outside Grenoble, France. In 1997, 5 members of the Solar Temple killed themselves in Saint Casimir, Quebec, Canada. In the same year, 39 members of a religious group committed mass suicide in a mansion near San Diego, USA. In short, it is possible to find individuals with extreme idiocentric tendencies in collectivist nations, and individuals with extreme allocentric tendencies in individualist nations.

Aside from individual differences, in the United States there are also appreciable regional differences in individualism and collectivism. Using the following eight indicators, Vandello and Cohen (1999) created an individualism index for the 50 states in the US: (1) percentage of people living alone (individualism item), (2) percentage of elderly people living alone (individualism item), (3) divorce to marriage ratio (individualism item), (4) percentage of people with no religious affiliation (individualism item), (5) percentage of people voting Libertarian over the last four presidential elections (individualism item), (6) percentage of households with grandchildren in them (collectivism item), (7) ratio of people carpooling to work to people driving alone (collectivism item), and (8) percentage of self-employed workers (individualism item). The collectivist tendencies are strongest in the Deep South, and the individualist tendencies are strongest in the Mountain West and Great Plains. It was also found that relative to collectivist states, individualist states have lower poverty rates, lower population density, smaller numbers of ethnic minorities, higher suicide rates, higher prevalence of binge drinking, and greater gender equality.

Finally, the same individual may adhere to some individualist values and some collectivist values. For example, based on Hofstede's international survey, the United States should be an individualist nation and Japan a collectivist one. Consistent with the characterization of these two nations, Japanese have a greater preference to work in a group than do Americans. However, in other life domains, Americans on average are more collectivist than Japanese. For example, compared to Japanese, Americans are more willing to accept hierarchy, and to strive for group harmony. They also have a greater tendency to define themselves contextually, as well as a stronger sense of belonging to groups (Oyserman et al., 2002).

Given the huge intra-national and inter-domain variability, it is dangerous to generalize from the results of international surveys of values and beliefs to the psychology of a national group. The fact that the United States is a more individualist nation than Japan does not imply that all Americans are individualists. To derive the global cultural dimensions, researchers often eliminated all intra-national variations in the data and considered only the national averages on the measured values or beliefs. By doing so, they have reduced a distribution to a single point on the cultural dimension. This research strategy helps to highlight differences in values/beliefs between nations, while at the same time obscuring rich intra-national and inter-domain variations. Indeed, when researchers consider both intra-national and international variability in values and beliefs simultaneously, differences between nations are often not discernible. For example, when both international and intra-national variability in individualism and collectivism are considered, researchers have not been able to discern a consistently higher level of individualism or lower level of collectivism among North Americans relative to Japanese (Takano & Osaka, 1999).

The Focal Approach

Imagine yourself in the following scenario. You are planning a trip to a warm and sunny place in the winter break. You check the climate of the world cities on the Internet, and find that Cape Town, South Africa is situated in the Mediterranean (dry summer subtropical) climate zone. Therefore, you expect the climate in Cape Town to be similar to that in coastal central and southern California, with a hot and dry summer, and a cool and wet winter. You also find on the Internet that the latitude of Cape Town is 33°S. Bingo! It is summer in Cape Town during your winter break, and this South African city will be the destination of your vacation. As you pack your bag for this trip, you wonder whether you should take an umbrella and a jacket.

The global information (climate type, latitude) you have gathered will not be very useful for making these decisions. In a typical week in December in Cape Town, the maximum daily temperature could range from 70°F to 90°F, and the weather may range from hot and sunny to cool and rainy. Global climatological information (such as climate types) helps us make rough estimations of what the weather is like in a particular place, and how similar or different the weather is in different places. However, it is not helpful for predicting meteorological variations in a particular place. Similarly, global dimensions of culture give us teleoscopic pictures of national cultures. To view the fine texture of a national culture, we need different empirical lens.

As an alternative to the global approach, the focal approach applies local constructs, or constructs indigenous to the culture being studied, to describe a culture. This approach attends to the culture-specific meanings of local constructs, and examines subtle local variations in the constructs' meanings in different cultural milieux and epochs. As such, this approach complements the global approach in several important ways.

In the global approach, a global dimension of cultures is assumed to have the same meaning in all cultures, and therefore can be used as a universal dimension to describe similarities and differences between national cultures. For example, power distance refers to the extent to which a nation values equality or accepts inequality between people in the nation. The meaning of this dimension does not change when it is applied to study different national cultures. What changes is a particular nation's position on this dimension. In the focal approach, two nations may be characterized as nations with a large power distance for different reasons. For example, in both India and China there is high acceptance of unequal power between different social groups (Meade & Whittaker, 1967; P. Singh, Huang, & Thompson, 1962). Despite this, there are important differences in the social construction of power relations in these two countries.

Inequality in India

It is impossible to understand the power relations in India without referring to its caste system. The origin of the caste system in India is in Hinduism. In Hinduism, there exist four hierarchically arranged castes, and anyone who does not belong to one of these castes is an outcast, who is *untouchable* to the four castes. The caste system affected the social structure of traditional India. Each caste (or *Varna*) had certain duties and rights, and a certain diet. Members of each caste were allowed to work in certain occupations only. The highest caste was the *Brahman*, who were priests and the educated people of the society. The next highest caste was the *Kshatria*, who were the rulers and aristocrats of the society. After the Kshatria were the *Vaisia*, who were landlords and business people. The *Sudra* were peasants and the working class, who performed "nonpolluting" jobs. The outcasts or untouchables worked in degrading jobs like cleaning and sewage (Dirks, 2001).

Unequal power distribution was strictly enforced in the traditional Indian caste system. The first three castes (Brahman, Kshatria, and Vaisia) possessed social and economical rights that the Sudra and the outcast did not have, whereas the untouchables suffered from harsh social discriminations. Their dwellings were at a distance from the settlements of the four caste communities. The outcasts were not allowed in the temples, or to drink from the same wells used by people from the four castes. They were also not allowed to enter the houses of the four castes or to touch people from the four castes. If for any reason a contact was made between an untouchable and a member of the castes, the untouchable could be beaten or murdered, and the caste member had to purify himself or herself by going through the prescribed religious rituals (Moon, 2001).

In modern India, the practice of the caste system is unlawful, and the government has an affirmative action policy to reverse historical discriminations against the degraded groups in the society. Despite this policy, most of the communities that were low in the caste hierarchy remain low in today's social hierarchy, and those that were high in the caste hierarchy remain high in today's social hierarchy (Figure 2.4). Most degrading jobs are performed by the outcasts, while the Brahmans remain at the top of the social hierarchy, taking up prestigious jobs such as doctors, engineers, and lawyers (Das, 2001).

Filial Piety in Chinese Societies

In Chinese societies, Confucianism impacts the organization of social relationship heavily (Hwang, 2001). In Confucianism, all major social relations are supposed to be modeled on the father–son relation. Filial piety (or *hsiao*) was the primary duty of every Chinese. In traditional China, filial duties included complete compliance with the wishes of the parents during their

FIGURE 2.4. A snapshot of social inequality in India: young children begging for money in Mumbai.

lifetime, taking best possible care of them as they grew older, performing ritual sacrifices at their grave site or in the ancestral temple after their death, winning prestige for the whole family by passing the Civil Service examinations, and continuation of the family line.

The father–son relation in traditional China provided a model for organizing other social relations (Hwang, 2000). Thus, most other social relationships were regulated by extensions of filial duties. Just as the son was expected to demonstrate respect, obedience, and deference to the father, respect, obedience, and deference were expected from the ministers to the emperor, from the subordinates to the leader, from the students to the teacher, from the wife to the husband, and from the daughters-in-law to the parents-in-law.

The precept of filial piety takes two forms depending on whether the emphasis is placed on submission to paternal authority or reciprocal obligations between the father and the son (Yeh, 2003). The psychological tendency to accept the unbounded authority of parents in Chinese societies has been referred to as *authoritarian moralism* (Ho, 1987, 1996) or *authoritarian filial piety* (Yeh, 2003). Authoritarian moralism embodies two significant features of traditional Chinese societies: a hierarchical structure of authority ranking in family and other social institutions, and a pervasive tendency to judge other people against the moral standards embodied in the moral imperative of filial piety.

Authoritarian filial piety is premised upon the assumption that one's body exists solely because of one's parents (Hwang, 1999). Thus, in traditional China, children's obligations to the parents had no limits, and filial obligations took precedence over the affection between husband and wife, and between parents and children. We will illustrate this with two examples. First, in traditional China, a husband could divorce his wife if she did not get along with his mother. When there was a conflict between the wife and the mother, filial piety demanded that the man should get rid of his wife to please the mother. According to filial piety, a man could always get another wife, but he would only have one mother (see Figure 2.5).

Second, the *Twenty-Four Paragons of Filial Piety* compiled by Guo Jujìng in the Yuan Dynasty (AD 1260–1368) has been a widely circulated text for teaching Chinese children the meaning of filial piety. One story in this collection portrays a case of filicide as an admirable example of filial conduct. According to the story, Kuo Chi was a very poor man with a 3-year-old son. Although there was little food, Kuo Chi's mother often gave part of her share to her grandson. One day, Kuo Chi said to his wife, "We are poor, and cannot give mother enough to eat. Besides, our son is eating mother's food. We better bury him alive." As Kuo Chi started to dig a grave, he found a pot of gold under the Earth. His filial piety had touched the heart of Heaven.

FIGURE 2.5. The inscription on the panel over the door of this traditional Chinese house in the Jiangxi Province says, "Enter and be filial."

Although filial piety demands compliance and deference from the son, it also demands virtuous and benevolent conduct from the father. By extension, although all social interactions are expected to follow the principle of respecting the superior, those who assume the role of the father, elder brother, husband, or the ruler should act in accord with the principles of benevolence and kindness (Hwang, 2000). This notion of *reciprocal filial piety* emphasizes acceptance of unequal power in social relations, as well as reciprocal obligations between the superior and the subordinate (Yeh, 2003).

In contemporary Chinese societies, both authoritarian and reciprocal filial piety are still important guiding principles of social interaction. A recent survey showed that in Beijing, China, old people continue to hold high filial expectations for young people and young people still endorse strongly filial obligations for old people (Yue & Ng, 1999). Teachers enjoy very high occupational status in the society (Fwu & Wang, 2002) and are regarded as authority figures. Many students tend to adopt a passive, uncritical orientation toward learning (Ho, Peng, & Chan, 2001). In business and educational organizations in China and Taiwan, there is a strong emphasis on loyalty to the supervisor. Many employees are willing to dedicate themselves to the supervisor and protect the supervisor's welfare even at the expense of personal interests. They are willing to exert considerable effort on behalf of the supervisor, desire to be attached to and follow the supervisor, and respect the accomplishments of the supervisor. Furthermore, loyalty to supervisor in

Chinese business organizations is positively related to employee perform-ance in the organization (Z. Chen, Tsui, & Farh, 2002; B. Cheng, Shieh, & Chou, 2002; Farh & Cheng, 2000).

The above analysis illustrates the utility of the focal approach. Both Indian and Chinese cultures are cultures with a large power distance. Despite this, unequal distribution of power in Indian and Chinese societies originated from different cultural sources. In India, it originated from Hinduism and is instituted in the caste system; in China, it originated from Confucianism and is embodied in the indigenous idea of filial piety.

In the case of filial piety in Chinese societies, the focal approach has also enabled researchers to identify different shades of meaning of this cultural precept. Indeed, taking a focal perspective, research has revealed markedly different psychological ramifications of the two variants of filial piety for indi-vidual attitudes and behaviors. For example, Chinese parents who adhere to the norm of authoritarian filial piety are likely to advocate impulse control, display of proper behaviors, and inhibition of self-expressions in child train-ing. They are likely to hold relatively fatalistic, superstitious, stereotyped beliefs, be authoritarian, dogmatic, and conforming (Ho, 1994, 1996), support male dominance and submission to authority, and adhere to social conven-tion (Yeh, 2003; Yeh & Bedford, 2003). However, Chinese who believe in recip-rocal filial piety tend to value egalitarianism, gender equality, and fairness. They also tend to see empathy, self-closure, and perspective-taking as impor-tant in interpersonal relationships (Yeh, 2003; Yeh & Bedford, 2003).

Meet the Researcher: Kuang-Hui Yeh

"The ethos of a culture plays a central role in the devel-opment of people's mind and behavior. Indigenous psychology as a body of knowledge reflects a group of social scientists' collective effort to organize people's worldviews into a form of scientific inquiry that captures the distinctive sensibilities of a culture. However, when a culture becomes highly pluralistic, indigenous psychol-ogy needs to consider and integrate voices from various cultural sources into a comprehensive framework. 'Let noble thoughts come to us from all directions.' "

Kuang-Hui Yeh is an Associate Research Fellow at the Institute of Ethnology, Academia Sinica, Taipei, Taiwan. He also teaches personality and family psy-chology courses at National Taiwan University, where he received his M.A. and Ph.D. in social and personality psychology.

Focal Analysis of Culture Change

The focal approach also affords a deep analysis of how core ideas and practices in a cultural tradition are transformed in response to social change. In Beijing and Taiwan, filial piety is still highly valued; many young people still believe in looking after their aged parents, assisting them financially, and retaining close contact with the elders. However, obeying the elders is no longer perceived to be very important (Yeh, 1997; Yue & Ng, 1999). In Taiwan, over the past three decades, there has been a persistent decline in the importance of living with elderly parents as a filial obligation (Yeh, 2002). Additionally, parents' power to make decisions for their children regarding marital and consumption choices has drastically decreased. Finally, in Hong Kong, there has also been a gradual shift from authority-centered to affect-centered father–child interactions (Ho & Kang, 1984).

In India, caste system reforms were handed down from the government. When India became an independent state, its leaders decided to separate the state from religion. The practices of untouchability or caste-based discrimination were made illegal. To reverse the effects of historical discrimination against the degraded classes, affirmative action policies were introduced. According to central government policy, each state must allot a fixed percentage of government jobs and places in the universities to each Backward Class (e.g., the untouchables, the Sudra Varna), and the percentage is calculated on the basis of the distribution of the Backward Class in the population of the state. As a consequence, in the major cities in India, it is not uncommon to see members of different castes mingling with each other, although separatism, caste-based discrimination, and violent clashes connected to caste tensions are still prevalent in some rural areas.

The affirmative action policy has also created new caste tensions. The high caste communities feel that they are discriminated against by the government policy. Oftentimes, many high-caste members have to compete for a few places reserved for them, while the Backward-Classes members face little competition because of the large number of reserved places for them. Sometimes in order to fill the quota, unqualified candidates from the lower classes are awarded government jobs or admitted to the universities. Among the Backward Classes, different groups also compete for their entitlement, and a person's class identity has become a subject of political, social, and legal interpretation (Das, 2001).

Summary and Conclusion

In this chapter, we have introduced two major approaches to describing cultures. The global approach seeks to describe differences and similarities between national cultures in terms of a few pan-cultural dimensions. This approach offers a telescopic view of world cultures. The focal approach seeks to describe the pattern of ideas and practices in a single culture, using local or indigenous constructs (such as caste and filial piety) that are linked to the culture's unique historical, religious, and intellectual traditions. As such, the focal approach gives forth historically grounded and highly contextualized descriptions of the culture. We have illustrated the differences between the global and focal approaches with national cultures, although both approaches can be applied to describe other cultures, such as organizational cultures and campus cultures.

It is important to emphasize that the two approaches offer different, complementary views of culture. It would be erroneous to assume that one view is more accurate than the other. Going back to the meteorology analogy, climate types and local weather variations are both valid and useful meteorological information on a region, although they serve different functions. Similarly, global and local information on a culture are useful for understanding a culture. Culture travelers need both small- and large-scale maps to guide their navigation. As the traveler begins to approach a new country from a distance, global information on the country, like a small-scale map, will provide a bird's-eye view of the country's cultural profile. As the traveler begins to enter the destination, local information, like a large-scale map, will provide a nuanced understanding of the culture in the country. Both kinds of maps are indispensable to successful navigation in a culture (Morris, Leung, Ames, & Lickel, 1999).

We should also emphasize that both the global and focal approaches are descriptive approaches to culture. As descriptive approaches, they do not explain cultures (Rohner, 1984). We opened this chapter with a discussion of the different cultural versions of the Cinderella story. Cultural variations in the themes of the Cinderella story may reflect the different dominant ideas in the places and times the story was circulated. The image of Raisel, the Jewish reincarnation of Cinderella, embodies the values of intellectuality and generosity in Jewish culture. Compared to the image of Sabrina (Audrey Hepburn) in *Sabrina*, the image of Marisa Ventura (Jennifer Lopez) in the movie *Maid in Manhattan* reflects an increasingly permissive attitude toward Latino American single mothers in contemporary American society. However, culture does not explain cultural variations in these stories. It would be circular to say that Raisel, as an embodiment of Jewish culture, is portrayed as an intellectual and generous woman *because* Jewish culture values intellectuality and generosity. Similarly, individualism in North America does not explain why Americans define the self as an entity separate from the group, because the independent self is part of North America's individualist culture.

To explain culture, we may adopt several approaches. First, we can try to understand how biological evolution enables culture by examining how the cognitive and environmental support for culture emerged in human evolutionary history. This is the subject of the next chapter. Second, we may seek to identify the social and psychological functions that culture serves. We will introduce the functional explanations in Chapter 4. Finally, we can explain culture in terms of a set of social cognitive principles that govern the organization and application of cultural knowledge in concrete situations, and this will be the subject of Chapters 5–8.

Psychological Foundation of Human Culture

3

Culture in the News

In Pierre Boulle's novel *Planet of the Apes* (1963), a primate civilization, by imitating human behavior, eventually replaces human culture. For most people, ape cultures exist only in fictionists' imaginary world. It is generally believed that culture distinguishes humans from other animals, as it does one human group from others. Because culture is specific to humans, *Homo sapiens* are superior to their sister species in the primate family. Therefore, the prospect for Boulle's planet of the apes is dim. Dim as it is, decades of detailed observations of primate behavior have led to a ground-breaking discovery: the discovery that ape cultures may exist. This discovery shatters the romantic belief that human beings own a monopolistic claim to culture.

    Aside from challenging the doctrine of human supremacy, this provocative discovery invites researchers to revisit the history of human evolution, as well as the evolution of human cultures. The story of the evo-lution of human culture is still a story in the making. As new scientific dis-coveries are made and new pieces of the hidden history of human civilization are unearthed, many parts of this chapter will need to be rewritten. Yet these fascinating discoveries, which have raised questions about the very nature of humanity, have never failed to catch the spotlight in the media.

*****

On January 2, 2003, CNN reporter Marsha Walton began her story entitled "Study Reveals Complex Orangutan Culture" by drawing atten-tion to how humans and orangutans perform a similar learned routine before they go to sleep. "Remember how the television show *The Waltons* used to end each evening: Good night, John Boy. Good night, Mary Ellen. Good night, Grandpa," Miss Walton reminded her readers. Then, she con-tinued, "In orangutan culture, there's a a little less formal way to say good night: Ppppffffffffftttttttttt."

*****

Orangutans are large tailless apes with long powerful arms. They live in the forests of Borneo and Sumatra in Southeast Asia. Orangutans learn the spluttering "raspberry" sound described in Miss Walton's article by observ-ing and mimicking their peers. This signal and the 23 other signals and skills observed in wild orangutans are geographically distinct; the behaviors com-mon in one orangutan population are absent in at least one other popula-tion. In other words, the complex behaviors and skills displayed by the different orangutan populations are geographically distinct patterns of socially transmitted behaviors. The discovery of these orangutan behaviors has led some scientists to believe that ape cultures exist.

Before the orangutans, the chimpanzees in Africa's rainforests had twice made headlines in the *Boston Globe*, first on June 17, 1999 and then on November 26, 2002. To date, primatologists have tallied at least 65 separate behaviors that are either performed differently by different chimpanzee troops, or performed by some but not all troops.

What do we learn from these recent discoveries other than that humans do not monopolize the rights to culture? Why should social psychologists care about ape cultures? What do ape cultures tell us about the nature of human cultures? On the same day that CNN covered the story of orangutan cultures, the BBC ran a story entitled "Ape culture hints at earlier evolution." The BBC news article focuses on the implications of ape cultures for understanding early evolution and the nature of human cultures. To social psychologists, what lies beneath the story of ape cultures is a fascinating story concerning the cognitive evolution of the human mind that makes the development of human cultures possible.

Ape Cultures

In social sciences, *culture* has two meanings. First, culture refers to the network of knowledge characteristic of a human population. This sense of culture distinguishes one human group from another. Thus far, we have focused on this meaning of culture. Second, culture refers to the ability to create and transmit shared knowledge. This ability has long been assumed to be specific to humans. The news stories described above challenge this assumption. In the present chapter, we are concerned primarily with the second meaning of culture: the allegedly unique human ability to create and transmit shared knowledge.

Our story evolves around a couple of simple questions. If ape cultures have existed for millions of years, what has prevented apes from developing cultures that are similar to human cultures? What are the distinctive human qualities that are necessary for the development of human cultures? To answer these questions, we need to know what is special about human cultures.

Local Variations in Customary Behaviors

To appreciate the distinctiveness of human culture, it is important to know what ape cultures are like. For years, researchers have observed behaviors of chimpanzees in the rainforests of Africa. Andrew Whiten et al. (1999) provided a synthetic summary of the research findings from long-term studies that were conducted at seven research sites in Guinea (Bossou), Ivory Coast (Tai Forest), Tanzania (Gombe, Mahale M-group, and Mahale K-group), and Uganda (Budongo Forest and Kibale Forest). Sixty-five different categories of behaviors were observed and recorded in seven chimpanzee populations. Some examples of these behavioral patterns are: use leaves to clean their body, manually wipe ants off wand, use probe to extract ants, pull stems noisily, slap on a branch to attract attention, use objects to tickle themselves, throw an object directionally, and rip off the parts of a leaf with mouth. Most of these behaviors are related to chimpanzees' tool use, grooming, and courtship.

Whiten et al. (1999) coded the behavioral data from the seven research sites to determine if the 65 behaviors were customary, habitual, present or absent at each site. According to the coding scheme, a behavior is *customary* if it occurs in all or most able-bodied members of at least one age–sex class (e.g., female adults). A behavior is *habitual* when it has occurred repeatedly in several individuals, an indication of some degree of social transmission. A behavior is *present* if it is clearly identified in a population, but is neither customary nor habitual at the site. A behavior is *absent* if it has never been recorded at the site. Finally, when a behavior is absent in a chimpanzee population, caution was taken to ascertain whether the absence was explicable because of a local ecological feature. For example, algae fishing was recorded at Bossou simply because of the rarity of algae in the local conditions of other research sites.

Of the 65 behaviors, 39 are customary or habitual in some chimpanzee populations, but are absent in others for no apparent ecological reason (Whiten et al., 1999). Figure 3.1 depicts the local variations of eight chimpanzee customs at the seven research sites. It is obvious that these behaviors vary widely from one group to another. For example, chimpanzees at Mahale customarily use a probe to extract ants, but they do not manually wipe ants off the wand, as the chimpanzees at Gombe do. The troops at Kabale use leaves as napkins for grooming, but they do not slap on tree braches to attract attention, as the troops at Bossou, the Tai Forest, and Budongo do. In short, each of the seven chimpanzee populations has a distinctively different profile of customary behaviors.

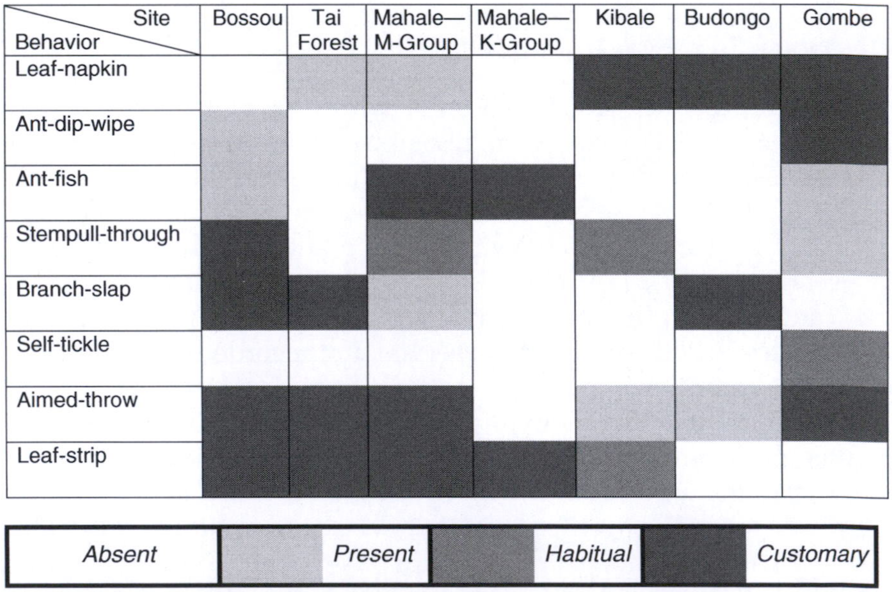

FIGURE 3.1. Local variations of customary or habitual behaviors in seven chimpanzee populations.
Leaf-napkin: use leaves as napkins to clean their body; *ant-dip-wipe*: manually wipe ants off wand; *ant-fish*: use probe to extract ants; *stem pull-through*: pull stems noisily; *branch-slap*: slap a branch to attract attention; *self-tickle*: use objects to tickle themselves; *aimed-throw*: throw an object directionally; and *leaf-strip*: rip off the parts of a leaf with mouth. Based on Whiten et al.,1999.

To Whiten et al. (1999), the presence of local variations in learned behaviors among chimpanzees suggests that chimpanzees have culture. At least, the local variations of chimpanzee behaviors fit the definition of culture customarily accepted in the biological science: Cultural behaviors are behaviors that are transmitted repeatedly through social and observational learning to become a population-level characteristic.

Social Transmission of Customary Behaviors

However, Whiten et al. (1999) do not have direct evidence that the chimpanzee customary or habitual behaviors observed in their research are socially transmitted. Cultural behaviors are learned behaviors. Local variations in customary or habitual behaviors do not by themselves prove that these behaviors are acquired by imitation or social learning. The chimpanzees at the seven research sites belong to two subspecies. Those at Bossou and Tai are *verus*, whereas those at the other sites are *subweinfurthii*. Whiten et al. (1999) found that customary behaviors vary as much between sites associated with the same subspecies as between subspecies. This finding rules out the possibility that local variations in customary behaviors are genetically transmitted. Still, this does not constitute direct evidence for social transmission of chimpanzee customary behavior.

The most often-cited anthropological evidence for social transmission of behavior in primate troops has to do with potato washing. On the tiny Japanese island of Koshima, one juvenile female macaque started the habit of carrying sweet potato to the water to wash off the dirt. Her mother and peers observed and imitated her behavior. Within a decade, washing potatoes became a customary habit in the troop (Kawamura, 1959).

The interpretation of these observations in terms of social learning presents two major problems. First, it assumes that potato washing is a novel behavior. Accordingly, it is inconceivable that individual macaques could have learned this behavior on their own. However, brushing sand off food is something many monkeys do naturally, and has been observed prior to the Koshima observations of macaque potato washing (Tomasello, 1999). Shortly after Kawamura's report was released, Kawai (1965) observed potato washing in four other troops of Japanese macaques. Visalberghi and Fragaszy (1990) also reported that captive individuals of other monkey species learn to wash their food on their own quite rapidly when they are provided with sandy fruit and water. These findings suggest that potato washing may not be a novel behavior among monkeys, and it could just have been the result of individual discovery. In other words, each and every macaque could have discovered the technique anew.

Second, if potato washing is learned through imitation, the rate at which potato washing is spread within the group should increase as the number of macaques who carry this habit increases. However, this is not the case. Spread of potato washing is far slower than what is expected if the new habit is spread through social learning (Galef, 1992).

Compelling evidence for social transmission of customary behaviors among nonhuman primates was obtained in another large-scale observational study conducted by van Schaik et al. (2003). They applied the same approach developed by Whiten et al. (1999) to study geographical variations of customary or habitual behaviors in six different wild orangutan populations on the islands of Borneo and Sumatra in Southeastern Asia. They identified 19 behaviors that are present at one or more sites at customary or habitual levels and absent elsewhere without clear ecological reasons. Figure 3.2 illustrates the geographic variations of seven orangutan customs. These behaviors involve specialized feeding techniques, and alternative forms of social signals. Some examples are: making spluttering raspberry sounds in the final phase of nest building; using a handful of leaves to wipe latex off their chin; riding on a pushed-over snag as it falls,

Behavior \ Site	Gunung Palung (Borneo)	Tanjung Putting (Borneo)	Kutai (Borneo)	Lower Kinabatangan (Borneo)	Leuser, Ketambe (Sumatra)	Leuser Suaq (Sumatra)
Snag riding	Absent	Customary	Absent	Absent	Absent	Absent
Kiss-squeak	Customary	Absent	Habitual	Absent	Absent	Absent
Play nests	Customary	Habitual	Present	Absent	Habitual	Customary
Bunk nests	Absent	Present	Absent	Habitual	Absent	Absent
Autoerotic tool	Absent	Present	Present	Absent	Habitual	Absent
Raspberry sound	Absent	Absent	Absent	Habitual	Absent	Customary
Leaf napkin	Absent	Absent	Customary	Absent	Absent	Absent

Legend: Absent — Present — Habitual — Customary

FIGURE 3.2. Local variations of customary or habitual behaviors in six orangutan populations. *Snag riding*: ride on pushed-over snag as it falls, then grab onto vegetation before it crashes on ground; *kiss-squeak*: use a leaf on mouth to amplify sound, and then drop it; *play nests*: build nests for social play, not to rest; *bunk nests*: build a nest as a rain cover for a short distance above the nest; *autoerotic tool*: use tool for sexual stimulation; *raspberry sound*: make spluttering raspberry sounds in the final phase of nest building; and *leaf napkin*: use a handful of leaves to wipe latex off chin. Based on van Schaik et al., 2003.

and grabbing on to vegetation before it crashes on ground; using a leaf on mouth to amplify sound, and then dropping it; building a nest as a rain cover for a short distance above the nest; building nests for social play, not to rest; and using a tool for sexual stimulation. Some signals invented by the orangutans (e.g., the spluttering raspberry sound described above) may reflect shared meanings (e.g., *I'm going to bed now*) based on arbitrary symbols.

To test whether social learning is responsible for emergence of local orangutan customs, van Schaik et al. (2003) examined the relationship between the geographic distances between the research sites and how different the customary or habitual behaviors are at these sites. If a custom invented in one orangutan troop is spread to the troops in the neighborhood, troops that live within a short distance are more likely to share the custom than those that live far apart. This is indeed the case. There was a strong negative correlation between geographic distance and similarity in customary or habitual behaviors ($r = -.60$), suggesting that orangutan customs or habits spread from the location where they originate to the neighboring areas.

More importantly, the number of customary or habitual behaviors in an orangutan troop increases as individuals within the troop spend more time with other individuals other than their mother or children. According to van Schaik et al. (2003), association time is directly related to the amount of opportunities for social learning. As the amount of social learning opportunities increases, the repertoire of ape customs and habits also expands. In short, it seems that ape customs and habits, like human customs and habits, are socially transmitted.

Human Cultures

The discovery of ape cultures has brought human beings closer to their sister species in the primate family, as de Waal (1999) proclaimed in his comments on the Whiten et al. (1999) findings: "The *culture* label befits any species, such as the chimpanzee, in which one community can readily be distinguished from another by its unique suite of behavioral characteristics. Biologically speaking, humans have never been alone—now the same can be said of culture." (p. 636). Van Schaik et al. (2003) also believe that finer distinctions need to be made to separate human cultures from ape cultures.

What might the "fine" distinctions between ape cultures and human cultures be? Obviously, human cultures are much more complex than ape cultures. Human beings use a sophisticated system of symbols to convey meanings, and the great apes do not. Compared to the skills possessed by the great apes, those innovated by human beings are far more numerous and complex.

However, complexity is only a surface feature that distinguishes human cultures from ape cultures. What sets human and ape cultures apart is the unique human capability to reproduce and cumulate cultural knowledge. Simply put, human culture builds upon itself and ape culture does not. Some orangutans at Kutei learned to build a cover on their nest

(a)

(b)

FIGURE 3.3. After the wheel was invented, humans built on it and invented the carriage (a), and then the motor vehicle (b). The car shown in (b) is decorated with various cultural artifacts and has become a symbol of New Orleans tourist culture.

during bright sunshine, but they do not pass this knowledge on to the next generation. Because orangutans do not accumulate modifications of their invention over time, this primitive practice of providing shelter from the sun has been around for millions of years. By comparison, human culture is cumulative. When humans discover a piece of knowledge, they start from there, and go on. In human societies, once the wheel is invented, the new generations do not have to invent it again. Instead, they build on it and invent the carriage, and then the motor vehicle (Figure 3.3). This uniquely human process is referred to as *ratcheting*, and is the engine for human cultures. Cultural complexity ensues from ratcheting; through ratcheting, sophisticated cultural knowledge and complex cultural practices *evolve* over time (Tomasello, 2001).

Cognitive Foundation of Human Cultures

Emergence of Humanlike Cultures

About 14 million years ago, the ancestors of orangutans and those of African apes diverged. The presence in orangutans of humanlike culture suggests that human culture started to develop about 14 million years ago (van Schaik et al., 2003). For much of the 14 million years over which hominids have been developing, they remained within the confines of their birthplace, Africa.

If hominids had never left Africa, human culture might not be as diversified as it is today. Differentiation of human cultures began with migration of hominids. Paleoanthropologists have sought to chart the routes of hominids' migration by dating the hominid fossils unearthed at the archeology sites in Africa, the Middle East, Asia, and Europe. The oldest undisputed fossils in Africa (Bahrel Ghazal, Chad; Hadar, Ethiopia) are from about 3 million years ago, and those in the Middle East (Damansi, Republic of Georgia) are from about 1.75 million years ago. The oldest hominid fossils unearthed in East Asia (Donggutuo, China; Gongwangling, China) are little more than 1 million years ago, whereas those in Europe (Ceprano, Italy; Atapuerca, Spain) are around 0.8 million years ago. These archeological discoveries have led most paleoanthropologists to believe that hominids migrated from Africa to the Middle East about 1.75 million years ago. The early hominid explorers reached East Asia about 1.1 million years ago, and hominid settlements in Western Europe were established far later (Wong, 2003).

The first representatives of *Homo erectus* had emerged as early as 1.9 million years ago in Africa. Early hominoids did not migrate northward until the advent of stone tools such as hand axes 150,000 years later. The rapid biological evolution that took place in the transition to *Homo erectus* set the stage for invention and use of tools. Indeed, the evolution of the physical features of the hominids coincided with the beginning of inter-continental migration of the hominids. Based on the archeological evidence from China, the first intercontinental travelers who made it to East Asia were *Homo erectus*, who possessed long limbs, large brains, and an upright posture.

However, the early hominoid adventurers were not particularly brawny and brainy. The skulls unearthed in Damansi, Republic of Georgia had a cranial capacity of 600–775 cubic cm, which was about half the size of a modern brain. From the bones of unearthed ribs, clavicles, vertebrae, and limbs, it is clear that the early hominoid pioneers did not possess a broad, strong looking physique (Gabunia et al., 2000; Vekua et al., 2002). In addition, the stone tools early hominoid adventurers brought with them in their expedition were primitive tools. The stone tools found at Damanisi are simple flakes and choppers that were used by African hominoids nearly a million years ago (Vekua et al., 2002).

In short, the evolution of an upright posture allowed early *Homo erectus* to use their free hands to grasp and manipulate small objects. The invention of crude stone tools greatly enhanced early hominoids' capacity to penetrate into the northern latitudes. We can picture how early ancestors of humankind, who were beneficiaries of biological and technological evolution, ventured into unknown territories, creating and spreading early human civilizations in different parts of the world.

Cognitive Limitations of the Early Hominids

Figure 3.4 depicts the time line of hominid evolution. Throughout the history of hominid evolution, the brain, the mind, and culture have coevolved in close interaction with each other. There appear to be two major break-points in the evolution of hominid culture, which coincided with the speciation of *Homo erectus* about 1.8 million years ago, and the speciation of *Homo sapiens* about 0.4 million years ago. According to Merlin Donald (1993), the first breakpoint in the evolution of the human mind seems to have occurred with *Homo erectus*. Before this breakpoint, hominids had the mental capability to store their perceptions of specific episodes. However, their ability to retrieve these episodic memories was poor. They could not retrieve these memories in the absence of appropriate environmental cues.

It is possible to get some idea of the limit of early hominid intelligence by examining the cognitive abilities of the great apes. Evidence from the observational studies reviewed above indicates that chimpanzees are

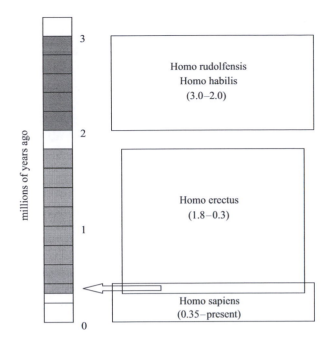

FIGURE 3.4. Time chart of hominid evolution.

capable of imitative learning. They can learn how to use a tool from their peers. However, as Tomasello (1996) pointed out, although chimpanzees are good at learning what a tool can do for them, they are not good at discerning the strategic significance of tool use. For example, if a mother rolls over a log and eats the insects underneath, her children may learn that there is food underneath the log, and they may roll over a log and eat the ants. They will remember this event, and subsequently retrieve the memory and repeat the action sequence when they see a log again. What they fail to discern is the mother's behavioral *intention*. They do not understand that the mother was searching for food, and she knew that there were ants underneath the log. The chimpanzees could have learned the same skill if the wind had caused the log to roll over and exposed the ants.

Moreover, the great apes cannot voluntarily access their memories in the absence of the appropriate environmental cues. They cannot selftrigger their memories of the skills they have learned, and therefore cannot voluntarily reflect on the skills they have acquired (Donald, 1993). This implies that the great apes will not voluntarily rehearse a learned behavioral sequence in order to teach their children and peers a learned skill. In short, the limits of ape intelligence tie ape learning to the immediate environment, and forbid modifications of learned skills and ratcheting of ape cultures.

Mimetic Skills and Gestural Communication

Speciation of *Homo erectus* was accompanied by evolution of some cognitive abilities that are necessary for the emergence of human culture. The increase in hominid brain size accelerated sharply and was sustained until the emergence of *Homo sapiens*. Apparently, there was a rapid expansion of brain size in the early phase of *Homo erectus*, which laid the biological foundation for the development of complex cognitive abilities to support the rapid improvement in tool making skills throughout the *Homo erectus* period.

Still *Homo erectus* had very limited speech production capabilities. However, these early hominids had developed the ability to use their body as a communicative device to represent knowledge and ideas. Anthropologists have observed male chimpanzees performing a rain dance, while being witnessed by females and the young (Goodall, 1988). In transitional hominid cultures, male hominids danced and sang during communal celebrations or demonstrations. The singers communicated not by words, but by gestures or tones (Lehman & Bernsten, 2003). The animal dances performed by early hominids contained mimicry of animal movements. Some early prehistoric sites also indicate that early hominids used animal remnants such as bones and horns from hunting or scavenging as props or costume elements in animal dances (Hewes, 1973). In addition, the rapid increase in cerebral volume in the transition to *Homo sapiens* was concentrated in the association cortex, hippocampus, and cerebellum. These brain areas modulate complex cognitive and motor functions, including long-term memory, short-term memory, and control and coordination of motor activities. During the transition from *Homo erectus* to *Homo sapiens*, sophisticated stone tools and long-distance hunting techniques were invented. Taken together, the evidence indicates that mimetic skills and gestural communication played an important role in the evolution of *Homo erectus* cultures.

The presence of mimetic representations of knowledge in *Homo erectus* indicates that at this stage, hominids were capable of *mentally* representing an action sequence (e.g., the movement sequence in a dance). The learned action sequence became an object of consciousness. As a mental object detached from the physical environment, the learned action sequence could be mentally manipulated. For example, *Homo erectus* were able to store and retrieve their memory of the action sequence in a dance voluntarily, and could hence purposively rehearse, edit and perfect the action sequence for ceremonial performance. These newly acquired cognitive abilities enabled early hominids to reflect on and refine their learned skills (Donald, 1993). Ratcheting or cumulative modifications of cultural knowledge was evident during this period. Tool making skills and long-distance hunting routines improved rapidly throughout this period, and have been considered to be the most notable accomplishments of *Homo erectus*. Refinement of these skills would not have been possible if it were not supported by the evolution of mimetic representation.

In early hominid cultures, meanings were often mapped onto mimetic signs, of which gesture is a major category. As a result, mimetic representations and gestures had important communicative values. Orangutans and chimpanzees also have shared signals. For example, a "kiss squeak" is a common orangutan signal. Some orangutans use a leaf on mouth to amplify a kiss sound when an unwelcome intruder or predator comes near them. The same gestures sometimes have different meanings in different ape populations. Tearing a leaf along the mid-rib to make a nice shearing sound means *I'm ready to mate* in one group, and means *I'm ready to play* in another. However, there is a fundamental difference between ape signals and early hominid mimetic communication. Ape signals are called out by environmental cues. By comparison, early hominid mimetic representations could be voluntarily retrieved for a variety of purposes, including ceremonial performance and emotional expression. They could also be used to direct imitation (Donald, 1993). The use of mimetic representations to direct imitation marked the beginning of conscious, self-directed teaching of cultural knowledge, which is a hallmark of human culture (Tomasello, 1999). Active instruction had speeded up social transmission of cultural knowledge significantly.

Language and Evolution of Human Culture

Mimetic representations emerged 1.5 million years ago. It took hominids more than 1 million years to reach the second milestone of cognitive evolution, when hominids finally found the words to express themselves.

Several remarkable anatomical changes came before the development of spoken languages. These include another large brain expansion, descent of the human larynx, redesign of the supralaryngeal vocal tract, and evolution of specialized auditory and memory devices for processing speech (Levelt, 1989). Compared to gestures, spoken language has several advantages. It works at a distance and in the dark, and does not interfere with other motor activities. Because humans can produce an infinite number of sound patterns, a vocal language can support a large number of different words. As such, speech is much more efficient in conveying meanings than are hand gestures (see Krauss & Chiu, 1998).

The importance of spoken languages in the evolution of culture cannot be overstated. As mentioned, apes invent signs by mapping meaning to some arbitrary signals. However, for every signal invented in an ape population, there is one and only one meaning. In human languages, the same expression can mean different things, and the same object can be referred to differently. For example, the expression *She is hot* can mean she feels warm or she is sexy. In the United States, some people call television *TV* or the *tube*. In London, *the tube* may refer to the underground railway system.

Because there are indefinite ways sounds can be mapped onto meanings in a spoken language, people can describe the same event in different terms, and therefore assign different meanings to it. Individuals in a collective may share many experiences, but different individuals may describe these experiences differently. As these individuals interact, they will collaborate to find a mutually acceptable expression to describe their experiences. Shared meanings arise and are encoded in the resulting shared expressions (Lau, Chiu, & Lee, 2001). Through this meaning negotiation process, symbolic cultures emerge. As Bruner (1990) said, "Our culturally adapted way of life depends upon shared meanings and shared concepts and depends as well upon shared modes of discourse for negotiating differences in meaning and interpretation" (pp. 12–13). Because different human groups may agree upon different ways of referring to their group experiences, different variants of symbolic cultures gradually evolve in different populations.

Later in this book (Chapters 5 and 9), we will review the extant literature on the role of language in cultural processes. The essence of our contention is that language encodes shared cultural meanings, as evident in many instances of everyday language use. Consider a cartoon published in the December 1, 2003 issue of the *New Yorker*. Four men and a woman congregate in an office. One of the men reads from a memo, "Our parent company wants us to be in bed by ten." The word *parent* and the expression *be in bed by ten* call out a socially approved belief about good parental practice in the United States: Good parents make sure that their children are in bed by ten. The word *company* calls out the shared knowledge that office hours usually end at 5 o'clock. The irony is felt when a holding company that exploits its employees' time is referred to as *our parent* company. Moreover, in the cartoon the word *parent* does not refer to a father or a mother. As such, this cartoon also underscores how mapping of multiple meanings onto multiple words in human languages facilitates generation of creative elements of culture, such as humor and poetry.

Invention of External Memory Devices

Language facilitates creation of shared knowledge. However, if social transmission of knowledge relied exclusively on individual memory, the rate of ratcheting would have been slow. At the beginning of the Stone Age, early human beings began to innovate the first external memory devices. External memory devices create collective storage and retrieval systems of knowledge. Knowledge stored in these devices is relatively permanent. Whereas human memory is limited in capacity, external memory devices have virtually unlimited capacity. Whereas only one individual can directly access a person's memory, external memory devices usually have many retrieval paths and can be accessed by multiple users (Donald, 1993). The Internet is an example of an external memory device. Other examples include DVDs, videotapes, microfilms, photographs, books, paintings, and stone carvings. The development of external memory devices modified the configuration of the human biological and cognitive systems. For example, the invention of written symbols led to the development of brain areas that specialize in processing pictorial, phonetic, and ideographic symbols. It also increased people's reliance on external devices to store, retrieve, reorganize, and edit a huge amount of information.

External memory devices give each of their users access to knowledge created by other individuals and knowledge accumulated over generations. Each user has at his or her disposal a huge amount and variety of knowledge for reflections and innovations. External memory devices also provide physical records of cultural histories. When new knowledge is created and stored into an external memory device, the new knowledge goes down in cultural history, is rendered public, and may be used as materials for further refinement and innovation. This iterative process enables cumulative modification of cultural knowledge to progress at an exponential rate.

Finally, changes in the accessibility of external memory may alter the way a cultural group is defined. When wall paintings and carvings were the major external memory devices, cultural diffusion was slow, because these media are not portable, and direct access to them was restricted largely to a small population of people who lived close to these cultural artifacts. In those days, it was relatively easy to identify the physical boundary of a culture. The invention of writing paper and printing allowed cultural knowledge to spread rapidly within a linguistic group. For a long time, language has been a useful criterion for determining the boundary of a cultural group. In the first edition of the *Handbook of Cross-Cultural Psychology*, Triandis et al. (1980–1981) proposed to use *cultunit* as the operational definition of culture. Two persons belong to different cultunits if the languages they speak are mutually unintelligible to each other. With the rapid development of the Internet and other electronic external memory devices, people find themselves increasingly enmeshed in global symbolic environments (Bandura, 2002), and it becomes increasingly difficult to determine the physical boundaries of cultures. For example, Hollywood movies are recorded on DVDs, dubbed into different languages, and distributed worldwide. American cultural knowledge encoded in Hollywood movies has spread across geographic and linguistic boundaries. With the advancement of globalization, physical boundaries of culture have become less clear and important than before. We will discuss the phenomenon of globalization and its psychological effects in Chapter 11.

In summary, unlike great ape cultures, human cultures ratchet; they build on themselves. Ratcheting occurred in conjunction with 1.8 million years of biological, cognitive, and technological evolution. The evolutionary process took several discrete steps. At each step, new biological and cognitive properties emerged. Biological evolution has resulted in the expansion of brain size, development of speech production and perception devices in the brain, and evolution of specialized brain regions for processing language and other symbols. Cognitive and biological evolutions occurred in parallel, supporting each other. Through cognitive evolution, humans developed the ability to represent a state of affairs in mimetic format, in language, and in other symbols used in various external memory media. These cognitive abilities facilitated the development of several important human competencies: the ability to unchain the learning processes from the immediate environment, the ability to voluntarily retrieve stored knowledge, the ability to encode their experiences in different terms, and the ability to externalize their knowledge. These human competences have increased the rate of social transmission of cultural knowledge, led to negotiation of meanings and construction of shared knowledge, and fostered the creation of cultural histories.

Like humans, great apes also possess socially transmitted shared knowledge. Some primatologists call such knowledge culture. We believe that ape cultures resemble human cultures in some respects. Where humans and the great apes diverged in the process of hominid evolution is the emergence of the human abilities to perpetuate the evolution of culture.

Social Psychological Foundation of Human Culture

In Chapter 1, we describe culture as a social process. Thus far, in this chapter we have focused exclusively on the biological, cognitive, and technological foundations of culture. The picture is not complete if we attempt to understand a social process exclusively in terms of biological and cognitive evolution. Before we review the literature on the distinctively human social competencies that give rise to culture, we should emphasize that these social competencies may evolve from a biological disposition. After all, humans are social *animals*.

Primatologists who studied chimpanzee behaviors have reported many socially competent behaviors in their subjects. In one experiment, a chimpanzee participant was seated in front of a computer. On each trial, a black and white portrait of a mother chimpanzee was shown. Next, two comparison portraits were shown. One of them was a different portrait of the same mother chimpanzee and the other one was a portrait of another chimpanzee. The chimpanzee participant used a joystick-controlled cursor to choose the comparison portrait that matched the previously seen portrait. The participants' performance in this experiment was significantly better than chance. This finding indicates that chimpanzees can recognize the faces of other members of their species. In a different experimental condition of the same experiment, following the presentation of the mother chimpanzee's portrait, the participant saw a portrait of the mother chimpanzee's son and the portrait of an unrelated chimpanzee. In this condition, the participant was able to match the mother's face with her son's face, indicating that chimpanzees can distinguish kin from nonkin based on physical appearance (Parr & de Waal, 1999).

This experiment is one of the many studies that have shown the availability in primate species of the abilities to recognize individuals in their group, and to relate to other individuals based on kinship, friendship, and dominance rank (Tomasello, 1999). Other researchers have reported that primates engage in cooperative behaviors, actively seek reconciliation after a conflict, and mediate conflicts between their peers (see Conniff, 2003). Because primates live in a group, they have to get along. The prosocial behaviors displayed by primate species, often referred to as *reciprocal altruism*, may thus have adaptive value.

Humans share these prosocial traits with their sister species in the primate family. However, humans possess some species-unique social cognitive skills, which are necessary for humans to participate in culture. Tomasello (1999) believes that at the heart of these skills is the assumption that other individuals are *intentional agents* who would engage in an activity with the intention to produce a certain effect. In other words, other individuals are seen to have goals, and be capable of making active choices among behavioral means for attaining these goals.

Representing others as intentional agents fosters *cultural learning*, a process necessary for transmitting and preserving a learned routine in the culture. For example, when a child sees his mother walk to a mirror, he understands that she *wants* to look at her image in the mirror. When he wants to see his image, he will walk to the mirror. For cultural learning to occur in this example, the child needs to follow the gaze of the mother, see things from the mother's perspective, and act on the environment as the mother does. This complex of social skills is known as *joint attention*. Joint attention, which develops early when the infant is 9 to 12 months of age, is a necessary precondition for cultural learning, which begins to mature when the child is 2 years old (Tomasello, 2001).

When children represent others as intentional agents, they assume that other individuals have their own perspectives. After children have mastered the ability to use language, they begin to use language to separate their own perspective from that of others. A child facing her father may say something like *I like the cup on your left hand side more*. In this utterance, the child separates her spatial perspective from that of the father. The child may also say something like *Father disapproves of my choice*. In this example, the child tries to separate her preference from that of the father.

In both examples above, the child does not only separate her own perspective from that of the father, she also tries to construct the meaning of the situation by coordinating the two perspectives. As the child articulates the perspective of the other person, she takes the perspective of the other person into consideration, and enters another person's subjective world. As children learn to articulate the perspective of the generalized other (e.g., *People love to have chocolates and ice-cream for dessert*), they assume the organized attitudes in the culture. Through perspective taking in language use, the mind of a child is turned into a cultural mind (Chiu & Chen, 2004; Ho & Chiu, 1998).

In summary, joint attention, cultural learning, and perspective taking constitute the complex of uniquely human social skills that are necessary for people to engage in culture. These skills rest on the assumption that other people are intentional agents who make active choices between behavioral means for attaining their goals.

Nature, Culture, and Mind

A common bias in the discussion of culture is that what is culture is not nature, and what is nature is not culture. There is also a tendency to characterize culture as a collective phenomenon. As such, individual cognitive processes can never get to the heart of cultural processes.

As mentioned at the outset, culture is a polysemous term, with both a generic sense and a specific sense. The generic sense of culture refers to the uniquely human capability to create and cumulate cultural knowledge. It is this sense of culture that distinguishes humans from other primate species. In the present chapter, we deal with this sense of culture. We argue that the brain, the mind, and culture coevolve. Human culture could not have emerged if humans were not biologically and cognitively prepared for it. In fact, biological and cognitive evolution did not take place for the purpose of cultural evolution. The concept of *culture* did not even exist in much of the 1.8 million years the brain and the mind have been evolving. New cognitive strategies and their supporting biological structures evolved because these strategies have new properties with high adaptive value. For example, mimetic representations emerged because they afford voluntary retrieval of episodic memories. Spoken languages emerged because they allow communication at a distance and in the dark, do not interfere with other motor activities, and can support a large vocabulary. Similarly, new technology and species-unique social skills evolved because they have adaptive value. External memory devices emerged because they extend the limits of individual memory. Joint attention, social learning, and perspective taking evolved because they help individuals adapt to collective life.

Once cultural evolution is set in motion, the ratchet effect is activated, leading to accumulation of cultural knowledge. As knowledge generates new knowledge, and is applied to create and refine the environment, culture plays an increasingly important role in shaping human civilizations. Since human history stepped into the Age of Progress in 1850, culture has been the dominant force that drives the development of the economy, technology, and various social and political institutions. Nowadays, many social scientists refer to the economies in advanced industrial societies as "knowledge economies." An expanding occupational category in these societies is "knowledge workers." The Internet, the latest and the most powerful external memory device humans have invented, has changed the mode of social discourse in many societies (Figure 3.5). The Internet did not evolve in reaction to environmental pressure. It was generated from

FIGURE 3.5. The Internet and various electronic memory devices allow mass storage and fast access to a large amount of knowledge.

the vast reservoir of cultural knowledge humans had accumulated. As we marvel at the "complexity" of the great apes' skills, which have been around for millions of years, we should celebrate our own culture, a highly distinctive human accomplishment that has liberated us from the confines of the physical environment and our limited biological endowment. Imagine how life would be if every person needed to reinvent the wheel on his or her own!

Culture also has a specific sense. As defined in Chapter 1, this sense of culture refers to the network of shared knowledge characteristic of a population. This sense of culture distinguishes one human group from another, and is primarily a product of symbolic social interactions.

To understand human culture, it is important to consider the generic and specific senses of culture, as well as their interactions. The generic sense of culture focuses on the universal qualities that make all humans alike, and the specific sense of culture focuses on the diverse manifestations of the universal human qualities in different populations. Research on the generic sense of culture leads to the recognition of a common core that defines our humanity. Research on the specific sense of culture leads us to appreciate and celebrate the diverse forms of sociality that have branched out from the common core. For example, people in all societies view others as intentional agents. However, people in different societies have constructed different models of agency to guide their practices (Hernandez & Iyengar, 2001; Markus & Kitayama, 2003b; Menon et al., 1999; Miller, 2003). These diverse manifestations of humanity emerge as creative and adaptive responses from different human groups in response to their unique physical, social, and historical environments. In the subsequent chapters, we will focus on the dynamic interplay of the generic and specific senses of culture.

What is Culture For?

Fact or Hoax?

You've got mail …

THE $250 COOKIE RECIPE
Okay, everyone … a true story of justice in the good old U.S. of A.
Thought y'all might enjoy this; if nothing else, it shows internet justice, if it can be called that.

My daughter & I had just finished a salad at Neiman-Marcus Cafe in Dallas
& decided to have a small dessert. Because our family are such cookie lovers,

we decided to try the "Neiman-Marcus Cookie." It was so excellent that I asked if they would give me the recipe and they said with a small frown, "I'm afraid not." Well, I said, would you let me buy the recipe? With a cute smile, she said, "Yes." I asked how much, and she responded, "Two fifty." I said with approval, just add it to my tab.

Thirty days later, I received my VISA statement from Neiman-Marcus and it was $285.00. I looked again and I remembered I had only spent $9.95 for two salads and about $20.00 for a scarf. As I glanced at the bottom of the statement, it said, "Cookie Recipe—$250.00." Boy, was I upset!! I called Neiman's Accounting Dept and told them the waitress said it was "two fifty," and I did not realize she meant $250.00 for a cookie recipe. I asked them to take back the recipe and reduce my bill and they said they were sorry, but because all the recipes were this expensive so not just everyone could duplicate any of their bakery recipes … the bill would stand.

I waited, thinking of how I could get even or even try and get any of my money back. I just said, "Okay, you folks got my $250.00 and now I'm going to have $250.00 worth of fun." I told her that I was going to see to it that every cookie lover will have a $250.00 cookie recipe from Neiman-Marcus for nothing. She replied, "I wish you wouldn't do this." I said, "I'm sorry but this is the only way I feel I could get even," and I will.

So, here it is, and please pass it to someone else or run a few copies … I paid for it; now you can have it for free.

(Recipe may be halved):

2 cups butter; 2 tsp. soda; 5 cups blended oatmeal**; 2 cups brown sugar; 1 8 oz. Hershey Bar (grated); 2 tsp. baking powder; 2 tsp. vanilla; 4 cups flour; 2 cups sugar; 24 oz. chocolate chips; 1 tsp. salt; 4 eggs; 3 cups chopped nuts (your choice)

** measure oatmeal and blend in a blender to a fine powder.

Cream the butter and both sugars. Add eggs and vanilla; mix together with flour, oatmeal, salt, baking powder, and soda. Add chocolate chips, Hershey Bar and nuts. Roll into balls and place two inches apart on a cookie sheet. Bake for 10 minutes at 375 degrees. Makes 112 cookies.

Have fun!!! This is not a joke—this is a true story. That's it. Please, pass it along to everyone you know, single people, mailing lists, etc. ... Ride free, citizen!

This is a widely circulated e-mail. Will you use the recipe and/or pass it along?

*****

In 1994, an Ohio man called 911 from his hotel room in Las Vegas, and was rushed to the hospital in an ambulance. He struck up a conversation with an attractive young woman at a bar in his hotel, the two hit it off, and after several drinks, the man blacked out. When he regained consciousness, he found himself lying in a hotel bathtub, covered with ice. A phone was placed on the floor beside the tub, with an attached note that said, "Call 911 or you will die." According to the doctors in the hospital, he had undergone massive surgery, and one of his kidneys was removed, apparently by a gang selling human organs in the black market. Similar crimes were reported subsequently along the Vegas strip, leading Las Vegas police to issue warnings to travelers visiting the city.

Will you warn your friend visiting Las Vegas of the organ harvesters in the strip?

*****

There is a good chance that you have heard these stories. Both stories are widely circulated urban legends, or modern, *fictional* stories that reach a wide audience quickly by being passed from one person to another as truth. One individual has received the Neiman-Marcus e-mail about 300 times, and feels so annoyed by it that he sets up a web page and urges people to stop spreading this chain letter (http://www.bl.net/forwards/cookie.html). Indeed, the $250 cookie recipe may make tasty cookies, but Neiman-Marcus did not make such a chocolate chip cookie when the story was first circulated. Similarly, the Las Vegas Police Department has never received any report of organ harvest, but thousands of people have passed the legend on in the course of 10 years. The legend also inspired an early episode of the popular TV show *Law and Order*.

Urban legends are numerous, and most of them have similar features. They are usually fictional stories told as truth, tinted with a shade of horror and humor, and completed with a cautionary note and a moral lesson. In the Vegas organ harvester legend, the horror of waking up in a bathtub with a kidney removed warns travelers to the strip of the danger and indignity of engaging in flirtatious behaviors with a mysterious woman at a bar.

A cultural idea is reproduced when it is transmitted from one person to another. Urban legends interest cultural psychologists because they are highly transmittable cultural ideas (Heath, Bell, & Sternberg, 2001). Although urban legends are by definition legendary, they spread rapidly. This raises an intriguing possibility: Some highly reproducible cultural ideas may not be good representations of reality. If cultural ideas serve some psychological functions, such functions are not restricted to representation of reality. What other psychological functions does culture serve? In this chapter, we review a number of possible answers to this question. We begin with a brief discussion of biological and cultural evolution, and proceed to discuss the possible role culture plays in the evolution of the human species. Next, we review how culture can be viewed as a shared resource jointly cultivated by a collective to coordinate social actions, to cope with the changing social environment, and to fulfill the psychological needs of the individual.

Biological and Cultural Evolution

Natural selection theories have been applied to explain the emergence, evolution, and differentiation of human cultures. According to some evolution theorists (Fox, 1970, 1989; Meggers, 1971), cultures emerged because natural selection favored those who could develop cultural traditions. Because instinctive behavior and genetic materials change slowly, they do not adapt rapidly enough to changing circumstances. By comparison, cultural traditions adapt more quickly to the changing environment. In other words, culture allows humans to adapt to environmental changes more rapidly than they could through the process of natural selection acting on genetic variation (Dawkins, 1976). In essence, human culture does not stand apart from biological evolution; it grew out of it and remains inextricably intertwined with it. As Fox (1970, p. 40) put it, "culture does not represent a triumph over nature." Rather, "in behaving culturally we are behaving naturally."

Other evolution theorists believe that through the action of natural selection, organisms are designed to respond to local conditions in fitness-enhancing ways. Thus, cultural evolution is a form of phenotypic adaptation to varying social and ecological conditions (Boone & Smith, 1998). This view has been heavily influenced by contemporary biological evolution theories, which we review briefly below.

Biological Evolution

The story of biological evolution is a story about the reproductive success (or failure) of genes. In essence, evolution under natural selection is a process that produces genetic variation and biological adaptation to the changing environment.

Genetic variation results from mutation and recombination of genes. The genes of a population of sexually interbreeding organisms constitute a gene pool. Genes may stay in the body of an organism (the host), or travel from one body to another via sperms or eggs in the process of sexual reproduction. Through sexual reproduction, new copies of the genes are made. Random errors in the gene-copying process may lead to mutation of genes, producing a "new" gene in the gene pool. Once a new mutated gene has been formed, it can spread through the gene pool via sexual reproduction. In short, genetic variation arises from sexual reproduction and genetic recombination.

Biological adaptation is a consequence of the interaction between genetic variation and the external environment. Some genes are rare in the gene pool, and others are common. Genetic evolution is the process through which the relative distribution of the genes in the gene pool is altered. Natural selection is one reason for change in gene frequencies. Genes influence the development of phenotypic traits in the body. Genes that generate phenotypes that are good at surviving and reproduction will be duplicated frequently and be widely represented in the gene pool. When offspring inherit some of their parents' genes, they tend to develop the phenotypes associated with the inherited genes. The proliferation of more successful genotypes results in increase in genotypes that are better adapted to the local environments (Boone & Smith, 1998).

Through natural selection, genes that make adaptive phenotypes will come to predominate in the gene pool, and genes that do not will be removed from it. However, when environmental conditions change, selection may lead to evolutionary change. Changes in the environmental conditions may result from natural catastrophes or through evolutionary improvement of other creatures (e.g., predators, prey, and parasites; Dawkins, 1996). Accordingly, the frequencies of the genes in the gene pool are constantly being redistributed or updated as the environmental conditions change, for the sake of maximizing the species' adaptability.

Cultural Evolution

Although natural selection is a theory of biological evolution, it has been applied to explain cultural evolution. The cultural analog of genes is *memes*, a term coined by Dawkins (1976) in his classic book *The Selfish Gene* to refer to a cultural idea held by an adherent or host. Related memes are often connected to each other and form a network (Gabora, 1997). Culture is like an organized network of associated memes that are relatively successful in surviving and reproducing. Like genes, memes are replicators; replication occurs when representations of memes are transformed into action or language, transmitted through social processes such as imitation and communication, and reproduced in the brain of another host.

The organ harvester legend is a quintessential meme with great reproductive success. It has been relayed to thousands of people by word of mouth, electronic mails, and even printed fliers, although there is no evidence that any such incident ever occurred in the United States. Another example of a highly successful meme is the legend that drug dealers are giving temporary tattoos coated with LSD to children, who put them on and absorb the LSD through their skin. Despite public announcements that this story is not true, the legend continues to spread. Some concerned individuals even posted warnings in police stations, schools, and other public places.

Variations in memes are created when their representations are combined, transformed, and reorganized consciously or unconsciously. The Neiman-Marcus cookie recipe story has been around since the 1940s. In an urban legend widely circulated in the 1980s, Mrs. Fields was accused of overcharging its customer for a cookie recipe. Years before that, in another widely circulated urban gossip, Waldorf Astoria Hotel in New York was accused of overcharging its customer for a red velvet cake recipe.

Some cultural evolution theorists believe that a meme's content determines its reproductive success, or the number of new adherents it can spread to. For example, some memes (e.g., the Gospel) encourage their adherents to tell them to others (spread the good news to the world), some (e.g., Atkins' diet) encourage preservation of the organisms, some (e.g., the values of chastity and virginity of women in the Brahman caste in traditional India) threaten a penalty for abandoning them, and some influence their hosts to attack or sabotage competing movements (e.g., prolife extremism influences its adherents to attempt abortion-clinic bombings). These memes have an advantage in surviving and reproducing (Lynch, 1996).

Other theorists believe that as memes compete for reproductive success, they are subjected to the law of demand in the social marketplace: Memes that are instrumental to fulfilling basic personal and collective goals will have greater demand in the market, and higher likelihood of being passed on (Heath et al., 2001). In essence, people pass on memes or cultural ideas that have worked for them or the society (Triandis, 1996). The question is: What functions does culture as a network of widely circulated memes serve? In the following sections, we review three possible answers to this question: (1) culture confers benefits to the survival of the species; (2) culture confers benefits to the optimal functioning of the society; and (3) culture confers psychological benefits to the individual.

What Does Culture Do for the Survival of the Species?

Evolutionary Psychology

Some evolutionary psychologists hold that human culture evolved because human ancestors needed to find adaptive solutions to the recurrent problems they faced regularly (Kenrick, Li, & Butner, 2003). These problems include selecting mates and maintaining relationship with one's mate (mating), gaining and maintaining respect from and power over others (status), establishing cooperative alliances (coalition formation), defending the self and one's in-group members (self-protection), and providing care to the offspring (Bugental, 2000; Kenrick, Maner, Butner, Li, Becker, & Schaller, 2002).

Mating

Through biological evolution, a set of adaptive decision rules were developed and applied to solve each key problem. Mate selection is of critical significance to the reproduction of one's own genes. Thus, individuals are particularly attentive to information that would enable them to select a mate who would increase the chance of reproductive success. This information includes the potential mate's sex, physical attractiveness, health, age, resources, and status. For men, optimization for reproductive success involves finding a healthy and fertile female agent to carry their genes. Consistent with this idea, investigators (D. Singh, 1993; Kenrick, Groth, Trost, & Sadalla, 1993; Kenrick & Keefe, 1992) found that men weigh information pertinent to physical attractiveness (a cue of health and fertility) more than do women. Moreover, men's commitment to their female partner may be undermined when other physically attractive females are available (Kenrick, Neuberg, Zierk, & Krones, 1994). Conversely, because of the scarcity of eggs (relative to sperms) and the costs and risks associated with pregnancy, for women, reproductive success depends on whether a resourceful and reliable mate can be found to ensure the survival of the infants. Accordingly, in mate selection, women weigh information pertinent to resources and status more than do men. Additionally, women's commitment to their male partners may be undermined when other males with higher status or richer resources are available. There is also evidence that women tend to be more restricted in obtaining multiple mates than do men, probably because the costs of a poor mating decision weigh more heavily for women than for men (Kenrick et al., 1993).

Status

To address the problem of status differentiation, decision rules were developed for placing individuals into a network of hierarchies. Recall that females have a greater tendency to use male status as a cue for mate selection. Hence, according to evolutionary psychology, compared to females, males have been designed by natural selection to be more sensitive to possible gain and loss of status (Li, Bailey, Kenrick, & Linsenmeier, 2002). In other words, because of the stronger association of status with reproductive success for men than for women, status and social dominance may be more valued in male culture than in female culture (Gutierres, Kenrick, & Partch, 1999).

Coalition Formation

When there is uncertainty associated with the supply of vital resources, resource sharing is a means to reduce the amount of uncertainty in the supply of these resources (Kameda, Takezawa, & Hastie, 2003). In several simulation studies and experiments, Kameda and Diasuke (2002) demonstrated that when there is uncertainty associated with the supply of vital resources, people tend to share their resources in order to reduce the amount of uncertainty in the supply of these resources. These findings concur with some ethnographic observations. Among Ache foragers in Paraguay, acquisition of collected resources (vegetables and fruits) is much more predictable than acquisition of meat. Thus, these foragers share hunted prey (peccary and deer) with all members in the hunting community, but they share vegetables and fruits with their kinsmen only (Kameda et al., 2003).

Sharing resources and engaging in cooperative behaviors with those who share genes with the self increases the reproductive success of one's own genes. Thus, according to evolutionary psychology, the tendency to share resources with genetically connected others is greater than the tendency to share resources with genetically unconnected individuals. Thus, as the above example illustrates, resource sharing with genetically unconnected individuals in the community occurs only when the uncertainty in the supply of resources is high. By contrast, the threshold for communal sharing among kinsmen is relatively low. In addition, most human groups have developed rules for altruism to ensure that people would likely engage in cooperative behaviors with neighbors who are genetically closely related (Burnstein, Crandall, & Kitayama, 1994).

Self-Protection and Parental Care

Organisms have also been designed by natural selection to apply rules for self-protection and parental care to ensure survival of their own genes. For example, people would likely reciprocate aggression and violence directed toward the self and those who are genetically related to the self, particularly when aggression was initiated from those who are genetically unrelated. In addition, parents would likely invest heavily in their offspring, because parents share half of their genes with their offspring. By contrast, stepparents are more likely to abuse or neglect their children than biological parents, possibly because stepparents are not genetically related to their stepchildren (see Kenrick et al., 2002).

In short, the objective of the evolutionary psychology research program is to explain how in the course of biological evolution, shared decision rules emerged in key problem areas, and how individual differences (such as gender differences) in decision rules emerged as biologically adaptive responses (Kenrick et al., 2003).

Evaluation of Evolutionary Psychology

Returning to the example of urban legend, evolutionary psychology may provide some insights into the factors that determine which cultural idea will succeed in the social marketplace. Specifically, evolutionary psychology holds that cultural ideas that serve the fundamental goals in the key problem areas are likely to win the competition of the market. It is noteworthy that urban legends that enjoy wide circulation often contain a cautionary note. The organ harvester legend reminds people of the danger of engaging in flirtatious behaviors with a mysterious woman in Las Vegas. A recurrent theme in many urban legends (such as the LSD-coated tattoo legend) concerns the negative consequences of accepting free gifts or food from strangers. These legends appeal to common fears, and seem to serve the self-protection goal.

However, not all widely circulated urban legends evoke fear. Indeed, some of them evoke positive emotions. For example, according to a chain letter that was widely circulated on the Internet in 1997–1998, Bill Gates was testing a new e-mail-tracing software; a monetary incentive was offered to encourage people to forward the chain letter to others. Each person was promised a $1000 award when the letters reached 1000 people. Indeed, research has shown that people are likely to pass on urban legends that carry either surprisingly positive or surprisingly negative news (Heath, 1996).

Some evolutionary psychologists hold that if there are seemingly universal decision rules in each key problem area, a biological explanation is needed. According to them, although different societies wear different symbolic disguises and exhibit a great deal of differences in the details of their culture, beneath these differences is a remarkable uniformity of social structure and social institutions (e.g., laws and property, rules about incest, a system of social status, and courtship practices). Accordingly, cultures are different phenotypic expressions of the outcomes of the interaction between genotype and environmental conditions (Fox, 1989; Rubinstein, 2004).

Unfortunately, the above assumption is difficult to test. Some authors (e.g., Reynolds, 1976) have questioned whether a biological explanation is needed to explain universal decision rules. It may be that societies developed the same solutions to ever-recurrent problems because these are the most practical solutions.

All cultural evolution theorists acknowledge the role of natural selection in the emergence of human cultures. However, they disagree on the specific role natural selection has played in the evolution of human cultures. Evolutionary psychology holds that natural selection acts directly on culturally transmitted variation, producing variations in behaviors in different human groups. For example, they believe that the uneven distributions of some sex norms and behaviors in male and female cultures described above result directly from natural selection. However, other cultural evolution theorists believe that earlier evolutionary processes have led to the development of fitness-enhancing cognitive and behavioral strategies (e.g., language and encoding of information into external memory devices; see Chapter 3). These strategies have enabled people to respond adaptively to the changing physical and human-made environments they live in, producing diverse cultural patterns (Boone & Smith, 1998; Fiske, 2000; Kashima, 2000a).

Today, most social scientists disavow the view that natural selection acts on cultural evolution directly. Instead, they submit that natural selection enables cultural evolution, and that culture has evolved in response to historical events. In other words, culture has evolved in response to itself. We now turn to the implications of this view.

What Does Culture Do for a Society?

Culture as Collective Solution to Coordination Problems

It is widely accepted that culture is a collectively constructed device to solve coordination problems (Cohen, 2001; Fiske, 2000; Heylighen & Campbell, 1995; Y. Kashima, 1999). The following example offers an illustration of this argument. The French drive on the right side of the road, and the British drive on the left side of it. With the opening of the Channel Tunnel (Chunnel), the amount of traffic from Europe in Britain has increased. Should the Britons switch to driving on the right, or should the French cars switch over? In effect, both solutions will work. However, if

British drivers		French drivers	
		Stay put	Switch over
	Stay put	−10/−10	10/10
	Switch over	10/10	−10/−10

FIGURE 4.1. A hypothetical payoff matrix for the joint decisions of British and French drivers.

both British and French cars follow the customary driving convention in their own country, or if both switch over, both parties will suffer.

Figure 4.1 shows the payoff matrix for the Britons and the French described above. The entries in the table represent the utility or disutility associated with each joint decision. For example, if both British and French drivers switch over, both groups will suffer a disutility (−10). If one group switches over, and the other group stays put, both groups will gain 10 utility points. If both groups have perfect information about the payoff matrix, but cannot communicate with each other, can they solve this coordination problem?

To make the coordination problem more complex and realistic, we will bring in the cost of switching over. Assume that the trouble of having to overcome one's driving habit will generate 5 disutility points. The new payoff matrix is presented in Figure 4.2. According to the new payoff matrix, from the perspective of a British driver, it makes sense to stay put, because the potential maximum utility associated with this option is 10 and the maximum potential disutility is −10, compared to 5 and −15 for the alternative option (switching over). However, the French drivers have exactly the same payoffs. If both groups try to maximize their own potential utility and minimize their potential disutility, they will both stay put, and both groups will suffer. This scenario corresponds to what Heylighen and Campbell (1995) refer to as the *mixed partially competitive system*, where increase in utility for one group implies decrease in utility for another group, and where there is some but not enough incentive for cooperation.

British drivers		French drivers	
		Stay put	Switch over
	Stay put	−10/−10	10/5
	Switch over	5/10	−15/−15

FIGURE 4.2. A hypothetical payoff matrix for the joint decisions of British and French drivers, taking into consideration the cost of switching over.

Coordination is a major issue in all societies, and coordination problems, characterized by interdependent decisions and codependence of interests, similar to the one depicted above, have been extensively studied in economics. The significance of solving complex coordination problems could not be emphasized more, because almost every kind of social activity (e.g., cooperation, competition, communication, exchange, division of labor, conducting a ritual, making joint decisions, and relating to outsiders) that defines human sociality involves solution of complex coordination problems (Fiske, 2000).

To ensure that individuals facing coordination problems will make joint decisions that produce optimal outcomes to all parties involved, several major types of social control mechanisms have evolved in human societies. The most rudimentary type is mutual monitoring. Through informal face-to-face transmissions, the involved parties agree on some common beliefs and practices, and those with deviating beliefs or patterns of behaviors are held in check by different forms of ostracism. Individuals may also internalize and identify with these beliefs and practices. In this case, shared beliefs and practices are cultural devices for solving complex coordination problems (Fiske, 2000). Indeed, according to Heylighen and Campbell (1995), in human societies, beliefs spread through conformist transmission and internalization are often the predominant mechanisms of social control.

When the cultural mode of social control fails, the system may rely on other social control mechanisms, such as market mechanism, and legal control. In the Chunnel example, absence of coordination will cause accidents and long delay. Drivers who want to minimize their costs will learn from their mistakes and ultimately agree on and comply with some rules. Alternatively, the British authorities can decide to switch to driving on the right, and drivers who are caught disobeying the rule will be fined.

Going back to our urban legend example, one current view is that urban legends and gossip in general are a potentially powerful and efficient means of transmitting information about the rules, norms, and other guidelines for living in a human group (Baumeister, Zhang, & Vohs, 2004). Indeed, the most widely spread urban legends contain a moral lesson (e.g., do not be greedy). In one study, participants were asked what they had learned from a gossip, and most of them mentioned generalized maxims for their own social life, like "Don't forget your true friend" (Baumeister et al., 2004). A gossip may ring true after being repeated many times, and the moral lesson behind it may become accepted wisdom. Although it seems likely that only young children would believe in the contents of gossip, in reality, compared with younger children, older children are likely to believe in the contents of gossip (Kittler, Parker, & La Greca, 2002).

Thus far, we have focused on the social control function of culture in solving complex coordination problems. Successful solution of complex coordination problems also requires coordination of plans and actions. In addition to being a social control mechanism, culture also provides the shared, standard operating procedures, unstated assumptions, tools, norms, and values for grasping experiences (Triandis, 1996). As such, by virtue of culture, individuals are capable of constructing shared representations of their experiences, and coordinating their plans and actions (Y. Kashima, 1999).

In addition, culture also provides conventionalized solutions to recurrent coordination problems (Y. Kashima, 1999). Culture is to society what memory is to individuals (Kluckhohn, 1954). Culture encodes collective memories of schematized approaches to solving coordination problems (Y. Kashima, 1999). These conventionalized solutions are widely accepted solutions in the community. Competent members of the culture can retrieve such conventionalized solutions to solve emergent coordination problems.

In short, coordination problems arise in all human communities in which people need to make joint decisions on problems with more than one possible optimal solution. Culture provides different means for solving such coordination problems.

Culture Adapting to Institutional and Historical Changes

Culture also adapts to changes in institutional and historical events. As the institutional and historical conditions supporting a culture change, culture will change accordingly (Yamagishi & Takahashi, 1994).

For example, in the 1980s, the Japanese employment system was one of the main factors contributing to the economic success in Japan. Two major characteristics of the Japanese employment system are long-term employment and seniority-based wage. According to a recent report by the Bank of Japan, long-term employment and seniority-based wage are still widely practiced in Japanese business organizations. Specifically, compared to workers in other major world economic powers (Germany, France, the United States, Canada, and the United Kingdom), workers in Japan have the longest average tenure of a worker, the lowest ratio of employees working in short-term employment, and the strongest association between seniority and wage (Hattori & Maeda, 2000).

With low job mobility and the absence of formal sanctioning mechanisms in Japanese organizations, social reputation of individuals and mutual monitoring of behaviors become the major social control mechanisms. Individuals who violate organization norms will receive a negative reputation, which will be widely circulated in the organization. Such individuals risk being ostracized and becoming a social outcast in the organization. In such institutional contexts, the motivation to accommodate the self to the organization culture is particularly strong. Shaped by this institutional context, Japanese tend to adhere to the value of interdependence, pay attention to context, and prefer conformity to uniqueness (Markus & Kitayama, 1991).

However, when the institutional context changes, such cognitive and behavioral tendencies may become maladaptive, and ultimately be replaced by another set of tendencies that are adaptive in the new institutional environment. A number of demographic and economic changes have cast serious doubt on the desirability and sustainability of the Japanese employment system. For example, in many Japanese firms, the middle-age group and older-age employees receive higher salary than their productivity justifies, whereas younger employees receive lower salary than their productivity justifies. For the system to be sustainable, the proportion of middle-age and older employees should be smaller than that of young employees. The system's sustainability also relies on high economic growth, and the continued existence of firms. However, as the baby boomers born just after World War II get older, and with the unexpected rapid decline in economic growth, and the increased number of firm bankruptcies, the continued survival of the traditional employment system is facing many challenges. Indeed, since the 1980s, the average working years in a single company have shortened in the young-age group, and the association between seniority and wage has weakened, particularly among university-graduate male workers (Hattori & Maeda, 2000).

The potential long-term impact of such institutional changes in Japan on Japanese people's cognitive and behavioral styles is highlighted in a study conducted by Suzuki and Yamagishi (2004). These investigators had Japanese undergraduates participate in a trading game. For half of the participants, social reputation and mutual monitoring were the dominant social control mechanisms in the game. A player who was found to have cheated would earn a bad reputation, and each player knew other players' reputation. For the remaining participants, there was a formal system that punished unfair traders. After the participants had played the game for 2 hours, they completed measures of cognitive styles.

Previous research has shown that compared to European Americans, Japanese are more attentive to contextual information and have greater preference for conformity vs. uniqueness (see Chapters 5 and 6). In this study, after 2 hours' social interactions in a simulated environment where formal social control mechanisms dominated, the participants were less attentive to object–context relation, and had a greater preference for uniqueness (vs. conformity), compared to those who had engaged in extensive social interactions in a simulated environment where social reputation and mutual monitoring were the dominant social control mechanisms. In short, this study demonstrated how social institutions afford certain culture-specific cognitive styles, and how changes in social institutions can alter such seemingly well-learned cognitive styles.

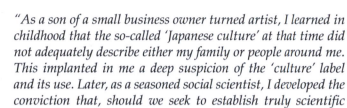

Meet the Researcher: Toshio Yamagishi

"As a son of a small business owner turned artist, I learned in childhood that the so-called 'Japanese culture' at that time did not adequately describe either my family or people around me. This implanted in me a deep suspicion of the 'culture' label and its use. Later, as a seasoned social scientist, I developed the conviction that, should we seek to establish truly scientific social sciences, the term 'culture' ought to be vanquished utterly. Ironically, eliminating 'culture' from social science vocabulary requires explaining 'cultural' phenomena on non-cultural grounds, rather than pretending that they don't exist. This demands of me a profound understanding of 'culture.' I now realize that 'culture' is like quicksand; the harder I try to escape, the deeper I am drawn in."

Professor Toshio Yamagishi was born in Nagoya, Japan. He earned his doctorate in sociology from the University of Washington in the United States. Recently, he established the Center for the Study of Cultural and Ecological Foundations of the Mind at Hokkaido University in Sapporo, where he directs studies in human sociality.

Culture change in post-communist Albania provides another illustration of how culture adapts to historical change. After the collapse of communism, villagers in some former communist states (e.g., Albania) face the advent of economic incentives for adopting individual- and household-centered economic strategies. As a consequence, traditional culture that emphasizes the power of the household head and the key role of the clan in social and economic life declines. At the same time, the villagers develop new consensus on status ranking, and they now view personal (vs. social) qualities (e.g., intelligence and honesty) as the key determinants of status (Lawson & Saltmarshe, 2002).

In summary, evolutionary theories offer a fresh perspective to cultural phenomena, and confer new insights on how culture as distributed cognitions emerges, reproduces, and transforms. Whereas some theorists (e.g., evolutionary psychologists) believe that uneven distributions of cultural ideas or decision rules result from the interaction between the fundamental goal of genetic reproduction, the biological constitution of the individuals, and the environment, others believe that cultural variations result from the application of the cognitive and behavioral proclivities humans developed in the course of biological evolution to manage the increasingly complex coordination problems in group life. Despite these differences, a recurrent theme in cultural evolution theories is that culture is an adaptive tool jointly constructed by a group of interconnected individuals to solve practical problems they regularly encountered in group life.

What Does Culture Do for the Individual?

The cultural evolution theories reviewed above seek to expound on culture's importance to the human species or the society. In this section, we review the functional theories that seek to explicate what culture does for the individual. These theories examine how, via culture, specific social and psychological needs are fulfilled. To understand the psychological benefits culture confers to the individual, it is useful to review some characteristics of culture as a knowledge tradition.

What is Special about Cultural Knowledge?

A major difference between cultural and personal knowledge is that cultural knowledge is widely shared, whereas personal knowledge is not. The relatively wide distribution of cultural knowledge implies that many people in the culture apply this knowledge. More importantly, the more widely distributed a piece of knowledge is, the more frequently it is used in everyday communication.

Imagine yourself as a research participant in a referential communication task. You are presented with an array of four drawings, like those in Figure 4.3, and asked to describe one of them, say drawing (d). Later, another student in your university will see the same drawings, but arranged in a different order. The second student will listen to your description and try to identify drawing (d) based on your description. How would you describe this drawing to enable your fellow student to successfully identify the drawing?

Like most participants in this experiment, you may use expressions like "It looks like a brick wall," rather than expressions like "It looks like the pattern on my roommate's shower curtain." This is because most undergraduates are expected to know what a brick wall is like, but few undergraduates are expected to have seen the shower curtain of a particular

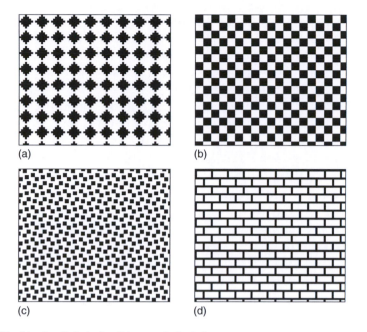

FIGURE 4.3. Stimuli in a hypothetical referential communication task.

person (Fussell & Krauss, 1989a, 1989b). In general, people would use what they believe their addressee would know when they formulate their communicative messages in everyday social interactions (Fussell & Krauss, 1991, 1992; Krauss & Fussell, 1996; Lau, Chiu, & Hong, 2001). If you have no reason to believe that your addressee has seen your roommate's shower curtain, it is unlikely you would refer to it when you describe the pattern. The more widely shared a piece of knowledge is, the more likely it would be applied in daily communication.

Generally speaking, a shared belief or attitude is usually perceived to be more valid than one that is not shared. When a person holds a certain belief or attitude, knowing that other people share this belief or attitude would increase the person's adherence to this belief or attitude.

In a study conducted by Sechrist and Stangor (2001), European American undergraduates completed a measure of prejudice toward African Americans. On the basis of their scores on this measure, participants were preselected to have either high or low prejudice beliefs toward African Americans. Later, the participants were given feedback on how widely shared their attitude was among their fellow undergraduates. Half of the participants, randomly selected, were told that 81% of the students on campus agreed with their belief, and the remaining half learned that only 19% of the students on campus agreed with their belief. Next, the investigator led the participant to the hallway and asked the participant to wait there while the experimenter prepared the materials for the next part of the study. In the hallway, an African American (the experimenter's confederate) was sitting in a chair, and next to the confederate was a row of seven empty chairs. The question of interest is: Would the participant choose to sit closely to the confederate?

Not surprisingly, high-prejudice participants generally sat further away from the African American confederate than did low-prejudice participants. However, the association between prejudice level and sitting distance was much stronger when the participants learned that their own attitudes were widely shared by others. In this condition, those who had favorable attitudes toward African Americans sat much closer to the confederate than did those with unfavorable attitudes. Conversely, when the participants learned that most undergraduates did not share their attitude, those who had favorable attitudes toward African Americans also sat closer to the confederate than did those with unfavorable attitudes, but the difference was small. In short, when people believe that their attitudes are widely shared, they are certain of their attitudes, and are prepared to use their attitudes to guide their behaviors.

Epistemic Security

The foregoing analysis implies that cultural knowledge affords a sense of epistemic security, or the feeling of having certain answers to questions in life. When people need certain answers, they may tend to rely on cultural knowledge.

Arie Kruglanski uses the term *need for cognitive closure* to refer to this need for epistemic security. Individuals with high need for cognitive closure prefer certainty to ambiguity. They desire certain answers that would enable them to construct a structured, orderly, unambiguous, and predictable reality (Kruglanski & Webster, 1996). There are individual differences in the need for cognitive closure, and such individual differences can be reliably measured by the Need for Cognitive Closure Scale (Webster & Kruglanski, 1994). If you agree strongly with items such as "I think that having clear rules and order at work is essential for success," and "I don't like situations that are uncertain," you have a relatively high need for cognitive closure. Conversely, if you agree strongly with items such as "I enjoy the uncertainty of going into a new situation without knowing what might happen," and "I dislike the routine aspects of my schoolwork," you have a relatively low need for cognitive closure.

The need for cognitive closure may vary from situation to situation. For example, people who ordinarily would consult many different opinions and consider many possible options on an issue before forming their own view would desire closure when they are physically or mentally exhausted, or need to make decisions under time pressure (Kruglanski, Webster, & Klem, 1993).

As mentioned, when people need epistemic security, they may increase their adherence to cultural convention. This point was illustrated in several cross-cultural studies of causal explanation. Compared to North American societies, most Chinese societies have many norms, and punish deviant behaviors more severely (see Chapter 7). In North America, the society is expected to accommodate to individual interests. Individuals feel that they are in control and that they can make things happen. By comparison, in Chinese societies, people are expected to follow group norms. Individuals may feel powerless when confronted by the group. In these societies, the group is seen as an entity that makes things happen (Hernandez & Iyengar, 2001; Su et al., 1999). Consistent with this idea, research has shown that European Americans agree more strongly with statements like "In my society, individuals take control of situations around them and exercise free will" than with statements like "Organizations set a course for themselves independent of the influences surrounding them." The reverse is true for Chinese Singaporeans (T. Menon et al., 1999).

These beliefs impact the way European Americans and Chinese explain social events. European Americans tend to explain a social event in terms of the dispositions of the individual: Something about the individual is the cause of the event. Conversely, Chinese tend to explain a social event in terms of the dispositions of the group: Something about the group is the cause of the event (T. Menon et al., 1999).

In one study (C. Chiu, Morris, Hong, & Menon, 2000), European American and Hong Kong Chinese undergraduates were presented with the following event, and asked to judge how likely the event was caused by some dispositions of the pharmacy worker (individual dispositions) or by some dispositions of the clinic (group dispositions):

One hundred and forty-five children aged two months to six years were affected in a medicine mix-up in a city medical clinic. A pharmacy worker who was dispensing medication gave these children mouthwash (instead of the prescribed cough syrup) to drink. A spokesman from the Medical Board announced later in the week that many children were affected by this blunder. At least 101 children had taken the "syrup" by the time the error was discovered. Two were sent to the Emergency Room after having taken the "medicine."

In response to this case, European American undergraduates made stronger individual dispositional attributions than they did group dispositions, whereas Hong Kong Chinese displayed the reverse trend. More importantly, in this study, the investigator also measured the research participants' need for cognitive closure. Among European American undergraduates, those who had a higher need for cognitive closure believed more strongly that something about the pharmacy worker (e.g., the pharmacy worker was not conscientious about service) caused the event. Conversely, among Hong Kong Chinese undergraduates, those with a higher need for cognitive closure believed more strongly that something about the clinic (e.g., the clinic was incompetent in maintaining proper usage of the medical products) caused the event. This finding shows that differences in causal attribution between European Americans and Hong Kong Chinese is particularly pronounced among people with high need for cognitive closure.

In another study where causal attributions of European American and Hong Kong Chinese undergraduates were compared (T. Menon et al., 1999), half of the participants in each cultural group read the following story:

> A farmer was grazing a small herd of cattle. One day, things unexpectedly went wrong. At first, a bull seemed agitated by something near the farmer. Moments later, the bull charged directly at the farmer, who fell to the ground as he was hit by its impact. The bull managed to break free from the enclosed area. It escaped and ran free.

In this story, the agent is an individual bull. The remaining participants in each cultural group read a different version of the story. In this version, the agent was changed from the individual (the bull) to a group (the herd): The herd charged at the farmer.

When asked to explain why the incident depicted in the vignette happened, European Americans made stronger dispositional attributions when the agent was an individual bull than when the agent was a herd. In their view, when an individual was out of control, something about the bull (e.g., the bull was aggressive and dominant) was the cause. However, when a herd was out of control, the herd's dispositions were not good explanations of the incident. By contrast, Hong Kong Chinese undergraduates made stronger dispositional attributions when the agent was the herd than when it was an individual bull. In their view, if a herd was out of control, something about the herd was the cause. However, the bull's dispositions could not explain very well why an individual bull was out of control.

This pattern of results was particularly pronounced when the participants responded to the scenario under time pressure. In one study (C. Chiu et al., 2000), half of the participants were put under time pressure when they responded to the bull vs. herd scenario. Recall that the need for epistemic security increases under time pressure. As expected, when put

under time pressure, European American students made stronger dispositional attributions when the agent was an individual bull than when the
agent was a herd, and the reverse was true for Hong Kong Chinese
students. However, when the participants were not under time pressure,
cultural differences in causal attribution disappeared.

Aside from social judgment, the need for epistemic security also moderates cross-cultural differences in the way people present themselves and
how they would respond in social situations.

To maintain one's standing in the society, individuals are expected to
present the self in a socially appropriate or desirable manner. There are at
least two ways people can present themselves positively. First, people can
exaggerate their positive personal qualities. For example, they may say, "I
am a completely rational person," or "I am fully in control of my own
fate." This self-presentation strategy has been referred to as *self-deceptive
enhancement* (Paulhus, 1984). Alternatively, people may exaggerate how
conscientious they are in following social norms. They may say, "I always
obey laws, even if I'm unlikely to get caught," or "I have never dropped
litter on the street." This self-presentation style is generally known as
impression management (Paulhus, 1984).

Although both self-presentation strategies are found in almost every
society, they are unevenly distributed across societies. For example, in
North America, where self-confidence and personal excellence are heavily
emphasized, self-deceptive enhancement is more common than impression
management. Conversely, in East Asian societies where there is a heavy
emphasis on following societal norms, impression management is the more
widely practiced self-presentation strategy (Lalwani, Shavitt, & Johnson, in
press).

In a cross-cultural study (Ip, Chen, & Chiu, 2004), the self-presentation strategies of European American and Hong Kong Chinese undergraduates were compared. As expected, European American
undergraduates gave more self-deceptive enhancement responses than
impression management responses, and Hong Kong Chinese undergraduates gave more self-deceptive enhancement responses than impression
management responses. More importantly, this cross-cultural difference
was particularly pronounced among individuals with high (vs. low) need
for cognitive closure.

Research on conflict resolution offers another illustration of the role
of epistemic security in cross-cultural differences. Chinese and Western
traditions of using third parties to mediate conflicts differ with regard to
the presence of prior relationships: Chinese prefer a trusted familiar person as the mediator, whereas Westerners prefer a neutral stranger
(LeResche, 1992). In one study, Fu, Morris, Lee, and Chiu (2002) presented

the following case to European American and Hong Kong Chinese under-graduates.

> Amy and Linda work in the Marketing Division at a large candy com-pany. Amy is in the team of print advertising and Linda is in the team of TV commercial advertising. They are at the Associate level, below the level of Manager, which in turn is below the level of VPs. The Marketing Division is located in the same building as the Human Resources Division. For the past several months, Amy and Linda have been developing an integrated print/TV advertising package for a new candy. The VP told them that whoever came up with the best idea would receive a bonus. Amy and Linda were told to talk about the preliminary ideas with each other but ultimately presented their pol-ished proposal at a meeting. At the end of the meeting, the VP selected Amy's plan. Linda was surprised that the plan Amy presented was quite similar to an idea that Linda had sketched out weeks before; Amy had rejected it, suggesting that it had little potential. After the meeting, Linda checked her records and became even more convinced that her original plan had inspired Amy's idea. Linda approached Amy and shared her impression that she deserved partial credit for the idea. Amy was surprised and angered because she didn't see much similarity between the rough ideas she remembered Amy having men-tioned and the polished plan that she had worked hard to perfect. After an increasingly awkward and angry conversation, the two women stormed off to their respective offices. A few hours later, Linda called Amy and suggested that they needed to resolve this misunder-standing. Linda agreed and suggested that they find a third party to be mediator to help them sort out the issues.

After studying the case, participants rated the desirability of a connected person (Manager A, who has worked with both Linda and Amy before, has offered valuable advice to both, and has a close friendship with both) and an unconnected person as the mediator (Manager B, who knows nei-ther of them, and is known to be willing to give advice).

As expected, European American undergraduates preferred the unconnected mediator and Hong Kong Chinese undergraduates the con-nected one. Again, this pattern was more pronounced among participants with high (vs. low) need for cognitive closure.

The foregoing analysis seems to suggest that when the need for epis-temic security is high, people adhere rigidly to cultural convention and do not consider alternative viewpoints. However, this is the case only when the individual's cultural tradition offers a shared reality that is perceived to be valid and useful in the current situation. In situations where the cultural tradition fails to offer valid, certain answers, individuals who seek epistemic security may be particularly motivated to look for new information that will provide them with a sense of epistemic security (see Kruglanski et al., 1993).

To illustrate this point, Chao (2005) presented Asian and European American undergraduates with the following hypothetical case:

> Donna is a pharmacist in a drug chain store. One day, Sue, the Manager of the store, receives a phone call from Chris, who bought a bottle of cough syrup a few days ago from the store. According to Chris, Donna was the pharmacist who sold him the cough syrup. When Donna gave him the medicine, Chris noticed that the package of the cough syrup was torn, but Donna assured him that the medicine was good. She also told him that it was the only bottle they had in the store. Chris bought the medicine. When he went home, he found that the quality seal of the bottle was broken. Nonetheless, he took the medicine after dinner, and got a severe stomach upset in the evening. He calls Sue, the store manager, to file a complaint, and demands that Donna be removed from her job. When Sue asks Donna for an explanation, Donna insists that although the package was a bit torn, the medicine was in good condition when it was sold. According to Donna, Chris checked the quality seal of the bottle before he paid for it, and she suspects that Chris might have broken the quality seal himself when he checked the medicine. Donna has worked in the store for five years, and has recently been recommended for promotion to Senior Pharmacist. Donna is also a regional advocate in a pharmacist organization, which is an active labor organization in the country.

If you were Sue, what kind of information would you consider to be important for resolving the conflict?

How you would answer this question may depend on your cultural background. In American culture, the major goal in conflict management is to understand what really happened and to find a solution that is fair to all parties involved. To achieve this goal, it is important to gather antecedent information, or information that can help to determine the causal responsibility of the disputants (e.g., whether the pharmacist has a record of making similar mistakes). In East Asian cultures, the major goal is to maintain harmonious relationship in the group or community. To achieve this goal, it is important to gather consequent information, or information pertinent to how the involved parties may feel in response to the possible actions the mediator may take (e.g., how the pharmacist's coworkers would feel if the pharmacist is fired).

Consistent with this idea and the idea that the need for epistemic security increases adherence to cultural convention, among European American students, those with higher need for cognitive closure perceived antecedent information to be more important. Conversely, among Asian American students, those with higher need for cognitive closure rated consequent information to be more important.

What would happen when participants needed to manage a conflict in a culturally unfamiliar situation? For example, how would European American students respond if they were asked to maintain harmonious relationship within the group and the community? How would Asian American students respond if they were required to be fair and to punish the wrongdoer? In both situations, the participants could not rely on their cultural knowledge for a well-accepted, certain answer. Those who sought epistemic security would now be motivated to consider *any* information that would lead to a certain answer. Indeed, when European American students were asked to pursue a relationship maintenance goal, those who had higher need for cognitive closure considered *both* antecedent and consequent information to be more important. Similarly, when Asian American students were asked to pursue a retributive fairness goal, those with higher need for cognitive closure considered *both* types of information to be more important.

This finding has important implications for understanding the psychological experiences of individuals who move to an unfamiliar culture (e.g., expatriates or new immigrants in an unfamiliar culture). In a series of studies, Kosic, Kruglanski, Pierro, and Mannetti (2004) found that immigrants who are surrounded by other members of their ethnocultural group (e.g., those who migrated together with friends and families) perceive the knowledge of their home culture as valid and applicable. For them, a higher need for cognitive closure is associated with a stronger motivation to adhere to the culture of origin. Conversely, immigrants who are surrounded by members of the host country (e.g., those who migrated to a new country alone) no longer perceive the knowledge of their home culture as valid or applicable. For them, a higher need for cognitive closure is associated with a stronger motivation to assimilate into the host culture.

In short, when individuals need to acquire or maintain epistemic security, they tend to adhere to cultural convention, probably because culture as a shared knowledge tradition can provide them with certain answers to recurrent problems in social life. The findings reviewed in the current section suggest that epistemic security is a major psychological benefit of culture. Because the need for epistemic security varies between individuals and across situations, the strength of adherence to culture may also increase or decline depending on the individuals' chronic need for cognitive closure and the specific features of the situation.

Sense of Belongingness

The need to belong, to attach psychologically to one's significant others or a group is a fundamental human motive (Brewer, 1991; Hogg & Abrams, 1988; Taifel & Turner, 1979; Turner, Oakes, Haslam, & McGarty, 1994). Participation in culture is a means to fulfill the need to belong (Hong, Roisman, & Chen, 2006).

In social identity theory, some central features of a group define what the group is (Hogg, 2004; Turner, Hogg, Oakes, Reicher, & Wetherell, 1987). A defining feature of a cultural group is the knowledge tradition believed to be mutually shared by the members of the cultural group (D'Andrade, 1987). This idea has several important theoretical implications. First, when the need to belong to a group is activated, people who identify strongly with their in-group will be motivated to adhere to the group's shared cultural tradition, and to attribute to the self the attributes that are associated with the cultural tradition. The need to belong to the in-group will be stronger either when people realize that they are different from other members of the in-group, or when they realize that they are not different from members of an out-group (Brewer, 1991; Pickett & Brewer, 2001). In one study (Pickett, Bonner, & Coleman, 2002), members of different sororities in an American public university received feedback on how similar or dissimilar they were to other members of their sorority or to members of other sororities. Those who identified strongly with their own sorority tended to attribute to themselves the stereotypic attributes associated with the sorority when they learned that they were dissimilar to other members in the sorority. The tendency to self-stereotype also increased when these participants learned that their personal qualities did not distinguish them from members of other sororities. These results were much less pronounced for those who did not identify with their own sorority.

Second, when people are reminded of their cultural tradition, they tend to see themselves as members of a group rather than as individuals. In one study, Briley and Wyer (2002) reminded half of the American undergraduates in their sample of their cultural identity by presenting to them icons of American culture (e.g., a Dixieland band and Marilyn Monroe). The remaining participants saw some culture-unrelated drawings. Subsequently, the participants completed a measure that tested their tendency to think of themselves as individuals or as members of a group. Each item of the measure consisted of five words (e.g., *to, go, work, we, I*), and the participant's task was to underline the four words that could be used to construct a meaningful sentence. Participants who were reminded of American culture were more likely to form sentences using a first-person plural pronoun (*We go to work*), rather than sentences using a first-person singular pronoun (*I go to work*), indicating that the cultural icons increased the participants' likelihood of seeing themselves as members of a group (vs. individuals). The same findings were obtained in a study where Hong Kong Chinese undergraduates viewed either Chinese cultural icons (e.g., the Great Wall and a Chinese dragon) or culture-unrelated drawings prior to completing the sentence construction task.

Third, people who identify with their culture tend to adhere to the core values that define the tradition, whereas those who do not identify with their culture may not endorse such values (Wan et al., 2004; Wan, Chiu, Peng, & Tam, 2004). For example, in Australia, people who identify themselves as socialists are more likely to endorse welfare-related values and less likely to endorse independence, relative to those who identify themselves as capitalists (Heaven, 1999). In South Africa, self-identified black South Africans have a greater tendency to endorse values of international harmony and national order than do self-identified white Afrikaners (Heaven et al., 2000). In Hong Kong, self-identified Hong Kongers see values related to modernity as more important and values related to Confucianism as less important, compared to self-identified Chinese (Hong, Chiu, Yeung, & Tong, 1999; Lam, Lau, Chiu, Hong, & Peng, 1999).

In a series of studies, Jetten, Postmes, and Mcauliffe (2002) showed that people might use cultural knowledge to express or defend their social identity. Collectivist norms are emphasized in Indonesia, and individualist norms are emphasized in North America. In their first study, Jetten and her colleagues found that Indonesians who identified with Indonesian culture scored higher on collectivism and lower on individualism than those who did not, and Americans who identified with American culture scored higher on individualism than those who did not. In their second study, Australian employees who identified with their company described themselves as more individualist when they learned that their organization culture was individualist and more collectivist when they learned that it was collectivist. Those who did not identify with their organization were not affected by the organization culture feedback. In their third study, the disciplinary culture of psychology was described as either collectivist or individualist. Psychology students (in the Netherlands) who identified with their discipline presented themselves as an individualist when they learned that psychology was an individualist discipline, and presented themselves as a collectivist when they learned that psychology was a collectivist discipline. This effect was particularly pronounced when the disciplinary identity was under threat. Students who did not identify with psychology did not engage in self-stereotyping and were not affected by the identity threat manipulation.

Finally, when people are made accountable to their cultural group for their behaviors, they tend to adhere to the group's cultural tradition (Briley, Morris, & Simonson, 2000; Gelfand & Realo, 1999). As an illustration of this idea, consider the following three computers that differ in terms of memory and hard disk capacity. Computer A has 48 MB of RAM and 1 GB of hard disk space, Computer B has 16 MB of RAM and 3 GB of hard disk space, and Computer C has 32 MB of RAM and 2 GB of hard disk space. In this example, Computer A has the largest RAM size and the smallest disk space, Computer B has the largest disk space and the smallest RAM size, and Computer C represents a good compromise on both product attributes. To most consumers, Computer C is most attractive, but there are cultural differences. There is a stronger emphasis on avoiding extremes in East Asian cultural traditions than in the European American cultural tradition. Accordingly, one would expect East Asians, relative to European Americans, to have greater preference for Computer C.

Briley et al. (2000) assessed preference for compromise options among Asian Americans, European Americans, Hong Kong Chinese, and Japanese. Their results indicate that Asians have a greater preference for the compromise options than do European Americans, but *only when* they are required to explain their choice to members of their cultural group.

Meet the Researcher: Donnel A. Briley

"The global community offers a tremendous breadth of diverse peoples, adding an inexhaustible source of intrigue and revelation to our world and lives. This realm of discovery has traditionally been available to those who leave familiar surrounds to pursue it. But our world is becoming smaller, as more and more people visit and immigrate to foreign lands, and open communication with those from other parts of the globe. Now, cultural surprises often come to us—and when this happens, we might not expect or be fully receptive to these surprises. I hope to increase our understanding of why those from other cultural groups are sometimes different—and reveal the ways in which we are all quite similar—so that these inevitable cultural surprises stimulate fascination and mutual discovery rather than apprehension and conflict."

Donnel A. Briley was born in southern California, has lived in France and Hong Kong, and now resides in Sydney, Australia where he is Associate Professor of Marketing at the University of Sydney.

Gelfand and Realo (1999) have reported similar effects of accountability on cultural differences in the preference for intergroup negotiation strategies. In this study, American and Estonian participants engaged in a hypothetical intergroup negotiation task. The participants in the low-accountability condition were told that they had complete authority for making decisions, whereas those in the high accountability needed to justify their decisions to their manager. The collectivists in the sample were more willing to concede and to cooperate when accountability was high than when it was low. Conversely, the individualists were less willing to do so when accountability was high than when it was low.

In short, there is clear evidence that adherence to cultural tradition is a widely used means to express identification with a cultural group, and to derive a sense of belongingness. Returning once again to our urban legend example, it has been suggested that a primary function of gossip is to facilitate the bonding of social groups (Dunbar, 2004). Dunbar (2004) posits that primates protect themselves against predation by living in groups. To foster cohesion of large social groups, primates spend a lot of time in social grooming. However, as evolution proceeded, group size also increased. In human societies, gossip has replaced social grooming as the primary means for fostering group cohesion. It is estimated that humans now spend about 65% of their speaking time on social information exchange (or gossiping; see Dunbar, Duncan, & Marriott, 1997). Gossip serves the function of facilitating social bonding in large social groups well because it allows individuals to broadcast news within the social network to a large audience.

There is also evidence that in cultural evolution, urban legends are frequently selected and retained because they evoke a widely shared emotional reaction. Accordingly, rumors and legends may serve the important function of bonding people with others who are sharing the same emotion. Consistent with this idea, Heath et al. (2001) found that most widely circulated urban legends have the ability to evoke emotions like anger, fear, or disgust. Furthermore, during the Mad Cow crisis in France in the mid-1990s, the disease was either referred to in the mass media as Mad Cow disease, or by its scientific terms, bovine spongiform encephalopathy (BSE) or Creutzfeldt–Jakob disease (CJD). Detailed analyses performed on French people's responses to the media coverage of the crisis revealed that the public reduced beef consumption when the media referred to the disease as Mad Cow disease, a term that evoked strong negative emotions. However, beef consumption was unaffected by news articles featuring scientific labels for the disease, because the scientific labels did not provoke anxiety (Sinaceur, Heath, & Cole, in press). In short, cultural ideas that help to foster social bonding are likely to be selected and retained, and become part of the cultural tradition.

Purpose of Existence

Through evolution, humans have developed the cognitive abilities to represent nonimmediate events (D'Andrade, 2002). This unique human capability enables the evolution of human culture (see Chapter 3). However, it also makes humans intellectually adept enough to be aware of the inevitability of their finitude (see Figure 4.4). The juxtaposition of the desire for self-preservation and the awareness that death is inevitable gives rise to an overwhelming *terror of death* (Becker, 1973). In this sense, human evolution has presented to humans a universal existential question: What is the purpose of one's existence?

According to terror management theory (Greenberg, Solomon, & Pyszczynski, 1997; Pyszczynski, Greenberg, & Solomon, 1999; Solomon, Greenberg, & Pyszczynski, 1991), the mere thought of death can spontaneously call out this existential question, and hence evoke a surge of existential terror. Until the existential question is satisfactorily addressed, the terror will remain, creating psychological disturbance in the individual. Defending one's own cultural worldviews or distancing oneself from others who hold dissimilar worldviews are two strategies people can use to address the existential question. Terror management theorists refer to these

(a)   (b)

FIGURE 4.4. The mortality motif is represented in many cultural and religious practices: (a) the tombs of a holy family in the Mughal Empire in the Fatehpur Sikri Fortress, India; (b) a priest guarding the tomb of a child in the holy family.

strategies as distal defense. Distal defense strategies can mitigate the terror of death because they can turn the otherwise chaotic world into a well-organized system of beliefs. This system of beliefs provides answers to fundamental questions of life and death (e.g., what is the meaning of life?) and a sense of literal immortality via religious concepts (e.g., afterlife and heaven). In addition, cultural worldviews provide to those who live up to the standards delineated by the worldviews a sense of symbolic immortality, both via a sense of being a valuable member of an imperishable culture, and via a sense of contributing to the culture (Solomon et al., 1991).

According to the *mortality salience hypothesis* in terror management theory, "if a psychological structure provides protection against the potential terror engendered by knowledge of mortality, then reminders of mortality should increase the need to maintain that structure" (Greenberg et al., 1997, p. 78). As cultural worldviews can provide protection against the terror of death, when people are reminded of their mortality, they would be motivated to maintain and validate their cultural worldviews. This motivation, as Pyszczynski, Greenberg, and Solomon (2000) posit, is an unconscious one, and its behavioral and cognitive manifestations are often referred to as mortality salience effects.

There is consistent support for the mortality salience hypothesis. In some studies (e.g., Greenberg et al., 1990, 1995; Greenberg, Pyszczynski, Solomon, Simon, & Breus, 1994; Harmon-Jones, Simon, Pyszczynski, Solomon, & McGregor, 1997; McGregor et al., 1998), some American undergraduates were reminded of death, and the remaining ones were not. Next, participants in both conditions read an essay that explicitly praised the United States, and another essay that explicitly criticized the United States. The results showed that making mortality salient increased participants' negativity toward the writer of the critical essay relative to the writer of the appreciative essay. Under mortality salience, participants were less tolerant of people holding worldview-threatening (vs. worldview-supporting) beliefs, less willing to interact with them, and more hostile to them. In addition, a recent cross-cultural study shows that making salient the threat of mortality strengthens adherence to individualist values among Australians and collectivist values among Japanese (E. Kashima, Halloran, Yuki, & Kashima, 2004), again suggesting that mortality salience strengths adherence to cultural tradition.

Summary and Integration

Culture serves manifold psychological functions for the individual, including providing a sense of epistemic security, a sense of belongingness, and a buffer against existential terror. Epistemic security, belongingness, and terror management are inter-related motives. For example, group identification can reduce uncertainty and provide a sense of epistemic security (Hogg & Mullin, 1999). In addition, individuals with high need for cognitive closure identify more strongly with their in-groups, particularly when members of the in-group are similar to each other (Kruglanski, Shah, Pierro, & Mannetti, 2002). Accordingly, identification with a relatively homogenous culture may provide certain answers to problems the individual faces, and hence give rise to a sense of epistemic security.

The three motives may also work in concert to increase adherence to cultural tradition. Mortality salience may increase the need for epistemic security and affect intergroup perception. Research has shown that when mortality is made salient, individuals would prefer a structured and stable environment (Landau et al., 2004). In addition, according to terror management theory, in-group members are more likely than out-group members to share similar cultural worldviews with the self. Therefore, when reminded of death and hence motivated to protect their cultural worldviews, people are more likely to derogate out-group members and favor in-group members. Consistent with this hypothesis, Greenberg et al. (1990) found that when participants with Christian religious background were reminded of death, their evaluations of a Jewish target person became more negative, and their evaluations of a Christian target person became more positive, compared to the mortality nonsalient control participants. In another study (Castano, Yzerbyt, Paladino, & Sacchi, 2002), Italian participants responded to an in-group identification measure, and then rated Italians and Germans on ten traits. Compared with mortality nonsalient control participants, mortality salient participants showed higher identification with their in-group and more pronounced in-group bias on the group perception measures. Similar effects were also observed among 11-year-old children participants (Florian & Mikulincer, 1998). Finally, among Aboriginal Australian bicultural individuals, mortality salience increases adherence to Aboriginal values when they are reminded of their Aboriginal identity, and adherence to Australian values when they are reminded of their Australian identity (Halloran & Kashima, 2004). In short, the activation of one basic need may activate the other needs, which together exert confluent influence on the tendency to follow cultural tradition.

Conclusion

In the first part of this chapter, we discuss what culture does for the survival of the human species, and for the society. In the second part, we discuss what culture does for the individual. The specific theories reviewed in this chapter differ in the theoretical assumptions they make about cultural evolution, and in their focal emphasis. Nonetheless, they share a similar perspective: Culture is functional. From the research reviewed in this chapter, we begin to understand what culture means for the human species, for human societies, and for individual adjustment.

The idea that culture serves basic psychological needs implies that culture is a means rather than an end in itself. Thus, culture does not determine behavior. Instead, individuals appropriate shared ideas from their cultural traditions to fulfill their psychological needs, although they may not be consciously aware of the motivational processes that underlie their behaviors. Later in this book (Chapter 10), we will elaborate on this idea of culture as a resource when we discuss the notion of cultural competence.

In addition, as the strength of these basic motives may change from one situation to another, and from one person to another, adherence to cultural tradition will change accordingly, producing *systematic* variations in behaviors within a cultural group. Such within-group variations are interesting and important topics in social psychology of culture.

However, it is important to note that although culture confers important evolutionary, social, and psychological benefits, adherence to cultural tradition could also lead to negative consequences. For example, rigid adherence to a cultural tradition may hinder the development of creativity via the synthesis of ideas from other cultures, and slow down cultural, social, and political reforms. In addition, in Chapter 1, we discuss the problems associated with ethnocentrism. The need to achieve epistemic security, to belong a group, and to manage terror may exacerbate the problems associated with ethnocentrism, which range from discrimination against out-groups to genocide. Finally, when an antisocial and self-destructive idea is widely distributed in a group (e.g., suicidal bombing in terrorist groups), it may seem to provide certain answers to the problems the group faces. In some Middle Eastern states, the prevalence of warfare and violence can make mortality and the need for epistemic security particularly salient. Under such circumstances, emphasis on group identification and wide circulation of extremist beliefs can further increase the likelihood of individuals acting on such beliefs. In short, adherence to a cultural tradition serves manifold functions. However, it is also important to develop a reflective and critical attitude toward one's cultural tradition.

Culture as Mental Habits: Shared Unintended Thoughts

5

Culture Travelers' Journal

In North America, it is traditional to say "thank you" when someone does you a favor. Indeed, it probably strikes many Americans as rude not to say it. However, in Somali culture, it is not traditional to say "thank you," and because of this, many Somali immigrants in the United States often give their fellow Americans the impression of being rude, arrogant, and aloof.

*****

In the United States, people engaged in conversation will assume a distance of roughly 4–7 ft. However, in the Arab world, the expected distance is much shorter. Consequently, while Americans traveling overseas often experience the urgent need to back away from a conversation partner who seems to be getting too close, Arabs frequently complain that Americans are cold, aloof, or "don't care" (Hall, 1966).

*****

The ways we see the world are often filtered through a cultural lens, and the ways we behave are often guided by our cultural tradition. We seldom think about this, but can easily feel it when we meet people from other cultures.

In the early 1960s, anthropologist Edward T. Hall found himself in a hotel lobby in Washington, DC, waiting for a friend. Wanting to be both visible and alone, he seated himself in a solitary chair outside the normal stream of traffic. There he encountered a shocking cultural experience. Recounting this experience, he wrote:

> In such a setting most Americans follow a rule, which is all the more binding because we seldom think about it, that can be stated as follows: as soon as a person stops or is seated in a public place, there balloons around him [sic] a small sphere of privacy which is considered inviolable. … Anyone who enters this zone and stays there is intruding. … as I waited in the deserted lobby, a stranger walked up to where I was sitting and stood close enough so that not only could I easily touch him but I could hear him breathing. … If the lobby had been crowded with people, I would have understood his behavior, but in an empty lobby his presence made me exceedingly uncomfortable. Feeling annoyed by his intrusion, I moved my body in such a way as to communicate annoyance. Strangely enough, instead of moving away, my actions seemed only to encourage him, because he moved even closer. Instead of the temptation to escape the annoyance, I put aside thoughts of abandoning my post, thinking, "To hell with it. Why should I move? I was here first and I'm not going to let this fellow drive me out even if he is a boor." (Hall, 1966, pp. 155–156)

At this point, Hall's tormentor was joined by his companions, and from their mannerisms, he found out that they were Arabs.

*****

Robert Suter was a Swiss gentleman who became the president of ABB Korea (a global technology company in Korea). Like many other expatriates, Suter experienced culture shock. In an article in the *Korea Herald* (December 11, 2001), he wrote:

> My current range of tasks is similar to that when managing a company in Europe. … But my present role as a leader differs substantially from

my former position as CEO in Switzerland in that not only am I CEO 24 hours a day, but I am also more recognized as a sovereign commander rather than the first among peers.

A company president in Korea has almost unlimited power. At the same time, he also carries an extensive amount of responsibility and cares about the well being and the success of his staff. A company president in Korea is more comparable to the Swiss conception of a father.

*****

These stories illustrate that even experienced culture travelers could be surprised by their experiences with other cultures, probably because these experiences contradict the entrenched beliefs or unstated assumptions in their own culture. These experiences prime reflections on how routinely we have used knowledge from our culture to guide our cognitions, emotions, and behaviors.

Reflecting on his experiences with the Arab "intruder," Hall (1966) realized that culture is a hidden dimension in human perceptions of physical space. In his view, we see space through a cultural lens. As such, differing cultural conceptions of space, internalized in all people at an unconscious level, can lead to serious failures in cross-cultural communication. Most Americans believe that they have the "right" to their circle of privacy in a public place, but this belief strikes most Arabs as strange and puzzling. To them, public space, after all, is public space, and there is no such thing as intrusion in the public domain.

In Chapter 4, we discuss why people adhere to their cultural tradition. In this and the next three chapters, we discuss *how* people apply cultural knowledge to guide their thoughts and behaviors. It is possible that culture consists of learned habits. As people participate in culture, they develop habitual, shared ways of responding to the physical and human-made environment (e.g., Whorf, 1956). It is also possible that culture consists of distributed ideas. By virtue of participating in culture, people develop shared knowledge, and use this knowledge to grasp experiences and navigate social situations (Brenneis, 2002; D'Andrade, 1987; Y. Kashima, 2000; Shore, 2002). In our view, culture consists of both learned habits and shared ideas. In addition, how people apply cultural knowledge in a particular situation may depend on the type of cultural knowledge that is applicable to the situation. To flesh out these ideas, we begin with a short introduction to the taxonomy of knowledge.

Taxonomy of Knowledge

Culture can be treated as a network of distributed knowledge characteristic of a group. This definition of culture enables researchers to borrow insights from the literature of knowledge representations to understand the relation of culture, thought, and behavior.

Cognitive psychologists have distinguished between two major types of knowledge representations: *procedural* knowledge (knowing *how*) and *declarative* knowledge (knowing *that*) (see Wyer, 2004). Procedural knowledge, also referred to as *production*, consists of cognitive representations of how to achieve a particular result. It consists of a learned sequence of responses to situation cues. Through frequent practice, a learned response sequence may become a routine or habit, and its performance requires little cognitive deliberation.

Declarative knowledge is knowledge that is either true or false. It describes objects and events by specifying the properties that characterize them; it does not attend to the actions needed to obtain a result, but only to its properties (Turban & Aronson, 1988). Activation of a declarative representation in a given situation often has important behavioral and judgmental consequences. The three types of declarative knowledge that have received most research attention in social psychology of culture are representations of persons, events, and norms. In Figure 5.1, we present a schematic representation of the different types of knowledge representations, and their inter-relations.

Different groups have different shared habits. For example, for American drivers, it is habitual to drive on the right side of the road. However, British drivers "naturally" drive on the left side of the road. This chapter focuses on the role of shared mental habits in cultural differences in perception, attention, cognition, emotion, and performance. The next two chapters focus on the role of shared declarative knowledge.

For theoretical reasons, it is useful to distinguish mental habits (which are likely to be procedural knowledge) from declarative knowledge. In reality an observed cultural practice can arise from the *joint effect* of mental habits and declarative knowledge. For example, saying "thank you" after having received a favor from others may be a learned habit in American culture. However, this habitual response is supported by the belief in American culture that altruistic behavior is a voluntary act (see Chapter 7), and we should be grateful to people who voluntarily extend a favor to us. In Islamic countries, helping one another is considered a fundamental obligation. Thus, thanking someone for simply fulfilling a religious requirement could be construed as an insult, and it is not customary to thank others for their help.

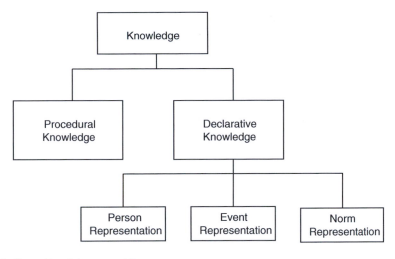

FIGURE 5.1. Types of knowledge representations.

Interpretive Cautions

In the current and the next two chapters, we review many well-documented cross-cultural differences. Our objective is not to provide a comprehensive catalog of all known cross-cultural differences in psychological processes and behaviors. Instead, we aim to use representative research findings to illustrate how different types of cultural knowledge may mediate a broad range of psychological phenomena.

Because of the markedly different physical and social environment in the East and the West, most cross-cultural studies compared individuals from Western cultures with individuals from East Asian cultures. Additionally, because of convenience in recruitment of research participant, most studies compared undergraduate students with different cultural backgrounds. There are obvious limitations in these research strategies, particularly when we want to generalize findings from these studies to other national cultures (e.g., Eastern European cultures, South American cultures), cultures other than national cultures (e.g., organization culture), and noncollege populations (Medin & Atran, 2004). Thus, when we describe research findings, we try to include information about the specific populations that were compared in the studies.

Awareness of alternative cultural beliefs and practices increases our sensitivity to cultural variations in thoughts and behaviors, and thus invites us to reflect on our own cultural tradition critically. However, an exclusive focus on cultural differences may also lead to attribution of an inordinate level of homogeneity in cultural groups (see Chapters 1 and 2). We may, for example, be led to believe that all Japanese think alike, and all Japanese are different from us. We may hence overlook individual and subgroup differences in cognitions and behaviors among Japanese. To overcome the tendency to stereotype a culture, it is important to interpret cultural differences as *differences in central tendencies* (e.g., differences in mean response tendencies). The presence of differences in central tendencies between two groups does not entail absence of variability within either group. Thus, in this book, when group differences are described, collective nouns that denote a collectivity (e.g., Westerners) refer to an average member (statistically speaking) of the collectivity (e.g., an average Westerner).

Finally, our primary objective is to illustrate how different types of cultural knowledge mediate basic psychological processes. To achieve this goal, instead of focusing on the cultural differences themselves, we seek to identify consistent patterns of cultural differences, and use these differences to illustrate how basic cultural processes operate. More specifically, instead of cataloging cultural differences, the current chapter and the next two chapters focus on: (1) identifying replicable cultural differences in different kinds of cultural knowledge; (2) explicating the mediating role of culture-specific knowledge in interesting psychological processes; and (3) relating the development of cultural knowledge to the processes whereby individuals in the same culture interact in a shared physical and social environment (e.g., acculturation processes, cultural affordances).

Mental Habits as Procedural Knowledge

We divide this chapter into two major sections. In the first section, we describe how cultural experiences may lead to the development of cognitive and perceptual habits that mediate cross-cultural differences or similarity in cognition, emotion, and performance. These habits resemble procedural knowledge shared in a cultural group, as they are acquired and made perfect through frequent, repeated applications of the knowledge item, and are often applied without conscious deliberation.

Language and culture evolved together (see Chapter 3). In addition, language processing occasions repeated performance of the perceptual and cognitive productions required to process a language's characteristic form. Because languages differ in forms, different languages may foster the development of different cognitive–perceptual productions (Chiu, Leung, & Kwan, in press). In the second section, we review the literature that examines the role of language experiences in habitual thought processes. We also discuss a number of important conceptual issues in the relation of cultural experiences and habitual thoughts.

Perception and Attention

Many cultural patterns of perception, attention, thinking, emotion, and performance result from frequent interactions with the shared physical and social environment.

Visual Illusion

Early cross-cultural research has provided extensive evidence for the role of shared experiences in perception. For example, many studies have examined cultural differences in the experience of visual illusion. Figure 5.2 depicts the Muller–Lyer illusion. Although the vertical line in Figure 5.2a and the one in Figure 5.2b have identical length, people tend to see the one in Figure 5.2a as significantly shorter than the one in Figure 5.2b. Moreover, Europeans living in a highly carpentered world tend to experience this illusion more sharply than non-Europeans who do not live in a carpentered world (see Triandis, 1964).

Europeans living in a highly carpentered world may spontaneously interpret Figure 5.2a as a drawing of the outer edge of a building, and Figure 5.2b as a drawing of a corner in a room. From the viewer's perspective, the "shorter" vertical line looks closer, and the "longer" line looks further away. Operating from the assumption that things further away from the viewer should look smaller, the perceiver may see the "longer" line as representing a bigger object and the "shorter" line as representing a smaller object in the drawings. People who do not live in a carpentered world would less likely infer depth in these two-dimensional drawings, and therefore would be less susceptible to the illusion.

Attention Strategies

A society's social organization may determine the contents of the mental habits that are widely shared in the society. The term *high context* is used to characterize societies (e.g., East Asian, Mediterranean, and Middle-Eastern societies) where people have long-term relationship, knowledge is situational and relational, and verbally explicit communications are infrequent. Likewise, the term *low context* is used to characterize societies (e.g., American and Northern European societies) where people tend to have many connections

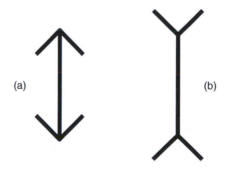

FIGURE 5.2. The Muller–Lyer illusion.

but of shorter duration or for some specific reason, knowledge is codified, public, external, and accessible, and cultural beliefs and expectations are spelled out explicitly (Hall, 1990). Compared to inhabitants in low context societies (e.g., European Americans), people in high context societies (e.g., Chinese, Japanese, Koreans, Greeks) have much more opportunities to develop a habitual tendency to attend to contextualized meanings.

The foregoing analysis implies that people from high context cultures should have a greater propensity to attend to context than do people from low context cultures. This idea has received strong support from a series of studies that compared the attention processes of European Americans (a low context group) and Japanese (a high context group). In one study (Masuda & Nisbett, 2001), participants viewed several underwater scenes briefly. In each scene, there were various types of living things floating around: fish, sea animals, and water plants. Subsequently, participants were asked to report what they had seen in each scene by memory. As expected, compared to European Americans, Japanese were more likely to report information in the background, like the color of the water, plant formation, and inert animals.

Meet the Researcher: Takahiko Masuda

"One day in Kyoto, an ancient capital city of Japan, I left my dormitory very early to set up an experiment session for my Masters' thesis. As I rode to school, I came across a party of Buddhist monks chanting in the early grey dawn. I still remember the faces of these monks, their deep and clear voices, the scent, the crisp air, and the color of haze. Spending so many years of my life in various cities, both in Japan and North America, the variety of my experiences has persuaded me that people do not live in a vacuum—we are surrounded by 'context'. Our thoughts and feelings are interwoven with patterns of social interaction in rich contexts which even include environmental temperature, sounds, and smells associated with the experiences we have. As a student of cultural psychology, I have always tried to conduct research with both analytic and scientific rigor, while at the same time maintaining a sense of perceiving contextual cues as a whole. I believe that such 'context sensitivity' may be the key to further developments in this field of research."

Takahiko Masuda is a cultural psychologist at the University of Alberta, Canada. As a Fulbright scholar, he moved to the United States, and received his Ph.D. from the University of Michigan in 2003.

In another study (Masuda & Nisbett, 2004), European Americans and Japanese watched several movie clips, each depicting an industrial scene with various machines and backgrounds: an airport, a construction site, an American city, an American farm, an American harbor, a Japanese city, and a Japanese farm. In each movie, there were a similar number of changes in a machine's attributes (e.g. changes in colors of a car), a machine's location, a machine's speed, and the background information. After each movie, the participants described the changes that they saw. Compared to American undergraduates, Japanese undergraduates were more likely to detect changes in a machine's location and the background information, and less likely to detect changes in a machine's attributes.

In a third study (Masuda & Nisbett, 2001), European American and Japanese viewed pictures of animals and fish with a surrounding background. Later, participants were shown pictures of animals or fish they had seen as well as pictures of new animals or fish. The old or new fish/animals appeared either with the same background or in a new background. Japanese participants were more likely to correctly recognize previously seen fish or animals when they were seen in their original settings than in novel settings. Among American participants, the setting had no effect on their recognition. Apparently, when Japanese register an object, they spontaneously bind the object to its surrounding background. As such, the object and background form a holistic percept. By contrast, for European Americans, the object is abstracted from the background, and perceived as a bounded entity.

The culture-specific patterns of attention strategies described above may be afforded by the perceptual environment of each culture. As illustrated in Figure 5.3a, in a typical scene in American cities, objects are usually distinctive and stand out from the background. Thus, living in the

(a)   (b)

FIGURE 5.3. A scene of (a) New York City, and of (b) Tokyo. Courtesy of Yuri Miyamoto, Richard Nisbett, & Takahiko Masuda.

American environment may direct one's attention to the distinctive and focal objects rather than to the background. By contrast, as illustrated in Figure 5.3b, in a typical scene in Japanese cities, objects are more ambiguous and difficult to distinguish from the background. Living in the Japanese environment may direct one's attention to the object–context relationship (Miyamoto, Nisbett, & Masuda, 2006).

To test the connection between environmental affordances and attention strategies, Miyamoto et al. (2006) had Japanese and European American undergraduates view either Japanese or American city scenes, imagine that they were placed in the scenery, and rate how much they liked the scenery. Subsequently, all participants responded to the change-detection measure used in the Masuda and Nisbett (2004) study. For both Japanese and American participants, viewing Japanese city scenes increased attentiveness to contextual changes, whereas viewing American city scenes increased attentiveness to changes in focal objects. These findings demonstrate the causal role of environmental affordances in the development of culture-specific pattern of attention strategies.

Cognition

Cognitive Style

Japanese people's sensitivity to context is also reflected in their cognitive style. In one study (Kitayama, Duffy, Kawamura, & Larsen, 2003), European American and Japanese undergraduates performed two simple matching tasks. In the *absolute matching* task, participants first saw a square frame with a straight line extended downward from the center of the upper edge of the square (see Figure 5.4a). Next, they were given a second square frame that was either larger than, smaller than, or the same size as the first frame. Their task was to draw a line from the upper edge of the square that was the same absolute length as the line in the first frame (see Figure 5.4b). The *relative matching* task was similar to the absolute matching task, except that the proportion of drawn line to the size of the second frame was expected to match the proportion of the first line to the size of the first frame (see Figure 5.4c).

To perform well on the absolute judgment task, participants would need to ignore the sizes of the first frame and the second frame (contextual information) and focus on the length of the first vertical line (attribute of the focal object). In contrast, the relative matching task requires participants to use the square frames as the frames of reference. To do well on this task, the participants need to attend to the proportion of the first line to the first frame, as well as the proportion of the second frame to the first frame. As expected, Japanese undergraduates performed better on the relative

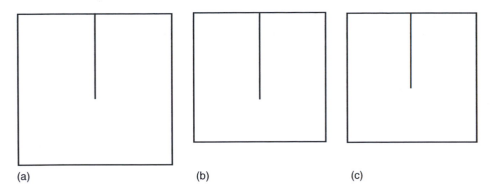

(a) (b) (c)

FIGURE 5.4. The original stimulus (from Kitayama et al., 2003): (a) the correct response in the absolute matching task; (b) the correct response in the relative matching task.

matching task than did European American undergraduates, who in turn performed better on the absolute matching task.

Similar results have been obtained in another study (Ji, Peng, & Nisbett, 2000) that compared East Asian (Japanese, Koreans, Chinese) and European American undergraduates on the Rod and Frame Test. Participants in the study viewed a tilted frame with a line placed at the center (see Figure 5.5a). Their task was to rotate the line so that it would be perpendicular to the earth's surface while ignoring the frame (see Figure 5.5b). In other words, participants were required to ignore the contextual information (the frame's orientation), and failure to meet this requirement would produce errors. As expected, East Asians had greater difficulty in ignoring the field information and made more errors than did European Americans on the Rod and Frame Test.

If frequent practice can increase the strength of a mental habit, Japanese in North America should have plenty of opportunities to practice the American cognitive style. Likewise, Americans in Japan should have plenty of opportunities to practice the Japanese cognitive style. In a

FIGURE 5.5. The tilted frame with the line in its original orientation (a), and the correct response from the participant (b) in the Rod and Frame Test.

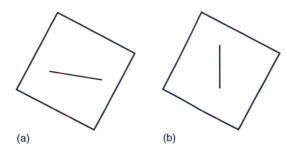

(a) (b)

follow-up study, Kitayama et al. (2003) administered the framed-line tests to four different groups: Japanese undergraduates in Japan, European American undergraduates in the United States, Japanese studying in an American university, and American exchange students in a Japanese university. As in the first study, Japanese in Japan had better performance on the relative matching task than did European Americans in the United States, and European Americans in the United States did better than the Japanese on the absolute matching task.

Interestingly, the performance of American students in Japan was more similar to Japanese in Japan than to European Americans in the United States. Compared to American students in the United States, American students in Japan were more accurate in the relative matching task and less accurate in the absolute matching task. Similarly, Japanese students in the United States performed better on the absolute matching task than did Japanese students in Japan. This study showed that even a well-learned mental habit could be altered with new cultural experiences.

Illusory Covariation

Screen 1

Screen 2

Screen 3

Screen 4

Individuals who habitually try to discern relationships between events may be prone to perceive illusory covariation between events; they may perceive two unrelated events as related. To test this idea, Ji et al. (2000) compared the performance of Taiwan Chinese and European American students on a covariation detection task. In the test, participants saw on a bifurcated computer screen pairs of schematic drawings. For example, they saw on the left side of the screen either a light bulb or a medal, and on the right side of the screen either a pointing finger or a coin (see Figure 5.6). There was *no covariation* between figures on the left and figures on the right. When a light bulb appeared on the left, there was equal chance

FIGURE 5.6. Examples of the stimuli presented to the participants in a covariation detection task. As illustrated in these four screens, there was no actual association between the figures that appeared on the left side of the screen and the figures that appeared on the right side of the screen.

that a pointing finger or a coin would appear on the right. Similarly, when a medal appeared on the left, the figure on the right was equally likely to be a pointing finger or a coin. After viewing ten pairings of these drawings, participants rated how strong the association between what appeared on the left and what appeared on the right was. Both European Americans and Taiwan Chinese perceived some covariation between the two sets of figures, but Taiwan Chinese perceived a higher level of covariation than did European Americans.

Categorization

Categorization is a cognitive process that renders otherwise meaningless patterns of sensations into meaningful percepts. The habitual tendency to attend to information in the field and relationship between objects may also affect the criteria people use to categorize objects. In high context societies, people habitually attend to relationships between objects, and would likely categorize objects based on relational themes. For example, when presented with the following three items, *monkeys, bananas,* and *pandas,* these individuals would likely group monkeys and bananas together because monkeys eat bananas. In low context societies, people habitually attend to internal attributes of objects, and would likely categorize objects based on the objects' shared attributes. For example, when presented with the same three items, they would likely group monkeys and pandas together because both are animals. The data generally support this idea. When presented with the categorization task described above, compared to European American undergraduates, Chinese undergraduates are more likely to group objects based on their thematic relationships, and less likely to group them based on their common attributes (Ji, Zhang, & Nisbett, 2004).

Reasoning

The foregoing analysis suggests that social organization directs attention at some aspects of the social environment at the expense of others. Additionally, attentional preferences are often accompanied by the development of supporting reasoning strategies (Nisbett, Peng, Choi, & Norenzayan, 2001). Aristotle, who laid the foundation of logic, asserted that truth and reason are within things, the truth of something is in its essence or nature, and logic is a tool that guides the intellectual search for truth residing in the object. Not surprisingly, attention to objects and application of logic have found each other good company in the Western intellectual tradition. In contrast, social organization and social practices that direct attention to the context may also support the reasoning strategies that situate causality of events in the context or field (Nisbett et al., 2001). Accordingly, when individuals believe that event causality resides in the object, they rely on the object's internal essences rather than its surface appearance when rendering judgment. Conversely, when individuals believe that event causality resides in the context, they rely on their experiences with the object in the context to form inferences.

Several cross-cultural studies of reasoning strategies showed that European Americans rely on essential features of an object more and East Asians rely on experiential knowledge more in categorization and reasoning. First, consider the following experimental task. The participant is presented with a flower with a long stem, and two sets of flowers. Set A consists of four flowers with long stems, and Set B consists of four flowers with short stems. Accordingly, stem length is an essential feature that determines the categorical membership of the flowers. However, the target flower looks more similar to the flowers in Set B than the flowers in Set A. Both the target flower and most (but not all) flowers in Set B have a leaf on the left side of the stem, and *most* (but not all) flowers in Set A have leaves on both sides of the stem. Additionally, the target flower and *most* flowers in Set B have five petals, whereas most flowers in Set A have four petals. If the participants judge the target flower to be similar to the flowers in Set A, they rely on essential features more than on surface appearance in categorization. Conversely, if they judge the target flower to be more similar to the flowers in Set B, they rely more on surface appearance than on essential features to form categories. When given this and other similar categorization tasks, most European American undergraduates categorize on the basis of essential features, whereas most Korean and Chinese undergraduates categorize on the basis of surface resemblance (Norenzayan, Smith, Kim, & Nisbett, 2002b).

As another illustration, consider the following two arguments.

1. All birds have ulnar arteries.

    Therefore all eagles have ulnar arteries.

2. All birds have ulnar arteries.

    Therefore all penguins have ulnar arteries.

Because both eagles and penguins are birds, the conclusions in both arguments are valid. If people need to judge how convincing each conclusion is, formal logic dictates that the two conclusions should be rated as equally convincing. However, compared to penguin, eagle is a more typical exemplar of bird. If judgments are colored by this experiential knowledge, people may be tempted to rate the eagle argument to be more convincing than the penguin argument. Again as expected, Korean undergraduates rate arguments that reference typical exemplars to be more convincing than arguments that reference atypical exemplars. In contrast, European American undergraduates rate the two kinds of arguments to be equally convincing (Norenzayan et al., 2002b).

In another experiment, the role of experiential knowledge in logical reasoning was further examined by having participants evaluate the convincingness of the following two types of arguments:

I.   Valid/Believable Arguments, e.g.,

Premise 1: No police dogs are old.

Premise 2: Some highly trained dogs are old.

Conclusion: Some highly trained dogs are not police dogs.

II.   Valid/Nonbelievable Arguments, e.g.,

Premise 1: All things that are made of plants are good for health.

Premise 2: Cigarettes are things that are made of plants.

Conclusion: Cigarettes are good for health.

If experiential knowledge does not interfere with application of logic, these two types of arguments should be seen as convincing regardless of whether the conclusion is believable. The results showed that for both American undergraduates and Korean undergraduates, the argument's believability impacted judgment. Both groups rated the valid, believable arguments to be more convincing than the valid, unbelievable ones. However, the bias was considerably greater among Korean undergraduate students (Norenzayan et al., 2002b).

Finally, when individuals believe that event causality resides in the field, they would examine situational information carefully before rendering causal judgments. As expected, compared to their American peers, Korean undergraduates see more situational information as relevant in determining the motive of a behavior, regardless of whether the behavior is a positive behavior (e.g., an altruistic behavior) or a negative one (e.g., a murder; I. Choi, Dalal, Kim-Prieto, & Park, 2003).

Meet the Researcher: Ara Norenzayan

"Consider the life of an ancestral modern human in a Eurasian valley forty thousand years ago. She lives with fewer than 150 hunters and foragers who are her genetic relatives, the only people she would regularly interact with in her short lifetime. She is a fully-fledged modern human—genetically identical to you and me. Accordingly we share many of our mental capacities with this human ancestor. Yet the gulf that divides us is staggering—agriculture, animal domestication, cities devoid of plants and animals, material technology beyond stone and bone tools, counting, writing, calendars, money, organized religion, formal schooling, and diverse forms of political and social institutions transcending kinship are all recent cultural inventions. What separates us is cultural inheritance—a vast and complex network of socially transmitted ideas and their material effects accumulated over time that have radically transformed human lives and the course of human evolution itself. Humans, more than any other species, have a dual biological inheritance— genetic and cultural. Cultural psychology aims to understand how they interact and shape minds in astonishingly diverse ways around the world."

Ara Norenzayan is a social psychologist at the University of British Columbia (UBC), Vancouver. He received his Ph.D. from the University of Michigan in 1999.

Emotion

Perception of Emotions

Background information also impacts heavily on recognition of emotions among individuals from high context cultures. In one study (Masuda, Ellsworth, Mesquita, Leu, Tanida, & van de Veerdonk, 2004), Japanese and European Americans viewed a set of cartoons, each depicting a central figure and four background figures. The central figure wore an emotional expression on the face (e.g., sadness, happiness), which might be the same as or different from the emotion expressed by the background figures (see Figure 5.7). The participants' task was to judge the intensity of the emotion expressed by the central figure. The results indicated that changes in the background figures' facial expression had a greater impact on the emotion intensity judgments of the Japanese than on those of European Americans. Consistent with these results, other studies have shown that when responding to oral presentation of an emotional word, Japanese respond automatically to its vocal tone (contextual information), whereas European

FIGURE 5.7. Stimulus used in the Masuda et al. (2004) emotion intensity judgment task. *Source:* http://lynx.let.hokudai.ac.jp/~tmasuda/takahtml/TMstimuli.html. Courtesy of T. Masuda.

Americans respond automatically to its verbal contents (Ishii, Reyes, & Kitayama, 2003; Kitayama & Ishii, 2002).

In short, there is impressive evidence for the spontaneous tendency to attend to contextual information among individuals in high context cultures. In these cultures, people rely on situational and relational cues rather than explicit communication to navigate social situations. Thus, the social life in high context societies provides many opportunities to practice decoding of situational and relational cues. As a result, individuals living in high context societies might have developed a habitual tendency to bind the focal object, the background, and other objects in the field into a holistic percept.

In-group Advantage in Emotion Recognition

Cultural experiences also play an important role in the accuracy of decoding emotions from facial expressions. In a typical emotion recognition experiment, perceivers view emotion faces on slides or photos and identify the emotion each face is intended to portray by selecting an emotion term from several alternatives. In most studies, perceivers are more accurate in judging the emotions of expressors from their own culture than emotions of foreign expressors. Such in-group advantage in emotion recognition is found in 146 out of the 182 studies included in a meta-analytic review (Elfenbein & Nalini, 2002).

The seemingly universal in-group advantage in recognizing facial expressions of emotions may arise from more frequent practices in decoding facial expressions of members of one's own culture (vs. members of foreign cultures). For example, Chinese in China have greater exposure to emotion faces of Chinese people than do Chinese Americans and non-Asian Americans. Conversely, non-Asian Americans and Chinese Americans have greater exposure to emotion faces of Americans than do Chinese in China. Consistent with the "practice makes perfect" idea, Chinese in China are faster and more accurate in recognizing emotions from Chinese emotion faces than from American emotion faces, and the reverse is true for non-Asian Americans and Chinese Americans. In addition, among Chinese Americans, the advantage for recognizing American over Chinese expressions is greater among later-generation Chinese Americans than among immigrant-generation Chinese Americans. Finally, Tibetans residing in China are faster and more accurate when they decode emotions from Chinese faces than from American faces. Likewise, Africans residing in the United States are more skilled in recognizing emotions from American faces than from Chinese faces (Elfenbein & Ambady, 2003). In short, proficiency (as measured by accuracy and speed) in recognizing the facial expressions of emotions of a certain group increases with exposure to the group and hence with the frequency of practicing emotion recognition from facial expressions posed by members of the group.

Performance

Differing mental habits in different cultures also have important implications for problem solving and task performance. For example, American undergraduates often use internal speech to keep track of their thoughts during problem solving. Requiring them to think aloud while solving reasoning problems does not affect their performance on the problem-solving task. However, thinking aloud is not a common cognitive strategy for most East Asian undergraduates (Tobin, Wu, & Davidson, 1989). To them, thinking aloud requires cognitive deliberation and could lead to impaired performance in problem solving.

This idea was tested in a study conducted by H. Kim (2002). In this study, European American and East Asian undergraduates performed two sets of nonverbal problems. They completed the first set of problems in silence. The performance on this set of problems provided the baseline measure of their performance. Next, half of the participants were instructed to verbalize their thought processes while working on the second set of problems. The remaining participants were instructed to repeat the alphabet from A to Z aloud while they were working on the second test. European American students were accustomed to using internal speech to keep track of their thoughts. Requiring them to externalize their speech had no effect on their performance. When they were asked to think aloud while working on the second set of problems, they performed at the same level as they did on the first set of problems. However, their performance on the second set of problems deteriorated markedly (compared to their baseline performance) when they needed to repeat the alphabets when working on these problems. Presumably, having to repeat the alphabets had prevented these participants from engaging in internal speech, and hence hindered their performance.

For East Asian participants, repeating the alphabets had no debilitating effects on their performance, probably because they did not rely on internal speech as a thought monitoring strategy in problem solving. However, articulating their thoughts was distracting. When they were instructed to think aloud, their performance suffered.

Summary

The foregoing analysis seems to suggest that even very basic cognitive processes, such as attention and perception, are malleable and can be altered through cultural experiences. In addition, through repeated applications, a cognitive process or strategy may become a spontaneous, automatic response, and may influence behaviors and performance without conscious deliberation.

Although cultural experiences could have enormous impact on basic cognitive processes, the human mind is not a blank slate. The perceptual order imposed by properties of the biological system limits the range of the effect cultural experiences can have on cognition. In addition, procedural knowledge, like other types of knowledge, has a specified range of applicability; it is applied only when its activating conditions are met, and when it is relevant to the local situation. If a mental habit is like a procedural knowledge item, it should have local rather than general influence on behaviors. The theoretical significance of these issues will become clear as we review the literature on the linguistic relativity hypothesis.

The Linguistic Relativity Hypothesis

The linguistic relativity hypothesis holds that individuals in an ethnolinguistic group are led by their shared language experiences to acquire shared, habitual ways of thinking, which influence cognitions in a general way. This hypothesis is premised on the following assumptions about perceptual experiences, language, and culture. First, perceptual experiences are presented in a kaleidoscopic flux of impressions that need to be organized by the human mind. Second, the formal structure of each language embodies a distinctive internal logic. Third, the distinctive internal logic of a language constrains its speakers' thought processes, creating marked differences in cognitions between speakers of different languages (Whorf, 1956). If the ways in which a language is organized stand in isomorphic relation to how its associated culture is organized, culture, like language, would also possess an internal logic, and be highly patterned, systematic, and distinctive. If this is the case, language should account for a broad range of cultural phenomena, and be the entry point for understanding cultural organization (see Brenneis, 2002). However, these assumptions fly in the face of the research evidence.

Is the Human Mind a Blank Slate?

Whorf (1956) posited that there is no inherent structure in people's experiences, and language is the major cognitive tool people use to categorize their experiences. This idea is most clearly articulated in Whorf's provocative writing:

> We dissect nature along lines laid down by our native languages … We cut nature up, organize it into concepts, and ascribe significances as we do, largely because we are parties to an agreement to organize it in this way—an agreement that hold throughout our speech community and is codified in the patterns of our language. The agreement is, of course, an implicit and unstated one, but its terms are absolutely obligatory; we cannot talk at all except by subscribing to the organization and classification of data which the agreement decrees. (pp. 213–214)

Despite its strong appeal, findings from color categorization research have cast serious doubts on this idea.

People in different language communities have more or less equivalent experiences with colors. However, variations in color vocabulary can be readily found in natural languages. For example, American English has 11 basic color terms, and Dugum Dani (a stone age tribe from Irian Jaya) has only two achromatic terms for color. According to Whorf's linguistic relativity hypothesis, Americans and Dugum Dani should experience colors very differently. The data do not support this prediction.

First, research findings reveal that, contrary to the linguistic relativity hypothesis, there may be a universal perceptual order independent of language. In one study, Berlin and Kay (1969) had informants (from 20 different language groups) list the basic color terms in their native language, and select a color chip to represent each term. Although the number of basic color terms varies across languages, the focal regions of the basic color terms in all 20 languages appear to be invariant. Moreover, in an extensive library research of color terms in 98 languages, Berlin and Kay found a seemingly universal evolutionary order in the emergence of basic color terms, which they later argue could be mapped onto the neurophysiological substrate of color perception (Kay & McDaniel, 1978).

Many cognitive psychologists now believe that despite the presence of linguistic and cultural variations, a universal fundamental structure of categories may exist. For example, in their studies of folk biological taxonomy, Medin and Atran (2004) found that young children from diverse cultures have similar understanding of what constitute a biological species. These investigators conclude that there is a core module for biological categorization in all cultures, although differences in experience and expertise can affect how this core module is put to use to grasp experiences. In color perception, the perceptual order imposed by properties of the visual system limits the range of language's effects on color categorization. For example, no language has color categories that include two color spaces (e.g., yellow and blue) and exclude the connecting color space (e.g., green, Davidoff, 2001). Within the constraints imposed by the visual system and the structure of the color space, different languages partition the color space differently (Roberson, Davies, & Davidoff, 2000).

Research on grammatical gender provides another illustration of how the perceptual order imposed by the external reality constrains object categorization. Languages differ in whether they assign a gender to all nouns that refer to animates (e.g., psychologist) or to nouns that refer to inanimates (e.g., moon). Some languages (e.g., Spanish, Italian, French, German, Arabic, and Hebrew) mark gender with morphorical information carried by pronouns, determiners, nouns, and adjectives, and others (e.g., English) do not. It is often assumed that at least in most European languages, the basis of grammatical gender assignments to inanimate objects is arbitrary. For example, in French, the word for "the moon" is feminine (*la lune*) and the word for "the sun" is masculine (*le soleil*). However, in German, "the moon" is masculine (*der Mond*) and "the sun" is feminine (*die Sonne*).

Some studies suggest that users of a language with a grammatical gender system tend to infer psychological gender properties from gender inflections of nouns. For example, French speakers conceptualize the moon in more psychologically feminine ways and the sun in more psychologically masculine ways than do German speakers. In a classic study, Ervin (1962) taught native speakers Italian nonsense words that possessed either the masculine Italian affix (*-o*) or the feminine one (*-a*). In this study, the participants rated the nonsense words with masculine endings as more like men than those with feminine endings, and vice versa. Similar results have been obtained in speakers of Arabic (Clarke, Losoff, McCracken, & Rood, 1984; Clarke, Losoff, McCracken, & Still, 1981). However, because participants in these studies were asked to judge the gender connotations of words, it is unclear whether these judgments reveal participants' knowledge of grammatical gender or the effects of grammatical gender on categorization (see Sera, Elieff, Forbes, Burch, Rodriguez, & Dubois, 2002). Nonetheless, other studies using more sophisticated tests of categorization (e.g., free classification, assignment of either a man's voice or a woman's voice to pictured objects) have found robust effects of grammatical gender on object categorization in speakers of Spanish (Martinez & Shatz, 1996; Sera, Berge, & del Castillio Pintado, 1994; Sera et al., 2002) and speakers of French (Sera et al., 2002). These findings seem to support the linguistic relativity hypothesis.

However, two problems undermine the validity of this conclusion. First, the effects of grammatical gender on object categorization are not uniform across languages with a grammatical gender system. For example, the cognitive effects of grammatical gender are absent in Finnish speakers (Clarke et al., 1981, 1984) and German speakers (Sera et al., 2002). Second, although assignments of gender to objects are mostly arbitrary in some languages (e.g., German), this is not the case in other languages. For example, in Spanish, a female gender is often attributed to an object that is used by women, natural, round, or light. Likewise, a male gender is often attributed to an object that is used by men, artificial, angular, or heavy. Thus, Spanish grammatical gender seems to be highly correlated with natural gender. By comparison, the basis of grammatical gender assigned to inanimates in German is far more arbitrary. Recall that grammatical gender effect has been reported in Spanish speakers but not in German speakers. In a series of computer and experimental simulation studies, Sera et al. (2002) found that overgeneralization of masculine and feminine traits to inanimate objects is likely to occur when the grammatical gender system has only two gender categories (feminine and masculine), and when there is a high correlation between grammatical and natural gender. Taken together, object categorization by gender may stem from the natural gender associations of objects. Natural and grammatical gender may or may not correspond. Only when they do are grammatical gender effects likely to be found.

In short, consistent with what we maintain in Chapter 4, the culture vs. nature dichotomy is a false dichotomy. Cultural learning does not require the assumption of the mind as a blank slate, which the mind is not.

How General Are the Effects of Linguistic Experiences?

More importantly, linguistic experiences do not seem to have any general effects on cognition. For example, although colors are represented very differently in English and Dugum Dani, speakers of the two languages organize their memory representations of the colors in strikingly similar ways (Heider & Olivier, 1972; see also Roberson et al., 2000). Although unlike English, some languages (the language of the Dugum Dani, and the language of the pastoral Himba people of northern Namibia) do not have monolexemic terms for circles, triangles, and squares, speakers of these languages categorize variants of these three shape categories into "circles," "triangles," and "squares" based on perceptual similarity between the variants (Roberson, Davidoff, & Shapiro, 2002; Rosch, 1973). Americans use the same word (*cup*) to refer to a paper drinking vessel, and a vessel for drinking tea. Israelis call them by different names (Kronenfeld, Armstrong, & Wilmoth, 1985). Despite their different naming patterns, speakers of Hebrew and English categorize drinking vessels in a similar way (Kronenfeld et al., 1985). In one study, when speakers of American English, Mandarin Chinese, and Argentinian Spanish named 60 common objects, both the number of categories and the composition of the named categories differed across the three languages (Malt, Sloman, Gennari, Shi, & Wang, 1999). For example, the 16 objects named "bottle" in English were spread across seven different linguistic categories in Spanish. Again, cross-linguistic diversity in object naming is not accompanied by cross-linguistic diversity in object categorization. Despite the presence of divergent naming patterns in English, Spanish, and Chinese, speakers of these languages use similar criteria to categorize containers.

Whorf (1956) submitted that experiences with a specific language could lead to the development of global cognitive styles. However, despite their persistent effort, researchers have failed to demonstrate such effects of language experiences. For example, in Navaho (a native American language), inanimate objects are classified into "round objects" and "long objects," and a different verb stem is required for a "round" or a "long" subject (or object) in a sentence. However, Navaho-speaking children were not more inclined than English-speaking children to group objects with a similar shape together (Carroll & Casagrande, 1958).

Unlike English, Chinese lacks formal grammatical markers (the subjunctive mood) to express counterfactual thoughts. The lack of the subjective mood in Chinese does not hinder Chinese speakers' ability to understand counterfactual ideas. In several studies, Chinese speakers and English speakers read a passage that contained counterfactual statements in their native language, and later answered questions that tested their comprehension of the passage. Chinese speakers performed at the same level as English speakers (Au, 1983, 1984; Liu, 1985).

The absence of general effects of language experiences does not imply that language experiences are irrelevant to cognition. However, the effects of language experiences are local rather than general. A recent study on language and false beliefs has offered evidence supporting this point.

Puerto Rican (PR) Spanish and Turkish have specific verb forms for marking false-belief states explicitly. For example, PR Spanish uses *creer* to denote that the speaker is neutral on whether the grammatical subject in the sentence holds a true belief or not, and adds a reflexive clitic to the verb phrase (*creer-se*) to denote that the speaker is sure that the grammatical subject holds a false belief. English and Brazilian (BR) Portuguese have no such specific forms. In a recent study, Shatz, Diesendruck, Martinez-Beck, and Akar (2003) compared the performance on a false-belief understanding task of PR Spanish- and Turkish-speaking preschoolers with their English- and BR Portuguese-speaking counterparts. In this study, one experimenter showed the preschooler a crayon box and a blue box in the presence of a second experimenter. Then, the second experimenter left the room to get some paper. After the second experimenter had left, the first experimenter opened both boxes, remarked that the crayon box was empty and the blue box contained crayons, and asked the preschooler, "Where does [Experimenter 2] think the crayons are?" and "Where is [Experimenter 2] going to look for the crayons when [he/she] returns to draw?"

Note that in the first question, the verb *think* provides an explicit marker of the false belief in the two languages with formal markers for false beliefs. If having explicit grammatical markers for false beliefs in one's own language improves understanding of false-belief states, PR Spanish and Turkish speakers should do better than BR Portuguese and English speakers on the comprehension task. In addition, if false-belief markers helped by improving children's general ability to represent false-belief states irrespective of whether the explicit marker (*creer-se*) was included in the question, Turkish and PR Spanish speakers should do better than BR Portuguese and English speakers on the general question about false beliefs (*Where is [Experimenter 2] going to look for the crayons?*) as well as the explicitly marked question (*Where does [Experimenter 2] think the crayons are?*). However, if the grammatical markers for false-belief states help only locally without influencing reasoning in a more general way, the Turkish and PR Spanish speakers should outperform the BR Portuguese and English speakers only when the explicitly marked question was asked. The results showed that Turkish- and PR Spanish-speaking children outperformed the two other groups in the comprehension test only on the explicitly-marked question, but not on the general question. Apparently, the effects of explicit grammatical markers are limited to the local context of language use.

Effects of Language Processing on Perceptual and Cognitive Productions

In short, experiences with a language with particular linguistic features do not lead to development of global habitual cognitive styles that affect cognition in a general way. However, language processing does require repeated performance of the perceptual and cognitive productions involved in processing the language's characteristic form. Languages differ in forms. Accordingly, different languages may enhance the efficiency in performing different *specific* cognitive-perceptual productions. However, it is important to recognize that these productions consist of learned sequences of responses that accompany language use, and the effects of such productions should therefore be specific to situations that involve language use (Wyer, 2004). Data from visual scanning and apparent motion research support these ideas.

Visual Scanning

Try to find the symbol "Ж" in the following row of symbols.

♏ Ж ♏ ♏ ♏ ♏ ♏ ♏ ♏ ♏ ♏ ♏

Now, try to find it again in the following row of symbols.

♏ ♏ ♏ ♏ ♏ ♏ ♏ ♏ ♏ ♏ Ж ♏

If it takes you longer to find the symbol in the second trial, you may have a habitual tendency to scan from left to right. For most Americans, the preferred direction of visual scanning is left-to-right.

However, Israelis' preferred visual scanning direction is right-to-left (Braine, 1968). Why might this be the case? As you read through the printed pages of the book, you scan from left to right consistently, because English is read from left to right. As a proficient user of English, you perform visual scanning in this direction every time you read an English text. For you, scanning from left to right has become a habitual perceptual process. By contrast, Hebrew is written from right to left, and Israelis are used to reading from right to left. Thus, they have developed the habit of scanning from right to left.

Americans are not used to scanning from top to bottom, because English texts are seldom written in that direction. Thus, Americans often find it harder to perform vertical scanning than horizontal scanning. In contrast, Chinese characters are sometimes read from top to bottom. Not surprisingly, Chinese speakers can perform vertical scanning just as efficiently as horizontal scanning (Freeman, 1980). More importantly, Chinese American children who do not have any experience with written Chinese perform more poorly in vertical scanning than in horizontal scanning, just

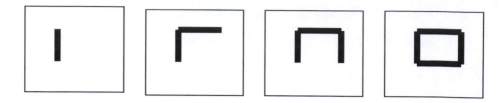

FIGURE 5.8. Sample sequence of frames presented in an apparent motion experiment.

as the American adults do (Hoosain, 1986), suggesting that experience with reading Chinese texts is responsible for the cultural differences in the preferred direction of visual scanning.

Apparent Motion

When a Chinese character is presented stroke by stroke on a computer screen, Chinese readers (but not English readers) perceive an apparent motion in the last stroke in the direction predicted by the stroke's writing direction (Tse & Cavanagh, 2000). For example, when presented with the sequence of frames on a computer screen depicted in Figure 5.8, for the Americans, the bottom horizontal line in the last frame seems to move from right to left. To them, the first three frames suggest that a rectangle is being drawn, and to complete the figure in a continuous line as illustrated in Figure 5.9a, the bottom horizontal line in the last frame should run from right to left.

However, for users of the Chinese language, the bottom horizontal line in the last frame seems to move from left to right. To them, the computer is generating the Chinese character "口" (*mouth*) stroke by stroke, and the writing sequence depicted in Figure 5.9b suggests that this line should run from left to right.

These results again illustrate how language processing can set up habitual patterns of thoughts. However, the apparent motion perceived by Chinese speakers is obtained only in the presence of writing cues. For

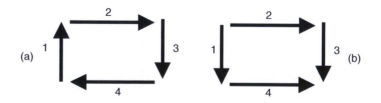

FIGURE 5.9. The directions for drawing a rectangle in a continuous line (a); the conventional directions for writing the Chinese character "口" (b).

example, the presented sequence must follow a writing sequence in a handwritten script. In the absence of cues suggesting that a Chinese character is being produced, the difference in perceived apparent motion between Chinese and Americans disappears (Li & Yeh, 2003).

Conclusion

By virtue of participating in similar cultural practices and using the same language, people in a culture may come to develop similar habitual cognitive and perceptual styles. These cognitive and perceptual styles resemble what cognitive psychologists refer to as procedural knowledge, which consists of a learned sequence of responses to situation cues. Like procedural knowledge, a habitual cognitive and perceptual style consists of a learned response sequence with a specified range of applicability, and is evoked by the presence of relevant cues. As mentioned, a procedural production is an automatic response sequence whose application requires little cognitive deliberation. If habitual cognitive and perceptual styles are procedural knowledge, individuals with a certain habitual cognitive style may not consciously exhibit the style in the situation. Instead, the situation evokes the style automatically, and people would exhibit this style even when they were cognitively busy. In addition, some cognitive habits can be so strong that once activated, they cannot be suppressed even if individuals want to do so. These possibilities merit future research attention.

Culture, Self, and Others: Who Am I and Who Are They?

6

Culture and Architecture

Figure 6.1 shows the entrance to an American house, and the entrance to a Chinese house. Do they look very different to you? To anthropologist Francis Hsu, these entrances not only lead to American and Chinese homes, they also open the passages to American and Chinese cultures. In his book *Americans and Chinese: Passages to differences*, Hsu (1981) wrote:

Let us begin with Chinese and American homes. An American house usually has a yard, large or small. It may have a hedge, but rarely is there a wall so high that a passerby cannot see the windows. The majority of American houses have neither hedges nor outside walls.

(a)

(b)

FIGURE 6.1. The entrance to an American house (a), and the entrance to a Chinese house (b).

Usually the interior is shielded from exterior view only by window curtains or blinds, and then during but part of the day.

The majority of Chinese houses are, in the first place, surrounded by such high walls that only the roofs are visible from the outside, and solid gates separate the interior grounds from the outside world. In addition, there is usually a shadow wall placed directly in front of the gates on the other side of the street as well as a four-paneled wooden screen standing about five feet behind the gates. The outside shadow wall keeps the home from direct exposure to the unseen spirits. The inside wooden screen shields the interior courtyard from pedestrians' glances when the gates are ajar.

Inside the home, the contrast between China and America is reversed. The American emphasis within the home is on privacy. There are not only doors to the bathrooms but also to the bedrooms, and often to the living room and even the kitchen. Space and possessions are individualized. Parents have little liberty in the rooms of the children, and children cannot do what they want in those parts of the house regarded as preeminently their parents' domain. Among some sections of the American population this rule of privacy extends to the husband and wife, so that each has a separate bedroom.

Within the Chinese home, on the other hand, privacy hardly exists at all, except between members of the opposite sexes who are not spouses. Chinese children, even in homes which have ample room, often share the same chambers with their parents until they reach adolescence. Not only do parents have freedom of action with reference to the children's belongings, but the youngsters can also use the possessions of the parents if they can lay their hands on them. If children damage their parents' possessions they are scolded, not because they touched things that were not theirs but because they are too young to handle them with proper care … .

The American child's physical environment establishes strong lines of individual distinction within the home, but there is very little stress on separation of the home from the outside world. The Chinese child's environment is exactly the reverse. He finds a home with few demarcation lines within it but separated by high walls and multiple gates from the outside world.

Indeed, findings from recent research comparing East–West differences in the conceptions of the self–other relation agree with Hsu's observations: In American culture, the boundary between the in-group and out-groups is soft and thin, but the boundary between individuals is sharp and impermeable. In Chinese culture, the walls separating the in-group from outgroups are solid and thick. Inside the walls, the boundary between in-group members is fuzzy.

Person Representations

In this chapter, we review major cultural differences in person representations, which are a type of declarative knowledge. A person representation is a network of associations between a central concept and a number of individual features. The referent of the central concept can be the self, a person other than the self, a group or a social category. A person representation is shown in Figure 6.2. The central concept in this representation is Samuel L. Clemens. The features that are associatively linked to the referent may include alternative labels of the referent (Mark Twain), traits (humorous), identity (American writer), prototypic behaviors (gave lectures), or physical characteristics (wore a mustache). The associations between individual features and the central concept differ in associative strength, and may be specific to a particular type of situation.

Several different representations may be constructed for the same referent, each with a different set of associated features. For example, a person can construct a personal self that is associatively linked to a set of personal attributes, a social self that is linked to a set of social roles and role expectations, and a collective self that is linked to a set of collective memberships. Moreover, each person representation is a separate cognitive unit that can be independently retrieved from memory (Triandis, 1989). When an individual has constructed for the same referent several

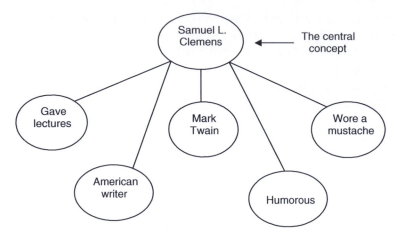

FIGURE 6.2. A person representation of Samuel L. Clemens.

representations, each with different implications for a judgment or behavior decision, the response that is made will depend on which representation is retrieved and used (see Wyer, 2004).

Representations of Other People

Cultures differ in what the most widely distributed mental representations of other people are. When individuals describe the referent of a person representation, they retrieve a person representation from memory and report the features that are associatively linked to the referent. When several different representations of the same referent are available in memory, description may depend on which representation is most accessible in memory and, therefore, is most likely to be retrieved and used.

Research has shown that for European Americans, the most cognitively accessible mental representation of other people consists of general traits, whereas the one for Asians includes social roles and situation-specific behaviors. For example, compared to European Americans, Asians weigh situational information more heavily when they form social judgments. When somebody performs a helpful behavior, the perceiver may predict that this person may perform similar behavior in the future. Confidence in this prediction should increase when the perceiver learns that this person has gone out of his way to help others (situational information that would augment trait inferences). This was the case for both European Americans and South Koreans. However, South Koreans weigh such situational information more heavily than do European Americans (Norenzayan, Choi, & Nisbett, 2002a).

Causal Attribution

In addition, compared to Asians, European Americans are more likely to use abstract traits to explain others' behaviors, and less likely to use contextual factors (J. Miller, 1984; Morris & Peng, 1994; Norenzayan et al., 2002). In one study conducted by Joan Miller (1984, Study 1), participants of different age groups from India and the United States were asked to narrate two prosocial and two deviant behaviors, and offer explanations for the behaviors. As expected, American participants offered more trait explanations than did Indian participants, who in turn offered more contextual explanations. Moreover, the magnitude of these cultural differences increased with age, suggesting that as participants gained more experiences in their culture, they would more likely display the culturally characteristic pattern of causal explanation.

In another study (J. Miller, 1984, Study 2), the explanations for deviant behaviors offered by American and Indian adults were compared. Again, American participants were more likely to offer trait explanations and less likely to offer contextual explanations. For example, when explaining a motorcycle accident, in which a passenger was hurt and the driver (who was an attorney) took the passenger to the local hospital and left, an American participant said:

> The driver is obviously irresponsible; the driver was in a state of shock; the driver is aggressive in pursuing career success (J. Miller, 1984, p. 972).

For the same incident, a typical response from Indian participants was:

> It was the driver's duty to be in court for the client whom he's representing; secondly, the driver might have gotten nervous or confused; and thirdly, the passenger might not have looked as serious as he was (J. Miller, 1984, p. 972).

Similar cross-cultural differences were obtained between Chinese and European Americans. In one study, Morris and Peng (1994) compared the attribution styles of Chinese and European American high-school children. The participants saw animated displays of a blue fish swimming on a trajectory that deviated from that of others, and rated the extent to which the blue fish's movements seemed influenced by internal and external factors. Compared to Chinese participants, European American participants gave higher ratings to internal factors and lower ratings to external factors.

This cross-cultural difference was also reflected in how a crime was narrated in the newspaper. In 1991, a Chinese graduate student shot his advisor after he lost an award competition and failed to get an academic job. At about the same time, an Irish-American ex-postal worker shot his ex-supervisor, after he lost his job, and failed to find a full-time replacement job. The two murders were covered in *The New York Times* and the *World Journal* (a Chinese newspaper widely circulated in the United States). *The New York Times* attributed both murders more to personal dispositions (e.g., "very bad temper"), whereas *World Journal* attributed more to situational factors (e.g., "isolation from Chinese community"; Morris & Peng, 1994).

In an analysis of how sports events are reported in American newspapers (*Los Angeles Times*, *The Boston Globe*, and *The New York Times*) and a Hong Kong newspaper (*South China Morning Post*), F. Lee et al. (1996) also found that attributions from US newspapers are more dispositional than attributions from Hong Kong newspapers.

The Fundamental Attribution Error

Perceivers commit the fundamental attribution error when they explain a person's behavior in terms of the person's dispositions, even when there is an obvious situational explanation for the behavior. In an experimental demonstration of this attribution bias (I. Choi & Nisbett, 1998), European American and South Korean undergraduate students read an essay written by another student in the university. In both conditions, the participants learned that the essay writer was asked by the course instructor to write a pro-capital punishment or an anti-capital punishment essay, regardless of the writer's own attitudes toward the issue. The participants also learned that the course instructor had provided a list of pro- or anti-capital punishment arguments to the essay writer and demanded that he use these arguments in the essay. The participants in the study were asked to infer what the essay writer's genuine attitude toward the issue was.

In this experiment, there was no reason to believe that what the essay writer wrote in the essay would reflect his genuine attitude toward the issue, because the essay writer had no choice over the position he could take on the issue or the arguments he could include in the essay. South Korean undergraduates did not commit the fundamental attribution error; they did not think that the essay reflected the essay writer's genuine attitudes. However, American undergraduates, biased by their belief that people's behaviors are consistent with their attitudes, inferred that the author of the pro-capital punishment essay had a more favorable attitude toward the issue than did the author of the anti-capital punishment essay (I. Choi & Nisbett, 1998). Other studies have similarly shown that relative to European Americans, Japanese and Hong Kong Chinese are less likely to commit the fundamental attribution error (Knowles, Morris, Chiu, & Hong, 2001; Masuda & Kitayama, 2004; Miyamoto & Kitayama, 2002).

Boundary Conditions

Although consistent cross-cultural differences between European Americans and Asians in social perception have been reported, these differences emerge only when a number of conditions are met. First, when European Americans have sufficient cognitive resources to process contextual information, the tendency to commit the fundamental attribution error decreases significantly, and cross-cultural differences in the tendency to exhibit the fundamental attribution error disappear (Knowles et al., 2001; F. Lee et al., 1996). According to the two-step model of causal attribution (Gilbert, 1989; Gilbert, Pelham, & Krull, 1988), dispositional information is easy to process, whereas situational information is usually more complex. Thus, dispositional information is processed automatically, and processing situational information is effortful. Accordingly, when perceivers have limited cognitive resource or low motivation to be accurate, they process dispositional information only, resulting in a strong dispositional bias in their judgment of others. When individuals have sufficient cognitive resource and are motivated to be accurate, they also consider situational attribution and moderate their strong initial dispositional judgment (Gilbert et al., 1988; Gilbert, Krull, & Pelham, 1988).

The two-step model also predicts that both European Americans and East Asians would exhibit the fundamental attribution error when situational information becomes difficult to process. Consistent with this prediction, Norenzayan et al. (2002) reported that South Koreans weigh situational information more heavily when they make future prediction of behavior than do European Americans, but only when situational constraints on behaviors are highlighted. The difference disappears when information that pertains to situational constraints on behaviors is not salient. I. Choi and Nisbett (1998) also found that South Koreans commit the fundamental attribution error just as European Americans do when information on the situational constraints is not sufficiently highlighted.

In addition, cultural differences in the likelihood of committing the fundamental attribution error disappear when the situational forces are perceived to be not strong enough to dominate the essay writer's behavior. For example, Japanese display a significant fundamental attribution error when the essay writer is perceived to have some control over the quality of the essay. If the essay writer has choice over the arguments to be included in the essay (Masuda & Kitayama, 2004), or if the essay writer writes a long and persuasive (as opposed to a short and unconvincing) essay (Miyamoto & Kitayama, 2002), Japanese undergraduates, like their European American counterparts, also exhibit a significant fundamental attribution error.

Representations of the Self

Mental representation of the self is the most widely researched person representation in cultural psychology. Much contemporary research on culture and self is inspired by two theories published at about the same time, which together form the theoretical backbone of contemporary social psychology of culture.

Major Theories of Culture and Self

Culture and Self-Construal

Markus and Kitayama (1991, 2003a) identified two different cultural meaning systems, each organized around a distinctive construal of the self. The meaning system that characterizes the European American view of personhood evolves around an independent self-construal, which emphasizes separation of the self from others. The independent self is represented as a bounded, distinctive, autonomous, and self-contained entity. By contrast, the self-construal that characterizes the prototypic Japanese view of personhood emphasizes the fundamental connectedness of human beings to each other. The self is embedded in a network of social relations, and defined in relation to one's position in it.

In the independent self-system, major life tasks include attaining personal goals, actualizing one's own potentials, and individuation of the self. In contrast, the major life tasks in an interdependent self-system include living in harmony with the social context, living up to group standards, and following group norms.

The Tripartite Model of Self

According to Triandis (1989) and Y. Kashima, Kashima, and Aldridge (2001), people are active agents who selectively appropriate symbolic ideas about the self from their cultural environment to further valued goals. Triandis (1989) identifies three major kinds of self: the private self (knowledge about a person's traits, states, or behaviors), the public self (knowledge about the generalized other's view of the self), and the collective self (knowledge about some collective's view of the self). Every person possesses these three kinds of self, although people in different cultural groups sample these three kinds of self with different probabilities.

The likelihood that the private self and the collective self will be sampled depends in part on the relative emphasis on personal vs. collective goals in the cultural context. In some cultural contexts (e.g., individualist contexts), pursuit of personal goals is widely accepted and highly valued (Triandis, Bontempo, Villareal, & Asai, 1988). The private self (self-reliance, independence, self-esteem, self-concept clarity, and self-realization) is likely to be sampled in such contexts. In such cultural contexts, higher rates of sampling the private self are expected, and there are greater emphases on personal agency, self-esteem, personal distinctiveness, and competition between individuals.

In other cultural contexts (collectivist contexts), the widely accepted view is that people should avoid pitting their personal goals against the collective goals. If a conflict between personal and collective goals is inevitable, people should subordinate their personal goals to the collective goals (Triandis et al., 1988). In such cultural contexts, higher rates of sampling the collective self are expected, and there are greater emphases on group agency, social acceptance, intergroup distinction, and competition.

According to this model, although most people in an individualist culture value personal goals, some people in an individualist culture (the allocentrics) emphasize collective goals. Similarly, although the prevailing norms in a collectivist culture emphasize collective goals, some people in a collectivist culture (the idiocentrics) place high priorities on personal goals (Triandis et al., 1985; see Chapter 2). Triandis (1989) also recognizes the role of context in determining the probability of sampling a particular kind of self. For example, the probability of sampling the collective self would increase as the salience of in-group–out-group boundaries increases.

The culture and self-construal model and the tripartite model offer different perspectives to culture and self. Whereas the culture and self-construal model offers a parsimonious framework to organize cross-cultural differences in self-processes reviewed below, the tripartite model offers a language to describe the dynamic interaction between culture and self. The theoretical significance of the tripartite model becomes obvious as we discuss such interactive processes in later chapters.

Cultural Differences in Self-Construal

Inspired by the culture and self-construal model and the tripartite model, most cross-cultural studies of self-construals have focused on cultural differences in the distributions of the independent (private) self, and the interdependent (collective) self. Because the distributions of these self-construals are markedly different in European American and East Asian cultural contexts, most studies have compared North Americans of European descent with individuals from East Asian contexts.

Spontaneous Self-Concept

The culture and self-construal model and the tripartite self model agree that the independent self is more widely distributed in Western cultures, and the interdependent self is more widely distributed in East Asian cultures. Consistent with this view, some studies (Bond & Cheung, 1983; Cousins, 1989) have shown that European Americans are more likely to describe themselves spontaneously in terms of abstract psychological attributes ("I am sincere"). In contrast, Japanese when describing themselves are more likely to list their social roles (e.g., "I am a student of Keio University"). Studies that compare European Americans with other East Asian groups on spontaneous self-descriptions reveal a similar pattern. Undergraduates in mainland China are much more likely than undergraduates in the United States to describe the self in terms of social categories and less likely to do so in terms of personal attributes (Triandis, 1989; Q. Wang, 2001). While American children often describe themselves in terms of positive personal attributes, abstract dispositions, and internal traits, children in Beijing often describe themselves in terms of social roles, context-specific characteristics, and daily activities in a neutral or modest tone (Q. Wang, 2004). Likewise, compared to European Americans, Hong Kong Chinese are more likely to mention their social roles, preference, and attitudes, and less likely to mention their physical attributes (Ip & Bond, 1995). South Koreans also mention more specific attributes and fewer traits than do European Americans (Rhee, Uleman, Lee, & Roman, 1995). Among Asian Americans, those who have a salient Asian American identity mention more social identities, and fewer traits than do those whose Asian American identity is not salient (Rhee et al., 1995; see Figure 6.3).

Shweder and Miller (1985) submit that those who believe that society is built up out of individuals in pursuit of personal interests and gratification of personal desires prefer to rationalize the moral order in terms of natural rights. Conversely, those who believe that society is built up out of statuses and roles prefer to rationalize the moral order in terms of duties. Consistent with this idea, spontaneous self-descriptions of Hong Kong Chinese contain more duties and fewer rights than self-descriptions of European Americans (Hong, Ip, Chiu, Morris, & Menon, 2001). In addition, Chinese Americans mention more duties and fewer rights when

(a)   (b)

FIGURE 6.3. Expression of individuality and uniqueness in a Mardi Gras parade in New Orleans, USA (a), and expression of interdependence in a parade in a suburb of Tokyo, Japan (b).

they are reminded of their Chinese identity than when they are reminded of their American identity (Hong et al., 2001).

Conception of Agency

Many psychological theories (Bandura, 2001; Ryan & Deci, 2000) take a motivational perspective to human motivation. In these theories, individuals are conceived of as efficacious agents, who believe that they can intentionally influence their functioning and life circumstances. More importantly, people can exercise their agency through the self (direct personal agency), other people who act on the self's behest (proxy agency), or group action (collective agency). Successful functioning requires an agentic blend of these three modes of agency. According to this view, agency is central to personal development, adaptation, and change in diverse cultural milieux (Bandura, 2002).

Different cultural representations of the self place differential emphases on the three modes of agency. Some cultural psychologists (Hernandez & Iyenger, 2001; Iyengar & DeVoe, 2003; Markus & Kitayama, 2003b; Menon et al., 1999; Su et al., 1999; Weisz, Rothbaum, & Blackburn, 1984) posit that countries that privilege the independent self also value personal agency, or the idea that individuals can influence existing realities. By contrast, countries that privilege the interdependent self tend to value group agency, or the belief that individuals should accommodate to existing social realities and yield to group influence. The evidence generally supports this idea.

First, European Americans believe more strongly in personal control than do Hong Kong Chinese (Hsieh, Shybut, & Lotsof, 1969). Compared to

Hong Kong Chinese, European Americans are more likely to attribute social events to the dispositions of the individuals and less likely to attribute them to the dispositions of the group (C. Chiu et al., 2000; T. Menon et al., 1999; see Chapter 4). Third, compared to Japanese and South Koreans, Australians and North Americans agree more strongly with beliefs like "I stick to my opinions even when others in my group don't support me," and "I based my actions more upon my own judgments than upon the decisions of my group," and disagree more with beliefs like "I feel uneasy when my opinions are different from those of members of my group," and "I think it is desirable for members of my group to have the same opinions" (Y. Kashima, Yamaguchi, Kim, Choi, Gelfand, & Yuki, 1995). Furthermore, relative to people in English-speaking cultures (Australia, UK, and the US) and continental European cultures (Belgium and Germany), people in Eastern Asian cultures (Hong Kong, Japan, and South Korea) are more likely to attribute intentionality to the collectives (family, friends, and society; Y. Kashima et al., 2005).

Selfway and Self-Esteem

Self-esteem refers to global, positive (vs. negative) feeling one has toward the self (James, 1890). People need to feel good about themselves. Thus, it is generally believed that self-esteem, broadly conceived, is a universal human need (Brown, 1988). However, individuals may take different routes to feel good about the independent self, and to feel good about the interdependent self (Heine, Lehman, Markus, & Kitayama, 1999). The way it takes to feel good about a culturally constituted conception of the self has been referred to as selfway (Heine, 2003; Heine et al., 1999). The independent selfway prescribes the means one would take to feel good about the independent self. These means include assertion of one's rights, needs, interests; a focus on one's strengths and potentials; a drive for excellence; and affirmation of one's distinctive positive qualities and achievement. By contrast, achievement of positive self-feeling through the interdependent selfway requires meeting one's obligations, acknowledgment of one's weaknesses, the motivation to learn from one's failures and to overcome imperfection of the self that may disgrace the group or community, and the motivation to pursue and attain goals that would reflect positively on the group or community and to earn respect from the group or community (Bempechat & Drago-Severson, 1999; Tao & Hong, 2000; Yu & Yang, 1994).

Most current measures of self-esteem assess feeling good about the independent self, and European Americans tend to score higher on these measures than East Asians or Asian Americans (see Heine et al., 1999). There are several possible reasons for such cultural variation. First, compared to European Americans, East Asians are less inclined to give extreme responses on a psychological survey (C. Chen, Lee, & Stevenson, 1995). Second, East Asian cultures place high premium on being modest in public self-presentation (Kurman & Sriram, 2002). These explanations account for some but not all of the East–West differences in self-esteem. For example, although Easterners (mainland Chinese and Malaysians) score lower than Westerners (Britons and European Americans) on self-esteem items that depict positive evaluation of self-competence, they score higher on self-esteem items that do not reference a positive independent self (e.g., "I like myself"; Tafarodi, Lang, & Smith, 1999; Tafarodi & Swann, 1996). The research findings described in Chapter 4 also show that Hong Kong Chinese are less modest than European Americans in impression management. These findings show that modesty and response set do not fully explain why East Asians report lower self-esteem than do European Americans.

Heine et al. (1999) reported that Japanese students' self-esteem (as measured by conventional self-esteem measures) increased over the course of a 7-month academic exchange program in Canada (Heine et al., 1999), indicating that submergence in Canadian culture could at least temporarily raise Japanese students' self-esteem. This evidence suggests that East–West differences in self-esteem are the result of cultural learning.

Kitayama, Markus, Matsumoto, and Norasakkunkit (1997) provided further evidence linking self-esteem to cultural experiences. First, they had their European American and Japanese participants list situations that would increase or decrease their self-esteem. Next, they had another set of European American and Japanese undergraduates rate how much the American- and Japanese-made situations would influence their self-esteem. Most European American undergraduates estimated that their self-esteem would be enhanced in both American- and Japanese-made situations, whereas most Japanese in Japan estimated that their self-esteem would decrease in both American- and Japanese-made situations. Thus, European Americans have a general tendency to anticipate self-esteem enhancement, whereas Japanese have a general tendency to anticipate self-esteem deflation. More importantly, both American and Japanese participants rated American-made situations as more self-esteem enhancing than Japanese-made situations, indicating that experiences in the US are generally more conducive to self-enhancement than are experiences in Japan. Finally, as in Heine et al. (1999), most Japanese students studying in the United States believed that their self-esteem would increase in American-made situations, and decrease in Japanese-made situations. These findings together suggest that culture-specific experiences support the development of culture-specific self-construals.

Research on *implicit self-esteem* also showed that European Americans and Japanese differ on how positively they view themselves. In these studies, the investigators (Hetts, Sakuma, & Pelham, 1999) compared the level of self-esteem of recent immigrants to the United States, European Americans, Asian Americans, and Japanese students who had or had not visited North America. An association task was used to assess how strongly the individual self ("me") and the collective self ("us") were associated with positive or negative attributes. On each trial of the task, either a singular first-person pronoun (*me*) or a plural first-person pronoun (*us*) was presented briefly. Shortly following this, two target words (*good* and *bad*) were presented on the computer display, and the participant's task was to decide by pressing a key as quickly as possible which of the two target words appeared in the center of the computer display. If the pronoun *me* called out positive associations, the participant should be able to identify the target word *good* quickly when *me* was presented shortly before *good*. Similarly, if the pronoun *us* called out positive associations, the participant should be able to identify the word *good* quickly if the preceding pronoun was *us*. Because it is unlikely that responses to this reaction time task are influenced by conscious deliberation, they may more accurately reflect the participants' genuine feelings toward the self. In these studies, Asian participants who had little or no exposure to North American culture (recent US immigrants from Japan) associated the collective self (*us*) with positive attributes, and the individual self (*me*) with negative attributes: They responded more quickly to the target word *good* when it was preceded by *us* than by *me*, and more quickly to the target word *bad* when it was preceded by *me* than by *us*. In contrast, Americans and Asian participants strongly acculturated to American culture only associated the individual self with positive attributes. When these findings are taken together, the independent selfway is better received in Western societies than in East Asian societies.

Psychological Implications of Cultural Differences in Self-Construal

Much research in cultural psychology has been devoted to explicating the psychological implications of the different culturally constituted self-construals.

Optimism

There is good evidence that culturally constituted self-construals are related to self-perception. For example, in societies that privilege the independent self, people have a tendency to be overly optimistic about their future. For example, compared to Japanese, North Americans have a greater tendency to see the self as "invincible" (Chang, Asakawa, & Sanna, 2001; Heine & Lehman, 1995). Specifically, both European Americans and Japanese believe that negative events would more likely occur to others than to the self, but European Americans hold this belief more strongly than do Japanese. In addition, Japanese expect positive events to be more likely to occur to others than to the self, but European Americans do not show such pessimistic bias (Chang et al., 2001). The prevalent belief in the invincibility of the personal self in Western societies is richly illustrated in the lyrics of an old Helen Reddy song, which asserts women's strength and determination to excel:

> If I have to I can face anything
>
> I am strong (strong)
>
> I am invincible (invincible)
>
> I am woman
>
> Oh, I am woman
>
> I am invincible
>
> I am strong

Self-Consistency

Individuals who attend to the independent self would be likely to comb through the inconsistencies in their self-perceptions. By comparison, individuals who attend to the interdependent self are less likely to do so. In a series of studies that compared the level of self-consistency between European Americans and South Koreans, I. Choi and Choi (2002) found that European Americans, who attend more to the independent self than to the interdependent self, have consistent self-perceptions. When presented with two seemingly contradictory statements about the self (e.g., "I am extroverted" and "I am introverted," or "Equality is more important to me than ambition," and "Ambition is more important to me than equality"), they agree with one more than the other. However, this is not necessarily the case among South Koreans. Compared to European Americans, South Koreans have a greater tendency to agree to *both* seemingly inconsistent statements of the self at the same time. Suh (2002) also reported that compared to South Koreans, European Americans' self-perceptions are more consistent across interpersonal contexts. In particular, they tend to think that they display similar personality characteristics when they are with their close friend, parents, professor, a younger person, and a stranger. Moreover, among European American undergraduates, those with more consistent self-perceptions tend to be happier with their life. By comparison, among South Korean undergraduates, life satisfaction depends less on consistency in self-perceptions.

Social Cognition

The influence of culturally constituted self-construals on social perception is equally evident. For example, in European American culture, when asked to predict how others would feel in a particular situation, people may project their own emotions to others: If I feel sad, people surrounding me would feel sad too. Such egocentric projection is less evident among East Asians. East Asians, however, are more likely than European Americans to project complementary emotions to others: If I feel sad, others would feel sympathetic (Cohen & Gunz, 2002).

Cultures with markedly different self-construals also differ in how people make decisions in social interactions. Suppose you are meeting a new coworker, with whom you would have to work very closely, or a potential romantic partner, with whom you may want to get acquainted. Now you are provided with some personal information about this person (the person's accomplishments, beliefs, and interests), and information about this person's relational background (whom the person has close relation with, the social groups the person belongs to, and the person's social status). Which type of information would you want to have before meeting this person? If you are given each type of information, how confident are you in your ability to predict how the stranger will behave? How confident are you in your ability to predict how you should act in this situation? How confident are you in your ability to predict what you should say in the interaction? In a cross-cultural study, Gelfand, Spurlock, Sniezek, and Shao (2000) asked European American and Chinese respondents the above questions, and found that personal information is perceived to be more useful for making predictions in social interactions among European American respondents, whereas relational information is perceived to be more useful among Chinese respondents.

Choice and Self-Justification

In societies where the independent self-construal is widely distributed, people tend to value personal uniqueness, and assume that how they make their choices reveals their internal attributes. In contrast, in societies where the interdependent self-construal is widely distributed, people would less likely consider choice as a form of self-expression, and uniqueness is not highly valued. Consistent with this idea, research shows that compared to Chinese Americans and Koreans, European Americans like a geometric figure that is different from other figures in the set more than they like a figure that is identical to other figures (H. Kim & Markus, 1999).

In North American culture, because the ability to make a choice reflects personal agency and the value of self-expression (e.g., taste, preference, and identity), people prefer "making a choice" on every new occasion. Thus, when European Americans make choices, instead of staying with the same rule in a situation, they prefer *choosing* a new rule. If they have used a rule (e.g., a risk aversion rule) in one context, they are likely to shift to a different rule in the second context. Such tendency to seek variety in choice rules is considerably weaker among Koreans (H. Kim & Drolet, 2003).

In American culture, the independent self is privileged and choice is considered good. People are motivated to perform well when they can decide what they want to strive for, and feel demotivated when others dictate what they should work on. In a series of studies, Iyengar and Lepper (1999) asked European American third-graders to solve anagrams. There were three experimental conditions in this study. In the choice condition, the children could choose to work on one of six categories of anagrams (e.g., animals and family). In the no-choice in-group condition, the children learned that they would work on a particular category of anagrams suggested by their mother. In the no-choice out-group condition, the experimenter assigned a category of anagrams to the children. The researchers measured the number of anagrams the children completed correctly (task performance), and the amount of time the children spent on the anagrams during the free-play period after the purported end of the experiment (intrinsic motivation). As expected, the European American children had much higher performance and intrinsic motivation in the choice conditions than in the two no-choice conditions.

Interestingly, when Asian American children were recruited to participate in the same experiment, they displayed a different pattern. Like their European American counterparts, they performed better and were more intrinsically motivated in the choice condition than in the no-choice out-group condition. However, when they learned that their mother (an important other) had chosen a category of anagrams for them, their intrinsic motivation and performance were just as high as the European American children in the choice condition. Apparently, in an independent culture, only personal choice is motivating, whereas in an interdependent culture, both personal choice and choice made by important others for oneself are motivating. This is the case probably because Asian American children identify strongly with the choices their important others have made for them.

Individuals who value the independent self not only want to make a choice, they also want to see themselves as having made a reasonable choice. Thus, in European American culture, individuals often justify their personal choice—If I choose to have a salad instead of a ham sandwich for lunch, that must be because I like salads more than ham sandwiches. Such self-justification is much less prevalent in Japan (Heine & Lehman, 1997).

However, this does not imply that Japanese do not care about whether the choices they have made are reasonable or not. In fact, Japanese are *more* likely than European Americans to justify their choices after they have chosen a gift for *their friend* (Fein, Hoshino-Browne, Davies, & Spencer, 2003). Taken together, these findings suggest that European American and Japanese cultures do not differ in the need to justify their choices. Instead, the two cultures differ in the kinds of choices that require self-justification. European

Meet the Researcher: Darrin Lehman

"Living in Vancouver, with its significant multicultural mix, one can't help but be interested in the ways in which culture shapes and influences self, social, and cognitive processes. Although some in our field have resisted the first major wave of findings of important cross-cultural differences, it is becoming increasingly clear that in fact "culture goes all the way down." This doesn't mean there aren't psychic universals (of course these exist), but it does mean that one must take seriously the notion that culture and self are mutually constitutive, and that a wide variety of fascinating cultural differences both make sense in this regard and necessitate inclusion in our discipline. Social psychology is in large part the study of how the situation (the "independent variable") affects people's emotions, thoughts, and behavior, and in this sense culture can rightfully be thought of as the "ultimate independent variable." This is perhaps why cultural psychology has had such a juggernaut feel to it, picking up lots of people along the way in just its infancy. I can only imagine how much this research area will expand in the years to come, and the intriguing and important things we will learn about culture's affects on personhood."

Darrin Lehman was born and raised in New York. He received his Ph.D from the University of Michigan, and is now a Professor at the University of British Columbia.

Americans feel the need to justify choices they make for themselves; probably these choices reflect on their personal self, the self that is highly valued in their culture. In contrast, the relatively interdependent Japanese feel the need to justify choices that could affect their interpersonal relation.

Interpersonal Processes

The East Asians' highly accessible interdependent self is also reflected in their sensitivity to interpersonal information. Relative to European Americans, East Asians have better memory of how other people think of the self (Cohen & Gunz, 2002), and of information about the collective self (Wagar & Cohen, 2003). In contrast, European Americans have better memory of information about the personal self (Wagar & Cohen, 2003). In addition, East Asians are more likely than European Americans to take other people's perspective when reading other people's emotions (Cohen & Gunz, 2002), pay closer attention to the common ground in communication (Haberstroh, Oyserman, Schwarz, Kuehnen, & Ji, 2002), and have a greater tendency to mimic other people's behaviors (van Baaren, Maddux, Chartrand, de Bouter, & van Knippenberg, 2003).

For example, in the van Baaren et al. (2003) study, the research participant, who was either a Japanese or a European American undergraduate, took part in a bogus pilot test with a confederate. The participant and the confederate took turns to describe what was in a set of photographs. During the experiment, the confederate rubbed her face or head-hair area constantly but naturally and subtly during the interaction. As expected, Japanese participants were much more likely than were their European American counterparts to mimic the confederate's behavior.

Self-construal also mediates cultural differences in interpersonal relationship. The interdependent self is more emphasized in Turkey than in Canada. When asked how close they feel and how close they ideally would like to be to family members, romantic partners, friends, and acquaintances, both Turkish and European Canadian undergraduates reported feeling closest and ideally wanting to be closest to their romantic partner, and then to their families and friends, followed by acquaintances. However, Turkish undergraduates desired more closeness with family members and acquaintances than did European Canadian undergraduates (Uskul, Hynie, & Lalonde, 2004).

Persuasion

People are more receptive to persuasive messages that are consistent rather than inconsistent with culturally emphasized self-construal. For example, magazine advertisements emphasizing personal benefits are more persua-sive in the United States than in South Korea. Conversely, magazine adver-tisements emphasizing family and in-group benefits are more persuasive in South Korea than in the United States (Han & Shavitt, 1994).

In addition, for the same product, European Americans like an adver-tising message that emphasizes personal uniqueness ("Timex watches. It embodies so much. It's like a person. It is an impressive personality, very individualistic, and with a strong focus and concern for oneself—in a pos-itive way") more than they do a message that emphasizes interpersonal connectedness ("Timex watches. It embodies so much. It's like a person. It is an impressive social being, very connected to others, and with a strong focus and concern for others—in a positive way"). Chinese participants showed the reverse preference (Aaker & Schmitt, 2001).

Furthermore, appeals to personal uniqueness, individual benefits and preferences, and personal success are more commonly employed in American magazine advertisements than in South Korean magazine adver-tisements. Conversely, appeals emphasizing conformity, in-group benefits, harmony, and family integrity are more common in South Korean maga-zine advertisements than in American advertisements (Han & Shavitt, 1994; H. Kim & Markus, 1999).

Life Satisfaction

Pursuit and attainment of goals consistent with culturally emphasized goals is a good predictor of life satisfaction (Oishi & Diener, 2001). Contemporary Western societies are built up out of individuals pursuing self-esteem, identity consistency, personal freedom, and happiness. Although in most countries people with higher levels of self-esteem and positive affect are more satisfied with their life, self-esteem and positive affect are better predictors of life satisfaction in societies that privilege the independent self than in societies that privilege the interdependent self (Diener & Diener, 1995; Kwan, Bond, & Singelis, 1997; Oishi & Diener, 2001; Schimmack, Radhakrishnan, Oishi, Dzokoto, & Ahadi, 2002; Suh, 1999, 2002; Suh, Diener, Oishi, & Triandis, 1998). In addition, within the United States, pursuing goals for fun and enjoyment and successfully achieving these goals is associated with higher levels of life satisfaction for European Americans, but not for Asian Americans (Oishi & Diener, 2001).

In contrast, in societies that privilege the interdependent self, individ-uals view their relationship with in-group or community members as of utmost importance. In Japan, pursuing goals to make one's parents and friends happy and successfully achieving these goals is associated with higher levels of life satisfaction (Oishi & Diener, 2001). For Hong Kong

Chinese, but not for European Americans, having harmonious relationship with important others contributes to a higher level of life satisfaction (Kwan et al., 1997). Within the United States, pursuit and attainment of goals to make parents and friends happy, and positive regard from important others are positively related to life satisfaction for Asian Americans, but not for European Americans (Oishi & Diener, 2001; Suh, 1999).

It is important to emphasize that in East Asian contexts, maintaining harmonious relationship and pursuit of collective goals are likely to be seen as self-identified choices rather than externally imposed goals. Indeed, research has shown that in East Asian societies, while successful pursuit of self-identified collective choices contributes to psychological well-being, attainment of externally imposed collective goals does not (Chirkov, Kim, Ryan, & Kaplan, 2003; Chirkov & Ryan, 2001).

Self-Regulation

Self-construal is related to how an individual regulates oneself. As noted, individuals with independent self-construal are motivated to distinguish themselves positively from others. These individuals would likely focus on the positive features of the self and potential gains in situations. Likewise, individuals with a dominant interdependent self seek to fit in harmoniously with others, and may therefore focus on fulfilling obligations and avoiding mistakes that would cause social mishap. A. Lee, Aaker, and Gardner (2000) provided evidence for the link between self-construal and the focus of self-regulation. They showed that European Americans with independent self-construal tend to focus on potential gains in situations, whereas Chinese with interdependent self-construal tend to focus on potential losses (see also Elliot, Chirkov, Kim, & Sheldon, 2001). In addition, compared to Chinese, European Americans are more likely to have regrets of inaction (feel bad for not having done something to improve the outcome), and less likely to experience regrets of commission (feel bad for having done something that produced the negative outcome; J. Chen, Chiu, Roese, Tam, & Lau, in press).

If the interdependent self-construal sets up a focus on fulfilling obligations and avoiding potential losses, individuals with such self-construals should be psychologically prepared to learn from their mistakes, and persist on a task that they have failed before. Consistent with this idea, there is evidence that individuals from Asian cultural contexts tend to remember a failure as a bigger failure than it actually was. In one study (Oishi & Diener, 2003), Asian Americans and European Americans were given 20 anagrams to solve. Asian Americans solved as many anagrams (about six to seven) as European Americans did. One month later, when asked to recall how many anagrams they had solved, Asian Americans remembered solving fewer anagrams (five to six) than did their European American peers, who remembered solving about seven anagrams.

Furthermore, in the face of failure, to maintain one's positive self-evaluation, people may engage in self-defenses. They may devaluate the importance of the task, and even derogate the strong performers. This tendency is considerably weaker among East Asians than European Americans. Compared with their European American counterparts, East Asian undergraduates are less likely to view criticism or negative feedback as a self-threat. In response to failure feedback, East Asian undergraduates do not defend their self-esteem by derogating their peer who outperforms them, as their European American peers sometimes do (Brockner & Chen, 1996).

Finally, when European Canadian undergraduates fail on a task, instead of persisting on the task, they prefer to shift to another task. If they succeed on the task, they would choose to work on the same task later (Heine et al., 2001; Oishi & Diener, 2003). For them, working on what they are good at makes them feel better than persisting on a task that they did not do well (Oishi & Diener, 2003). By contrast, among East Asian undergraduates, when they fail on a task, they tend to persist on the task, instead of shifting to a new one. If they do well on a task, they would move on to a new task. To them, it is more important to overcome a past failure than to show that one can do well on a new task. In summary, culturally constituted self-construals have important implications for a wide range of psychological phenomena.

Situational Activation of Self-Construal

By now, we have reviewed evidence on some cultural differences in self-construals and their associated psychological phenomena. We argue that a culturally constituted self-construal is a cognitive structure that is widely distributed in a cultural group. As people participate in culture, they acquire the prevalent self-construal in the culture, and apply it frequently to make sense of their experiences and to guide their actions. Consequently, this self-construal becomes a highly accessible cognitive structure; it can be readily retrieved from memory.

Comparative studies may lead to the erroneous impression that the relatively widely distributed self-construal has absolute authority over one's cognitions and behaviors. Recall that according to the tripartite model of self (Triandis, 1989), people in a culture may have acquired several different self-construals. As noted, in the Kitayama et al. (1997) study, Japanese students studying in the United States feel that their self-esteem will increase in American-made situations, and decrease in Japanese situations. This finding suggests that both the independent self and the interdependent self are available to individuals with experiences in both Eastern and Western cultures. Moreover, although many American-made situations promote self-enhancement, some dampen self-esteem. Likewise, although many Japanese-made situations promote self-efface-ment, some bolster self-esteem. If self-construals are acquired through cul-tural experiences, even within American (or Japanese) culture, people may acquire both independent and interdependent self-construals. According to this line of reasoning, the cultural differences reviewed in the last two sections do not result from the absence of interdependent self-construal in North American culture, or from the absence of independent self-construal in East Asian cultures. Instead, consistent with the tripartite model of the self, the differences stem from uneven distributions, and hence unequal levels of cognitive accessibility of the two self-construals in Eastern and Western cultures (see Chapter 8).

If self-construals are indeed learned cognitive representations, envi-ronmental cueing should be able to call out a relatively inaccessible self-construal. In line with this idea, researchers have used an environmental cueing procedure to activate either the independent self or the interde-pendent self in a controlled experiment. In the first self-construal cueing experiment, Trafimow and colleagues (1991, Study 1) and Trafimow, Silverman, Fan, and Law (1997) had their American and Chinese partici-pants either think of what made them different from their family and friends (the independent self-condition), or think of what they had in common with their family and friends (the interdependent self-cueing condition). Next, all participants were asked to describe themselves. Both American and Chinese participants mentioned more individual attributes (e.g., personal beliefs and qualities), and fewer collective attributes (e.g., group membership) in the independent self-cueing condition than in the interdependent self-cueing condition. The same results were obtained in another experiment (Trafimow et al., 1991, Study 2) that used a different cueing manipulation. In this experiment, American undergraduates read the story of how a warrior in ancient Sumer decided on a military appoint-ment. In the independent self-cueing condition, participants learned that the warrior made appointment to pursue personal goals (e.g., solidify his own dominion and enhance his own prestige). In the interdependent cue-ing condition, participants learned that the appointment was made to show the warrior's loyalty to his family, and to increase the prestige of the family. Again, subsequent to independent (vs. interdependent) self-cueing, participants mentioned more individual attributes and fewer collective attributes in their self-descriptions.

Self-construal cueing also influences value endorsement. In one experiment, Gardner, Gabriel, and Lee (1999) found that when participants were not exposed to any self-construal cues, European American undergraduates adhered more strongly to individualist values than to collectivist values. In contrast, Hong Kong Chinese undergraduates adhered more strongly to collectivist values than to individualist values. These findings reveal the higher accessibility of the independent self to European American undergraduates, and the higher accessibility of the interdependent self to Hong Kong undergraduates. However, both European American and Hong Kong Chinese adhered more strongly to individualist values than collectivist values in the independent self-cueing condition, and adhered more strongly to collectivist values than individualist values in the interdependent self-cueing condition. Again, this finding illustrates that both self-construals are available to European Americans and Chinese, and that environmental cues can activate either self-construal and push participants' responses in one or the other direction.

Earlier in this chapter, we described how culturally constituted self-construal might impact the tendency to mimic others' behavior. In one study, van Baaren et al. (2003, Study 2) cued the independent and the interdependent self with a scrambled sentence task. Each scrambled sentence consisted of five words that were not in the correct order, and participants were asked to make a grammatically correct four-word sentence. In the independent self-cueing condition, most sentences contained a word related to the independent self (e.g., unique and individual). In the interdependent self-condition, most sentences contained a word related to the interdependent self (e.g., group and cooperate). Participants in the control condition did not receive the scrambled sentence task. The participants were undergraduates in the Netherlands. In this experiment, mimicry in the interdependent self-condition was highest, followed by mimicry in the control condition, and finally by mimicry in the independent self-condition.

Using a different self-construal manipulation, H. Kim and Drolet (2003) illustrated the effects of self-construal cueing on choice behavior. In this study, the participants, who were American undergraduates, were randomly assigned to the independent or interdependent self-cueing condition. In the independent self-cueing condition, participants received three advertisements that promoted uniqueness and individuality (e.g., "Routine, the enemy" or "Ditch the Joneses"). In the interdependent self-cueing condition, they received three advertisements that highlighted relationality and connectedness among people (e.g., "Looks like we all share more in common than we think," or "E-mail when I want to talk to my best friend."). As mentioned earlier, European Americans have a greater tendency to shift their choice rules across decision-making situations than do

Koreans. In this study, cueing the independent self led to a considerably greater tendency to switch choice rules in new situations than did cueing the interdependent self.

Gardner et al. (1999) have also cued the independent and interdependent self in an experiment by having participants read a brief paragraph about a trip to a city and circle the pronouns in the text. In the independent self-cueing condition, the pronouns reference the individual self ("I" and "me"), while in the interdependent self-cueing condition, the pronouns reference the relational self (e.g., "we" and "us"). Using this manipulation, researchers (Haberstroh et al., 2002; Küehnen & Oyserman, 2002) showed that interdependent (vs. independent) self-cueing has a temporary effect on the way participants

---

Meet the Researcher: Daphna Oyserman

"A main contention of cultural and cross-cultural psychology is that societies differ in their chronic levels of individualism (independence) (IND) and collectivism (inter dependence) (COL) and that these differences have consequences beyond differences in relative endorsement of universal values. The cross-national evidence is suggestive of a relationship between these cultural factors and cognition; Americans are more likely to focus on dispositions in providing rationales for behavior or explaining causality than are participants from other, non-western countries. How are these findings to be interpreted? To me, the most provocative possibility is that culture influences not only the content but also the nature of our thinking. One possible model is that distal differences—in philosophy, religion, language, history—create proximal differences in how we think. Americans think like Americans, Chinese like Chinese and so on. A number of studies, including work from my own lab, suggest otherwise. Though Americans may routinely think in a certain way—looking for the main point, the central theme, and Chinese may routinely think differently—looking for the gestalt, the relationships among parts—all of us can shift and see differently, depending on what is cued."

Daphna Oyserman obtained her Ph.D. in 1987 from the University of Michigan. She holds joint appointments as Professor in the Department of Psychology and the School of Social Work at the University of Michigan, and Research Professor in the Research Center for Group Dynamics of Michigan's Institute for Social Research.

process information. For example, under interdependent (vs. independent self) cueing, German undergraduates were more sensitive to the question context in a survey. For example, when the participants were asked to report their happiness and satisfaction with life in one questionnaire, participants under interdependent self-cueing tended to believe that the experimenter would not ask the same question twice in the same survey, and therefore interpreted happiness and satisfaction to mean slightly different things. In contrast, participants under independent self-cueing were not sensitive to the context of questioning, and did not use the questioning context to infer the survey researchers' communicative intention. Hence, they treated the meaning of the two items as identical (Haberstroh et al., 2002).

In another study in which the same self-construal cueing procedure was used, American undergraduates were presented with a letter made of smaller letters (see Figure 6.4) on a computer screen. Their task was to identify the large letter in one block of the trials, and to identify the smaller letter in another block of trials. The speed of identifying the large letters indicates how efficient the participants were in processing global information (the global configuration of the display), whereas the speed to identify small letters indicates efficiency in processing local information (the local features of the display). As expected, interdependent self-cueing facilitates global information processing, whereas independent self-cueing facilitates local information processing. Participants under interdependent self-cueing were faster in identifying the large letter than the small letter. In contrast, participants under independent self-cueing were faster in identifying the small letter than the large letter (Küehnen & Oyserman, 2002).

As mentioned, in cultures with different dominant self-construals, life satisfaction is predicated on different psychological factors. In cultures that privilege the independent self, life satisfaction is related to positive affect, whereas in cultures that privilege the interdependent self, both positive affect and positive regards from important others predict life satisfaction. Self-construal cueing could produce a similar pattern of results. In one study (Suh, 1999), American undergraduates received one of Trafimow et al.'s (1991) self-construal cueing manipulations. Next, all participants completed measures of life satisfaction, positive and negative affect, and social appraisal (how important others evaluate the self). Under independent self-construal cueing, life satisfaction depended on affective experiences (the amount of positive affect over negative affect) only. Under interdependent self-cueing, life satisfaction depended on both affect balance and social appraisal.

```
KKKKKKK
K
K
KKKKK
K
K
K
```

FIGURE 6.4. Stimulus used to assess efficiency in global and local information processing.

In summary, researchers have used a wide variety of techniques to activate the independent self and the interdependent self in experimental settings, and found strong and consistent effects of independent vs. interdependent self-activation on self-perception, values, choice behaviors, social cognition, and life satisfaction. Moreover, the findings from the cueing studies parallel those from cross-cultural studies. These findings together suggest that the cross-cultural differences in self-processes reviewed in the current chapter are mediated by the relative accessibility of independent vs. interdependent self-construal. Moreover, self-construals are knowledge structures that are called out in concrete situations to grasp experiences and guide actions. Although the independent self and the interdependent self are unevenly distributed and hence have different levels of cognitive accessibility across cultures, they are available to individuals from very diverse cultures. This evidence provides strong support for the tripartite model of the cultural self (Triandis, 1989).

Meet the Researcher: Eunkook M. Suh

"By the time I was in 5th grade, I had lived in 5 different countries and needed to master 3 different languages simply to blend in as a 'normal kid' at school. Then, after finishing college in Korea, I went to the US to study psychology, minus the foresight that this time I'd be spending 14 years away from home. I had a luscious taste of the various cultural nuances of human thinking during my cross-cultural excursion. However, for me, the biggest highlight was not that cultural members subtly differed in how they construed the world. What struck me the most was that each cultural group seemed to be totally unaware of this perpetual influence of culture on their thoughts and behaviors. Culture, as Durkheim once said, indeed is like an 'invisible air'—omnipresent and powerful, yet deceivingly natural and unremarkable to those who are submerged within it. Recent cross-cultural research findings in social psychology, in a sense, are spraying color to this invisible sculptor of human mind. They enable us to see what we normally don't see."

Eunkook M. Suh was born in Seoul, Korea. He received his Ph.D. from the University of Illinois at Urbana-Champaign. Suh has recently returned to his alma mater, Yonsei University, to teach in the Department of Psychology.

Representations of Groups

We began this chapter with a metaphor introduced by anthropologist Francis Hsu. According to this metaphor, the dominant model of self in American culture is like a typical American house, with low fences and many internal partitions. Differentiation between individual selves in the group is clear, whereas in-group–out-group boundaries are relatively fluid. Conversely, the dominant model of self in East Asian contexts resembles a typical Chinese house, with high outside walls and few internal partitions. Differentiation between individuals within the group is fuzzy, but in-group–out-group boundaries are relatively impermeable.

Cultural differences in cognitive representations of groups are not as thoroughly investigated as cultural differences in cognitive representations of the self. However, some research findings have lent support to Hsu's idea. In one comparative study of European Americans and Japanese (Sethi, Lepper, & Ross, 1999), the investigators measured the tendency to reject the use of trait terms to describe the self, one's friend, and the enemy. People have more knowledge about the context in which their own behaviors occur than they have knowledge about the contextual nature of others' behaviors. Thus, there is a greater tendency for individuals to ascribe traits or dispositions to others than to themselves. In this study, both European Americans and Japanese were more reluctant to ascribe traits to themselves than to their enemy. Indeed, Japanese students used significantly more traits to describe their enemy (out-group) than did European American students, indicating a greater level of differentiation between the self and the out-group among the Japanese students.

Moreover, European American students were equally willing to apply traits to describe their enemy and their friend, presumably because they represented the self (*me*) as different from both their friend and their enemy (*others*). In contrast, Japanese students used much fewer traits to describe their friend than their enemy. Compared to European American students, Japanese students also used fewer traits to describe their friend, indicating that in terms of trait ascription, Japanese students treated their friend and self more alike than did European American students.

Furthermore, when European American students explained the behaviors of a wrongdoer, they made *slightly* stronger dispositional attributions than situational attributions, regardless of whether the target person was a friend (in-group) or a stranger (out-group). Asian American students made *much* stronger dispositional attributions than situational attributions when the wrongdoer was a stranger. However, they made stronger situational attributions than dispositional attributions when the wrongdoer was a friend (Sethi et al., 1999). Again, this finding illustrated a greater level of differentiation between in-group and out-group members among Asian American students than European American students.

Similar cultural differences were found in participants' self-reported communication styles. For example, Hong Kong Chinese and Japanese reported that they would use different patterns of communication strategies with members of in-groups and out-groups. Americans and Australians also reported that they would communicate differently with members of in-groups and members of out-groups, but the distinction was considerably less sharp (Gudykunst et al., 1992). Taken together, the level of differentiation between the self and others seems to be greater among European American students than Asian American students.

Cultures differ not only on the dominant conceptions of how the self, in-group members, and out-group members are related. They also differ in the dominant criteria for defining in-group membership. According to Yuki (2003), in American culture, belonging to the same social category is an important criterion for defining in-group membership. Individuals may treat a person who graduated from their university as an in-group member, even when they do not know this alumna personally.

By contrast, in East Asian cultures, people need to know the complex relational structure within the in-group to anticipate how others in the group would behave. Thus, East Asians tend not to depict their in-group members as depersonalized entities of a social category, but as interrelated members in a complex network. In other words, aside from considering categorical memberships, East Asians would likely include somebody as an in-group when they have personal connections with the person (e.g., she is my acquaintance), or when they know the person indirectly through a middle person (e.g., she is my acquaintance's niece).

Consistent with this idea, Yuki, Maddux, Brewer, and Takemura (2005) showed that although both European American and Japanese undergraduates trust people in their own university more than they do people from another university, compared to their European American counterparts, Japanese undergraduates are more trustful toward a person from another university, if there is an indirect connection between this person and the self (e.g., if they know someone in that university).

In short, compared to the dominant cognitive representation of groups in American culture, the dominant representation of groups in East Asian cultures seems to emphasize interpersonal connections as a criterion for defining in-group membership more, and have fuzzier distinctions between the self and other in-group members, and more discrete boundaries between the in-group and out-groups.

Conclusion

The previous chapter focuses on culture as shared learned habits. The current chapter deals with another aspect of culture: culture as learned cognitive representations of persons, including the self, others, and the group. The empirical evidence reviewed in the current chapter suggests that participation in a culture leads to acquisition of culturally constituted person representations, which impact a wide variety of psychological phenomena. The self-construal cueing experiments illustrate the causal impact of culturally constituted self-representations on self-perception, social perception, interpersonal processes, and life satisfaction. These experiments also show that although dominant cultural representations may have higher cognitive accessibility than less dominant ones, very different cultural representations of the self are available to people in most cultures. Moreover, situational cueing can push responses of individuals in the same culture in one or the other direction, depending on which cultural representation is activated. As such, culture does not rigidly determine individual behaviors. Instead, it provides a lens to make sense of reality, and people can flexibly change their cultural lens in response to the cultural cues in the environment. We will return to these dynamic processes in Chapter 8.

Events and Norms: How Events Unfold and What We Should Do

7

Contents at a Glance

Cultural Psychology in Public Bathrooms

In 1976, the *Journal of Personality and Social Psychology* published a field experiment conducted by Middlemist and his colleagues (Middlemist, Knowles, & Matter, 1976). The investigators hypothesized that the presence of others is arousing. The field in which the study took place was a men's public bathroom. In the control condition, the unwitting participant used the only urinal not closed for cleaning. In the first experimental condition, one confederate stood at the urinal next to the one the unwitting participant was using. In the second experimental condition, the confederate stood one urinal away. The question is whether the presence of a confederate who coactively engaged in private elimination would increase physiological arousal. If the answer is yes, the arousal would cause contraction in the muscles at the exit from the bladder, and so delay the onset of urination. The delay and the tension would then cause the urine stream to be faster and therefore to persist for a shorter time. To test the hypothesis, the experimenter hid in a cubicle behind the urinals, balanced a little periscope on some books under the door, and directed it upward so that the participant's urinal was visible. From there, he observed and recorded the delay and persistence of urination accurately with a timepiece. The evidence confirms the investigators' hypothesis.

This finding is often interpreted as a piece of supportive evidence for the social facilitation theory, which states that the presence of others generally increases physiological drive. However, from a cultural perspective, we must ask: Why would the presence of a confederate who coactively engaged in private elimination be arousing? In his critique of this experiment, Parker (1989) wrote, "The unwitting subject in the Middlemist et al. experiment could have publicly wet his trousers (to protest against the length of a lecture) or peed against a tree (to show off to the lads). In the lavatory he could have chatted amiably to the stranger next to him or huddled silently over the urinal" (p. 17). Why did these scenarios not happen in the Middlemist et al. experiment?

These questions bring to light the important fact that there are cultural mores regarding the display of bodily functions. Most people in the US hold very strong taboos against anyone seeing them when they are engaged in excretory activities, and they often feel uncomfortable when this happens. Additionally, in American culture, excretion is normatively considered to be a private event, to be executed privately without being watched in an enclosed space, and not publicly in a lecture theater, or the front yard. A public lavatory is not considered to be a public place for socializing. As Parker puts it, "Even a basic biological function like going to the loo, however, is organized in the expressive context of a culture" (p. 17).

The Middlemist field experiment violated research participants' basic rights to privacy and would unlikely be allowed to be carried out again. However, a "field experiment" of a different kind was recently conducted in London.

In early December 2003, Monica Bonvicini installed the sculpture *Don't Miss a Sec*, a usable public toilet on a construction site on a sidewalk near the River Thames. Unlike a regular public toilet, this one is enclosed in one-way mirrored glass, which allows the user to see out while passers-by cannot peep in. The toilet is free and open for use during certain hours of the day, and the stainless-steel potty within the glass cube is fully functional. As the user can see out, this contemporary art exhibit poses an obvious challenge to the cultural norms separating "the private" from "the public," and confronts its user with the embarrassing experience of performing the most private bodily function seemingly public on a street corner. This exhibit has drawn considerable public attention, and many people have posted their reactions to it in the Internet. Some posted reflections are as follows:

It looks strange so you would think twice before going inside. But come to think of it, it's a one way mirror so it would be safe to use coz you can see if people are peeking. But the question is will I use it? Well ... it's worth a try!)
Posted by Mitch on July 20, 2004 at 02:41 PM

yes of course!! with lots of newspaper to decorate the panel ...
Posted by Sharon Kim on July 20, 2004 at 06:18 PM

Oh my god! I wouldn't use it.
Posted by Lily on July 20, 2004 at 11:49 PM

I would definitely not use it ... who comes up with stuff like this in the first place ... its neat ... but seriously ... what in the world was that person thinking???:)
Posted by Utkarsh on July 21, 2004 at 03:59 AM

Norms, explicitly stated or unstated, regulate much of social life. Oftentimes, we follow cultural norms, like the norms governing the display of bodily functions, without thinking too much about them. In situations where these norms are violated, people may show strong reactions. Indeed, as we argue in this chapter, many cultural processes are normative in nature. Person representations, event representations, and norm representations are three major types of declarative knowledge that have been extensively studied in cultural psychology. In the last chapter, we discussed person representations. The current chapter focuses on cultural differences in event and norm representations.

Event Representations

People spontaneously construct mental representations of temporally- and thematically-related sequences of events. An event representation allows individuals to picture a state of affairs or an event in a specific situation and how it transforms into another state or event. To capture the gist of the event sequence, a caption or header (e.g., "visiting a restaurant") can be attached to the event representation (see Wyer, 2004). When an event representation becomes widely shared in human group, it becomes a *cultural script*.

Prototypic event representations are representations of events that routinely occur in a certain type of situation. A prototypic event representation can function as an *implicit theory* about the events that occur in a particular type of situation (Wyer, 2004). In the next subsections, we use culture of honor to illustrate the nature of cultural scripts, and discuss the role of implicit theories of change in event perception.

Culture of Honor

Thus far, we have focused on comparison of national cultures. Within the United States, there are cultural variations in behaviors that merit serious research attention, because failing to attend to such cultural variations could cause interpersonal hardship and even threats to one's physical safety.

Cohen (1996, 1998) and Cohen and Nisbett (1997) have conducted extensive studies on the culture of honor in the American South as an implicit cultural script that may reinforce violence in interpersonal and domestic settings. In the United States, Caucasian Americans in the South are thrice as likely as Caucasians in the North to commit homicide. Moreover, this regional difference is limited to conflict-, argument-, or brawl-related homicides, and does not exist in homicides related to other felonies such as robbery (Cohen, 1998; Nisbett, 1993; Nisbett & Cohen, 1996).

Additionally, compared to Caucasian northerners, Caucasian southerners are more likely to endorse the use of violence for self-protection, to answer an affront, or to socialize children (Cohen & Nisbett, 1994). Furthermore, the law in the Southern states is more accepting of the use of violence for self-defense and coercion (e.g., use of deadly weapons for self-defense, spousal abuse, corporal punishment, and capital punishment). For example, legislators in the South are more lax in gun control legislation, and are likely to vote against gun control than are legislators in the North. About half of the states (48%) in the North have statutes requiring an individual to retreat before using deadly force for self-defense. Only 25% of the states in the South have such statutes. About 40% (39%) of the states in the North have laws mandating arrest for a domestic violence incident, but none of the states in the South does. While almost 80% (78%) of the states in the North prohibit corporal punishment, only 13% of the states in the South do so. Capital punishment is legal in 94% of the states in the South, compared to 43% in the North (Cohen, 1996).

Cohen and Nisbett (1997) attributed these regional differences to the frontier mentality in the South. In the frontier areas in the Old South, the law was weak, and citizens had to depend on themselves to protect their

own life, families, and wealth. Tolerance of insults became a symbol of vulnerability to predation. Violence, or the threat of it, in response to aggression and insults became a means to communicate publicly one's toughness and determination to get even with the aggressor. Researchers have referred to this frontier mentality as *culture of honor*. Time has changed, and now the Southern states are as law-abiding as the Northern states. Yet, as shown in the data reviewed above, pockets of culture of honor still persist in the South (see Figure 7.1).

People who grew up in a culture of honor may develop an event representation that contains the following frames:

Frame 1: A man receives negative remarks on himself and his family.
Frame 2: He interprets the remarks as an insult and an attack on his honor.
Frame 3: This thought infuriates him, and he wants to retaliate.
Frame 4: He uses or threatens the use of violence to coerce submission from the perpetrator as a means to restore his honor.
Frame 5: Regardless of the outcome, he feels proud for standing up against an attack on his honor, and sees defending one's honor with violent acts as justified and honorable.

This event representation colors perception of events pertinent to defense of honor. In one study, Cohen and Nisbett (1997) provided reporters of college newspapers in the North, South, and West (where the culture of honor is also widely spread) with a set of facts and asked them to turn these facts into a news story. There were two sets of facts. One collection of "facts" described an incident in which Victor Jensen stabbed Martin Shell, after Shell shouted at a party that Jensen's sister was a "slut." The other set of "facts" depicted a robbery in which Robert Hansen robbed John Seger's convenience store and pistol-whipped him. The Jensen story (the honor story) involves an insult directed to the perpetrator's family, but the Hansen story (the control story) does not. The reporters' stories were content analyzed to determine the extent to which the reporters thought the perpetrator's action was justified or blameworthy. In the honor stories returned from colleges in the South and West, the perpetrator's action was portrayed as more justified and less blameworthy, compared to the honor stories returned from colleges in the North. This difference was not found in the control stories.

In another experiment (Cohen & Nisbett, 1997), letters inquiring about employment were sent to companies across the United States. There were two experimental conditions. In the honor condition, the letter writer admitted in the letter that he was convicted of manslaughter. According to the letter, the victim had an affair with the letter writer's fiancée, confronted the letter writer at the bar, told everyone at the bar of his affair with the letter writer's fiancée, laughed at the letter writer and challenged him to a fight. In the control condition, the letter writer admitted having been convicted of motor vehicle theft. According to the confession, he committed the theft because he needed money for himself and his family. The replies from the companies were analyzed. In general, a more sympathetic tone was communicated in the replies to the "killer" from companies in the South and West than in the North. No such regional differences were found in the replies to the "thief." Taken together, these findings suggest that violent acts in response to a family insult receive greater sympathy in the South and West than in the North.

It should be emphasized that culture of honor is not localized in the American South. Instead, pockets of it are distributed throughout the world. For example, in some South American countries (e.g., Brazil, Chile), there is also a heavy emphasis on avoiding shame and gaining respect for the self and the family. In Brazil, if the wife commits adultery, and this is known to others in the neighborhood, the husband will lose honor and respect from his peers. Moreover, if a husband responds to his wife's infidelity with violence (hitting his wife vs. just yelling at her), people in the United States would perceive the husband negatively. However, in Brazil, a husband hitting his unfaithful wife (vs. yelling at her only) would not be more negatively evaluated (Vandello & Cohen, 2003).

Women in cultures of honor are also expected to adhere to the code of honor. While men are expected to guard against any offenses to the family's grace and honor vigilantly and forcefully, women are expected to remain faithful to their spouse. To test this idea, Vandello and Cohen (2003) put their research participants in the following situation.

Participant arrived at the research laboratory and found a note saying that the experimenter would be a few minutes late. While the participant was waiting for the experimenter to return, another female participant (actually the experimenter's confederate) arrived with her boyfriend (also a confederate). The boyfriend asked the woman how long the experiment would take, and she said about half an hour but that she needed to go over to her former boyfriend's home to pick up a few things. The boyfriend was upset, grabbed the woman by her arm, and walked her down the hallway. At about 15 ft from where the participant sat, the couple began arguing loudly, and the boyfriend asserted that he did not want her to go to her former boyfriend's house, and demanded that she gave him her car keys. She refused, and he grabbed her by the wrist, and ripped the keys from her hand. When she tried to take them back, he shoved her very forcefully against the wall by her shoulders, making a crashing noise loud enough to be audible to the participant. She was shaken up, stood to see him walk away, and then tried to recompose herself, and walked over to where the participant sat. It should be emphasized that despite the convincing acting performance of the confederates, no physical harm had ever occurred to the woman.

Before the experimenter arrived, the woman had a few moments to interact with the participant. During those few moments, participants in the self-blaming condition heard the woman say, "That was my fiancé. He gets so jealous sometimes … I guess it was kind of my fault, huh?" Participants in the assertive condition heard her say, "That was my fiancé. He gets so jealous sometimes … I'm getting so damn tired of this, you know? He really makes me mad when he's like that." Later in the experiment, the participant had an opportunity to talk to the woman and rated their impression of her.

Would the assertive woman or the self-blaming woman receive greater sympathy from the participants? The answer depends on the participants' cultural background. The participants consisted of Latino Americans, southern US Anglos, and northern US Anglos. During the conversation with the woman, Latino Americans and southerners were more likely than northerners to voice tolerance of abuse. They were more likely to show support for the self-blaming confederate, encourage her to stay in the relationship, assure her that her fiancé was just concerned about her, encourage her to work out the problems with her fiancé, and state that jealousy is a good thing. Latino Americans and southerners also liked the self-blaming woman more than they did the assertive woman, whereas northerners showed the reverse pattern.

Culture of honor also directs individuals' responses to honor-related situations. Individuals, particularly men, in the American South who have internalized the culture of honor are expected to and would likely use violence to restore their honor when they feel that their reputation has been damaged, as when they are publicly insulted (Cohen et al., 1996).

To examine this idea, Cohen et al. (1996, Experiment 1) placed their research participants in the following situation. Shortly after the beginning of an experiment, the participant "completed" a short demographic survey and was asked to take it to a table at the end of a long, narrow hallway. As the participant walked down the hallway, someone

Meet the Researcher: Dov Cohen

"In graduate school, I had the opportunity to study with Dick Nisbett, who showed me just how fascinating culture research could be. I learned a lot, but at the time, I didn't even realize how tremendously useful studying culture would be outside of academics. My wife grew up in Brazil, meaning that life is now a cross-cultural project. However, the biggest thing that happened to me recently was the birth of our daughter. Now I feel like the man who suddenly realized he had been speaking prose all his life. You begin to notice the peculiar cultural practices that pervade everything you do with her, from encouraging her autonomy to building her sense of self-efficacy by praising her poop—with the appropriate lay theory of effort, of course ('Wow! Great job! You must have really been working hard on filling that diaper.') It also makes sense of all the advice you're given. In parenting classes, for example, we were told to first ask our baby's permission before burping her. (It's never too early to start building her sense of autonomy!) It explained my steadfast opposition to the pacifier—which lasted 10 minutes ('Get that thing out of her mouth. She'll become dependent on that in no time. That stuff is worse than crack …. What? You knew someone who sucked his thumb up until high school. Hmmm, I guess that won't be considered "socially appropriate." We can give her back the pacifier.') It explains why I (almost) had my daughter signed up for four days per week of enrichment activities. (There's nothing wrong with swim and music classes, but at the age of 1, it didn't seem right for her to become 'the overscheduled American' just yet.) And finally, it explains why, despite the occasional frustration, I'm gratified to see her sometimes foolish and reckless sense of independence. (Then again, at the age of 18, when she runs away to marry the lead singer of some band called Sewage Sundae or Earwax Attack or something like that—don't ask me how I'll feel about her sense of independence then.)"

Dov Cohen received his Ph.D. from the University of Michigan, and is now a Professor of Psychology at the University of Illinois, Urbana-Champaign.

(actually the experimenter's confederate) walked out of a door marked "Photo Lab," and began working at a file cabinet in the hall. The confederate closed the file drawer and yielded to the participant. The participant dropped the survey off the table and returned to the experimental room. In the second close encounter, the confederate, who had reopened the file drawer, slammed it shut, bumped into the participant's shoulder, and called the participant an "asshole." At this point in the experiment, unbeknownst to the participant, two observers stationed in the hall watched the participant's facial expressions, and rated the participant's emotional reactions.

As in many other studies on culture of honor, the participants were either male northerners or southerners. The two groups responded in markedly different ways to this situation. While 85% of the southerners displayed more anger than amusement, two-thirds of the northerners displayed more amusement than anger.

In another experiment (Cohen et al., 1996, Experiment 2), in which the participant was similarly bumped and insulted, southerners, compared with their northern peers, displayed a higher percent increase in cortisol and testosterone level, indicating that subsequent to being insulted, southerners were more upset and more prepared for aggression.

In yet another experiment (Cohen et al., 1996, Experiment 3), southern participants, when insulted, tended to believe that the insult lowered their status in the eyes of an onlooker. They also tended to assert their masculinity by displaying dominant behaviors. For example, when another person walked toward them in a narrow hallway, they went much farther before "chickening out" and deferring to the confederate. By contrast, northern participants did not display such tendencies.

In short, research on culture of honor richly illustrates important regional cultural variations within the United States, as well as the role of event representations in social perception and responses to honor-pertinent situations.

Implicit Theories

As mentioned, people may develop implicit theories to represent events that routinely occur in a certain type of situation. Two widely researched implicit theories are the beliefs in the malleability of personal characteristics, and the stability of social institutions.

Implicit Theories of Personality

Cultures differ in the distribution of different implicit theories. There is evidence that East Asians are substantially more likely to believe that the world is relatively stable (Chiu, Dweck, Tong, & Fu, 1997; Su et al., 1999) and individual persons relatively malleable (Norenzayan et al., 2002).

Implicit theories influence people's responses to a variety of situations. For example, when people believe that a person's personality is fixed, they tend to subscribe to a trait model of behavior, as illustrated in Figure 7.2. First, they tend to infer global traits from a small sample of trait-relevant behaviors (e.g., if Pat makes her bed in the morning, she is a good person), and to predict that a person with certain trait will display

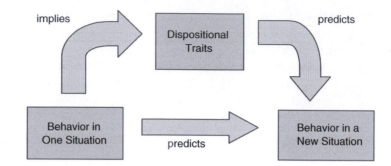

FIGURE 7.2. A trait model of personality.

trait-relevant behaviors in a particular situation (Pat is a conscientious person. Therefore, she makes her bed in the morning). They also believe that if somebody performs a trait-relevant behavior in one situation, they are likely to repeat the same behavior in another situation (Jack is friendlier than Joe in one particular situation. So, Jack will be friendlier than Joe in a completely different situation; C. Chiu, Hong, & Dweck, 1997). People who believe in fixed personality traits also have the tendency to spontaneously encode others' behaviors in terms of their evaluative meanings. When they see John clean up the table after his meal in a canteen, they immediately categorize that behavior as a good behavior. Likewise, when they see Peter interrupt somebody who is speaking, they immediately categorize the behavior as a bad behavior (Hong, Chiu, Dweck, & Sacks, 1997). They also tend to spontaneously categorize people into good vs. bad people, and organize their impressions of people into global, evaluative categories (Tong & Chiu, 2002). Finally, they rely on trait-relevant information to make important decisions about other people.

In one study (Gervey, Chiu, Hong, & Dweck, 1999), information about the defendant's respectability (trait-relevant information) and evident strength were manipulated in a murder case presented to the participants. What follows is the murder case presented in the high defendant respectability and high evidence strength condition:

Summary of the security guard's testimony: It was just after 6:00 in the evening, and most of the people had already left. I saw a Toyota pull up in the parking zone out front, and a guy got out. He went into the public library across the street. A little while later, he came out and headed across the street to this building. He was about average height and weight, brown hair, brown eyes. He walked up to the desk, carrying a book. He said he was going up to the fourth floor to see Mr. Foley, signed in, and walked past me. He seemed like he knew what he was doing, so I didn't think much of it. Anyway, I forgot about him, until a while later, when he came downstairs. He looked at me sort of funny, like all tense and wired up, and said I should call the cops because someone had killed Foley. I thought he was joking, but then I saw blood on his jacket and hands. So, I called the cops from the Security booth, and when I looked back towards the guy he was gone. When the cops came, I told them where to go, and described the guy to them. A few days later they called me down to the station, and I identified him in the line up. (Let the record show that the witness confirmed the Defendant was the man from the building.)

Defense attorney (DA)'s cross-examination of the witness (WIT):

DA: You said that my client looked funny ... all tense and wired up.

WIT: Yeah.

DA: Don't you think you would look tense if you just walked in for a meeting and the person you were supposed to see was lying dead on the floor?

WIT: Yeah, I suppose I would.

DA: Did you happen to notice with which hand my client signed his name?

WIT: Yeah. It was his *left hand*.

DA: You also said my client was upstairs for "a while." I wonder if you can tell me exactly how long a period of time that is.

WIT: Well, I guess ...

DA: Don't guess, sir. Was it 30 minutes? 23 minutes? 5 minutes?

WIT: I'm not exactly sure, but ...

DA: No further questions.

Summary of the detective's testimony: I responded to the call from the witness. We discovered and examined the victim's body. A knife was used to commit the murder. The victim was stabbed a couple of times in his stomach and once in the chest area. Forensic investigation confirmed that the wounds were inflicted by a person using his *left hand*. A fair amount of coordination was needed to stab someone in the manner the victim was stabbed.

In the low defendant respectability conditions, the description of the defendant in the security guard's testimony was changed to "It was just after 6:00 in the evening, and most of the people had already left. I saw his motorcycle pull up in the parking zone out front, and a guy got off. He went into the adult bookstore across the street. A little while later, he came out and headed across the street to this building. He was about average height and weight, brown hair, brown eyes. He walked up to the desk, carrying a magazine." In the low evidence strength conditions, the security guard testified that the defendant signed his name with his right hand.

The participants' task was to judge whether the defendant was guilty. For those who believed in fixed personality traits, the evidence strength manipulation had little influence on their verdict. However, these individuals were two times as likely to deliver a guilty verdict to the low-respectability defendant as to the high-respectability defendant. They also judged the less-respectable defendant to be more immoral than the more respectable defendant. Contrarily, for those who believed that personality can be changed, the defendant respectability information did not affect their verdict at all, and they were almost two times as likely to deliver a guilty verdict when the evidence was strong as when it was weak. In fact, the belief in fixed traits seems to set up a social perception framework in which personality traits (as opposed to situation-specific information) constitute the basic units of analysis (Dweck, Chiu, & Hong, 1995; Dweck, Hong, & Chiu, 1993).

If implicit theories of personal characteristics are used as guides for relating to the social environment and as premises for making causal inferences, East Asians, who tend to believe in the malleability of personality, should be more inclined to adjust to their social environment than to influence it, whereas North Americans, believing more strongly in fixed personality, should have the reverse preference. This notion was tested in a study conducted by Morling, Kitayama, and Miyamoto (2002). In this study, American and Japanese undergraduates described an actual influence event or adjustment event that happened to them recently. An influence event is one in which the participants had influenced or changed the surrounding people, events, or objects according to their own wishes. An adjustment event is one in which the participants had adjusted themselves to surrounding people, objects, and events. They also reported how many days had passed since the event. The median latency of the most recent US-made influence events was 2 days, compared to 5 days for the Japan-made influence events. Conversely, the median latency of the most recent Japan-made adjustment events was 1 day, compared to 7 days for US-made adjustment events. This evidence suggests that whereas influence events happen more frequently in the United States, adjustment events happen more frequently in Japan.

In addition, East Asians should be less inclined than North Americans to explain social behavior in terms of the actor's global traits, but relatively more inclined to reference external forces (dispositions of the group and situational constraints) in their social explanations. As mentioned in the last chapter, this prediction has received clear empirical support (J. Miller, 1984; Miyamoto & Kitayama, 2002; Morris & Peng, 1994; Norenzayan et al., 2002). Taken together, these findings suggest that culture-characteristic person representations are supported by culture-characteristic event representations.

Implicit Theories of the World

As noted, the belief in a fixed world is more prevalent in East Asia than in North America (C. Chiu et al., 1997). The belief in a fixed world is related to how people conceive of the moral order in the society. When people believe that they live in a fixed reality with a rigid moral order, the most important criterion for deciding the morality of a state of affairs is whether people have carried out the moral action prescribed by the existing moral order. When individuals believe that the world they live in is malleable, the authority of the existing moral order is no long absolute, and one's duty within it is not the primary concern. Instead, to them, the primary concern would be to identify, work toward, and uphold principles (such as respect for human rights) that will guide the society. The defining issue of morality becomes whether principles of human rights are respected and upheld.

Consistent with this idea, research shows that people who believe in a fixed world value adherence to norms and role expectations more than equal opportunity and individual rights (C. Chiu et al., 1997). Additionally, duty- vs. rights-based morality has important implications for how people respond to desirable and undesirable conduct. Because duty-based morality treats codes of conduct as of foremost importance, those who willfully misbehave deserve punishment. However, good behaviors do not deserve reward because one is merely delivering one's duties. Contrarily, under a rights-based morality, desirable conduct deserves appreciation because people display positive behavior *voluntarily*. If a belief in a fixed world is related to duty-based morality, people who believe in a fixed world should be more likely to punish undesirable behavior and less likely to praise desirable behavior, compared to those who believe in a malleable world. Indeed, this is what was found. Believers in a fixed world, compared with believers in a malleable world, are more likely to assign punishment when children display undesirable conduct (e.g., The teacher asked Larry to remove the old posters and notices on the students' notice boards. A week has passed and Larry does not do it), and less likely to praise children with desirable conduct (e.g., The teacher asked Jerry to remove the old posters and notices on the students' notice boards, and Jerry does what she requested as soon as possible; C. Chiu et al., 1997).

Again, if implicit theories of the world are used as guides for relating to the social environment, we would expect duty-based morality to be more prevalent in East Asia, and rights-based morality to be more prevalent in North America. There is clear empirical support for this idea (see the section Norm Representations below). Indeed, a guiding principle in Confucianism, the dominant social philosophy in Asia, is the belief that everyone has their role to play based on their relationship to others. In addition, the society will be stable and harmonious if everyone fulfills their duties and keeps their place in the society. This idea is in stark contrast to the guiding moral principle of human rights in the United States. As stated in the Declaration of Independence, "governments long established should not be changed for light and transient causes," but such changes are justified after "a long chain of abuses [of human rights]."

Implicit Theories about the Trajectory of Change

However, the foregoing analysis should not be taken to imply that in East Asia, people generally believe that the world is a completely static, unchanging reality. Indeed, some writers (Chan, Chan, Cheung, King, Chiu, & Yang, 2001; C. Cheng, Lee, & Chiu, 1999; C. Chiu, 2001; Peng & Nisbett, 1999) hold that East Asians also believe strongly in change. For example, the *I-Ching*, or *Book of Changes*, is the most widely read of the five Chinese Classics. The text originated from a prehistoric divination technique dated back to 5000 BC, and the principles of change and stability articulated in this ancient text still seem to have a strong hold on Chinese people's perception of change (Ji, Nisbett, & Su, 2001).

According to these principles, *yin* and *yang*, two opposing forces, manifest in various forms in Nature (e.g., the weak vs. the strong; evil vs. divine, illness vs. health, coldness vs. warmth, darkness vs. light, bad vs. good fortune), push themselves each into the place of the other, and hence changes take place. Fortune, good or ill, arises from these movements. However, *yin* and *yang* have their fixed and proper places. Therefore, their changes, however varied, are according to the requirements of the time when they take place (see Figure 7.3).

FIGURE 7.3. Depiction of *yin* and *yang*, two contradictory forces that push themselves each into the place of the other, creating short-term changes and ensuring long-term harmony and stability.

For example, as stated in the *I-Ching*:

> The sun goes and the moon comes; the moon goes and the sun comes; the sun and moon thus take the place each of the other, and their shining is the result. The cold goes and the heat comes; the heat goes and the cold comes; it is by this mutual succession of the cold and heat that the year is completed. That which goes becomes less and less, and that which comes waxes more and more; it is by the influence on each other of this contraction and expansion that the advantages (of the different conditions) are produced (the Great Appendix, Section II).

In other words, changes take place according to a predetermined time course, following an exact rule. Similarly to how the sun and moon continually emit their light, good fortune and ill are continually prevailing each against the other by an exact rule. This exact rule mandates a cyclical trajectory of changes: the continual prevailing of opposing forces ensures more stable reality, because all transient changes engendered by one force will be canceled out by the changes instigated by its opposing force. Thus, these beliefs about the trajectory of change may reinforce the belief in a fixed reality.

The Industrial Revolution in Europe brought the 19th century Western world into the Age of Progress. Since then, optimism and the belief in incremental change and progress have dominated the social philosophy in Western Europe and the New World. The intellectuals witnessed the increasing substitution of machinery for human effort, and of inanimate for animate supplies of power. They saw how their world was being transformed into one of iron, coal, and steam, of machinery and engines, and of railroads, steamships, and telegraph wires. They were optimistic about the future; they believed that a better world lay just around the corner, and the making of it was in people's own hands (Burchell, 1966). Theories of biological evolution and economic development that emerged at that time endorse the idea of linear change. The extinction of unfit species, the decline of maladaptive social systems, the domination of the superior species, and the rise of more advanced social systems were seen as irresistible trends. These beliefs about the trajectory of change support a malleable view of the world and its institutions.

Traces of the culture-characteristic beliefs about the trajectory of change are still detectable among Chinese and North American students. A recent survey shows that when things are moving in a particular direction, compared to their American peers, Chinese undergraduates are more likely to anticipate change in the movement's direction. For example, they believe more strongly that a couple who have been dating for 2 years will break up, someone who has been a chess champion for 3 years will lose in the next game, a student from a poor family will become rich one day, two kindergarten children who have been fighting will become friends one day, and a trend in the growth rates of the world economy or the world-wide death rate for cancer will reverse in the future (Ji et al., 2001).

Furthermore, individuals who expect the development of events to change course should be less surprised by unexpected events than those who expect events to develop following a linear track. In one study, I. Choi and Nisbett (2000) had American and Korean undergraduates read a scenario depicting a seminarian on his way to deliver a sermon. He was late, and on his way encountered a man lying in a doorway requesting help. Without being told whether or not the seminarian offered help, these participants estimated the likelihood that the seminarian would help. In this condition, both groups reported about an 80% probability that the seminarian would help and indicated they would be quite surprised if he did not.

Another set of American and Korean participants was told the seminarian had helped the victim. In this condition, both groups were not surprised at the "results," and reported that they would have thought the probability of helping was about 80%. In a third condition, a different set of American and Korean participants learned that the seminarian had not helped the victim. In this condition, American participants were surprised at the outcome, but still believed that the probability of helping was about 80%. In contrast, Korean undergraduates reported that they would have thought the probability of helping was only about 50%, and expressed little surprise that the seminarian had not helped.

An additional study (I. Choi & Nisbett, 2000) showed that Korean undergraduates expressed little surprise when they discovered that what they had been led to believe was untrue. In this study, American and Korean participants read about scientific research that examined two competing hypotheses: (1) people who are more optimistic are happier, and (2) people who are more realistic are happier. They learned that the finding supported the optimism hypothesis, and rated how surprising they found this result to be. Next, the experimenter "discovered" a printing error and told the participant that actually the finding supported the opposite hypothesis. When asked to rate how surprising they found the "actual" finding to be, American undergraduates were very surprised when they learned that after all, the less plausible realism hypothesis was the correct one. By comparison, Korean undergraduates expressed much less surprise.

When an American undergraduate learns a new scientific finding, they would be less surprised by it when it follows from a scientific theory than when one compelling theory predicts this finding, while another equally compelling theory predicts the opposite result. However, the Confucian notion of change embodies the idea that opposing forces push each in the place of the other, leading to transient changes and long-term stability. Thus, people who subscribe to this notion would expect an outcome to result from the dynamic interplay of opposing forces. Consonant with this idea, I. Choi and Nisbett (2000) found that Korean undergraduates are not more surprised when a scientific finding supports one theory and rejects a competing theory than when a scientific finding follows from one compelling theory.

The belief that opposing forces are always at play should increase the awareness of competing concerns in conflict situations and the motivation to reconcile them. In one study, Peng and Nisbett (1999) had Chinese and American students analyze everyday life situations that involve intrapersonal conflicts (e.g., a conflict between having fun and going to school) or interpersonal conflicts (e.g., a conflict between mothers and their daughters). Consistent with the idea that the Confucian notion of change is more widely distributed in Asia than in the United States, American responses tended to come down in favor of one side or the other ("mothers should respect daughters' independence"). In comparison, Chinese responses tended to reconcile the contradiction by considering merit and fault on both sides ("both the mothers and the daughters have failed to understand each other").

Cheung, Chan, Chan, King, Chiu, and Yang (2003) summarized a comprehensive ethnographic study of how people in four Chinese villages manage disputes by considering opposing concerns in the field. The study analyzed more than 150 cases of debates or disputes regarding the way village affairs should be managed in four villages, three located in Guangdong province and one in Anhui province of China. One representative dispute case is summarized below.

This case happened in Honglong Village at Nanhai County in Guangdong Province of Southern China. At the time the study was conducted (1993–1997), Honglong had a population of 190 individuals divided into 52 households. In addition, there were 200 nonlocal residents, who were mainly migrant workers, including their dependents, employed in the six factories situated at the outskirts of the village. Economically speaking, Honglong is a rather backward village.

This dispute concerns whether nonlocal residents have the right to send their children to the village nursery. This issue had led to an intense debate in the assembly of household representatives. Most villagers objected to admitting nonlocal children to the village nursery, on the grounds that the nursery was part of the village welfare system, subsidized by the village collective fund. The nonlocal workers did not belong to the community, and had no kinship ties with any of the local inhabitants. Accordingly, they were not entitled to the benefits of a villager.

A minority of the inhabitants led by Ai Bing, a female village leader, argued that because "everyone is a human being," the nonlocal children should not be discriminated against and had the right to go to the village nursery. After a long discussion, Ai Bing came up with a compromise proposal. She maintained her principle, but agreed to respect the interest of the local inhabitants as well. Therefore, she suggested that nonlocal workers' children be allowed to go to the nursery with a higher fee, thus increasing the collective fund in the village. Many villagers still felt reluctant to go along with this, but could not come up with more "reasonable" proposals. At the end, the new rule was passed. When asked how she came up with such a solution, Ai Bing had this to say:

> It is quite simple. You know the expression used by Mao, 'everything can be divided into two (parts).' I think it is very useful. So when there is a conflict, when people have different opinions, or even only when I need to make up my mind about a certain issue, I try to look at the situation from different angles. I know it would be wrong to consider it only from one perspective and then come up with a decision. Moreover, I listen to everyone during a discussion or a debate. I try to see what is correct in each position. And then I try to put all these correct perspectives together to form something like a core proposal. But I must admit that, once I found such a core position, or when I have formed a nucleus of all the valid principles, I will not change my mind easily. I will try to have other villagers accept it instead.

From her reflection, Ai Bing was aware that the two principles (equality and protection of village welfare) the villagers used to support their opinions might have conflicting implications. To her, the most reasonable solution lies in the identification of a position that would successfully integrate the two principles, and bring forth positive consequences for the group as a whole.

As indicated above, a common agreement was finally reached in the nursery dispute when Ai Bing offered a solution that reflects such a position.

Norm Representations

A norm representation is an implicative proposition consisting of three elements: the antecedent circumstances, the norm, and the consequent conditions (Lindahl & Odelstad, 2000). The antecedent conditions specify the activation circumstances of the representation. They include the range of concrete situations where the norm is applicable.

The norm refers to the state of affairs that is generally believed to be the case (e.g., the shared belief that the needy will receive help). In constructing a norm representation, individuals need to have access to the distribution of social knowledge in the society (e.g., they need to know the extent of agreement in the group with the idea of helping the needy; Ho & Chiu, 1998; Lau et al., 2001).

Finally, the consequent conditions specify the behavioral implications of the norm. When the antecedent circumstances are present in a given situation, a certain state of affairs is designated as the norm, and the individual (agent) is expected to see to it that this state of affairs will take place. Because norm representations are implicative propositions, they have direct authority over behavior (see Figure 7.4 on p. 176).

Cultural Differences in Norm Representations

Cultural norms are widely distributed norm representations. Cultural norms vary across cultures. A comprehensive review of cultural differences in normative behaviors is beyond the scope of this book. Here, we present a few illustrative research examples.

Emotion Display Rules and Decoding Rules

When people are presented with facial expressions expressing basic human emotions, they tend to be very accurate in identifying the emotion each face is intended to portray, regardless of whether the emotion expressers are members of their own culture or members of another culture (see Matsumoto, 2001). Such a high level of cross-cultural agreement in the judgment of facial expression suggests that facial expressions of emotion are universal (e.g., Ekman, 1972, 1994; Izard, 1971; Scherer & Wallbott, 1994).

FIGURE 7.4. An honor lot in Indianapolis. Many social behaviors are regulated by established norms, such as the code of honor.

Despite this, systematic cultural differences in emotion recognition accuracy have also been reported. For example, Japanese are less accurate than Americans in identifying unpleasant emotions such as anger, disgust, fear, and sadness (Matsumoto, 1992). Cultural differences in emotion recognition accuracy have been interpreted in terms of cultural variations in display and decoding rules.

Display rules are shared rules that prescribe how emotions should be displayed, whereas decoding rules are shared prescriptive rules of how emotions of others should be interpreted (Matsumoto & Ekman, 1989). The dominant display rules and decoding rules are different in Asian and American contexts. Specifically, whereas American display rules generally encourage outward displays of emotion, emotional displays are de-amplified in Asian societies (Matsumoto, Kasri, & Kooken, 1999). Accordingly, signal clarity is generally higher in American emotion displays than in Asian emotion displays, making it harder for perceivers to decode emotions from Asian emotion faces than from American emotion faces (S-l. Lee, Chiu, & Chan, 2005).

Furthermore, compared to Asian perceivers, American perceivers attribute greater intensity to facial expressions of emotion (Matsumoto et al., 1999). Interestingly, when asked to judge the intensity of the emotion the expresser feels, Asian perceivers tend to give higher ratings than American perceivers do (Matsumoto et al., 1999, 2002). Apparently, Asian perceivers believe that the expressers have de-amplified their emotions in their facial expressions. Thus, when they view an emotion face, they tend to scale up the inferred emotions experienced by the expresser. By contrast, American perceivers believe that the expressers have exaggerated their emotions in their facial expressions. Thus, when American perceivers view an emotion face, they tend to scale down the expresser's felt emotion.

Finally, in Asian contexts, there are sanctions against recognizing or acknowledging unpleasant emotions, because such emotions might threaten social harmony, which is heavily emphasized in Asian societies (Matsumoto, 1989). Consistent with this idea, East Asians have been found to be less accurate than Americans in identifying unpleasant emotions (Biehl, Matsumoto, Ekman, & Hearn, 1997; De Sonneville, Verschoor, Njiokiktjien, Op het Veld, Toorenaar, & Vranken, 2002); Matsumoto, 1992).

Helping Behavior

As noted, in North America, individual rights and freedom form the ultimate criteria for judging the moral correctness of social actions. Consistent with this notion, Miller and her colleagues (Baron & Miller, 2000; J. Miller & Bersoff, 1992, 1994, 1998) reported that reciprocal helping is more often categorized as a personal choice than a moral duty, and whether one feels the obligation to help another person is often affected by how likable the target is. According to J. Miller and Bersoff (1998), the American's tendency to consider liking for the target in assessing moral responsibilities to help may reflect a voluntaristic view of social relationship in American culture. In contrast, in India, duties form the ultimate criterion for evaluating the moral rightness of social action. Helping is morally required, and reciprocal prosocial behavior is seen as a moral obligation instead of a social exchange.

To test these notions, J. Miller and Bersoff (1994) conducted interviews with European Americans and Hindu Indians. The respondents were presented with a set of hypothetical situations in which a target person helped an acquaintance either spontaneously, or in response to prior reciprocity. When asked to explain why the target offered help, American respondents rated the target's liking to help as less important in the reciprocity condition than in the spontaneous helping condition. They also rated the target in the reciprocity condition as having lower satisfaction and being less helpful than the target in the spontaneous helping condition. Apparently, to American respondents, the presence of reciprocity turns a helping behavior into a social obligation, and hence an externally motivated behavior. If help is not given because the helper *likes* to help, the helping behavior is not perceived to be truly altruistic.

In contrast, for Hindu respondents, liking to help was rated as equally important in the spontaneous help and reciprocity conditions. They also saw the target offering spontaneous help and the one offering reciprocal help as equally helpful and happy to help. These findings reveal that Hindu Indians do not consider reciprocity (or social obligations) as either distracting from the altruistic characteristic of a helpful act, or diminishing the gratification involved in delivering the act.

Conception of Justice

Justice is the social basis of obedience, reforms, and revolution. It plays a critical role in guiding individuals' behavior, regulating social interactions, and maintaining the structure and organization of society as a whole. As such, deciphering the meaning of justice in a society is an important research task in the social sciences.

In the broadest sense, justice prevails when an individual fulfils the obligations to treat others according to their due (Furby, 1986). However, societies often disagree on what conditions, what conduct or what characteristics establish each person's due.

In American society, dominated by the Protestant work ethic and capitalist logic, ability and contribution are the two dominant claim-establishing conditions for reward. In the American conception of an ideal society, every citizen has equal opportunity, rendering ability and contribution the only legitimate considerations in administering rewards. This conception is epitomized in a quote from the inaugural address of Moon Landrieu, New Orleans' former mayor, which is inscribed on a monument installed in New Orleans' River Walk (see Figure 7.5):

> Let us be guided then by a sense of justice. Let us build a system of just laws and demand adherence to those laws. Let us create a city of equal opportunity for all, with all sharing in both the responsibilities and benefits.

> Let us create a city where neither the choice of religion nor the accident of color is an obstacle to opportunity and advancement, nor a substitute for effort or ability.

A very different conception of justice prevails in China. The emphasis on the enforcement of role behavior is an important theme in traditional Chinese social ethics and legal practice. For instance, in Confucian thought, *yi* (taking what is right and doing what is right) is the scheme of moral principles that regulates social actions. It prescribes different obligatory requirements for different role relationships; for example, loyalty of the ruled to their ruler, filial piety of sons and daughters to their parents, respect for brothers, and trust for friends. It also requires each person to fulfil the functions of one's position and observe the prescriptive rules implied in one's social role. Indeed, it demands that individuals do no more than fulfil the roles assigned to them. Individuals should not

FIGURE 7.5. A quote from Mayor Moon Landrieu's inaugural address is inscribed in a monument on River Walk, New Orleas.

seek to exceed their due, or fall short of what is expected from them (Young, 1981).

The principles of *yi* were enforced in the law in traditional China, which had been practiced for more than 15 centuries before it was abandoned at the beginning of the 20th century. The traditional Chinese law demands strict adherence to role-specific behavioral rules. For example, a son who injures his father even unintentionally could be punished by death, because the failure to shield one's parent from any form of physical danger violates the principle of filial piety (see Chapter 2). On the contrary, individuals might go unpunished for a crime committed to enforce role behaviors. For example, the law does not punish a father who kills an unfilial son (D. Chu, 1975; Ju, 1981; Zhang, 1984).

Several studies revealed that the traditional notion of *yi* is still a dominant conception of justice in some Chinese societies. In one study (C. Chiu, 1991a), Hong Kong Chinese undergraduates rated the level of fairness or unfairness of 18 local news events. The results reveal a high level of agreement between their fairness judgment and their evaluation of how much the protagonist in the news event had lived up to his or her role expectations. The event was seen as fair if role expectations were fulfilled and unfair if they were not. An additional study (C. Chiu, 1991a) shows that

Hong Kong Chinese students rate a positive behavior as more desirable when the behavior is role-consistent than when it is not. For example, behavior expressing empathy with the suffering of others is seen as more desirable when it is performed by a social worker than when it is performed by a news reporter. Furthermore, another study (C. Chiu, 1991b) shows that when asked to report an unjust event they had personally encountered, Hong Kong Chinese undergraduates were likely to mention events in which role expectations were violated. For example, they were more likely to report events of senior people abusing their social power, and peers displaying nonreciprocal and inconsiderate behaviors, than to report events of senior people being inconsiderate or peers being dominant.

A few studies have examined East–West differences in the conditions that establish a person's legitimate claim to rewards. In one study, K. Leung and Bond (1982) asked Hong Kong and American college students to imagine themselves as a member of a work team and assign a reward to another team member who either had facilitated or hindered the completion of a group project. The results show that, as expected, contribution to the team impacted reward allocation decisions: Both American and Chinese students distributed more money to the helpful team member than to the unhelpful one. However, American students weighed contribution more heavily than Chinese students did—Chinese students tended to distribute the reward more equally between themselves and the team member. An additional study (Hui, Triandis, & Yee, 1991) showed that when asked to allocate a monetary reward to the self and a friend, most people allocated more money to the self than to their friend when they had contributed more to the completion of the task than their friend had. However, this tendency to adhere to the proportionality rule was greater among American students than among Hong Kong Chinese students.

Chinese (vs. American) students' greater preference for equality in reward allocation may be related to the value they place on group cohesiveness (C. Chiu & Hong, 1997). Consonant with this idea, in both North American and East Asian contexts, when the situation emphasizes productivity, people like it more if reward is distributed in accordance with relative contribution than if it is distributed equally. When the situation emphasizes group harmony, people prefer the equality rule to the contribution rule (K. Leung & Park, 1986). Additionally, in Chinese culture, more popular sayings affirm rather than negate the value of cooperation and collective sharing of resources among group members, and more popular sayings negate rather than affirm the value of self-interest. Moreover, Chinese students tend to agree more with popular sayings that affirm cooperation and collective sharing of resources in the group than with popular sayings that affirm pursuit of self-interest (C. Chiu, 1990a). Taken together, the heavy emphasis on group cohesiveness in Chinese societies may set up a preference for equal allocation of reward.

If the value of group cohesiveness mediates Chinese participants' greater preference for the equality rule, this preference should be limited to situations where the reward is distributed between ingroup members. When a reward is distributed between the self and an outgroup member, Chinese would adhere to the contribution rule as much as their American peers do. Consonant with this idea, K. Leung and Bond (1984) had their American and Hong Kong Chinese participants rate the likability of an allocator who distributed a reward between the self and a friend in one condition, or a reward between the self and a stranger in another condition. The allocator distributed the reward either equally or in accordance to relative contribution. When a reward was distributed between friends, American participants liked the allocator more if the contribution (vs. the equality) rule was applied, whereas Chinese participants liked the allocator more if the equality rule was applied. When the reward was distributed between the self and a stranger, the two groups did not differ in their liking of the allocator, irrespective of whether the contribution or equality rule was followed.

Similarly, we would also expect the preference for the equality rule to be more pronounced in Chinese groups when group cohesiveness was high than when it was low. In a couple of field studies conducted in Hong Kong (C. Chiu, 1990b; C. Yang & Hui, 1986), students in a psychology class formed small teams and worked on a group research project. After they had submitted their project, they rated how fair it would be to give each member of the team the same grade, and the extent to which the team had worked as a group. The results showed that the more the students perceived that the team had worked as a group, the more they considered an equal distribution of course credit as fair.

In short, the evidence indicates that in Chinese societies there is a greater allowance for departure from the contribution rule. However, this does not imply that Chinese prefer equal distribution of reward to the contribution rule. In all studies where research participants distributed a reward, both Chinese and American participants adhered to the contribution rule more than they did to the equality rule. Slight departure from the contribution rule is deemed appropriate among Chinese when the following conditions are met: (1) the distribution was between the self and an ingroup member, (2) the situation emphasizes group harmony, and (3) group cohesiveness is high. Additionally, the allocators must be accountable to the group for their allocation decision. When Chinese allocators distribute a reward anonymously, they adhere to the contribution rule as much as their American peers do (K. Leung & Bond, 1984).

Indeed, during the Great Leap Forward Movement in China (1958–1961), when political ideologies dominated economic policies, achieving egalitarianism in income distribution was a major goal. During the movement, existing agricultural producers' cooperatives were amalgamated into communes, each averaging 5000 households, or 22,000 people. The individual commune controlled all the means of production and operated as the sole accounting unit. Private ownership of land and means of production was prohibited. Peasants surrendered their tools and farm animals to the commune and much of their personal property, including furniture and chickens. In the communes, all members participated in centrally planned economic activities, and revenues were centrally distributed in accordance with the principle of egalitarianism. Commune members ate in public canteens. Egalitarianism was also achieved through rationing of food and other daily necessities.

The Great Leap Forward movement caused a big step backward in China's economic development, and was a national disaster. Between 1958 and 1961, domestic productivity dropped drastically, food supply was in grave shortage, and many people starved. Some communist leaders blamed it on the weather, although a more plausible cause was the lack of economic incentive under extreme egalitarianism. The failure of these bold economic experimentations reveals that egalitarianism in reward allocation does not always lead to perception of distributive justice in Chinese societies.

The tolerance of departure from the contribution rule when dividing reward with ingroup members in some Asian societies raises an interesting issue: How can the society ensure that low contributors do not take advantage of the distributive norm and the generosity of their ingroup members, and take a free ride? It turns out that there is another set of distributive norms for low contributors. Some studies (J. Chu & Yang, 1976; Hui et al., 1991) revealed that Chinese low contributors would choose the contribution rule rather than the self-serving equality rule when they allocate reward. For example, in one study (Hui et al., 1991), when Chinese low contributors allocated a reward to their friend, they adhered strictly to the contribution rule. Interestingly, when American low contributors made the allocation, they allowed themselves to take slightly more than what their contribution entitled them to.

In summary, the dominant conception of justice in the United States focuses primarily on contribution and achievement as the criteria for establishing one's due. Although contribution and achievement are also important due-establishing criteria in the dominant conception of justice in many Asian societies, Asians have been found to place heavy emphasis on the relational implications of allocation decisions. Accordingly, they also attend to relational information when assessing a person's due. This information includes role expectations, the situational goal, and ingroup membership, as well as group cohesiveness.

Conflict Resolution and Negotiation

The dominant conceptions of conflict in the Far East and North America differ. In one study (Gelfand, Nishii, Holcombe, Dyer, Ohbuchi, & Fukuno, 2001), one set of American and Japanese participants described a conflict they personally experienced in the recent past. Next, another set sorted the conflicts generated by the first set into different categories. Multidimensional scaling, a statistical procedure, was used to identify the dimensions the participants used to classify the conflicts. When American participants classified America- and Japan-made conflicts, they thought in terms of whether the conflict involves a compromise (e.g., the conflict requires a compromise or mutual cooperation) or a concession or submission from one party (e.g., the conflict requires a concession by one party). Another dimension they used is whether the conflict involves intellectual or emotional issues. Japanese participants also used the compromise vs. win or yield dimension to categorize conflicts. However, instead of classifying conflicts in terms of whether intellectual or emotional issues are involved, they used the dimension of whether the conflict involves *giri*-related issues. *Giri* is a Japanese moral concept similar to the concept of *yi* described above. An example of a *giri*-related issue is whether the conflict revolves around an individual's sense of duties and obligations. Additionally, Japan-made conflicts are more likely to require compromise, whereas America-made conflicts are more likely to require yielding.

Consonant with these findings, other studies have shown that in resolving conflicts, the prevailing norms in some East Asian societies prescribe the use of mediational and accommodating strategies to minimize interpersonal animosity (see Figure 7.6 on p. 185). In contrast, the prevailing norms in the United States prescribe the use of more direct, confrontational strategies to win the negotiation game.

We have described an ethnographic study that illustrates the compromising strategy Chinese prefer to use to resolve interpersonal conflicts. In another study (K. Leung, 1987), Americans and Hong Kong Chinese read a scenario depicting a car accident-related dispute. In the scenario, the main character was in a hurry and did not stop when the light turned from green to amber. The car hit a pedestrian who suddenly ran out from the sidewalk. The victim turned out to be the driver's colleague. Later, the victim accused the driver of reckless driving, and demanded compensation for his medical expenses and salary loss due to

Meet the Researcher: Michele J. Gelfand

"To me, the study of culture is a life-long passion and one that I feel so lucky to have discovered. As a high school biology nerd, and later neuropsychology geek at Colgate University, the study of culture couldn't have been farther from my aspirations. I was fascinated with the brain and behavior and was 'destined' to be a medical doctor. I was a sheltered Long-Island kid, and 'culture' to me referred to the rare visits my family took to New York City to see a show. This changed during my junior year when I ventured off to England for a semester abroad. I remember being completely discombobulated being faced with different accents, foods, smells, and ways of life. I recall calling home to talk to my Dad—himself a sheltered guy who grew up in Brooklyn, New York (pronounced, New Yawk)—trying to make sense of the fact that my fellow students would, on a whim, travel to Amsterdam, Paris, Edinburgh, and Italy. To my surprise, his response was 'Well, just think about it like it's going from New York to Pennsylvania!' Armed with a new and comforting metaphor, the next day, with some 'Chutzpah,' I decided to book a long trip on the Nile in Egypt. Why not go to California, I reasoned (much to the dismay of my Pop, however!). It was that decision that forever changed my career path and development as a person.

My travels to Egypt, and later work on a Kibbutz in Israel, all left me with so many questions: How was I, as a person, profoundly shaped by American culture? What are the 'deep' aspects of culture and how and why do they vary? How do cultures develop and how do they change? ... Culture seemed so obvious, yet so elusive. So powerful, yet so rarely acknowledged in everyday conversations. How can that be, I asked (and continue to ask) myself! I went back to Colgate with a new view of the world and myself, enrolled in a crosscultural psychology class, and a year later, began my doctoral studies at the University of Illinois. I've never turned back."

Michele J. Gelfand is a Professor of Organizational Psychology at the University of Maryland, College Park. Her doctorate (social–organizational psychology) is from University of Illinois, Urbana-Champaign where she was a student of Harry Triandis.

hospitalization. The driver, however, felt that he was not responsible for the accident. The participants were asked to take the role of the driver, and evaluated the desirability of the following four conflict resolution procedures: (1) *Bargaining*: The disputants will attempt to resolve the

FIGURE 7.6. The inscription on the outside wall of this Chinese village reminds the villagers of the Chinese norm of moderation. Literally, the inscription means "Leave extra space." Its figural meaning is "Don't be excessive in asserting yourself; leave room for others."

conflict and arrive at a mutually acceptable outcome through negotiation and bargaining, without enlisting a third party; (2) *Mediation*: A third party appointed by the court will facilitate the negotiation and bargaining process in an attempt to arrive at a mutually acceptable outcome; (3) *Inquisitorial adjudication*: A judge will conduct a hearing and make a binding decision about the case based on the report from an independent investigator; and (4) *Adversary adjudication*: A judge will conduct a hearing and make a binding decision about the case, based on the evidence presented by two investigators, one representing the driver and the other, the victim.

The results showed that compared to Americans, Hong Kong Chinese preferred mediation and bargaining more, because they thought that these two procedures were more capable of reducing the animosity between the disputants. Additionally, other studies have shown that if a mediation procedure is to be adopted, Americans prefer an impartial mediator who has no prior relationships with either disputant, whereas

Chinese prefer a mediator who is known to and respected by both disputants (Fu et al., 2002; see Chapter 4).

In another study (Ohbuchi, Fukushima, & Tedeschi, 1999), the investigators had American and Japanese students recall a conflict experience and describe it. They were encouraged to remember what they did and what they wanted to achieve in the situation. The results reveal clear group differences in the main goals in the conflict situation. American students were oriented towards achieving justice, whereas the Japanese students were more concerned about relationships with others. The two groups also differed in the tactics they used in the conflict situation. American students preferred asserting their own request, whereas Japanese students favored indirect communication of expectations, and identifying compromise solutions that are compatible with their own goal and that of the other party.

The tendency to avoid confrontation in social situations may lead East Asians to remain passive when responding to social and personal injustices. Aversion of confrontation is a major theme in Chinese popular sayings. Almost every saying referencing confrontation or seeking legal settlement says that confrontation and seeking legal settlement are bad ideas. On the contrary, most other sayings related to conflict management endorse the ideas that those who inflict harm on others will have ill fortune or be punished by Heaven, and recommend nonaction (C. Chiu, 1991c).

In one study (C. Chiu, 1991c), Hong Kong college students recalled an unfair event they experienced recently, and reported how they felt and what they did in the situation. Most participants reported feeling angry in the situation. However, only 13% of the respondents confronted or negotiated with the perpetrator. In a field experiment conducted in the university sports facility in Hong Kong, the investigators placed canned cold drinks with the key for opening the can removed in a vending machine. However, only 32% of the thirsty and frustrated consumers who got the drink from the machine registered a complaint. The complaint rate dropped to 15% when the unsatisfied consumer needed to return the drink to the store located next to the vending machine, and hence could not avoid confronting the storeowner (C. Chiu, Tsang, & Yang, 1988).

These findings, however, should not be taken to imply that Asians always prefer nonconfrontational strategies in conflict management. Contrarily, when Asians negotiate with an outgroup, they may prefer confrontational strategies. In a conflict situation, people from individualist societies (e.g., Americans) are relatively unwilling to accept the situation and yield to arguments of the other party, and may threaten the other party and say that they would publicize the other party's action and thus damage their image and reputation. Moreover, they display these tendencies regardless of whether they negotiate with an ingroup member (classmate or neighbor), a group (e.g., a campus group, an investment group), or another country. People from collectivist countries (e.g., Asian countries) are more willing than people from individualist countries to accept the situation only when negotiating with an ingroup member. However, they are more willing than people from individualist countries to use threat when negotiating with another country (Derlega, Cukur, Kuang, & Forsyth, 2002).

Hong Kong Chinese's aversion to confrontation is also limited to ingroup interaction. In one study (K. Leung, 1988), Hong Kong Chinese and American students read a scenario in which one disputant bought a household appliance from the other disputant. The seller promised the buyer that if the appliance broke, the buyer would get a full refund. The appliance broke the next day, but the seller refused to refund the buyer, arguing that the appliance broke because of the buyer's mishandling of the machine. The disputants were described either as good friends or strangers to each other. The participants were instructed to take the role of the buyer and rated the likelihood of bringing the case to a court of law and suing the seller for monetary compensation. When the seller was a friend to the buyer, Chinese students were less likely than American students to sue the seller. However, when the seller was a stranger, Chinese students were more likely than their American peers to take legal actions against the seller. Consistent with K. Leung's finding, another study (Bond, Wan, Leung, & Giacalone, 1985) shows that although Chinese students see verbal insults from high-status ingroup members as more acceptable than American students do, both groups disparage verbal insults from high-status outgroup members.

Compared to American undergraduates, Hong Kong Chinese undergraduates also make sharper distinction in the patterns of negotiation with ingroup and outgroup members. In a computer-simulated negotiation task, compared to their American peers, Hong Kong Chinese undergraduates made more concessions when their opponent was a friend and fewer concessions when their opponent was a stranger. Additionally, when the opponent was a friend, Hong Kong Chinese undergraduates sent more cooperative messages to their opponent than American undergraduates did (see Carnevale, 1995).

Responsibility Attribution

Differences in cultural norms are also reflected in the ways responsibility is assigned. Lay people's conception of responsibility and justice is often reflected in the prevailing legal institutions (Fincham & Jaspars, 1979). In the American–British legal system, whether or not an act was intended plays a central role in determining the extent to which the actor can be held responsible for it. In everyday judgment, the intentionality of an act also plays an important role in determining responsibility. Thus, information pertinent to causality, foreseeability, and intentionality are usually considered when rendering responsibility judgment (Heider, 1958). For example, a person's responsibility for an outcome increases progressively from omission (e.g., John forgot to put on the safety belt for his child, and the kid was killed in an accident) to intentionally causing it without justification (a premeditated murder). This idea has received strong empirical support (Fincham & Schultz, 1981; Schultz, Schleifer, & Altman, 1981).

Evidence for intentionally causing harm is also an important consideration in the ascription of legal responsibility in the traditional Chinese law. In the Jin Code (267 AD), a distinction is made between omission and intentional commission, and less severe punishment is prescribed to omission than to commission. The same distinction can be found in the Tang Code (651 AD), which was practiced in China until 1911 (Nishida, 1985).

A distinguishing feature of the traditional Chinese legal system is the notion of collective responsibility. Starting from 746 BC, the system of *yuan zuo*—holding offenders' superiors, kinsmen, and neighbors responsible for their crime simply because they are related to the offenders—was widely practiced in China (Nishida, 1985; Zhang, 1984). The rationale underlying the practice of *yuan zuo* is the belief that one's superiors, neighbors, and kinsmen have the obligations and opportunities to monitor the offender's behavior, and therefore should have been able to prevent the offender from doing the harm. In other words, in Chinese societies, collective responsibility assignment is a means for enforcing social norms.

Consonant with these ideas, Tetlock (2002) proposes to use an intuitive prosecutor metaphor to understand collective blame. The intuitive prosecutor's primary information processing goal is to defend rules and regimes that are endowed with legitimacy. Within this framework, collective punishment is seen as a strategy. By linking a group member's action to his or her fellow group members' welfare, the intuitive prosecutor can effectively enforce the conventional rules in the society.

This idea has received some support from several studies. In one study (C. Chiu & Hong, 1992, Experiment 1), Chinese junior business executives in Hong Kong read about an industrial accident in which a foreman in a factory intentionally or unintentionally removed the safety shield of a power tool, causing a serious cut in a worker's hand. The participants assigned greater responsibility to the foreman when the harm was intended than when it was due to negligence, indicating that intentionality was a relevant factor in responsibility assignment. More important, the respondents also blamed the foreman's superior, who could not have foreseen the accident. In another study (C. Chiu & Hong, 1992, Experiment 2), Chinese junior business executives in Hong Kong read a scenario in which unbeknownst to his parent, a child intentionally or unintentionally let loose his dog, and the dog attacked and hurt another child in the neighborhood. Again, intentionality of the act impacted responsibility judgment. Additionally, as in the first study, the participants also blamed the child's parent for the child's act.

Collective responsibility also prevails in modern day Japan. Bell and Tetlock (1989) noted that in American organizations where individual performance is emphasized, blame is handled by identifying the individual "bad apple" as the target of blame. In contrast, in clan-like Japanese organizations, the emphasis is on group values and mutual trust. In such organizations, blame is handled by "cleansing" the organization; the head of the organization often becomes the sacrificial lamb, who is forced by the situation to step down.

Consonant with this idea, Zemba, Young, and Morris (2003, Study 1) found that when Japanese students read a scenario in which a truck driver of a moving company speeded and hit a pedestrian, they blamed the moving company more when the driver was on duty at the time of the accident than when he was off duty. More importantly, the participants also blamed the driver's supervisor at the time of the accident, and a *new* supervisor. Furthermore, the more the participants saw the company as responsible for the accident, the more they blamed the supervisor, who became the sacrificial lamb in the company blunder.

In another study (Zemba et al., 2003; Study 2a), American and Japanese students read a food poisoning case in a school, in which a student got sick after eating contaminated eggs prepared by the school cook. In this study, Japanese and American respondents did not differ in the amount of blame they assigned to the cook. However, compared to their American peers, Japanese students attributed greater responsibility to the school and the school principal. Again, the more the Japanese viewed the school as responsible, the more they blamed the principal.

The idea of collective responsibility and group punishment is foreign to most North Americans, even Americans with Asian descent. Park Sunjae was born in the US and raised in Korea since middle school. One of the first culture shocks he encountered in Korean school was group punishment. "I was very shocked that I had to be punished for something I did not do," Park said as he recalled the incident, "Surprisingly, my Korean friends were okay with it" (*Korea Herald*, June 21, 2003). Indeed, for most Westerners, collective punishment may seem uncivilized.

Summary

In summary, the evidence reviewed in the current section illustrates marked cultural differences in normative behaviors. In North America, the dominant cultural norms emphasize self-expression, self-direction, and the use of abstract, universal principles in allocating reward and responsibility. The emphasis on self-expression is clearly revealed in the emotion display and decoding rules, and the preference for direct communication and direct confrontation in conflict management and negotiation. The emphasis on voluntarism in defining altruistic behaviors reflects the value American culture places on self-direction. The use of abstract, universal principles such as contribution in establishing one's due, and intentionality in assignment responsibility, underscores the American ideal of allocating reward and punishment on the basis of what a person does rather than who the person is.

A different picture is revealed when we examine the dominant cultural norms in East Asia. Like American societies, East Asian societies apply abstract principles such as contribution and intentionality when distributing reward and assigning punishment. However, some Asian societies also consider the relational implications of applying these principles in concrete situations, and allow departure from the contribution rule in reward allocation in some relational contexts. Likewise, self-expression is permitted as long as it does not bring interpersonal discord or disgrace to the group. For this reason, collective responsibility could be an effective social control mechanism for keeping people in their place—if they do not behave, the negative behavior will bring disgrace and even punishment to the group. For the same reason, the decision to confront an ingroup member's unfair behavior is a sensitive issue that demands careful deliberation, because a rash move can easily upset the relational equilibrium in the group.

Conclusion

In this and the last two chapters, we describe cultural differences in terms of differences in the contents of the knowledge structures (procedural knowledge, person representations, event representations, and norm representations) that make up a culture, as well as the varying psychological implications of these knowledge structures. Knowledge structures that have higher levels of sharedness and chronic accessibility in a culture have greater authority over behaviors in the culture. Because of the uneven distribution of varying knowledge structures, cultural differences in thoughts, emotions, motivation, and behaviors emerge.

Defining a culture tradition in terms of its component knowledge items invites researchers to articulate clearly the type and nature of each knowledge item, as well as its range of applicability, activation circumstances, and judgmental and behavioral implications. When the structural and functional properties of each knowledge item are clearly specified, basic principles of knowledge application can be applied to predict how culture works in concrete situations. Although for the sake of presentation clarity we have described each type of knowledge structure separately, a knowledge structure perspective to culture also invites researchers to address the question of how the widely distributed knowledge structures in a culture are connected. After all, culture is a loosely organized network of knowledge, not a set of unrelated knowledge items (see Chapter 1). To complete the picture, the next chapter focuses on the organization and application of cultural knowledge.

Organization and Application of Cultural Knowledge

8

Cultural Icons

Moonwalk, Campbell's tomato soup, Elizabeth Taylor, Jackie Kennedy, James Dean, Coca-Cola, Marilyn Monroe, the dollar sign, Superman, Popeye, and Mickey Mouse. What do all these have in common?

First, they are all subjects in the prints of American artist Andrew Warhola, who is more widely known to the world as Andy Warhol. Second, they are all icons of contemporary American culture.

A cultural icon is a person or thing regarded as a representative symbol, especially of a culture or movement. It is usually a very famous person or thing considered as representing a set of beliefs or a way of life. For example, in the United States, Albert Einstein is the archetypal absent-minded scientific genius, and James Dean is the classic young man who rebels without a cause (Figure 8.1).

Cultural icons represent something bigger than themselves: They are enduring symbols of some aspects of the culture's social history, and

FIGURE 8.1. An icon of American culture.

represent to mass audiences certain aspects of their shared culture. The images of cultural icons repeatedly appear in the media. They are immediately recognizable, and what they represent is just as recognizable as the images themselves. Viewers confronted with these images will spontaneously access their cognitive representation of the shared culture the icons symbolize.

Finally, every cultural icon represents a certain part of the culture shared by *a specific social group*. Therefore, no cultural icon speaks to everyone; the icons of one group may be completely unknown to another.

Andy Warhol made American cultural icons a prominent subject in many of his most celebrated pictures. Instead of painting icons by hand, he applied a repeat-printing technique similar to techniques used to create advertising posters. By doing so, he effectively communicated the idea that these icons, like his art, are both products of and commodities in the mass culture. Social psychologists have made use of the unique properties of cultural icons to answer an important theoretical question: How do people apply cultural knowledge in concrete situations?

Organization of Cultural Knowledge: Is Culture a Coherent Meaning System?

In the last three chapters, we review cultural variations in four major types of knowledge structures (procedural knowledge, person representations, event representations, and norm representations) separately. The current chapter focuses on the organization and application of these structures. As noted in Chapter 1, it is widely accepted that culture consists of a *network* of distributed knowledge (C. Chiu & Chen, 2004; Gabora, 1997; Hong & Chiu, 2001; Y. Kashima, 2000a; Shore, 1996; Sperber, 1996). Therefore, to complete the analysis of culture as a network of knowledge characteristic of a group of interconnected individuals, we need to consider the organization of different cultural knowledge items.

Although we have presented the four types of cultural knowledge separately, it is easy to discern the interconnectedness of the different types of cultural knowledge. For example, in the last chapter, we characterize the culture of honor as an event representation. However, culture of honor is also supported by a code of honor, or a set of shared norms, which defines the conditions that establish a person's honor, and prescribes a course of actions to protect one's honor (Cohen & Nisbett, 1997). In addition, many East–West differences in procedural knowledge, and person representations, event representations, and norm representations, seem to revolve around a common theme: Asian societies value attention to the context, particularly the relational context, more than American societies do. There appears to be a common thread running through many East–West psychological differences.

As mentioned in Chapter 2, Hofstede (1980) has identified four major dimensions of culture: power distance, uncertainty avoidance, individualism–collectivism, and masculinity–femininity. Of these four dimensions, the dimension of individualism–collectivism has received most research attention. People in individualist cultures view the self as being independent. They also see the self as stable and the environment as changeable. Conversely, people in collectivist cultures view the self as interdependent with some in-group. They also see the environment as stable and themselves as changeable, ready to "fit in" (Triandis, 1995). As such, the dimension of individualism seems to epitomize many of the East–West psychological differences reviewed in the last three chapters. Indeed, some writers (e.g., Greenfield, 2000) see individualism–collectivism as the "deep structure" of cultural differences, from which all other differences evolved. The view that culture consists of a coherent system of meanings with an identifiable central theme around which all cultural meanings are organized has been referred to as the *systemic* view of culture (see Shore, 2002).

We acknowledge the presence of loose connections between cultural knowledge items within a culture. However, we are skeptical of the systemic view of culture. Indeed, the systemic view of culture, which justifies the use of a broad cultural dimension to characterize a culture, has been severely criticized for conflating different forms of sociality in the culture (Bandura, 2002; Fiske, 2002). Moreover, the empirical evidence does not support this view.

Recall that in their review of the extant literature on country differences in individualism and collectivism, Oyserman et al. (2002) found that "European Americans were not more individualistic than African Americans, or Latinos, and not less collectivistic than Japanese or

Koreans" (p. 3). In addition, there are remarkable inter-domain variations in country differences in individualism and collectivism. For example, in the case of US–Japan differences, North Americans are *more collectivist* than Japanese in most domains, including accepting hierarchy, striving to maintain group harmony, defining oneself contextually, as well as sense of belonging to groups. Japanese are more collectivist than North Americans only in the domain of preference for working in a group. Comparisons of North Americans with other Asian groups have yielded very similar results (see Chapter 2).

Similarly, having reviewed the literature in six major areas of cross-cultural research (perception, cognition, language, personality, emotions, and social behaviors), Poortinga (2003, p. 275) reached a similar conclusion: "The evidence for a system of values or meanings in one culture that differs in essential ways from the systems of other cultures appears to be rather limited." He urges researchers to stop explaining cultural differences in behavior in terms of broad and inclusive concepts, and instead consider culture as "a loose set of mentifacts with incidental interconnectedness." (p. 275)

Inter-domain variability in cross-cultural differences raises the question of whether it is useful to employ broadly and diffusely defined psychological constructs to explain group differences in cognition, motivation, and behavior. In response to this challenge, Kitayama (2002) argues that attitude and value measures have failed to capture the coherence of culture, because culture resides in external, public representations, not in people's minds. Thus, culture cannot be reduced to knowledge represented in the mind of individual members of a cultural group. Instead, culture is "out there" in the form of external realities and collective patterns of behavior, which include verbal and nonverbal symbols (e.g., language and media), daily practices and routines (e.g., gossips and behavioral scripts), tools (e.g., mobile phones and Internet), and social institutions and structures (e.g., reward allocation and legal systems).

Deciphering the meanings of culture in public representations is very important in cultural inquiry. However, public meanings of culture are not homogenous either. On the contrary, inconsistent and contrastive cultural ideas are often represented in the same external carrier of cultural meanings. For example, popular sayings and idioms carry widely shared evaluative, prescriptive, or proscriptive beliefs, and are embedded in many conversation scripts. In a content analysis of over 2000 Chinese popular sayings and idioms, Ho and Chiu (1994) found that ideas supporting individualism and ideas supporting collectivism are equally prevalent in Chinese sayings. Likewise, Zhang and Shavitt (2003) analyzed the values promoted in Chinese advertising and found that both modernity and individualism predominate in current Chinese advertising. They also discovered that individualism and modern values are more pervasive in magazine advertisements than in television commercials, whereas collectivism and traditional values are more pervasive on television than in magazine advertisements. The prospect of finding a homogenous culture in external carriers of cultural meanings is dim.

In the light of these findings, instead of trying to explain away inter-domain variability in cultural knowledge, it may be more useful to explain culture in terms of domain-specific and situation-specific distributed knowledge (Shore, 2002). The range of applicability is broad for some cultural knowledge items, and much more restricted for others. Knowledge items with a broad range of applicability mediate a wide range of cultural differences, whereas those with a restricted range of applicability mediate a smaller set of cultural differences. Knowledge items with very broad range of applicability have been referred to as foundational cultural schemata (Shore, 1996) or primary cultural syndromes (Triandis, 1994). However, given the substantial inter-domain variability in cultural knowledge, it is not justified to automatically credit an observed cultural difference in judgment and behavior to cultural variation in these broad cultural knowledge items.

How then do we account for the "common thread" that appears to run through many East–West psychological differences? First, cultural knowledge items are tools for relating and adapting to the physical and social environment (see Chapter 4). Second, in the long history of a human group, to solve the same problem, multiple knowledge tools are invented, and new tools are evolved from old ones. Third, culture is a cumulative process; the emergence of new or modified tools would not necessarily replace old or original tools (see Chapter 3). The availability of multiple tools for solving the same problem in a human group may give rise to the perception that all tools are part of a coherent cultural system, although in reality, these functionally equivalent tools are not necessarily connected to each other (Heylighen & Campbell, 1995). For example, both religious individualism (which emphasizes salvation through personal faith rather than mediation of the Church) and political collectivism (which emphasizes the application of the majority rule in making political decisions) were evolved to end the ruling classes' exploitation of the masses in the Middle Ages. Although both beliefs empower the individual, they did not arise from the same individualist logic.

Moreover, a tool that is useful for solving one problem may inspire the invention of similar tools to solve another problem that may or may not be related to the first problem. For example, the belief in religious individualism inspires the development of economic individualism (the ideology that encompasses the beliefs that God helps those who help themselves, and that people will be rewarded in accordance to their achieved rather than ascribed status), which was evolved as a response to the changing mode and means of production preceding the Industrial Revolution. We submit that the loose connections between knowledge items within the same culture may result from the incidental functional relatedness that emerged in the developmental history of these knowledge items, rather than from the culture's internal logic.

Multiple Determinants of Cultural Behavior

In the systemic view, all cultural behaviors evolve from the same deep structure. In contrast, the idea that culture consists of loosely interconnected cultural knowledge items leads to a more complex view of the causation of cultural behaviors. According to this view, the same cultural behavior can have several different causes. For example, the same cultural behavior may arise from the joint influence of a culture-characteristic self-representation and a culture-characteristic norm representation. Sometimes, the two knowledge items may act in concert to produce the same behavior, as in the case where the honor code and the honor-pertinent cultural script reinforce honor-related violence in the American South. Sometimes, two knowledge items may push behaviors in opposite directions, as in the case of self-enhancement in Japan (see below). When a culture-characteristic self-representation and a culture-characteristic norm representation have conflicting behavioral implications, self-expressions are subdued when normative influence dominates, and unleashed when normative influence recedes. In this section, we illustrate this idea with a heated debate in the social psychology of culture: Do East Asians need positive self-regard?

Do East Asians Self-Enhance?

The Need for Self-Enhancement in American Culture

Self-esteem is one of the most researched topics in psychology. In February 2005, we conducted a keyword search in PsycINFO, the most comprehensive database of psychological studies, and found 14,113 papers on self-esteem. High self-esteem has been found to be related to measures of mental health, subjective well-being, achievement, motivation, resilience, and positive coping outcomes. In addition, low self-esteem is associated with depression, suicidal tendencies, and other emotional and behavioral problems, such as substance abuse and teenage pregnancy. Because of these findings, in the United States, starting from the 1980s, many educators accept the assumption that higher self-esteem will help all students, particularly girls, and members of minority groups who see their sense of self diminished by an indifferent public school system. Increasingly, teachers focus on helping students identify their strengths, and encourage students to actualize their potentials. Many teachers believe that bolstering self-esteem will lead to success experiences, and is *the* psychological cure for most social, emotional ills. In mainstream American culture, self-improvement is often taken to mean development of one's talents rather than working on one's weaknesses (see Hong, Chiu, & Dweck, 1995).

Some critical reflections on the psychological costs of high self-esteem began to surface in American society in the 1990s. Some teachers feel that in some instances, they are pressurized to accept work that they should not accept because there is a fear that children will not feel good about themselves. Some researchers point out that despite the strong positive correlation between self-esteem and achievement, self-esteem does not cause achievement, because simply bolstering individuals' self-esteem does not increase the likelihood of future achievement. Conversely, individuals who have higher levels of achievement develop higher self-esteem. These findings indicate that self-esteem is a product, not a cause, of success experiences (Hong et al., 1995; Seligman, 1995). Other researchers also point out that when individuals have high but unstable self-esteem, they are vulnerable to depression and other psychological problems. These individuals think highly about themselves, but also feel insecure in ego-threatening situations. In situations where their abilities or achievements are questioned, they may defend their self-esteem with maladaptive, dominant behaviors, like aggressive behaviors and alcoholism (Baumeister, 1991).

Despite these, the heavy emphasis on self-esteem in American culture has fostered a need to present oneself positively to both the self and others. This need for self-enhancement is vividly portrayed in several memorable episodes of Stuart Smalley's *Daily Affirmations* in *Saturday Night Live,* a popular American TV Show. Smalley's self-affirmation always began with recitation of the following lines, "I'm good enough, I'm smart enough, and doggone it, people like me." The daily affirmation proceeds in the form of an inner dialogue, through which the tension between the need to self-enhance and the awareness of one's weaknesses and vulnerabilities gradually unfolds. In one episode, he recited the following affirmation: "I am fun to be with. Because I'm good enough, I'm smart enough and doggone it, people like me. Well, not everybody. But that's their problem. And your problem. Okay, I'm sorry, this is not my best show. I'm Stuart. I'm an over eater."

In another episode, Michael Jordan was Smalley's guest. Smalley told Michael Jordan that he probably woke up at night, saying to himself, "I'm not good enough, everybody's better than me, I'm not going to score any points." Next, Stuart asked Michael Jordan to recite an affirmation: "Hello, Michael. I don't have to be a great basketball player. I don't have to dribble fast or throw the ball in the basket. All I have to do is be the best Michael I can be" (Cader, 1994).

Many studies have demonstrated a strong need for self-enhancement in American society. For example, research in North America has found a robust self-serving bias in attribution: Individuals take credit for successes and evade responsibility for failures by attributing success to their own qualities and attributing failure to external causes (Davis & Stephan, 1980; D. T. Miller & Ross, 1975).

Do East Asians have the Need for Positive Self-Regard?

In 1999, Steven Heine (Heine et al., 1999) asked a provocative question: Do Japanese have the need for positive self-regard? According to Heine, "the empirical literature provides scant evidence for the need for positive self-regard among Japanese and indicates that a self-critical focus is more characteristic of Japanese" (Heine et al., 1999, p. 766).

The lack of self-serving bias in causal attribution is the most often cited supportive evidence for Heine's claim. In a review of 23 studies that assessed how Japanese explain their success and failure, Kitayama, Takagi, and Matsumoto (1995) found no evidence for the presence of self-serving bias among Japanese. In one study (Gelfand et al., 2002, Study 4), American and Japanese students participated in a negotiation task, and received positive, average, or negative feedback on their negotiation effectiveness. Next, they judged whether their performance was indicative of their negotiation abilities. American students thought the feedback was more indicative of their abilities when the feedback was positive than when it was average or negative. Conversely, Japanese students viewed the feedback as *less* indicative of their abilities when the feedback was positive than when it was average or negative.

Cultural differences in the extent of self-serving bias have been observed in moral judgments as well. For example, in an additional study, Gelfand et al. (2002, Study 1) had their American and Japanese participants write down as many fair and unfair behaviors as they could think of, and indicate whether they engaged in such behaviors more than others, or others engaged in such behaviors more than them. Compared to American students, Japanese students wrote down fewer fair behaviors performed by themselves, and fewer unfair behaviors performed by others.

Cultural divergence in self-enhancement motivation has also been found in social comparison. In general, North American undergraduates rate themselves more positively across a wide variety of personality traits than they do their peers. By contrast, Japanese rate their peers more positively than they do themselves. Moreover, American students display greater self-enhancement when the traits are more desirable. In contrast, Japanese students become more self-critical when the traits are more desirable or important to the self (Heine & Renshaw, 2002).

A similarly low level of self-enhancement motivation has been reported in Chinese culture. In the face of failure, Chinese students are more willing than European American students to accept responsibility by attributing the failure to lack of effort (an internal attribute) (Hess, Chih-Mei, & McDevitt, 1987; Salili, 1995).

Furthermore, after writing about a positive personal experience or reading about another's negative experience, European Americans spontaneously think that they possess some stable internal attributes that positively distinguish their life experiences from other people's life experiences. Accordingly, they tend to attribute a high level of stability to their level of life satisfaction, believing that they will be as satisfied with life in the future as they are now. In contrast, Asian Americans do not show this pattern (Oishi, Wyer, & Colcombe, 2000). In short, the evidence seems to suggest that the self-enhancement motivation is either absent or very weak in East Asian cultures.

One explanation for the attenuated self-enhancement motive in East Asia is that East Asians are socialized to overcome obstacles and hardship in life, and to meet expectations of important others. Consequently, they have learned to be sensitive to others' expectations and their personal weaknesses, and to derive pride and satisfaction from their determination to overcome failures and from meeting expectations of important others (Heine, 2003; Heine et al., 1999).

East Asians' focus on self-criticism is reflected in their lower self-esteem. As mentioned in Chapter 6, East Asians tend to report lower self-esteem than do European North Americans. They also tend to use more negative and fewer positive self-descriptions than do European North Americans to describe themselves, particularly when they do so in front of an authority figure (Bond & Cheung, 1983; Kanagawa, Cross, & Markus, 2001). They are also more modest than European Americans when describing their achievement (Akimoto & Sanbonmatsu, 1999). Furthermore, as mentioned in Chapter 6, situations that afford self-enhancement are more available in the United States than in Japan, whereas situations that afford self-criticism are more available in Japan than in the United States (Kitayama et al., 1997).

Some studies have also found stronger self-critical and self-improvement attitudes among East Asians than North Americans. For example, compared to their North American peers, Japanese undergraduates reported a greater discrepancy between who they are and who they aspire to become (Heine & Lehman, 1999). In addition, East Asian students are more eager to seek upward social comparison than downward social comparison: They are more curious about how they perform relative to the high performers than about how they stand relative to low performers. Presumably, they believe that comparing the self to high performers will provide more learning opportunities for self-improvement. Consistent with this interpretation, East Asians' tendency to seek upward social comparison is particularly pronounced when they fail on a task, and have the opportunity to improve their performance in the future. By contrast, European Canadian students do not have a preference for upward or downward social comparison (White & Lehman, 2005).

Normative Influence

Taken together, the data seem to suggest a stronger self-improvement motive in East Asian cultures, and a stronger self-enhancement motive in North American culture. However, it would be premature to conclude from these findings that in East Asian cultures, the relatively prevalent self-critical attitude and self-improvement motivation have attenuated or even eliminated the self-enhancement motivation. This conclusion is valid only if we assume that in East Asian cultures, self-enhancement and self-improvement motivations are mutually exclusive motivations: An East Asian cannot seek self-enhancement and self-improvement at the same time. In the United States, self-enhancement and self-improvement are not rival motivations. Indeed, self-esteem enhancement is an integral part of many self-improvement books and programs in the United States. For example, a recent popular American self-help e-book by Teresa King is entitled, *"Your attitude, your self-esteem—It's all about self-improvement."* In Japan, in a recent international forum, some Japanese educators learned from their international peers that an area that Japanese students need to improve is their relatively low level of self-confidence. The *Japan Times* has an interesting coverage of this intercultural dialogue:

Visiting educators find confidence lacking

Efforts urged to nurture student self-expression

By YUMI WIJERS-HASEGAWA

Staff writer

Japan should make greater efforts to instill a sense of self-confidence in its children and help them to develop the ability to express themselves, according to foreign educators invited to speak at a recent discussion session in Tokyo.

The July 10 event was part of an annual Keizai Koho Center Fellowships program in which 15 social studies teachers from the United States, Canada, Britain, and Australia were invited to deepen their understanding of Japan and take their experiences back to their students.

In addition to the 15 educators, Japanese teachers and business-people also took part in the discussion.

Partly due to an experience the teachers had during a school visit as part of the program, the discussion focused on children's self-confidence and the ability to express themselves.

The group of teachers visited a public high school in Tokyo, whose students' academic performance is on a medium level, the previous day. In an effort to better understand the situation of Japanese school education, they asked questions to the students in a friendly way.

However, all attempts to communicate with the students were completely ignored. Uninterested and unmoved by their visitors' efforts, the students simply chatted among themselves.

It was only when Colleen MacLeod, from Canada, suggested distributing a piece of paper and asking them to write down what they were thinking that the situation changed. The students responded with comments and questions that were very to the point, such as queries about the problem of guns in the US and whether it was true that Western companies rate their employees purely based on their performance.

The encounter indicated that the children's psychological conditions were not as bad as the educators had initially feared. Still, it confirmed that today's Japanese students are very reluctant to speak out.

"The children in yesterday's school were very shy," said MacLeod, "In Canada, people are less shy to speak out. In the school where I work, if a student is not good at something, teachers try to find what he or she is good at. For instance, one student who is terrible at math is acknowledged to be a great writer among the teachers."

Toru Matsuzawa, a teacher of civic education at Tokyo Metropolitan Tagara High School, believes Japanese adults look more at the negative attributes of a student than his or her positive aspects—a situation that clearly will not nurture self-esteem.

The Japan Times: July 24, 2001

The North American educators articulated the American view of self-confidence and self-improvement very well. The Japanese educators were self-critical and serious about self-improvement. The whole picture is very consistent with what we have learned from the research literature. However, the Japanese teachers do not seem to have difficulty in acknowledging that low self-confidence is a problem area that Japanese educators need to address.

If self-improvement motivation does not suffocate the self-enhancement motivation, then what does? The Japanese participants' responses in the forum provide a hint: When Colleen MacLeod suggested that the students write down their thoughts on a piece of paper, one student with gold-dyed hair apologized in her note for not speaking out, adding that it was out of shyness, even though she actually "really wanted to talk." Matsuzawa, a Japanese teacher, said children were afraid that if they asserted themselves, their peers would judge them to be "strange and weird" rather than "unique and different." Kataoka, a parent, also said he found the situation in Japan sad and irritating, but reluctantly admitted that this is the norm among Japan's modern-day students. Apparently, some Japanese students do want to assert themselves, feel the normative pressure, and decide to remain silent.

In keeping with this observation, research has shown that East Asians also have a need for positive self-regard. However, because the cultural norms in East Asian societies discourage outward expressions of positive self-evaluations, direct communications of one's strengths are relatively infrequent. However, even in East Asian societies, self-enhancement is not discouraged in all situations, and the self-enhancement motivation is often expressed through some subtle, indirect outlets.

Indeed, there is evidence that European Americans like people who self-enhance more than people who self-efface, whereas Asians have the reverse preference. In one study (Bond, Leung, & Wan, 1978), Hong Kong Chinese participants observed two persons (who were actually the experimenter's confederates) working on an intellectual task. In one condition, the confederates were incompetent. When asked to predict their performance on a similar task in the future, the self-enhancing confederate said, "I don't know what has happened to me today. I am not so useless. If I can do it again, I will get more answers correct." The self-effacing confederate said, "I have already tried my best. If I have to do it again, it is hard to say what the result would be." The participants liked the self-effacing confederate more than the self-enhancing one. Similar findings have also been reported in Korea (J. Kim, Kim, Kam, & Shin, 2003). These findings illustrate that in Asia, being modest is considered a socially desirable way of presenting the self in social situations.

Jenny Kurman (Kurman, 2001, 2003; Kurman & Sriram, 1997) has examined the role of modesty in self-enhancement in Asian cultures, and found that the heavy emphasis on modesty in Asian societies explains why Asian participants did not self-enhance as much as did their American peers in previous studies. In several studies, Kurman had participants in Singapore, Japan, and Israel, who reported their school grades, and compared their reported grades to the actual grades. In all national samples, reported grades were significantly higher than the actual grades, reflecting a self-enhancing bias, although the extent of self-enhancement bias was significantly stronger in Israel than in Singapore and Japan.

More importantly, Kurman (2003) also measured individual differences in self-construal (how important the independent and the interdependent self is) and perceived desirability of and the motivation to adhere to the modesty norm, using items such as "Bragging about oneself in a group is always socially inappropriate," and "Telling people about my strengths and successes has always been an embarrassing thing for me." In these studies, considerable cultural differences were found in the perceived desirability of and motivation to adhere to the modesty norm: Compared to the Israelis, Singaporeans viewed the modesty norm as more desirable, and were more inclined to adhere to it. Furthermore, mediation analysis revealed that cultural variations in self-enhancement are related to cultural differences in modesty, but not to cultural differences in self-construal (Kurman, 2003).

Moreover, students who displayed a stronger self-enhancement bias also reported a higher level of self-esteem, more positive emotions and fewer negative emotions. Kobayashi and Brown (2003) also reported that among both Japanese undergraduates and European American undergraduates, the tendency to self-enhance is associated with higher self-esteem. These findings indicate that self-enhancement is not a psychological liability in Asian contexts. Instead, as in North America, self-enhancement is related to psychological well-being and adjustment.

If the attenuation of self-enhancement in Asian culture is due to the influence of the modesty norm, Asians should display self-enhancement

Meet the Researcher: Jenny Kurman

"Raised in the emerging Israeli Jewish state, I had been exposed to cultural diversity constantly. My generation, following the dominant policy of melting pot in Israel that instructed us to ignore the differences and focus on the commonalities, was not deeply impressed with cultural differences.

There were stereotypes and prejudice—many Israeli standupists make their living on ethnic jokes, but in my world, friends with different cultural origins were never considered to be different types of people. When I had the wonderful opportunity to live in Singapore and got acquainted with the East Asian culture, I took the same perspective to the obvious cultural differences I observed. Contrary to the zeitgeist of the time, I saw, and still see, cross-cultural differences as mostly strategic responses to the same motives. I believe that we all have the same basic motives, but constraints and opportunities in a culture channel identical motives into different behaviors. The varying culture-characteristic strategies are not necessarily reflections of basic differences, nor should they be evaluated in terms of their efficiency in achieving certain prescribed or desired goals. These differences most likely reflect adaptive responses to culture that make our social world interesting."

Jenny Kurman was born in Israel. Her parents emigrated from Greece, escaping the Holocaust. She received her Ph.D. in psychology from the University of Haifa, where she is currently a Senior Lecturer.

when normative concerns from the situation are removed, as in the case when the participants are guaranteed complete anonymity of their responses. However, if Asians' weaker self-enhancement tendency is due to an internalized self-improvement motive, Asians should not display self-enhancement even when normative concerns are removed. Recall that one consistent finding in the research literature is that Japanese do not display the self-serving bias in attribution as North Americans do. In one study (Kudo & Numazaki, 2003), Japanese participants were promised complete anonymity and confidentiality of their responses when they made attributions for their personal successes and failures. Under this condition, Japanese participants displayed the self-serving bias: They attributed more personal responsibility for their success than for their failure.

Another implication of the normative explanation is that Asians would also display self-enhancement when it is measured using indirect, hidden measures. For example, it has been shown that Japanese like an alphabetical letter more if it is part of their name than if it is not, and a number more if it is part of their birthday than if it is not (Kitayama & Karasawa, 1997). Kobayashi and Greenwald (2003, Study 1) applied the implicit association test to assess implicit self-enhancement among Japanese and European Americans. The implicit association test is a sophisticated method that uses response competition to assess the strength of association between two cognitive elements. In one experimental condition, the participants were required to give the same response (press the same key on the keyboard with a finger) to words that denote the self and words that denote a pleasant attribute. In another condition, they were asked to give the same response to words denoting the self and words denoting an unpleasant attribute. If the participants associated the self with a pleasant attribute, they should respond more slowly when the same response was required for self-related words and words denoting unpleasant attributes (incompatible trials) than for self-related words and words denoting pleasant attributes (compatible trials). Accordingly, a longer response time for the incompatible (vs. compatible) trials can be used to indicate more favorable implicit self-evaluation. Using a similar procedure, the investigators also measured the participant's implicit evaluation of another student in the participant's university. It is worth noting that in this experiment, participants did not know that self-enhancement was being measured. In this study, both Japanese and European Americans displayed implicit self-enhancement: They viewed themselves more favorably than they did another student on campus. Indeed, the magnitude of implicit self-enhancement was slightly higher among Japanese than European Americans. Kitayama and Uchida (2003) reported a similar pattern in another study that also used the implicit association test to assess Japanese and European American undergraduates' implicit self-enhancement. Taken together, these findings illustrate the important role of cultural norms in mediating cultural differences in self-enhancement.

In an additional study, Kobayashi and Greenwald (2003, Study 2) obtained from European American undergraduates overt or explicit evaluations of themselves and another student on campus, in addition to their response to the implicit measure of self-enhancement. They found that European Americans self-enhance more on the explicit measure than on the implicit measure. Because self-presentational concerns impact explicit measures more than implicit measures, this finding suggests that self-enhancement is part of the self-presentation norms in North America. Recall that in Stuart Smalley's daily affirmations, although one may not feel good about the self, one may still feel the pressure to follow cultural expectations and present a positive self in social situations. This points to a major cultural variation in self-enhancement: Although self-enhancement is prevalent in both Asian and American cultures, in American culture, the dominant norms reinforce the self-enhancement motive, whereas in Asian cultures, the dominant norms discourage overt display of self-enhancing behaviors.

The modesty norm, which is more widely distributed in Asian societies than in North American societies, discourages asserting one's agentic characteristics (e.g., intelligence). However, asserting one's communal qualities (e.g., cooperation) is permissible under the modesty norm. Consistent with this idea, although compared to Israelis, Singaporeans tend to self-enhance less on agentic traits, the two groups do not differ in self-enhancement on communal traits (Kurman, 2001). Another study shows that while European American undergraduates self-enhance more on agentic traits than do their Japanese peers, Japanese undergraduates self-enhance more on communal traits (Sedikides, Gaertner, & Toguchi, 2003). Furthermore, as discussed in

Chapter 4, European American undergraduates have a greater tendency than their Hong Kong Chinese peers to describe themselves in unrealistically positive terms. However, Hong Kong Chinese undergraduates have a greater tendency to describe themselves as good followers of social norms and conventions (Figure 8.2).

The modesty norm encourages the use of self-criticism as a means to maintain interpersonal relationship. However, a self-effacer can self-criticize in public, and privately hold a favorable view of the self (Kitayama & Uchida, 2003). In one study

FIGURE 8.2. A statue in Jing-gang Mountains, China: Although Chinese culture discourages public expressions of individualist traits, it approves expressions of one's commitment to the collective's welfare. This young defender of the weak and the poor wears a proud expression on his face.

(Muramoto, 2003), when asked to make attributions for their successes and failures, Japanese undergraduates displayed the typical Japanese response pattern: They attributed personal successes to situational factors and failures to internal factors. Despite their self-critical responses, participants expected their important others to make supportive and appreciative attributions, and believed that these supportive attributions reflected how the participants really thought about their achievements. These participants expected their close friends and families to attribute the participants' successes to internal factors and failures to situational factors, although they did not expect their classmates to do the same. The participants also believed that their close friends and families understood the participants more than did their classmates, and the participants were more willing to share personal successes and failures with their friends and families than with their classmates.

The modesty norm is particularly applicable in noncompetitive situations where maintenance of interpersonal harmony is the dominant goal. One study (Takata, 2003) showed that when placed in a noncompetitive situation, Japanese undergraduates tend to be humble and self-critical. For example, they would express lower confidence in their performance, and spend less time reviewing the performance feedback when their performance is good than when it is bad. However, when they are placed in a competitive situation, the goal of winning becomes more important than the goal of maintaining harmony. In this situation, Japanese undergraduates do not follow the modesty norm. Instead, they display self-enhancing behaviors: Feeling confident in their performance and spending more time reviewing the performance feedback when they outperform (vs. being outperformed by) their competitor.

In short, the available evidence supports the following conclusions: First, compared to North Americans, East Asians have stronger self-criticism attitudes and self-improvement motivation. Second, both North Americans and East Asians have the need for positive self-regard, and both groups self-enhance. Third, in North America, the dominant cultural norms encourage self-enhancement, whereas in Asia, the dominant cultural norms (e.g., the modesty norm) discourage public display of self-enhancement on agentic traits, and permit and even encourage public display of self-enhancement on communal traits.

From this research example, we learn an important lesson. First, culture is complex; it consists of a collection of connected knowledge structures, such as the self-enhancement motive (a self-representation) and the modesty norm in East Asian cultures. The knowledge structures that make up a culture may suppress and seek to dominate each other, reinforce each other, or be unconnected. To understand a culture and cultural variation in behaviors, it is important to understand not only the relative distributions of individual knowledge items, but also how individual knowledge items are related to one another.

Relative Influence of Different Determinants

Thus far, we have focused on cultural variations in the interconnection and interaction of cultural knowledge structures. Cultures also differ in the relative importance of self-representations and norms in determining behaviors. Some early studies show that normative influence is stronger in Asia than in North America. For example, Indian adolescents value conformity more than American adolescents do (Sundberg, Rohila, & Tyler, 1970). Hong Kong Chinese students are more likely to shift their opinions in the direction of the majority than are American undergraduates (Meade & Barnard, 1973). In a quiz, compared to their American peers, Taiwan Chinese are more likely to conform to their co-participant's answer, particularly when the co-participant seems to be knowledgeable about the topic (Huang & Harris, 1973). In a large-scale international survey of life satisfaction, Suh, Diener, Oishi, and Triandis (1998) found that in individualist countries (e.g., USA, Britain, Canada, The Netherlands), emotion (positive and negative affect) is the best predictor of life satisfaction. In these countries, people who have higher satisfaction have more intense positive affect and less intense negative affect. By comparison, in collectivist countries (e.g., China, Indonesia, Colombia), both emotional experiences and norms regarding life satisfaction (how satisfied the ideal person would feel about their life) predict life satisfaction. In these countries, people who have high life satisfaction have pleasant emotional experiences, and expect the ideal person to have high life satisfaction (view having a high level of life satisfaction to be a socially desirable characteristic cherished by the ideal person in their culture).

However, these findings do not imply that norm representations have little authority over North Americans' behaviors. As mentioned earlier, in American culture, self-presentation norms also influence overt evaluation of the self and others (Kobayashi & Greenwald, 2003, Study 2). Similarly, in their study of norms for experiencing emotions, Eid and Diener (2001) found that the United States is one of the nations that are most uniform in norms with regard to pleasant affect—Americans agree that they *should* feel happy. Americans who can live up to cultural expectations for experiencing positive emotions also have higher levels of life satisfaction (Schimmack, Radhakrishnan, Oishi, Dzokoto, & Ahadi, 2002). Indeed, the founding fathers of the United States believed that to be happy is so American that it deserves to be written into the *Declaration of Independence*:

> We hold these truths to be self-evident, that all men are created equal, that they are endowed by their Creator with certain inalienable rights, that among these are life, liberty, and the pursuit of happiness.

The Context of Cultural Knowledge

In the last section, we describe the interconnection and interaction of different types of cultural knowledge. A goal of social psychology is to predict people's behaviors in concrete situations. Our discussion thus far has focused on cultural variations in general behavioral tendencies. Application of cultural knowledge is context-dependent (Higgins, 1996). To permit precise predictions of how a person from a particular culture will behave in a particular situation, we need to understand how cultural knowledge is applied in that situation. In this section, we introduce several specific principles underlying application of cultural knowledge in concrete situations.

Contextual Shift in the Meaning of Cultural Knowledge

Cultural meanings are often assumed to be relatively stable across situational contexts. This assumption may be valid in most experimental situations, where contextual features are carefully sampled to ensure comparability of responses in different experimental conditions. In real life situations, the motivational context of behavior is usually much richer, and cultural meanings may shift as the motivational context changes. For example, effort is emphasized in East Asian achievement contexts (Blinco, 1992; C. Chen & Stevenson, 1995; Eaton & Dembo, 2001). However, the meaning of effort may change with the structure of interdependence as well as the teaching practices in the motivation context.

In a series of studies, Grant and Dweck (2001) found that the relationship of effort attribution with affect and behavior might change with context. Attributing achievement setbacks to lack of effort (vs. abilities) is usually accompanied by more task enjoyment, greater task persistence, and better performance after failure. However, in some East Asian contexts, students often feel a sense of responsibility to their group for their own performance. In this context, the emphasis on effort may lead one to believe that one has not tried hard enough to meet expectations from one's group, resulting in feelings of anxiousness, embarrassment, guilt, and humiliation following failures. Thus, the meaning of lack of effort may change across cultural contexts.

In a related study, Salili, Chiu, and Lai (2001) compared the achievement motivation of Hong Kong Chinese high school students with Canadian Chinese and European Canadian high school students. Compared to European Canadian students, Hong Kong Chinese students and Canadian Chinese students placed greater emphasis on teacher-, family-, and peer-oriented goals, but the two Chinese groups did not differ from each other in the perceived importance of these socially oriented goals, indicating that the Hong Kong Chinese and Canadian Chinese students share a strong socially oriented achievement motivation that is highly encouraged in Chinese culture. However, there are pronounced differences in the motivation contexts in Hong Kong and Canada. In Hong Kong, students with poorer academic performance are often made to work harder; there is a negative correlation between time spent on studying and academic performance. In Canada, students who work harder have higher performance; the correlations between effort and academic performance in both Canadian student groups are positive. Not surprisingly, Hong Kong Chinese students and Canadian Chinese students attribute different meanings to effort. Among Hong Kong Chinese students, time spent on studying is unrelated to self-efficacy, but positively related to test anxiety. Among Canadian Chinese students, time spent on studying is positively related to self-efficacy and unrelated to test anxiety.

Contextual Activation of Cultural Knowledge

Availability

A knowledge item may be available in one culture but not in another (Lillard, 1998). A knowledge item must be available for it to be used. For example, the Hindu emotion term *lajya* is foreign to most European Americans. The Hindu Newar in Nepal and Hindu Oriyas in India use the term to describe an emotion that combines shyness, shame, and embarrassment. People having *lajya* may blush and have a fast pulse. *Lajya* also carries specific social moral meanings in Hindu communities. For example, *lajya* lowers one's social and moral standing in the community. *Lajya* is a social evaluation: When people in the community say a person has *lajya*, that person feels *lajya* (Parish, 1991). *Lajya* also prescribes how individuals should behave in the community. For example, women are expected to avoid *lajya* by covering their face and "ducking" out of a room to avoid contact with certain relatives they are not supposed to see. Individuals who act rudely, or expose certain parts, might have *lajya* (U. Menon & Shweder, 1994).

Other examples of culture-specific constructs that are foreign to European American cultures include *caste* in India (see Chapter 2); *filial piety* (see Chapter 2), *face* ("the reciprocated compliance, respect, and/or deference that each party expects from, and extends to, the other party") (Ho, 1976, p. 883), and *yuan* (affinity, predestined relationship, or the cause of a predestined relationship) (K. Yang & Ho, 1988) in Chinese culture; *kapwa* (fellow being, a conception of the self that also includes others) in Filipino culture; *amae* (to depend and presume upon another's benevolence) (Doi, 1956) and *on* (a relational concept combining a benefit or benevolence given with a debt or obligation thus incurred) (Lebra, 1976) in Japanese culture; and *cheong* (human affection that acts like an emotional glue, binding its members together) (S.-C. Choi, Kim, & Choi, 1993) in Korean culture. Because the meanings and behavioral significance of these constructs are deeply rooted in a particular cultural tradition, a focal approach is most appropriate for deciphering their psychological meanings (Chapter 2). Knowledge derived from analysis of these constructs will give researchers access to understanding of how the natives understand themselves that may otherwise be inaccessible (Ho, 1998).

Chronic Accessibility

The chronic accessibility of a certain knowledge item refers to the likelihood that the item will be accessed from memory in the long term. A knowledge item gains chronic accessibility through repeated activation (Higgins, King, & Mavin, 1982).

As mentioned in Chapter 4, a broadly distributed cultural knowledge item will be frequently used in everyday interaction (Lau et al., 2001; Lyons & Kashima, 2001, 2003; Sechrist & Stangor, 2001). In addition, a broadly distributed knowledge item is also widely represented in external or public carriers of culture, such the mass media and old sayings (T. Menon & Morris, 2001). The wide representation of the item in the external environment affords plenty of opportunities for the item to be activated, which in turn further increases the item's chronic accessibility. A highly accessible knowledge item is often used as the cognitive default to guide interpretation and action. Indeed, many cross-cultural differences we reviewed in the previous three chapters can be understood in terms of cultural variations in the level of chronic accessibility of the pertinent cultural knowledge. For example, for many North Americans, the independent self has high chronic accessibility and is used as the default self-representation to guide self-processes. Conversely, for many East Asians, the interdependent self has high chronic accessibility and is used as the default self-representation to guide self-processes.

Meet the Researcher: Michael W. Morris

"I have always been intrigued by the ideologies and belief systems that shape people's perceptions. I was born in New York City into a family of Irish-Americans. After a family move upstate to the Catskill Mountains, my formative years were spent wandering the area, engaging in friendly if skeptical dialogue with Hasidim, hippies, and other local subcultures in which such conversations could be held. As a state champion debater in high school, I have always been good at arguing both sides of the question.

After several colleges, I found the pluralism, humor, and fun I was seeking at Brown University, where I studied literature and cognitive science. Wanting to connect culture and cognition, I headed to Michigan to study social psychology in the late 80s. I had the good fortune there to find the cultural psychology that was coalescing in the work of professors such as Richard Nisbett and Hazel Markus.

Among the fellow students I shared ideas with in those days were Kaiping Peng and Shinobu Kitayama. I have felt very fortunate in those days and since to befriend many likeminded psychologists from Asia, who've crossed greater distances than I have. Whatever insight my surveys and experiments have brought, they pale next to the insights that have come from the process of dialogue and collaboration with fellow travelers from different cultures."

Michael W. Morris is Professor of Management and Professor of Psychology at Columbia University.

Temporary Accessibility

Contextual cues may temporarily increase the accessibility of a knowledge item, and momentarily raise the likelihood of applying this knowledge item. In Chapter 6, we have described how priming an independent or interdependent self-representation calls out its associated cognitive and behavioral responses. Recently, researchers have applied the principle of temporary accessibility to illuminate the process of *cultural frame switching* (Hong, Morris, Chiu, & Benet-Martinez, 2000).

Flexible switching of cultural frames is an experience familiar to people with multicultural background. When individuals have extensive experiences with more than one culture, they have at their disposal knowledge they have acquired from different cultures, and can flexibly switch between cultural frames in response to the changing demands of the environment.

What Susanna Harrington, a multicultural informant of South American origin in an ethnographic study, said illustrates this point:

> I think of myself not as a unified cultural being but as a communion of different cultural beings. Due to the fact that I have spent time in different cultural environments I have developed several cultural identities that diverge and converge according to the need of the moment. (Sparrow, 2000, p. 190)

Margaret Earle reported the first known experimental demonstration of cultural frame switching in 1969. In this study, she had Chinese–English bilinguals in Hong Kong respond to a measure of dogmatism either in its original English version or in a Chinese translation of it. Previous research has reported higher levels of dogmatism among Asian students than British and American students (Meade & Whittaker, 1967). Earle found that her bilingual participants scored higher on dogmatism when they answered the Chinese questionnaire than when they completed the English one. Earle (1969, p. 23) offered the following interpretation of the results:

> The effect of language in this study could be reflecting a more general effect of cultural differences between a relatively less authoritarian English language culture and a relatively more authoritarian Chinese language culture. It might be that coordinate bilinguals, who have learned their two languages in distinct settings and live in a bicultural environment can maintain two somewhat differently structured belief systems …, reflecting the contexts in which the two languages are acquired and perhaps more generally the two language cultures.

Subsequent studies have provided further evidence for the idea that language can temporarily push bilinguals' responses in one or the other direction. For example, Trafimow et al. (1997) had Chinese–English bilinguals in Hong Kong describe themselves spontaneously in Chinese or English. The participants' self-descriptions contained more references to demographic and social categories and fewer references to personal beliefs, attitudes, and qualities when the self-descriptions were given in Chinese than in English. This finding suggests that bilingual individuals may organize knowledge acquired from two language cultures into separate "cognitive baskets," and select the knowledge from either basket depending on the language being used in the current situation.

In another study (M. Ross, Xun, & Wilson, 2002), China-born students studying in Canada responded to a set of questionnaires written in either Chinese or English. An English-speaking Canadian group was included as a control group. Compared to the bilingual Chinese group who responded to the English version of the questionnaires, and the Canadians, the Chinese bilingual participants who responded to the Chinese version of the questionnaires reported more collectivist qualities of the self, lower self-esteem, a more balanced (vs. predominately positive) mood, a more balanced (vs. predominately favorable) view of the self, and higher endorsement of Chinese values. This finding shows that the use of the Chinese (English) language in a survey could push bilingual respondents responses in the Chinese (Canadian) direction. This finding is also consistent with the anthropological observation that conversations among Japanese wives of Americans in the United States contain more assertive contents when they are conducted in English than in Japanese (Ervin-Tripp, 1964).

Language priming also affects nonverbal behaviors. Compared to North Americans, Venezuelans interact at closer physical distance (Watson, 1970), and Japanese at greater distance (Engebretson & Fullmer, 1970). In one study (Sussman & Rosenfeld, 1982), Venezuelans and Japanese had conversations with another member of their culture on their favorite sports and hobbies. Some were induced to hold the conversation in their native language, and some in English. When the conversation was conducted in their respective native language, Japanese sat farther away from their interaction partner than did Venezuelans. However, when the conversation was conducted in English, Japanese shortened their conversation distance (relative to their peers conversing in the Japanese language), and Venezuelans increased the distance (relative to their peers conversing in the Venezuelan language).

At the start of this chapter, we describe how cultural icons embody widely shared cultural meanings. Moreover, the cultural meanings embodied in a cultural icon can be readily decoded from the icon. Accordingly, the presentation of cultural icons can easily call out their associated cultural knowledge, rendering this knowledge highly accessible.

Recall that compared to American students, Chinese students have a greater tendency to attribute an event to external causes (Chapter 6). For example, Chinese students are more likely than American students to interpret a fish's swimming ahead of other fish as a result of external causes (e.g., it is being chased by other fish). In a series of studies, Westernized Hong Kong Chinese undergraduates were primed with either Chinese cultural icons (e.g., the Chinese dragon) or American cultural icons (e.g., Mickey Mouse) before they explained why in a picture a fish was swimming in front of other fish. The participants assimilated their responses into the primed culture (Hong, Chiu, & Kung, 1997; Hong et al., 2000). When primed with Chinese (vs. American) cultural icons, these bicultural individuals made more external attributions (Figure 8.3).

FIGURE 8.3. A building in Chinatown, Chicago: One can easily find icons of heritage cultures in ethnic neighborhoods. These icons activate knowledge of the heritage culture, and help to maintain the accessibility of the heritage cultural tradition and identity in the ethnic communities.

Verkuyten and Pouliasi (2002) used a similar priming technique to study children of Greek descent living in The Netherlands (Greek–Dutch biculturals). First, the investigators showed that compared to Dutch children living in The Netherlands, Greek children living in Greece use more external reasons to explain behaviors, value family integrity and obedience more, and have stronger identification with friends and more favorable evaluation of the group. Next, they primed one group of Greek–Dutch bicultural children with icons of Greek culture (e.g., the Acropolis) and another group with icons of Dutch culture (e.g., a windmill). Following this, all bicultural children completed measures of causal attribution, cultural values, and identification. Again, the children's responses assimilated into the primed cultural icons. Children primed with Greek (vs. Dutch) icons made more external attributions, identified more strongly with friends, valued family integrity and obedience more, and evaluated their group more favorably.

Culture priming studies have important implications for the study of cultural processes. First, in most cross-cultural studies, two or more cultural groups are compared. Group differences are interpreted as cultural differences or differences in cultural knowledge traditions. However, unless the groups being compared are matched on all pertinent variables (e.g., age, income, gender distribution), the observed group differences in a cross-cultural study may result from group differences that have little to do with culture. Because of logistic problems, researchers often find it difficult to match their cultural samples on all relevant characteristics. In a culture priming study, bicultural individuals are *randomly* assigned to one of the priming conditions. As a result, researchers can confidently eliminate alternative explanations and conclude that cultural traditions contribute to differences in behaviors (Hong et al., 2000).

Second, the findings from culture-priming studies underscore the dynamic nature of cultural processes. Although widely distributed cultural ideas provide the default premises for sense making, they do not rigidly determine an individual's behavior. Individuals may gain access to other cultural knowledge traditions, and switch cultural frames flexibly to meet the demand of the environment.

Applicability

The principle of applicability further highlights the adaptive nature of cultural processes. Individuals do not passively respond to environmental cues. A cultural cue may increase the temporary accessibility of its associated cultural knowledge. However, the activated knowledge may or may not be applied. According to the principle of applicability, the likelihood that a knowledge item will be applied depends on its applicability in the immediate context. Knowledge applicability is defined in terms of the extent of mapping between "the features of a stored construct and the attended features of a stimulus" (Higgins & Brendl, 1995, p. 220).

For example, when explaining why a fish swims in front of other fish, individuals may attribute the fish's behavior to something about the fish (e.g., the fish wants to get the food first—an individual agency explanation), or something about the remaining fish (e.g., other fish want to catch the fish in the front—a group agency explanation). As mentioned in Chapter 6, the individual agency model is more widely distributed in North American societies than in Asian societies, and the reverse is true for the group agency model. However, for the individual vs. group agency to be applicable, the perceiver must first interpret the current behavior in terms of individual–group relations.

In a series of culture priming experiments, Hong, Benet-Martinez, Chiu, and Morris (2003) found that among Chinese–American bicultural individuals, culture priming affects the likelihood of making group attribution or individual attribution only when the tension between group agency and individual agency in the stimulus event is highlighted, rendering the individual vs. group agency models applicable in the judgment task. For example, presentation of Chinese cultural icons pushes the participants to favor a group agency explanation only when the lead fish has a different color than the remaining fish. In this condition, the color difference highlights the contrast between the individual fish and the group, rendering the group agency model applicable. However, the Chinese culture primes had no effect on participants' attributions when all the fish had the same color.

Recall that the in-group–out-group distinction is more heavily emphasized in Chinese societies than in American societies (Chapter 7). In Chinese societies, individuals are expected to be cooperative with their friends. However, there is no normative expectation for Chinese individuals to be cooperative with strangers. In other words, in Chinese societies, the norm of cooperation applies to friendship but not to interactions with strangers. In one study, Wong and Hong (2005) had highly Westernized Hong Kong Chinese participate in a mixed motive game either with their friends or with some strangers. In a mixed motive game, the player can choose to cooperate or compete with the co-participant. If both players choose to cooperate, both sides will score points, and the joint outcome is maximized. If both players choose to be competitive, both sides lose points. If one player chooses to be cooperative and one player chooses to be competitive, the competitive player will score points, and the cooperative player will lose points. In this case, the competitive partner's personal outcome is maximized. Therefore, in this game, there are incentives for both cooperation and competition.

Prior to playing the game, the participants were presented with either Chinese or American cultural icons. Consistent with the principle of applicability, participants primed with Chinese (vs. American) cultural icons made more cooperative choices when the other player was a friend, but not when the other player was a stranger.

Motivation and Cognitive Load

In Chapter 4, we maintain that cultural knowledge may be conceived of as a collection of chronically accessible cognitive tools (DiMaggio, 1997), and review some evidence that people are more likely to apply cultural knowledge when the need for epistemic security, or the need to belong is salient in the situation. For example, East–West differences in decision-making and choice of negotiation strategies are particularly pronounced when people need to justify their decisions to their cultural group (Briley et al., 2000; Gelfand & Realo, 1999), or when people need certain answers (C. Chiu et al., 2000).

People also tend to rely on readily accessible cultural knowledge when they lack cognitive resources, because cultural knowledge can provide cognitively busy people with a decision shortcut or judgment heuristic. Findings from a study (Knowles et al., 2001) support this idea. Recall that compared to Chinese, European Americans have a greater tendency to commit the fundamental attribution error, attributing a behavior to a dispositional cause even when there is a convincing situational explanation. In this study, European American and Chinese judged whether an essay a student wrote under the direction of a professor reflected the student's attitudes. Some participants needed to engage in a cognitively demanding task while processing the essay, and the remaining participants did not. The cognitively busy European Americans showed a stronger dispositional bias in their judgment than did the cognitively busy Chinese. However, when the participants were not under heavy cognitive load, this cultural difference was significantly attenuated.

Self and Contrast Effect

People who are primed with a social category tend to assimilate their response into the primed category. For example, university students walk more slowly than they normally do after they have been primed with the "elderly" stereotype (Bargh, Chen, & Burrows, 1996). However, activation of social stereotypes can also result in automatic behavioral contrast if a comparison of the self to the stereotyped group is provoked. For example, when university undergraduates are primed with the self and the elderly stereotype, a comparison intention is activated. They feel that they do not belong to the elderly category and display a behavioral contrast (Dijksterhuis et al., 1998; Dijksterhuis, Spears, & Lepinasse, 2001; Schubert & Hafner, 2003; Spears, Gordijn, Dijksterhuis, & Stapel, 2004).

As noted, priming a culture often leads to assimilative responses. However, if the participants feel that they do not belong to the primed culture, culture priming may lead to contrastive responses. Bond and his colleagues have reported contrast effects in a study that used languages as culture primes. In this study (K. Yang & Bond, 1980), Chinese–English bilingual participants responded to a Chinese value survey. They showed stronger adherence to Chinese values when the survey was in English than in Chinese. It seems possible that the presence of an out-group language (English) reminded the participants that they did not belong to the primed cultural group. As a consequence, a contrast effect was found.

However, this finding is difficult to interpret because when the Chinese values are translated from Chinese into English, their evaluative meanings may change: Some Chinese values may have more positive connotations in Chinese than in English, and some may have more positive connotations in English than in Chinese. The findings in the Yang and Bond (1980) study are likely to have resulted from this translation problem (Marin, Triandis, Betancourt, & Kashima, 1983). This problem was addressed in another study (Bond & Cheung, 1984), in which Cantonese-speaking Hong Kong Chinese undergraduates filled out the same survey of traditional Chinese beliefs. Some participants received oral instructions in Putonghua (the official spoken language in Mainland China), while the remaining participants received oral instructions in Cantonese (a dialect used in Hong Kong). Mainland Chinese are generally seen as more traditional than Hong Kong Chinese (Hong, Chiu, Yeung, & Tong, 1999; Lam, Lau, Chiu, Hong, & Peng, 1999), and most Hong Kong Chinese have more favorable evaluation of Hong Kong people than of Mainland Chinese (Ho, Chau, Chiu, & Peng, 2003; Tong, Hong, Lee, & Chiu, 1999). Thus, in the presence of a Putonghua-speaking experimenter, the Hong Kong participants might have a heightened motivation to distinguish themselves from the Mainlanders. As expected, participants who received oral instructions in Putonghua disagreed more with the traditional Chinese beliefs, compared to those who received instructions in Cantonese.

Some Chinese Americans view their dual cultural identities as oppositional (e.g., I cannot be both a Chinese and an American at the same time), while others see them as independent or complementary (e.g., I am both a Chinese and an American) (Benet-Martinez, Leu, Lee, & Morris, 2002; Tsai, Ying, & Lee, 2000). Variations in how dual identities are managed are related to bicultural individuals' responses to culture priming. Those who view their dual identities as independent or complementary can flexibly switch between cultural frames. When they are primed with Chinese (vs. American) cultural icons, they make more external attributions. Conversely, those who view their dual identities as oppositional may feel ambivalent about either cultural identity. The presence of an American cultural icon may make them feel that they are not a full member of American culture. Likewise, the presence of a Chinese cultural icon may make them feel that they are not a full member of Chinese culture. Thus, they may respond reactively to the cultural primes, displaying contrastive responses (Benet-Martinez et al., 2002).

In summary, cultural differences emerge from the activation of specific cultural knowledge in concrete situations and from the psychological implications of the activated knowledge. Activation of cultural knowledge follows basic principles of knowledge activation, which govern the nature of the dynamic interactions between cultural knowledge, the situation, the individuals' current cognitive and motivational states, and cultural identities.

Conclusion

In this chapter, we have discussed the importance of considering the inter-connection and interaction of different kinds of cultural knowledge. We also describe the basic cognitive principles that govern the application of cultural knowledge in concrete situations. The research reviewed in the current chapter highlights a few important points. First, to understand a cultural community, it is not enough to assess how widely a particular knowledge item is distributed in the community. It is also important to examine how the different cultural knowledge items are connected and how they interact to influence behaviors.

Second, cultural processes are dynamic and context-dependent. Knowing that a particular cultural idea is widely distributed in a cultural community is not enough to predict whether an individual in the community will apply that item in a concrete situation. Predictions of this kind can be made only when the following factors are also considered: (1) the context-specific meaning of the knowledge item, (2) the presenting cultural cue in the immediate environment, (3) the applicability of the knowledge item to the current behavioral context, (4) the individual's cognitive and motivational state, and (5) how the individual defines his or her cultural identity.

Indeed, this perspective can explain several important findings we describe in the previous chapters. First, older children have a greater tendency than younger children to display culture-characteristic cognitive patterns (J. Miller, 1984; Chapter 6). This may result from a developmental shift in chronic accessibility of the knowledge items that support the culture-characteristic cognitive patterns. Older children have more experiences in applying a cultural knowledge item than do younger ones. Thus, the item is more accessible to older children than to younger children.

Second, members from a particular national group may change their behaviors when they are relocated to a new cultural environment. For example, North American students attend more to the context after they have lived in Japan for several months (Kitayama et al., 2003). This behavioral shift may result from the increased chronic accessibility of context-sensitive cognitive strategies following repeated applications of these strategies in Japan.

Third, a culture-characteristic behavior is observed only when its supporting knowledge item is applicable to the situation. For example, the preference for nonconfrontational conflict resolution strategies in Chinese societies is limited largely to in-group contexts (see Chapter 7). As another example, in Chapter 6, we reviewed evidence showing that East Asians are sensitive to others' perspective in making personal decisions. Although this tendency is often observed when Asians make social and academic decisions, it is not found when Asians make financial decisions. Apparently, the knowledge item supporting a social orientation in decision-making is not applicable to the financial domain (Fong & Wyer, 2003).

Fourth, a culture-characteristic behavior will be applied only when its supporting knowledge item is activated, either because that item has a high level of chronic accessibility, or is called out by transitory situational cues. The point is richly illustrated in self-representation priming studies reviewed in Chapter 6 and the culture priming studies reviewed in the current chapter.

Finally, the distribution and interrelationship of cultural knowledge in a cultural group may change over time, as the society develops (see Chapter 4). How culture changes over time is important topic of its own, and deserves a separate chapter (Chapter 9).

Reproduction of Culture and Cultural Change 9

▶ *Contents at a Glance*

Cultural Change across the Globe

In Chapter 8, we described the critical importance of the value of egalitarianism in China's economic policies in the late 1950s. The philosophy of "no worry about poverty but about inequality," which was handed down in history, had led to a strong sense of animosity toward the wealthy people in China's history. Interestingly, in mid-November 2002, at the 16th National Congress of the Communist Party of China, the Communist leaders openly denounced egalitarianism and hailed entrepreneurship, making the world wonder: How Communist is Communist China?

On January 20, 2003, an article entitled "Chinese Bid Farewell to Outgrown Doctrine of Egalitarianism" was published in *Beijing Times*, featuring Nan Cunhui (a local magnate) and Miao Shouliang (a real estate tycoon), both of whom recently made it to the Forbes List of the 100 richest Chinese people. These two middle-aged entrepreneurs have become a role model and a source of pride to people in their hometown, according to the article.

At about the same time, *The Nation (Thailand)* ran an article entitled "Need Is Apparent for a Thai–Western Cultural Synergy." The article reported an interview with Chawana Phawaganun, an associate professor of journalism who studied the behavioral and cultural changes in Thailand. During the interview, Professor Phawaganun made the following remarks:

> I don't mind the influx of pop culture. We can't stop that, but we can create a defensive plan in which the cultures can complement each other. For instance, Thongchai McIntyre's latest album (For Fan) is a great mix of the Thai dialect with Western melody.

However, the professor is critical of other Western influences. For example, on fashion shows, he holds the following opinion:

> The fashion show is a fine activity because it builds their [young girls'] confidence. However, if wearing two-piece bathing suits has become common practice among young girls, it means they are no longer aware of our conservative culture.

He believes that the Thai Government should be more focused on creating a unique Thai character, one that integrates the elements of Buddhism and selective pop culture. For example, he is in favor of having fashion competitions involving Thai characteristics in which Thai national dress is predominant, and TV commercials that showcase aspects of Thai art.

The year 2003 also offered Iraq, under US domination, an opportunity to practice Western-style democracy. On May 11, 2003, a story with the headline "Exiled Iraqi Ayatollah Returns, Rejects Western Democracy: Shiite Cleric Calls for Elected Gov't Representative of All" appeared in the *New York Times*. According to the article, the cleric, Ayatollah Muhammad Bakr al-Hakim, said, "Iraq must base its laws on Islamic structures and prohibit the kind of behavior that may be acceptable in the West but is allegedly forbidden under Islam."

Two lessons can be learned from these stories. First, large-scale cultural changes are happening throughout the world. Second, people can have different reactions to cultural changes. Some people embrace the changes, some seek to synthesize new cultural elements with traditional ones, and some categorically reject new cultural elements. Analysis of the social psychological processes that mediate support for or resistance to cultural change is a topic that should have a pivotal role in the social psychology of culture. Unfortunately, this is also one of the most seriously neglected research topics in psychological research (Lehman, Chiu, & Schaller, 2004).

Culture changes, but culture is also constantly being reproduced. We divide the current chapter into two parts, with the first part focusing on reproduction and maintenance of conventional culture, and the second part on cultural change.

Media of Cultural Transmission

In evolutionary theory (see Chapter 4), a cultural idea (or meme) is reproduced when it moves from one host to another. Some cultural ideas (such as those that encourage their hosts to tell them to others, or those that encourage preservation of the organisms) are more transmittable than others (Lynch, 1996). In addition, ideas that evoke a strong emotional bond between people are also very competitive in the social market place of cultural ideas (Heath et al., 2001; Sinaceur et al., in press).

Transmission of cultural ideas can take two paths. Specifically, an idea can be transmitted directly from one host to another. Direct transmission often occurs in interpersonal communication, parent–child interaction, and teacher–student interaction. Alternatively, an idea can be transmitted through an intermediate medium between one host and others. For example, writers (like us) encode their ideas in a book (an intermediate medium), with the goal of transmitting them to the readers. Writing a book is an example of making a *deliberate* attempt to transmit ideas through an external medium. However, oftentimes the transmission process is much less deliberate. Indeed, most media, institutions, and practices in everyday life are suffused with conventional ideas. In the previous chapters, we have illustrated how dominant cultural ideas are encoded in the news, fairy tales, urban legends, personal space, architecture, art, and cultural icons. As people expose themselves to the popular media or participate in the prevailing institutions and practices, they may unwittingly acquire the embedded cultural ideas. We will discuss both paths to cultural transmission, beginning with transmission of conventional ideas via direct communication.

Cultural Transmission via Direct Communication

Parent–Child Interaction

Parents play a pivotal role in integrating children into their culture. Not surprisingly, the role of parental practices in socialization is the most extensively studied mechanism of direct cultural transmission. A thorough review of this literature is beyond the scope of the current chapter. Instead, we use two research examples to illustrate how cultural variation in parental practices may lead to the development of divergent behaviors in children from different cultures.

Children are able to tell stories about themselves in conversation from a remarkably young age, and researchers are interested in how young children's storytelling reveals how children are socialized into their culture. To address this issue, Peggy Miller and her colleagues videotaped family conversations in American Midwest and Taipei families and analyzed how young children in these families spontaneously narrated their personal stories. In an earlier study (P. Miller, Fung, & Mintz, 1996), it was found that 2.5-year-olds in Taiwan were much more likely than their same age European American counterparts to mention past transgression in their personal stories. In addition, in Taiwan, the parent, who played the role of a co-narrator, often invoked moral and social rules repeatedly so as to feature the child's transgression as the point of the story. By comparison, mentioning of the child's past transgression was very infrequent in European American children's personal stories. The practice of invoking moral and social rules is also very rare among European American parents. When a past transgression was mentioned in the child's personal story, European American parents tended to downplay the child's wrongdoing. Apparently, whereas Taiwanese parents encourage the child to use a self-critical interpretive framework to construct personal stories, European American parents encourage the child to use a self-affirmative interpretive framework.

A subsequent study (P. Miller, Wiley, Fung, & Liang, 1997) reveals that in the co-narration of the child's past transgression, Taiwanese parents sometimes ended the story with a didactic coda in which the present or future implications of a rule or rule violation were explicitly stated. Two examples of such didactic codas are:

Mother: Do you still want to go there again?
Child: Next time I don't do it again.

———

Mother: Saying dirty words is not good.
Child: Wooooo.
Mother: Is that right? Saying dirty words is not good.

The purpose of ending the story with a didactic coda is to ensure that the child understands the rule, will learn from the negative consequences of the transgression, and will follow the rule in the future.

Meet the Researcher: Peggy J. Miller

"I am a developmental psychologist by training and a cultural psychologist by inclination. As a graduate student with an interest in language and social class, I realized that much of the existing research embodied powerful negative stereotypes of working-class children and their families. This left a lasting impression on me and helped to fuel my commitment to create a more culture-sensitive understanding of human development. At the most basic level, what is at stake, I believe, is our ability to imagine one another across the perilous categories of class, gender, culture, and so on. Ironically, one of the surprises of my initial foray, many years ago, into the study of working-class children's language was the discovery that they and their families were prodigious storytellers. They put narrative in neon lights for me, and that illumination led me eventually to Taipei, Chicago, Salt Lake City and other sites where stories abound."

Peggy J. Miller was born and raised in rural Pennsylvania. She received her M.A. and Ph.D. in developmental psychology at Teachers College, Columbia University, and is a Professor at the University of Illinois at Urbana-Champaign.

Another example concerns the use of praise to shape children's behavior. Praise is usually defined as "positive evaluations made by a person of another's products, performance, or attributes, where the evaluator presumes the validity of the standards on which the evaluation is based" (Kanouse, Gumpert, & Canavan-Gumpert, 1981, p. 98). In the United States, popular parenting experts typically urge parents to avoid "over-controlling" practices that assert parents' own desires, goals, and emotions in an attempt to mold their children. In European American families, parents would praise a child after the child has displayed self-initiated desirable behaviors. In one study (Y. Wang, Wiley, & Chiu, in press), the investigators observed parent–child interactions during dinnertime in 23 European American families and 22 first generation Chinese immigrant families in the United States, and identified all episodes that involved parental praise. All these families have at least one 2.5–5.5-year-old child. As expected, in European American families, most praise episodes (70.9%) involved praising the child after the child has initiated a desirable behavior. The remaining praise episodes (28.5%) involved praising a child for adherence to parental expectations. Rarely would a European American parent praise a child before a desirable behavior was displayed.

By contrast, praise following self-initiated positive behavior was much more infrequent in Chinese immigrant families. Only 46.1% of the episodes fall into this category. Many episodes (37.1%) involved praising the child for following parental expectations. Interestingly, in 16.9% of the praise episodes in Chinese immigrant families, the parents first communicated their expectation to the child, and then used praise as a means to elicit the desirable behavior. A representative episode of this type is as follows:

[Child and parents are standing near the table]

Father: Sit down! Sit down! [Indicating a chair facing the camera to the child]
Mother: We need to eat now.
Child: I want to sit there. [Pointing to a different chair]
Father: Where?
Child: There!
Mother: Why? Just sit here. [Pointing to the first chair]
Child: I want to sit there! [Insisting on own choice, still standing]
Mother: Why? No, you need to sit here.
Father: Please just sit here! [Child still standing] You are a good boy. Good boy.
Mother: Yeah, good boy.

(Finally, the child sat where the parents asked him to sit, and the interactions went on smoothly.)

In short, to most European Americans, praising children's desirable behaviors to foster their autonomy and self-competence is a common practice. In contrast, in many Chinese immigrant families, praise is a means to foster adherence to parental expectations. The episode presented above may seem strange and controlling to European American parents. Nonetheless, episodes of this kind are not uncommon in Chinese immigrant families. Both European American and Chinese immigrant parents may not be consciously aware that they are performing the role of socialization agents. Despite this, how they interact with their children naturally adheres to the parenting scripts widely distributed in their culture. The execution of these scripts is instrumental in bringing children's behaviors in alignment with the cultural expectations for independence and interdependence in European American and Chinese immigrant contexts.

Communication Practices

Yoshi Kashima (Y. Kashima, 2000b; Lyons & Kashima, 2001) examined the role of interpersonal communication in the reproduction of conventional knowledge. In several studies, he presented stories that contained both stereotype consistent and stereotype inconsistent information to the participant, and had them relay the stories to another participant. As the stories were being reproduced in a serial chain, some information was retained and some was lost. Interestingly, information that was inconsistent with cultural stereotypes was retained proportionately more than consistent information at the beginning of the chain. However, as the chain of reproductions continued, inconsistent information began to drop off drastically, leaving the consistent information to dominate the last reproductions. In addition, compared to individuals who use stereotype-inconsistent information when describing others, those who use stereotype-consistent information are perceived to be similar to the self (Castelli, Arcuri, & Zogmaister, 2003).

Aside from dyadic communication, group discussion may also reproduce and reinforce stereotypes and conventional knowledge. In one study (Brauer, Judd, & Jacquelin, 2001), participants were randomly assigned to groups of three. Each group member received a different set of stereotypic and counter-stereotypic behavioral information about a group of young adolescents in a youth camp, and was asked to rate their impression of the group. Some groups had a chance to discuss their impressions before rendering their judgments, and some did not. The results showed that discussion led to more stereotypical impressions of the target group.

One explanation for the collective reproduction of stereotypic information focuses on interpersonal communication. In order to present a coherent narrative to the next person, the communicators may prefer to include information that they believe the audience will understand and accept (see below). Stereotypic information, which presumably is widely shared in the culture, has an advantage over stereotype inconsistent information in this regard, and hence is more likely to be kept in the narrative. In short, interpersonal communication has an important role to play in the maintenance of cultural stereotypes.

Cultural Transmission via Intermediate Media

As emphasized in Chapter 3, culture is a cumulative process. Partly because humans store their knowledge in external memory devices (e.g., pictures, books, computer hard drives, DVDs, and the Internet), human cultures accumulate and develop at much a faster pace than do ape cultures (Donald, 1993). Some external memory devices are particularly effective means for distributing knowledge, either because they can broadcast ideas to mass audiences at low costs (e.g., TV commercials), or because they allow multiple users to retrieve information simultaneously (e.g., the Internet).

Architecture

Architecture is an important part of the human-made environment, and is therefore an integral component of human culture. Additionally, it is a major carrier of culture. We have already described in other chapters research that connects architecture to reproduction of culture. For example, in Chapter 6, we introduce Francis Hsu's (1981) analysis of the architecture of a typical North American home and a typical traditional Chinese home. Hsu's analysis highlights how a typical North American home is set up to reinforce distinction between the self and others. It also illustrates how a typical traditional Chinese home embodies the dominant Chinese conception of in-group–out-group relationship (Figure 9.1).

Similarly in Chapter 5, we describe how imagining oneself in a typical Japanese city scene may draw one's attention to the context rather than

(a)

(b)

(c)

FIGURE 9.1. Architecture is suffused with cultural meanings. In a Western garden (a), discrete objects stand out prominently from the background and are featured as points of interest (Warsaw, Poland). In a Chinese garden (b), objects blend in completely with the background (Portland, Oregon). The architecture in this Indian garden at Amber Fort reflects the importance of symmetry and balance in Muslim culture (c).

objects in the foreground. Likewise, imagining oneself in a typical American city scene may draw one's attention to the objects in the foreground (vs. information in the background; Miyamoto et al. (2006)).

Legal Institution

As mentioned in Chapter 4, culture evolved as a solution to increasingly complex coordination problems in human societies (Heylighen & Campbell, 1995). The legal institution is a coordination device established for regulating individual behaviors in groups. Accordingly, the law embodies the dominant conception of what constitutes a functional society. Cohen's (1996) analysis of the culture of honor in the American South richly illustrates how the law in the South supports the culture of honor by sanctioning the use of violence for self-protection. We have also discussed how the concept of *yuan zuo* in traditional Chinese law enforces collective responsibility for the behavior of an individual in a group (C. Chiu & Hong, 1992, Chapter 7).

Mass Media and Popular Culture

Cultural knowledge is also instantiated in the mass media and popular culture, as illustrated in many research examples described in the previous chapters. For example, Cohen and Nisbett (1997; Chapter 7) showed that reporters of college newspapers in the American South, compared with those in the American North, are more likely to express sympathy to a violent crime committed to protect one's honor.

Fiona Lee et al. (1996; Chapter 6) compared sports articles in Hong Kong and US newspapers and found that more dispositional inferences were mentioned in Hong Kong sports articles than in US sports articles. Similarly, Morris and Peng (1994; Chapter 6) analyzed the coverage of two murder cases in an English newspaper and a Chinese language newspaper in the United States, and found more dispositional attributions in English newspaper articles than in Chinese newspaper articles. Both studies support the idea that dispositional representations of persons are more widely distributed in US news media than in Chinese news media. It has also been found that in the news coverage of American and Japanese scandals, Japanese newspapers referred more to properties of the organization than to the individual, whereas the reverse ordering held in American newspapers (T. Menon et al., 1999). This finding shows that in US news media, the notion of individuals as causal agents is more prominent than the notion of groups as causal agents, and the reverse is true in Japanese news media.

In another study (Hallahan et al., 1997), sports news articles in Hong Kong and the United States were analyzed. Compared to Hong Kong news articles, American news articles are more likely to mention internal causes when reporting on the winning teams. Conversely, compared to US news articles, Hong Kong news articles are more likely to mention external causes when reporting on the losing teams. This finding suggests that showcasing the merits of the winning teams is more emphasized in American sports news, whereas protecting the losing teams from losing face is more emphasized in Hong Kong sports news (see Chapter 6)

Aside from news reports, dominant cultural ideas are also widely represented in other media. For instance, Rothbaum and Tsang (1998) compared the lyrics of Chinese and American love songs, and found that although songs from the two countries do not differ in the intensity of expressed desire, compared to American love songs, Chinese love songs more often mention sufferings, and describe love as being embedded within a larger context (e.g., natural world, extended time). This finding is consistent with the Chinese implicit theory of change, which conceptualizes change in terms of harmonization of contradictory forces (love and suffering, see Chapter 7), and the emphasis on contextual meanings in Chinese culture (see Chapter 5).

Rothbaum and Xu (1995) also compared Chinese and American songs with words related to parents in them. Consistent with the emphasis on filial piety (Chapter 2) in Chinese culture, almost all Chinese songs included in this analysis mentioned giving back to parents. By comparison, the majority of American songs conveyed dissatisfaction, indifference or anger toward parents.

Print and television advertisements contain messages targeting mass audiences in the culture. As such, recurrent themes in a country's advertisements may reflect what is believed to be the dominant values in the country. A cross-cultural study of magazine advertisements reveals that advertisements in Korean magazines use appeals to conformity more frequently and appeals to uniqueness less frequently than do advertisements in American magazines (H. Kim & Markus, 1999). Similarly, Han and Shavitt (1994) reported that American advertisements are more likely to employ appeals to individual benefits and preferences, personal success, and independence, whereas Korean advertisements are more likely to employ appeals to in-group benefits, harmony, and family integrity. This is particularly the case for advertisements for products used with others (vs. products for personal consumption only).

As mentioned in Chapter 6, European American culture privileges the independent self, whereas East Asian culture privileges the interdependent self. Several studies have directly linked the recurrent themes in a culture's advertisements to the dominant self-representations of individuals in the culture. In one study, Han and Shavitt (1994) found that compared to American participants, Korean participants found collectivist appeals to be more persuasive and individualist appeals less persuasive. Again, the effect was more pronounced for products used with others. In another study (Aaker & Schmitt, 2001, Study 1), Chinese rated a product that promotes similarity to the group more favorably and a product that promotes differentiation of the self from the group less favorably, compared to European Americans. Finally, Chinese Americans also remember consumer choices that differentiate a person from the group better than those that make an individual similar to the group, and European Americans display the opposite pattern (Aaker & Schmitt, 2001, Study 2). This is the case probably because for Chinese Americans, making choices that set the self apart from others is an unusual and hence relatively memorable experience. Likewise, for European Americans, making choices that make oneself similar to the group is an unfamiliar and hence more memorable experience.

Cultural Icons and Role Models

In Chapter 8, we have described how cultural icons represent shared knowledge in a culture, and how presentation of cultural icons may activate their associated cultural meanings and affect subsequent responses that range from self-construal to casual attribution and cooperative behavior (Hong et al., 1997, 2000, 2003; Wong & Hong 2005; Verkuyten & Pouliasi, 2002).

Role models represent a specific type of cultural icons. A role model could be an individual who has achieved outstanding success (a positive role model), or an individual who has experienced some misfortune or some kind of failure (a negative role model) when pursuing socially desirable goals (Lockwood, Marshall, & Sadler, 2005). Both positive and negative role models can motivate individuals in the culture. While a positive role model motivates individuals to pursue similar excellence, a negative role model motivates individuals to learn from the role model's mistakes and from the role model's persistence in pursuing socially desirable goals in the face of setbacks.

Role models can be a real person (e.g., Abraham Lincoln, Mahatma Gandhi) or fictional figures. In both cases, the public representations of role models are idealized legendary figures that embody certain highly valued virtues in the culture. For example, Martin Luther King is a real person who exemplifies the values of liberty and equality, and Kuo Chi in *Twenty-Four Paragons of Filial Piety* (Chapter 2) is a legendary figure that exemplifies the virtue of filial piety in Chinese culture.

While the recurrent messages in the mass media represent cultural ideas that are widely distributed in the society, and the law represents the society's consensus on what behaviors should be sanctioned, role models represent cultural ideals, which may or may not be attainable. For example, most Chinese role models included in grade school textbooks in Hong Kong exemplify moral values possessed by an ideal person in the Confucian tradition (e.g., righteousness, filial piety, and self-sacrifice). Most Chinese role models of Hong Kong undergraduates spontaneously retrieved from memory also exemplify these values (Fu & Chiu, 2004). Some role models have authority over most individuals in the culture (e.g., Jesus in Christian culture), while others' authority is largely limited to a subset of people in the culture (e.g., David Beckham in England's teenage culture).

Elitists and the government often use role models to represent their conception of an ideal society. One well-known example is the "Learn from Lei Feng" campaign in China. The campaign began in 1963. According to the most widely circulated version of Lei Feng's biography, Lei was born in 1940. His parents were poor peasants. The Japanese killed his father during the Japanese occupation, and his mother committed suicide after a landlord's son sexually harassed her. Lei grew up as an orphan under the care of the Chinese Communist Party, joined the People's Liberation Army, and became a party member. In short, Lei's demographic profile matches that of an idealized Communist: offspring from a humble peasant family and a victim of imperialism and feudalism.

Lei lived a life of extreme frugality, and devoted himself to performing many good deeds: He sent his savings to help the needy parents of a fellow soldier, served tea and food to officers and recruits, and washed his buddies' feet after a long march. In August 1962, Lei was killed in an accident when a truck knocked down a pole that fell on him. However, this ending does not match Lei's martyr-like character. In the most widely circulated urban myth, Lei was said to have been electrocuted while he was helping to raise a power line in the countryside.

To the extent that role models are cultural products, people with different cultural backgrounds may respond differently to different types of models. Recall that in Asian Canadian contexts, there is a heavy emphasis on learning from one's mistakes (White & Lehman, 2005, see Chapter 8). Some recent studies have sought to link role model emulation to the self-improvement motivation in Asian Canadian contexts. In one study (Lockwood et al., 2005, Study 1), Asian Canadian undergraduates perceived negative role models to be as motivating as positive role models. In another study (Lockwood et al., 2005, Study 2), Asian Canadian students rated negative role models as more motivating than positive ones. In both studies, European Canadian undergraduates rated positive role models to be more motivating than negative ones. Additionally, in both studies, compared to European Canadian undergraduates, Asian Canadian undergraduates perceived negative role models to be more motivating. In short, it seems that Asian Canadians are more motivated to learn from the mistakes of negative role models than from the achievements of positive role models, whereas the reverse is true for European Canadians.

Language

Language is another carrier of cultural knowledge. In Chapter 8, we review several studies that show how language calls out its associated cultural knowledge and influences behaviors (Earle, 1969; M. Ross et al., 2002; Sussman & Rosenfeld, 1982; Trafimow et al., 1997). Other studies have shown that the grammar of a language may encode cultural ideas pertinent to self–other relationship. In a series of studies, Emi Kashima (E. Kashima & Kashima, 1998; Y. Kashima & Kashima, 2003) examined how the linguistic system of pronouns may encode conceptions of the social self in the culture. The use of pronouns sustains attention on the referent of the pronoun, bringing the person out from the conversational background. For example, the use of the first-person pronoun (*I* in English) draws attention to the speaker, and maximally distinguishes the speaker's self from the conversational context. Likewise, the use of the second-person pronoun (*you* in English) maximally distinguishes the addressee(s) from the conversational context. In some languages (e.g., English), the use of both first- and second-person pronouns is grammatically obligatory. In other languages (e.g., Spanish), the subject pronoun can be dropped because the referent can be recovered from the verb inflections. There are some languages (e.g., Chinese) in which the subject pronoun can be dropped even though there is neither verb inflection nor the subject–verb agreement rule. The obligatory use of subject pronoun is suggestive of whether the self and the addressee must be made salient in the conversational context, and the omission of either one or both first- and second-person pronouns de-emphasizes the salience of their corresponding referent(s).

To examine the relation between individualism, collectivism, and pronoun use, E. Kashima and Kashima (1998) correlated a cultural–linguistic group's emphasis on individualism/collectivism with the grammatical tolerance for pronoun drop in the group's dominant language. Cultural scores of seventy-six countries from prior major cultural surveys (Hofstede, 1980, 1991) were re-analyzed. Languages spoken in these countries were scored for whether pronoun drop was grammatically licensed. As expected, in countries that have low individualism score, their dominant language has higher tolerance for pronoun drop.

Meet the Researcher: Emiko Kashima

"Language is closely tied to the ways in which we construct our reality, because it influences how we see and describe the relations among objects and express ourselves to others. When using my mother tongue, Japanese, compared with English, which I learned in my adolescence, I remember things and construe experiences in slightly different ways. For example, when speaking in Japanese I may be more subtle, indirect, and recall more about things that are commonly known to Japanese people; for example, its history. Speaking two languages in everyday life is not as much as a problem as it may seem. I enjoy using two languages because they give me a greater choice in expressing my ideas and feelings. In fact, it is said that two-thirds of the world's population today are bilingual or multilingual, so a majority of the people in the world live using multiple languages. I think this is wonderful because it suggests that personal stories, thoughts, and shared memories originated from one culture can be translated and shared by people from diverse backgrounds. People can then recognize many similarities that are shared within humanity as well as appreciating many cultural differences."

Emiko Kashima was born in Tokyo, Japan, and received her Ph.D. from the University of Illinois at Urbana-Champaign. She currently teaches at La Trobe University in Melbourne, Australia.

Language is more than a collection of grammatical rules; it is a system for representing thoughts. Indeed, the use of language as a means to represent nonimmediate events is a unique human accomplishment. Based on their pragmatic functions, speech acts can be classified into five major types: directives (e.g., orders, demands, requests), expressives (e.g., *Ouch* or *I love you*), representatives (use of linguistic symbols to represent an immediate, nonimmediate, or displaced event), commissives (commitments, promises), and declaratives (e.g., *You're fired*; Austin, 1962; Searle, 1975). Other mammals use directives and expressives extensively, but the use of representatives, commissives, and declaratives is predominantly human (D'Andrade, 2002). Additionally, while other mammals typically use representatives to refer to immediate events only, humans often use representatives to refer to something that is not immediately present (e.g., *In May of 1962, Marilyn Monroe sang Happy Birthday Mr. President at a televised birthday party for President John F. Kennedy*).

Indeed, D'Andrade (2002) believes that as human societies grew in complexity, to coordinate social activities and facilitate division of work, people needed to be able to represent nonimmediate events mentally. This in turn increases the demand for the development of grammar and true symbols (a sign that may refer to different referents) as opposed to indexical signs with rigid one-to-one mapping between a sign and its referent. Thus, the development of human language may be an adaptive response to the need to represent nonimmediate events symbolically.

If language evolved to represent collective experiences, in response to the distinctive input condition in the environment, different human groups may develop a different vocabulary to represent their experiences. Accordingly, the vocabulary in a language may reflect the implicit organization of knowledge evolved from the group's shared experiences. An idea that is widely used in a culture is likely to have a linguistic expression that allows it to be expressed easily, rapidly, briefly and uniformly. Moreover, the use of such economical expression to encode a state of affairs may influence the way the language user processes information pertinent to that state of affairs. In one study, Hoffman, Lau, and Johnson (1986) identified English- and Chinese-language personality adjectives that have no economical equivalent in the other language. For example, there is no single English term equivalent in meaning to the Chinese personality adjective *shì gù*, which depicts a person who, among other things, is worldly, experienced, socially skillful, and somewhat reserved. Likewise, there is no single Chinese adjective for someone who has artistic skills and interests, an "artistic" cognitive style and temperament, and leads a "bohemian" lifestyle. The appropriate English term is *artistic* (or, better, the *artistic type*).

There were three groups of participants in this study: a group of English monolinguals, a group of Chinese-English bilinguals who processed the information in English, and a group of Chinese-English bilinguals who processed the information in Chinese. Participants read a set of concrete behavioral descriptions of four fictitious characters, either in English or in Chinese. Two of the characters exemplified personality schemas with economical labels in Chinese but not in English (the Chinese-specific adjectives) and the other two characters exemplified personality schemas with economical labels in English but not in Chinese (the English-specific adjectives).

When the behavioral descriptions of the two characters exemplifying the personality types with English-specific labels were processed in English, participants' subsequent memory of the original description was biased in the direction of the labels: They tended to infer label-congruent attributes not found in the original descriptions. Similar memory bias was also observed when the behavioral descriptions of the two characters exemplifying the personality types with Chinese-specific labels were processed in Chinese.

Referring expressions particular to a language do not always influence the language user's subsequent representation of the referent of the expressions. However, when a particular referring expression is *used* to describe a state of affairs, an on-line linguistic representation of that state of affairs will be evoked, which in turn biases the referent's memory representation (C. Chiu, Krauss, & Lau, 1998; C. Chiu, Krauss, & Lee, 1999; Fallshore & Schooler, 1995; Schooler & Engstler-Schooler, 1990). Specifically, when the same state of affairs has been encoded in both verbal and visual representational formats, if it is difficult to describe the state of affairs in words, representations in different formats should contain different information. Under such circumstances, the verbal representation may compete with the visual representation when the state of affairs is later recalled, causing a memory distortion in the direction of the linguistic representation. In cognitive psychology, this phenomenon is known as recoding interference (Schooler & Engstler-Schooler, 1990).

Recall that in Chapter 5, we reviewed psychological studies on the availability of basic color terms in different languages, and concluded that speakers of a language that has many basic color terms do not necessarily categorize colors differently from speakers of a language that has only two basic color terms. However, as some other studies (Kay & Kempton, 1984; Roberson et al., 2000) have shown, when the speaker of a language *uses* the color terms in the language to describe colors, the speaker's subsequent memory of the colors may be influenced by the color terms used in the description.

In a cross-language study, Kay and Kempton (1984, Study 1) presented three color chips at a time to native speakers of English and speakers of Tarahumara (a Uto-Aztecan language of northern Mexico), and had them judge the perceptual distance among the stimuli. Unlike English, Tarahumara lacks the lexical distinction between the color categories of "green" and "blue." When the participants' judgments were compared to the physical distance of the stimuli, the English-speaking participants, but not Tarahumara-speaking ones, systematically overestimated the distance between two colors when they were on different sides of the green–blue color boundary. On the surface, this finding seems to suggest that the basic color terms in a language can influence color perception.

However, Kay and Kempton (1984) believe that the English-speaking participants might have used a naming strategy when they were performing the judgment task. For instance, when presented with two colors that fell in the green category and one color that fell in the blue category, they might have labeled the two greener colors "green" and the bluer color "blue." Due to recoding interference, they overestimated the perceptual distance between the two "green" colors and the "blue" color. However, the

Tarahumara-speaking participants could not use this naming strategy because their language lacks the lexical distinction between the color categories of "green" and "blue." Thus, they did not overestimate the dissimilarity between the bluer color and the two greener colors.

To test this idea, in a second study, Kay and Kempton (1984, Study 2) made English-speaking participants use both verbal labels ("blue" and "green") to encode the same color. First, the participants were shown the target color with a greener color. Under this circumstance, they named the target color as the "bluer" color. Next, they saw the target color with a bluer color. Now, they encoded the target color as the "greener" color. Following this, the participants evaluated the perceptual distances between the three colors. Because the same color had been encoded both as the greener and the bluer color, the effects of linguistic encoding cancelled out each other. As a result, English-speaking participants no longer displayed the perceptual distortion observed previously. Instead, their judgments corresponded closely to the stimuli's physical distances and agreed with the Tarahumara speakers' judgments.

Roberson et al. (2000) reported similar findings in a conceptual replication of the Kay and Kempton (1984) experiments. The participants in Roberson et al.'s experiments were English and Berinmo speakers. Like Tarahumara, Berinmo makes no lexical distinction between "blue" and "green" colors. However, English lacks linguistic labels that refer to "nol" and "wor" colors in Berinmo. When asked to judge the perceptual similarity between pairs of colors, English speakers judged two colors across the green–blue boundary as more dissimilar to the two colors within the green or blue category. However, they did not show such categorical perception for colors across the nol–wor boundary. The reverse was true for Berinmo speakers. Similar results were obtained among both English speakers and Berinmo speakers in color category learning and color memory. More importantly, in a subsequent study of Berinmo speakers' color cognition, when a verbal interference procedure was introduced to prevent subvocal encoding of the stimuli, the basic color terms in Berinmo had no effect on Berinmo speakers' memory representations of colors (Roberson & Davidoff, 2000). Again, these findings indicate that a lexical term must be used to encode an event for it to influence the language user's subsequent representation of the event.

Finally, because proverbs and popular sayings carry widely shared evaluative, prescriptive or proscriptive beliefs, and are embedded in many conversation scripts, they have also been studied as another linguistic carrier of cultural knowledge (Ho & Chiu, 1994). When we discuss the Chinese pattern of conflict resolution (Chapter 7), we note that a recurrent theme in Chinese popular sayings is aversion to direct confrontation in conflict situations (C. Chiu, 1990a). Also discussed in Chapter 7 are the marked differences in the dominant implicit theories of change in Chinese and American contexts. The one in Chinese culture emphasizes harmonization of opposing forces, whereas the one in American culture emphasizes progress and linear changes. Peng and Nisbett (1999, Study 1) found that Chinese participants preferred Chinese proverbs that depict the Chinese theory of change, whereas American participants preferred proverbs that depict the American theory of change. In addition, Chinese participants also preferred Yiddish proverbs that depict harmonization of opposing forces to Yiddish proverbs that depict the theory of linear change. American participants did not differ in their preference for the two kinds of Yiddish proverbs (Peng & Nisbett, 1999, Study 2).

     In summary, it appears that cultural knowledge is encoded in both the form (grammar) and the common expressions (as in the case of the vocabulary and proverbs) of a language.

Life Experiences

Social experiences in every society are organized into certain loose patterns. The organization principles of social experiences in a culture may also reflect widely distributed cultural knowledge. Kitayama (Kitayama et al., 1997, see Chapter 6) has examined how life experiences may vary across cultures along several major themes, and discovered that life experiences in the United States afford more opportunities for self-enhancement, whereas life experiences in Japan afford more opportunities for self-effacement. In another study, Morling et al. (2002, see Chapter 7) found that experiences of influencing others are more available in the United States, whereas experiences of adjusting to the social environment are more available in Japan. These results are consonant with findings on cross-cultural variations in self-representation and implicit theory of change (see Chapters 6 and 7).

Summary

In summary, cultural knowledge does not reside exclusively in the mind of the individuals. It is instantiated in many different external media, institutions, and practices. These carriers of culture play an important role in reproducing culture. As Kitayama and Markus (1999, p. 250) put it:

> Everyone is born into a culture consisting of a set of practices and meanings ... To engage in culturally patterned relationships and practices and to become mature, well-functioning adults in the society, new members must come to coordinate their responses to their particular

social milieu. That is, people must come to think, feel, and act with reference to local practices, relationships, institutions and artifacts; to do so they must use the local cultural models, which consequently become an integral part of their psychological systems.

Because culture is also "out there" in the form of external realities and collective patterns of behavior, there is limit to the plasticity of culture. When a cultural idea is fully integrated into various external carriers, modification to this idea entails restructuring of social institutions and reorganization of social practices. The integration of a cultural idea with the external carriers of culture would inevitably slow down and modify cultural changes. If culture changes, in most cases, it does not change overnight.

How are Shared Representations Constructed and Reproduced?

The foregoing analysis seems to imply that culture will always be reproduced faithfully. However, as Braumann (1999) pointed out, "social reproduction of culture is always problematic and never guaranteed. Maintaining cultural consensus across time and individuals required considerable effort." (p. 11)

Recently, some psychologists have begun to examine closely the dynamic interpersonal processes through which knowledge is spatially clustered, and conventional knowledge reproduced. Although these theories focus on different aspects of the culture reproduction process, they share a common focus: They all emphasize the role of communication processes.

Dynamic Social Impact Theory

Through communication, previously unconnected values and beliefs become correlated, and a set of values and beliefs become spatially distributed (or clustered). The dynamic social impact theory (Latane, 1996) describes how these processes unfold.

In general, the opportunity to communicate increases with physical proximity. People are more likely to communicate with people in the same neighborhood or workplace than with people living far away. According to the theory, people influence and are influenced by the proximal people they communicate with. Figure 9.2 (left panel) illustrates how 16 individuals spread out spatially in a hypothetical community. Some of them (A1, A3, B2, B4, C3, D1, D4) had a positive attitude toward affirmative action, and some (A2, A4, B1, B3, C1, C2, C4, D2, D3) had a negative attitude. In the

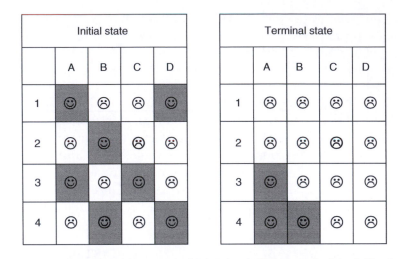

FIGURE 9.2. Illustration of dynamic social impact on spatial clustering of attitudes, assuming that anti-affirmative action individuals initiate social influence.

community, some members have greater influence than others. For example, B4 is the opinion leader in the pro-affirmative action group, and C2 is the opinion leader in the anti-affirmative action group, and they are more influential than other members in the community.

Assume that anti-affirmative action individuals start the chain of social influence first. Because people influence and are influenced by the proximal people they interact with, A1, B2, C3, D1, and D4, being surrounded by anti-affirmative action individuals, are likely to change their attitude and develop an anti-affirmative action attitude. At the same time, A4, being surrounded by a pro-affirmative action opinion leader and another pro-affirmative action individual, is likely to develop a pro-affirmative action attitude. An outcome of this dynamic process is spatial clustering of attitudes, as illustrated in Figure 9.2 (right panel). Clustering also protects individuals in the minority group (A3, A4, B4) from the influence of the majority group, and hence ensures continuing diversity.

The above conclusion also holds if the pro-affirmative action individuals start to influence their neighbors first. In this case, as illustrated in Figure 9.3 (right panel), A2, A4, B3, and C4 would be influenced by their neighbors and develop a pro-affirmative action attitude, whereas D1 will develop an anti-affirmative action attitude. Again, spatial clustering of attitudes emerges and continued diversity is ensured.

In addition to spatial clustering of attitudes, through interpersonal communication, previously unrelated attitudes and values would become correlated. For example, originally, individuals who believe in affirmative action may or may not adhere to other liberal values (e.g., free abortion).

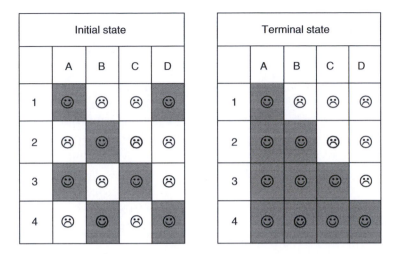

FIGURE 9.3. Illustration of dynamic social impact on spatial clustering of attitudes, assuming that the pro-affirmative action individuals initiate social influence.

However, through dyadic communication, previously unrelated attitudes and values may become increasingly integrated into a coherent liberal value system. Similarly, previously unrelated conservative values and ideas may become increasingly integrated into a coherent conservative value system.

Latané and his colleagues (Latané & Bourgeois, 1996; Latané & L'Herrou, 1996) simulated these dynamic processes in a series of computer-mediated human communication games using the electronic mailing system. They organized participants in these studies into groups of 24 and informed them of the majority opinions. Each participant could communicate with only a fixed number of individuals (approximating physical constraints in real life). Over a number of electronic sessions, clusters of opinions were formed along group boundary. Within each communication group, opinions were more homogeneous than before and previously uncorrelated issues were correlated. However, at the end of the study, even with incentives to agree with the opinions of the majority, there still remained pockets of different opinions.

Similar results were obtained in a 3-year longitudinal study of political socialization of business and social science students (Guimond & Palmer, 1996). In this study, over time, social sciences students became more likely than business students to attribute poverty and unemployment to systemic factors. Furthermore, beliefs about different causes of poverty that were unrelated in the first year became related in the third year. Toward the end of their studies, students developed social representations that are more structured and typical of their counterparts in their respective academic areas.

The 2004 Presidential Election in the United States was one of the most heated contests for the White House in US history. The American public's political opinions were highly polarized during and immediately following the election, and spatial clustering of conservative versus liberal values is obvious when we inspect the spatial distribution of the red (pro-Republican) states and the blue (pro-Democrat) states. The pro-Democrat states include states in the North East (e.g., Pennsylvania, New York, Connecticut), the West Coast (Oregon, Washington, California), and the Northern Midwest (e.g., Illinois, Minnesota, Wisconsin). The pro-Republican states include states in the South (e.g., Texas, Kansas, Arkansas), and states in the Mountainous Region (e.g., Idaho, Utah, Wyoming). The dynamic social impact theory can explain how spatial distribution of liberal and conservative political opinions emerges.

A Connectionist Model of Cultural Reproduction

Y. Kashima, Woolcock, and Kashima (2000) have developed a connectionist model to account for the reproduction and stabilization of cultural meanings in a group. The model assumes that culturally available knowledge and ideas are not evenly distributed across all members of a group. Individuals in a group resemble a network of simple processing units that receive information from each other and reproduce the information through the network. The network of connections is updated as serial reproductions proceed. Due to memory decay and schema-driven distortions, errors are introduced in the reproduced messages. In addition, to overcome the cognitive limits of the individual processing units, cognitive division of labor and externalization of memory are implemented. Through self-organization processes, cultural knowledge that is widely shared among group members (e.g., stereotypic and conventional knowledge) will have a high likelihood of being reproduced and consolidated in communication.

This model has several theoretical advantages. First, it explains how cultural knowledge and meanings are reproduced and maintained in everyday interpersonal communication. Second, it relies on a set of self-organizational processes to produce and maintain shared meanings spontaneously. Thus, it does not require a homunculus-like agent or a collective will to oversee or manage the reproduction of cultural meanings. Third, the model is specific enough to permit precise simulation of the postulated cultural-meaning reproduction processes in controlled experiments (Y. Kashima, 2000b). As mentioned, in these experiments, researchers track the likelihood that stereotypic and counter-stereotypic information in a story will be reproduced when one person transmits the story to the next person, who in turn transmits it to a third person, and so on. These experiments demonstrated that through serial reproduction, a story is conventionalized, as stereotypic information is retained and counter-stereotypic information lost (Lyons & Kashima, 2001, 2003).

Collaborative Construction of Shared Reality

The connectionist model and the dynamic social impact theory have offered two broad perspectives on the role of communication in the formation and consolidation of shared representations. Language is a primary medium in interpersonal communication. Not surprisingly, some researchers (C. Chiu et al., 1998, 1999; Lau et al., 2001, 2004) have sought to explain culture by analyzing the nature and cognitive consequences of language use in daily communication.

Sperber (1996) suggests that the best way to study how culture spreads and evolves is by examining how shared representations "are cognized by individuals and how they are communicated within a group" (p. 97). Similarly, Bruner (1990) asserts, "By virtue of participation in culture, meaning is rendered *public* and *shared*. Our culturally adapted way of life depends upon shared meanings and shared concepts and depends as well upon shared modes of discourse for negotiating differences in meaning and interpretation" (pp. 12–13).

In keeping with the essence of these assertions, some researchers have examined how shared reality arises as communicators tune their message to the assumed beliefs and attitudes of the addressee. This research reveals that speakers would estimate their addressee's knowledge about a referent when they formulate referring expressions (Clark & Carlson, 1982; Clark & Marshall, 1981; Clark & Murphy, 1982; Clark, Schreuder, & Buttrick, 1983; Krauss & Fussell, 1991, 1996; Krauss, Fussell, & Chen, 1995). Expressions tend to be briefer when the addressee is estimated to be knowledgeable about the referent, and vice versa (Fussell & Krauss, 1991, 1992; Lau et al., 2001). In addition, speakers tend to include in their communicative message expressions that are part of the established common ground (Fussell & Krauss, 1989a, 1989b; Krauss & Glucksberg, 1977; Krauss, Vivekananthan, & Weinheimer, 1968). Furthermore, when speakers learn that their addressee has a positive or negative attitude toward a target person, they would tune their descriptions of the target person in the direction of the addressee's attitude toward the target person. Consistent with the recoding interference hypothesis, the speakers' subsequent impressions of the target person become evaluatively consistent with the addressee's attitudes (Higgins & McCann, 1984; Higgins, McCann, & Fondacaro, 1982; McCann, Higgins, & Fondacaro, 1991).

To reveal how shared reality emerges in dyadic interaction, Wilkes-Gibbs and Kim (1991) presented to their participants ambiguous drawings that can be encoded with one of two alternate sets of labels. For example, an ambiguous figure can be labeled either as "a Viking ship" or "a person swimming" because it looks like both. The participants were led to encode each drawing with either one of the two alternate sets of labels. Following encoding, each participant was paired with another participant who either used the same (matched code) or a different set of labels (mismatched code) to encode the drawings. Each pair of participants, separated by a partition so that they could not see other, conversed to arrange the drawings in an identical order. The participants returned 15 min or 1 week later to reproduce the drawings they saw in the first session.

As expected, participants in the Matched Code Condition took less time than those in the Mismatched Condition to finish the communication task. Nonetheless, by the sixth trial, participants in both conditions had established a common way of referring to the drawings. Also as expected, participants in the Matched Code Condition used the same labels they used to encode the drawings to refer to the drawings. In contrast, participants in the Mismatched Code Condition generated new labels that were dissimilar to the labels they used to encode the drawings. Thus, irrespective of their initial encodings, participants collaborated to establish a common and definite way of naming each drawing as communication proceeds.

Again, consistent with the recoding interference hypothesis, participants' memory representations of the drawings changed in the direction of the established common referring expressions. In the Matched Code Condition, the participants' reproductions of the drawings were biased in the direction consistent with the labels used to encode the drawings, particularly when the established common labels matched the initial labels.

In short, when formulating a message, speakers are more likely to use expressions that presumably are widely shared and accepted in the culture (e.g., conventional and stereotypic knowledge) than expressions that are not. They would avoid idiosyncratic expressions, low-frequency words, and counter-stereotypic knowledge in their messages. As the connectionist theory posits, such practices contribute to the maintenance of shared representations. Additionally, when the shared linguistic representation established in communication is the same as the communicators' initial representation [as in the Matched Code Condition in the Wilkes-Gibbs & Kim (1991) experiment], the initial representation will be maintained. When the same linguistic representation is repeatedly communicated, it overshadows other representations, and becomes *the* shared representation in the linguistic community. As Sperber (1996) puts it, "(t)hose representations which are repeatedly communicated *and* minimally transformed in the process will end up belonging to the culture" (p. 88).

Summary

All three theories reviewed above treat culture as an interactive process. Individuals adjust to an existing cultural environment, but they also take an active role in shaping the evolution of culture. They influence, and receive influence from, others, sometimes deliberately and oftentimes not. They acquire knowledge about their culture and use such cultural knowledge to assess the common ground they have with the people they interact with. They take their addressee into consideration when formulating communicative messages, and through the process of doing so unwittingly collaborate to construct and maintain a shared reality.

Cultural Change

Cultural change has important psychological implications for the society and the individual. At the societal level, cultural change may involve modification, abolition and reestablishment of formal and informal institutions and life practices. At the individual level, cultural change may result in modification of a person's cultural frame, and/or development of alternative interpretive frames.

Sources of Cultural Change

In the process of reproducing culture, cultural change may occur because of endogenous and exogenous reasons. For example, endogenous cultural change may take place through the processes of differentiation. According to Triandis (2004):

> differentiation is important in culture change. A tool that works well may be replaced by a tool that works slightly better, but frequently the culture retains both tools. Random variation and selective retention result in different species of tools, just as they also result in different dimensions of cultural variation. Campbell (1965) argued that random variation provided the bases of cultural evolution. It is followed by selective retention, and propagation of the positively selected variants.

Indeed, invention of new tools is a major driving force of cultural change within a society. Inventions may be either technological or ideological.

Technological inventions include new energy sources and transportation methods. Ideological inventions include such things as socialism, constitutional law, and representational government. A recurrent debate in sociology is whether the emergence of capitalism in the Western world was driven primarily by technological inventions (which had drastically changed the mode and means of production) or by ideological inventions (the rise of Calvinism and Protestant work ethics; see Y. Kashima & Foddy, 2002, for review).

Necessity is the mother of invention. This idiom applies in the realm of cultural inventions as well. As noted in Chapter 4, oftentimes cultural conventions are created to solve a social coordination problem. Accordingly, cultural change may occur when the society needs to find solutions to new coordination problems. Cohen (1998) maintains that the culture of honor of the American South arose in part from the frontier conditions that pervaded the region (see Chapter 7). In the absence of any strong sense of order, men had to rely on themselves for protection. The society sanctioned the use of violence, and the idea that a good man must be prepared to protect his property as well as the honor of his family crystallized into a code of honor.

Exogenous-culture change often results from intercultural contacts, through which people from a culture are exposed to another culture. With rapid development of electronic communication, people find themselves increasingly enmeshed in global symbolic environments (Bandura, 2002). As cultural boundaries become increasingly permeable and fuzzy, intercultural contacts can take place without direct interactions with members of other cultures. For instance, intercultural contacts can result from things and ideas from one culture moving to another. For example, some aspects of American culture move to other countries when Hollywood movies are brought there. Sometimes, a foreign culture is brought to the entire indigenous culture. This happens, for example, when a country colonizes or takes over another country.

Intercultural contacts may also take place when individuals move from one culture to another, as in the case of migration. Immigrants from foreign countries are likely to be acculturated into the host country's dominant culture. However, they also carry with them their heritage cultures, and hence are also agents of cultural diffusion.

Endogenous cultural change may lead to exogenous cultural change. For example, the invention of the steam engine in Europe quickened the pace and widened the scope of colonization. Likewise, exogenous cultural change may lead to endogenous cultural change. For instance, ancient Egyptians invented their hieroglyphic writing system around 3050 BC after learning about the cuneiform writing system invented by Sumerians.

Once a new cultural idea is found to be valuable in coordinating collective life, it will be crystallized and integrated into various institutions and life practices. For example, once the culture of honor has crystallized, condoned violence becomes an integral part of the Southern culture, and more social organization gives rise to more condoned aggression. Consistent with this idea, Cohen (1998) reported that in the American South, the culture of honor is more integrated in the legal institutions (e.g., gun control laws, self-defense laws), and social practices (e.g., entertainment, recreation, and vocational activities) in socially organized states than in socially disorganized states.

Tracking Cultural Changes

One commonly used strategy for detecting and tracking cultural changes is longitudinal or cross-sectional studies of intergenerational similarities or differences in the psychological characteristics of a cultural group. Intergenerational comparisons are particularly useful for detecting cultural changes that occur within a relatively short period of time, such as changes in societies that are undergoing rapid industrialization and modernization. For example, intergenerational comparisons revealed that in Hong Kong, authoritarian parenting is more widely practiced among older parents than younger parents, who place more emphasis on developing affective bonds between the parent and the child. (Ho & Kang, 1984). Stewart, Bond, Deeds, and Chung (1999) also reported that among Hong Kong Chinese, the younger generation values autonomy more than does the older generation. As noted in Chapter 2, although filial piety is still highly valued in Beijing and Taiwan, the importance of obeying the elders and living with elderly parents as filial obligations has declined gradually in the past 30 years (Yeh, 1997, 2002; Yue & Ng, 1999). Although some traditional values are declining, some seem to be fairly resistant to change. For example, compared to Caucasian mothers, Asian mothers still place greater emphasis on conservative values (Stewart et al., 1999). In Taiwan, taking care of elderly parents is still considered an important filial obligation (Yeh, 2002).

Another strategy for tracking cultural changes is historical analysis of external carriers of cultural meanings (e.g., cultural artifacts, folklores, language use). For example, as noted earlier, collectivist commercial messages are more prevalent in East Asian countries than in the United States. However, in a recent study of the values promoted in Chinese advertising, Zhang and Shavitt (2003) found that individualist and modern values are more pervasive in magazine advertisements than in television commercials. Conversely, collectivist and traditional values are more pervasive in television than in magazine advertisements. Whereas magazine advertisements target younger consumers, television commercial messages are intended for mass audiences. This finding indicates that individualist values are gradually being integrated into the practices of younger people in China.

Meet the Researcher: Sharon Shavitt

"Although I had some experience living in two different cultures, my real cross-cultural experiences occurred within the family. At least 3 languages were spoken around our dinner table. Almost everyone in my family had left, or fled, their birthplaces in Eastern Europe before or after the war and had since lived in a number of countries. Accordingly, cultural and national differences were a common topic of conversation—both as a source of life lessons and as wry humor. This emphasis was reinforced in my early childhood in Israel, a society struggling yet eager to absorb waves of immigrants and refugees. As a result, I grew up believing that effectively traversing cultural boundaries was nothing short of a survival skill. In contrast, my later childhood in central Ohio presented a cultural environment with very different challenges. It was strikingly homogeneous yet largely unaware of its cultural particularities. This produced in me an 'outsider's perspective' on most of the cultural beliefs and practices observed in my broader environment. In short, I rarely felt any sense of wonder about cultural differences. These differences were a given; the wonder was that anyone might not recognize them."

Sharon Shavitt was born in Boston, MA. She earned her Ph.D. in social psychology at Ohio State University, and is now Professor of Marketing at the University of Illinois at Urbana-Champaign.

Conclusion

Culture changes, but it is also being constantly reproduced. There are dynamic processes operating that initiate changes and others that resist changes. Cultural changes occur when new knowledge is created or imported. However, social and psychological chaos would likely result if culture changes were not checked by conservative forces that operate to maintain a certain level of cultural stability. Integration of cultural ideas into social institutions and life practices is a major source of resistance to cultural change. In addition, as noted in Chapter 4, culture also confers many psychological benefits to the individual, including a sense of epistemic security, meaning in life, and a sense of belongingness. Individuals are particularly likely to resist cultural change when the needs for epistemic security, meaning in life, and belongingness are highlighted. Finally, as people spontaneously retrieve conventional knowledge to guide communication in interpersonal interaction, they unwittingly reproduce and consolidate the prevailing cultural conventions.

The meeting of old and new cultures, and of indigenous and foreign cultures, has important psychological consequences for the individual. On the one hand, it provides individuals with an alternative interpretive frame, and fosters culturally competent behaviors. (This issue is discussed in the next chapter.) On the other hand, when individuals are confronted with two or more cultural traditions, they may feel the need to affirm their traditional identity or reconstruct a new multicultural identity. In Chapter 11, we discuss how individuals define the self with reference to the different cultural traditions that are available in multicultural contexts.

Intercultural Contacts: Implications for Cultural Competence $\quad$ 10

The Rice Storm and the Butterfly Effect

The Rice Storm is very popular in Japanese organizations. It is a technique for making decisions through consensus, and for securing group commitment and team cohesion. The Rice Storm begins when the group leader identifies a problem area (e.g., issues arising from setting up a new job rotation system in a department). Each participant is given a pile of index cards and asked to write down all significant facts pertinent to the problem, with one fact on each card. The participants are reminded to disguise their handwriting, so that the author of each fact will remain anonymous. The leader collects all the cards and redistributes them. Next, the leader randomly draws a card and reads it aloud. In response, the participants go through their own pile of cards, select the cards that relate to the card that was read, and read them to the group. The leader places all the related cards into a pile and invites the group to summarize its essence and labels it. The process is repeated until all the cards go into one of the labeled sets. Next, the process is applied to bring all the labeled sets into a single, all-inclusive set. Finally, the group summarizes the all-inclusive set and labels it. The description and label of the all-inclusive set become the group's consensus definition of the problem.

The Rice Storm is seldom practiced in US organizations, where the work culture emphasizes personal achievement and accomplishment more than group consensus. At first glance, foreign practices such as the Rice Storm, interesting as they may seem, do not seem to have much relevance to American societies. However, a closer analysis reveals a different picture.

As the speed of globalization accelerates, increasingly the entire world is economically tied together, and complex webs of interdependence have gradually replaced regional economic independence. A large proportion of manufactured goods and produce sold in the US market is produced or grown in foreign countries. When an American consumer makes a toll-free call to an American company for support service, the customer service officer who answers the call may be an employee in a technological support center in India. China, Bangladesh, and Sri Lanka have become the world's factories, and many American manufacturing jobs are being moved to these countries to exploit the low labor costs there. When a financial crisis hit Asia in 1998, its impact was immediately felt in Wall Street. Any initial conditions in a regional economy can lead to large-scale and unpredictable changes in the future state of the world economy, resembling what chaos theorists refer to as the butterfly effect. More than half of the 100 biggest economies in the world are not nations, but multinational corporations. More than 20 million Americans now work for transnational corporations.

For American expatriates working in Asian contexts, aside from facing a different environment and changes in traffic, climate, and living standard, the biggest challenge is how to blend in with a new culture. Most multinational companies are aware of the importance of understanding cultural context in succeeding in doing business around the world, and provide global business skills and relocation training for their executives.

Psychologists are also aware of the increasing need to develop culture-sensitive and culture-relevant psychological theories and practices. In January 1999, approximately 550 psychologists and graduate students attended the National Multicultural Conference and Summit hosted by Divisions 17 (Counseling Psychology), 35 (Society for the Psychology of

Women), and 45 (Society for the Psychological Study of Ethnic Minority Issues) of the American Psychological Association (APA). The participants in the summit unanimously endorsed resolutions aimed at implementing cultural competence in all psychological endeavors, and strongly encouraged APA to take the lead in seeing that cultural competence becomes a defining feature of psychological practice, education and training, and research (Sue, Bingham, Porche-Burke, & Vasquez, 1999).

In this chapter, we discuss the nature of cultural competence and its major components. We also discuss the relationship between multicultural experiences and cultural competence, and other psychological effects of intercultural contacts.

Nature of Cultural Competence

Experts on cultural competence have different opinions on what cultural competence is, despite strong agreement on its importance (Cunningham, Foster, & Henggeler, 2002). Most practitioners believe that cultural competence involves self-understanding, knowledge of others whose cultural origins and values are different from their own, and adapting one's own behaviors to the needs of culturally diverse groups (e.g., Hansen, Pepitone-Arreola-Rockwell, & Greene, 2000; Offermann & Phan, 2002). However, little is known about what awareness, knowledge, and skills would enable people to function effectively in a variety of cultures.

Inspired by previous research on social competence, C. Chiu and Hong (2005) define cultural competence as the ability to use context-appropriate cultural knowledge in intercultural interaction, and the flexibility to switch cultural frames for sense making. In his seminal paper, Edward Thorndike (1920, p. 228) defined social competence as "the ability to understand and manage men and women, boys and girls—to act wisely in human relations." Inspired by Thorndike's idea, numerous attempts have been made to identify the specific expertise and skills (e.g., expertise in decoding communicative behaviors, expertise in judging people, tacit knowledge about managing other people) that define social competence (e.g., Sternberg & Smith, 1985). Many such attempts failed (e.g., Brown & Anthony, 1990; Ford & Tisak, 1983) before researchers realized that although expertise and specific skills are necessary for competent social behavior, they are not sufficient for attaining personal goals and promoting interpersonal relationships. As more recent studies (C. Cheng, Chiu, Hong, & Cheung, 2001; C. Chiu, Hong, Mischel, & Shoda, 1995) have shown, two crucial but previously overlooked components of social competence that predict competent social behaviors and positive affect in interpersonal interaction are sensitivity to subtle cues about the psychological meanings of *changing* situations and *discriminative* use of social knowledge and skills across situations. Similarly, a hallmark of competent cultural behavior is the ability to switch the mode of interpretation flexibly and adaptively as individuals navigate situations across different cultural contexts.

Psychological Benefits of Intercultural Contacts

Cultural Frame Switching

In Chapter 8, we discuss how individuals enmeshed in more than one culture can spontaneously switch their cultural frames in response to subtle cultural reference in the situation. For example, growing up in the British colony of Hong Kong, many Hong Kong Chinese undergraduates are familiar with both Chinese and American cultures. Hong Kong Chinese acquire their expertise in American culture through many different sources, one of which is cultural diffusion. For example, a total of 27 US TV channels are available in Hong Kong. From 1997 to 2003, among the 20 most popular movies in Hong Kong each year (in terms of box office records), 7 to 13 were US movies. During this period, half of the 100 most popular movies were US movies. By comparison, there are currently in total three Chinese TV channels in the United States. There are only 11 theaters in the United States that show Asian movies regularly (usually 1 day a week). The most popular foreign movie in the United States is *Crouching Tiger, Hidden Dragon*, which ranked 12 (in terms of box office records) in the United States in 2000, followed by *Life is Beautiful* (an Italian film), which ranked 35 in the United States in 1998.

Because of Hong Kong Chinese's fluency in both Chinese and American cultures, in response to subtle cues of the cultural requirements of a situation (such as the presence of Chinese or American cultural icons), their interpretation of social events is filtered through a Chinese cultural lens in one situation, and an American cultural lens in another situation (Hong et al., 1997, 2000). Anthropologists have referred to this phenomenon as cultural frame switching (LaFromboise, Coleman, & Gerton, 1993).

It is important to emphasize that bicultural individuals do not just passively respond to the cultural cues. Cultural cues activate their associated cultural knowledge, but a bicultural individual applies the activated cultural knowledge only when it is applicable to the current situation (Hong et al., 2003; Wong & Hong, 2005). In other words, their responses to cultural cues are highly discriminative. The adaptive nature of cultural frame switching is a recurrent theme in the self-reflections of multicultural individuals. For example, a Vietnamese immigrant in the United States reported that "As a result of all these (cultural) differences and having been forced to adapt to this new culture, I have developed another cultural identity which is capable of surviving in this new environment ... This identity functions like a second personality that appears when it is necessary to adopt a culturally appropriate behavior in the new culture" (Sparrow, 2000, p. 192).

Aside from cultural diffusion, individuals may also become expert in a foreign culture by studying abroad and by migration. In the United States, international students and members of ethnic minorities are often experts in both mainstream (European) American culture and their heritage culture. They can switch cultural frames spontaneously as they navigate situations in different cultural contexts (Benet-Martinez et al., 2002; Hong et al., 2000, 2003).

Flexibility in Behavioral Strategies

Aside from switching interpretive frames, bicultural individuals also switch their behavioral strategies in response to the situational cues of cultural demands. On December 31, 2004, the *Times of India* published the story of Christian R. Fabre (a.k.a. Swami Pranavananda Brahmendra Avadhuta). The title of the story is "Off label: Straddling two incongruent worlds." The story describes how Christian Fabre navigates Hindu culture and the Western business world.

Fabre is a Frenchman who came to India in 1971 to work for a French-Belgian exporter of semi-finished leather. When the Indian government banned exports of semi-finished leather, Fabre lost his job, and his wife divorced him and left with their young son in the early 1980s. Left with nothing, Fabre discovered yoga and Hinduism, and became a passionate practitioner of the traditional Indian religion. Later, Fabre became the CEO of Fashions International, which supplies clothing to European and American brands like Kenzo, Lee Cooper, and Haager. The company is one of the fastest growing and most profitable firms in India.

Fabre has straddled the diverse worlds of business and spirituality with poise. The company he runs exports 3.5 million pieces of apparel annually, and its profit is growing more than 25% a year. Fabre is also known to the business world as a sharp tactician and negotiator. However, he takes a modest monthly salary of $200, in keeping with his religious faith, which prescribes detachment from material comfort. For every 10 days he works, he retires to his hermitage for 2 weeks. When he is at work, he wears saffron robes, beads, and ash and vermilion on his forehead. In his hermitage, he goes without clothes, as his religion requires. In his ashram, Fabre meditates, naked. Fabre is connected to two different cultures through the Internet and makes momentary and adaptive shifts in behaviors when he is on line. At one moment, he uses the Internet to track business deals. At another moment, he discusses spiritual matters with his followers online.

Recently, social psychologists have started to investigate flexible switching of behavioral strategies in intercultural interactions. For example, Adair, Okumura, and Brett (2001) compared how American and Japanese international students in a US business school engaged in intracultural and intercultural business negotiation. Negotiation transcripts were coded and content analyzed to identify the negotiation strategies used. The results show that American business students, who knew relatively little about Japanese culture, used similar strategies when they negotiated with another American and when they negotiated with a Japanese. In both cases, they tended to exchange information directly. For example, they would tell the other party their reactions toward an offer or a proposal. They were comfortable sharing information about priorities, comparing and contrasting their preferences and those of their opponent, and providing direct feedback to their opponent's offers or proposals.

In contrast, Japanese international students, who were knowledgeable in both American and Japanese cultures, tended to exchange information indirectly with another Japanese, but would shift to more direct negotiation strategies when they negotiated with an American. For example, with another Japanese, they tended to respond to an offer with a new offer or a counter offer, and to infer from a chain of multiple offers and counter offers their opponents' priorities and preferences. However, with an American negotiator, Japanese international students tended to accommodate their strategies to the American norms; they reduced the use of indirect information exchange, and increased the use of direct information exchange.

Recall that Easterners have a greater tendency than Westerners to attend to object–context relations (Chapter 5). If East Asians are relatively sensitive to object–context relations, they may also be more adept at decoding indirect meaning in conversations. In one study (Sanchez-Burks, Lee, Choi, Nisbett, Zhao, & Koo, 2003, Study 3), East Asian and European American business students read the transcript of a meeting between a reviewer and a reviewee at an employee evaluation meeting. The participants did not have access to the reviewer's performance evaluation of the reviewee, and their task was to infer the performance evaluation based on the indirect information at the meeting. As expected, East Asian business students made fewer errors in recovering the original performance evaluation from the indirect information, compared to European American business students. More importantly, in an additional study (Sanchez-Burks et al., 2003, Study 4), Thai-English bicultural managers from two large multinational corporations in Thailand responded to a measure of indirectness written either in English or in Thai. When these bicultural individuals responded to the Thai survey, they were more sensitive to indirect cues than when they responded to the English survey. In short, these findings indicate that intercultural contact can increase flexibility in behavioral strategies in multicultural contacts.

Knowledge of a Second Culture

How do we account for bicultural individuals' behavioral flexibility? One possibility is that bicultural individuals, who are enmeshed in more than one culture, have acquired nuanced understanding of other cultures, which enables them to navigate situations in the second culture as experts. Several studies have compared Chinese American bicultural individuals' knowledge of Chinese and American cultures with that of European Americans. Although these studies generally show that Chinese American bicultural individuals seem to possess more nuanced understanding of Chinese culture, these findings should not be taken to imply that European Americans are less culturally sensitive than are Chinese American bicultural individuals. Chinese American bicultural individuals have better understanding of Chinese culture because they have much more experiences with Chinese culture than do European Americans. Indeed, European Americans may have more experiences and hence more nuanced understanding of cultures other than Chinese culture than do Chinese American bicultural individuals.

K. Y. Leung, Chiu, & Hong (2004, Study 1) tested the role of cultural knowledge in bicultural behavioral flexibility. They had European American and Chinese American undergraduates fill out a measure of regulatory focus (Higgins, Friedman, Harlow, Idson, Ayduk, & Taylor, 2001), which assesses one's personal history of fulfilling personal aspirations (promotion pride), and of meeting parental expectations (prevention pride). Although European and Chinese American students did not differ on prevention pride, European American students scored significantly higher on promotion pride. Next, the investigators had participants estimate how European and Chinese American students would respond to the regulatory focus measure. Compared to European American students, Chinese American students were more accurate in estimating cultural differences between European American and Chinese American on the two motivational orientations.

In an additional study, K. Y. Leung et al. (Study 2) asked Chinese and European American students to persuade a Chinese or American target to purchase an insurance policy. In this study, Chinese American students were more likely to tailor arguments according to the target's ethnicity based on their knowledge of Chinese and American cultures; they used more promotion-focused arguments (arguments that focus on possible gains) for an American target than for a Chinese target. In contrast, the target's ethnic identity did not affect European Americans' choice of persuasive messages. In contrast, irrespective of the target's ethnicity, European American students used more promotion-focused arguments than prevention-focused arguments (arguments that focus on preventing possible losses).

As noted earlier, Hong Kong people have more exposure to US culture than do Americans to Hong Kong culture. Consistent with the asymmetry in the direction of cultural contacts, S. L. Lee (2002) found that Hong Kong undergraduates are more accurate in estimating the distribution of knowledge among American undergraduates in New York than are New York undergraduates in estimating the distribution of knowledge among Hong Kong undergraduates. For example, Hong Kong undergraduates have very good knowledge of which flower is most widely known to New York undergraduate students. By comparison, New York students have relatively unrefined knowledge of which flower is most widely known to Hong Kong people.

In addition, Hong Kong undergraduates are capable of applying their knowledge about New York undergraduates when they formulate communicative messages for New York undergraduates. When they describe a flower that is not well known in New York to a New York student, they include more information in the description than when they describe a flower that is widely known among New York students. New York undergraduates, by comparison, have less accurate knowledge about Hong Kong undergraduates, and tend not to use such knowledge when they formulate messages for Hong Kong undergraduates (S. L. Lee, 2002).

In short, possession of nuanced understanding of a second culture increases behavioral flexibility. In addition, it also enables a bicultural individual to interact competently with a person from another cultural group. For example, in one study, Li and Hong (2001) found that Mainland Chinese students studying in Hong Kong differed among themselves in how well they knew the distribution of values in Hong Kong society. Those who possessed more accurate knowledge about what values are important to Hong Kong people had more competent social interactions with Hong Kong students.

Creativity and Openness to Experiences

When a cultural lens is repeatedly used to make sense of the environment, it becomes a learned routine, and a part of "routinized" culture (Ng & Bradac, 1993). For this reason, although culture provides conventional tools for sense making and problem solving, it also impedes creativity.

Most creative activities involve instances of conceptual expansion, in which people extend the boundaries of a conceptual domain by creating novel instances of the concept. For example, when psychologists propose a new theory, they extend the boundaries of a conceptual domain by mentally crafting new instances of some existing concepts (Ward, Patterson, Sifonis, Dodds, & Saunders, 2002), and this is also the case when architects design a new building, or when businesspersons propose a creative business plan. When people engage in creative conceptual expansion, it is difficult to avoid the influence of exemplars high in chronic accessibility (Ward et al., 2002). For instance, when people generate creative exemplars in a novel conceptual domain (e.g., animals on Planet Mars), even their most creative exemplars resemble the highly accessible exemplars in a preexisting conceptual category (e.g., animals on Earth, with eyes and legs; see Rubin & Kontis, 1983; Ward, 1994; Ward et al., 2002). Apparently, a major constraint on creative conceptual expansion is the influence of conventional knowledge.

To overcome this constraint, people can form new ideas by combining two seemingly incompatible ideas (Hampton, 1997; Wan & Chiu, 2002). In one study, participants were asked to integrate concepts that do not overlap. For instance, what is a fruit that is also a kind of furniture? What is a vehicle that is also a kind of fish? Subsequent to solving this kind of novel conceptual integration problems, participants tended to have higher performance on another unrelated creativity task (Wan & Chiu, 2002).

How may all these be related to intercultural experiences and creativity? As noted, the chronic accessibility of an exemplar increases with the frequency of exposure to the exemplar (Higgins, 1996, see Chapter 8). Thus, how accessible a particular exemplar of a given category is may vary from one cultural group to another, depending on how often the exemplar is found in the group's cultural environment. For example, many Singaporeans will readily think of durians (see Figure 10.1) when they think about fruits, because durians are highly available in Singapore. By contrast, most Americans do not immediately think of this foul-smelling fruit with a prickly rind when they think about fruits, because they seldom see one in the market. In short, an exemplar that is familiar to members of Culture A may appear novel to members of Culture B (Ip, Chen, & Chiu, in press). Thus, although conventional knowledge may limit creative

FIGURE 10.1. Durians, an exotic fruit from Asia.

conceptual expansion in all human groups, what is conventional knowledge in one culture may be unconventional in another.

If cultural differences in categorical accessibility norms reflect differences in cultural experiences, intercultural experiences may help foster creative expansion of ideas. To elaborate, Idea A may be highly accessible in Culture I but relatively inaccessible in Culture II. Conversely, Idea B may be highly accessible in Culture II but relatively inaccessible in Culture I. An individual who has extensive experiences in both Cultures I and II may be able to retrieve both Ideas A and B spontaneously, place the two ideas in juxtaposition, and through creative insights integrate the two ideas into a novel one. Indeed, many examples of creative conceptual expansion in daily life are outcomes of integrating indigenous cultural exemplars from diverse cultures. For example, furnishing a New York apartment with traditional Ming Dynasty furniture may give a creative postmodern feel to this apartment (see Figure 10.2).

Cultural psychological research affords many opportunities of this kind of creative expansion. For example, in the United States, the most accessible instance of the self is a bounded, distinctive, autonomous, and self-contained entity. When American psychologists learned that the most accessible instance of the self in Japan is defined in relation to a person's position in an interpersonal network, they became aware of the culturo-centric nature of their conception of the self. Through creative synthesis of

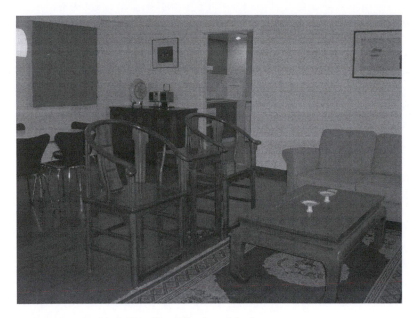

FIGURE 10.2. An apartment furnished with traditional Ming Dynasty furniture.

diverse cultural models of self, researchers have accomplished a more complete understanding of selfhood and crafted one of the most original theories in social psychology (Markus & Kitayama, 1991).

Through increased exposure to seemingly inconsistent strands of ideas from diverse cultures, multicultural individuals may gradually weave these ideas into their cultural life, and in the process of doing so become more creative (Nemeth & Kwan, 1987). Consistent with this idea, research shows that exposure to diverse cultural experience weakens the constraints of conventional knowledge on creative thinking (Simonton, 2000). For example, the experience of growing up when a nation breaks up into several peacefully coexisting independent states is conducive to the development of creativity (Simonton, 1975). In addition, when a country opens itself to foreign influences, the level of creativity in the country tends to increase (Simonton, 1997). Finally, children in some Eastern countries (e.g., China, Indonesia) tend to do more poorly on standardized tests of creativity than their European counterparts (Jellen & Urban, 1989). However, Asian children with rich multicultural experiences (e.g., Hong Kong Chinese children) and Chinese American children sometimes outperform European American children in standardized creativity tests (Niu & Sternberg, 2001; Rudowicz, Lok, & Kitto, 1995). In short, cultural diversity may facilitate creativity (Simonton, 2000).

Multicultural experiences may also increase openness to foreign ideas. In one study (K. Y. Leung, 2005, Study 1), European American undergraduate students with varying levels of multicultural experiences worked on a conceptual expansion task. Participants in this study had richer multicultural experiences if their parents were born outside the United States, spoke a foreign language, had close friends from other countries, and enjoyed foreign cuisines and music. Their task in this study was to expand a simple idea ("People who have more friends are happier") into a creative psychological theory of happiness that is suitable for an undergraduate honor thesis. Before they started the task, they could choose to consult *up to 7* sayings out of 15 written by famous scholars. They learned that the authors of five sayings were famous scholars in the United States, five were famous scholars in Far East, and five were famous scholars in the Middle East. Without looking at the sayings themselves, the participants made their choice based on the scholars' cultural background. The results show that participants with richer multicultural experiences were more willing to sample ideas from foreign cultures and use them for conceptual expansion.

Thus far, we have painted a rather rosy picture of the possible psychological effects of multicultural experiences. It seems that intercultural contact increases openness to other cultures' ideas, sensitivity to the distribution of knowledge in another culture, and to cognitive and behavioral flexibility. However, are there boundary conditions for the psychological benefits of intercultural contact? Would intercultural contact lead to any harmful psychological effects? We now turn to these questions.

Some Boundary Conditions

Intercultural contact does not always lead to openness or unbridle the effect of conventional knowledge on thinking. One boundary condition of intercultural contacts' psychological benefits is the need for cognitive closure (see Chapter 4). Among both Hong Kong Chinese and European American undergraduates, those who score higher on the need for cognitive closure generate more conventional exemplars when asked to list exemplars of a variety of conceptual categories (e.g., fruits, entertainment, birds, disease; Ip et al., in press).

Recall that people have a higher need for cognitive closure when they perform under time pressure. Earlier, we introduced K. Y. Leung's (2005, Study 1) finding that European American students with richer multicultural experiences tend to include more foreign ideas in a creative expansion task. In an additional study, K. Y. Leung (2005, Study 2) showed that the effect of multicultural experiences on openness to foreign ideas disappeared when European American students needed to perform the conceptual expansion task under time pressure.

Under some circumstances, cultural contact may also promote culturo-centrism and intercultural animosity. The Israelis and Palestinians do not lack opportunities for intercultural contact. Despite this, the two groups have a long history of inflicting harm on each other. A complete under-standing of the origin of the intercultural animosity between the Israelis and Palestinians requires collaborative research effort from political science, his-tory, religious studies, and other social sciences. From the perspective of social psychology of culture, once intercultural animosity has developed, conflicts may escalate with increased intercultural contacts, particularly when individuals are constantly bombarded with images of death (reminders of mortality) and reminded to pledge allegiance to their own group in the environment. In Chapter 4, we describe the research evidence showing how the need to reduce existential anxiety and the need to belong may increase individuals' adherence to cultural conventions. These psycho-logical factors may contribute partly to the maintenance of intercultural ani-mosity in the Middle East.

The foregoing analysis does not imply that intercultural bias cannot be corrected. Indeed, intercultural contact may reduce intercultural bias. However, for this to happen, a number of conditions need to be present. We will illustrate this point with research on countering negative cultural stereotypes of African Americans in the United States.

Intercultural tension between African and European Americans is one of the most researched topics in American social psychology. Some researchers (Allport, 1954; Gaertner, Dovidio, Anastasio, Bachman, & Rust, 1993; Gaertner, Dovidio, Nier, Ward, & Banker, 1999) believe and found that intercultural contact is conducive to reduction of bias toward African Americans. However, intercultural contact by itself is not sufficient to reduce intercultural bias. For intercultural contact to work, it needs to be conducted in an atmosphere that supports equal status, cooperative inter-action, interpersonal interaction, and supportive norms (Gaertner, Rust, Dovidio, Bachman, & Anastasio, 1994).

A study (Ensari & Miller, 2002) has provided detailed analysis of the conditions that must be present for intercultural contact to be effective for reducing intercultural bias. This study also takes us back to the Middle East. In Turkey, Islamic fundamentalists reassert Islam and Islamic values in Muslim politics and society. They dress in religious fashion, hold con-servative religious values, lead a traditional lifestyle, and vote for radical religious candidates in political elections. In contrast, secularists believe in modern lifestyle, dress in European fashions, and vote for liberal political candidates. Because of the sharp contrast in values and lifestyles, the two groups blame each other for the society's problems. On one side, Islamic fundamentalists blame secularists for pursuing Western models of political and economic development in Turkey, which Islamic fundamentalists believe are the source of moral decadence and spiritual malaise. Islamic fundamentalists also claim that secularists are atheist or even antireligious. On the other side, secularists blame Islamic fundamentalists for constraining others' behaviors and interfering with others' freedom. They perceive Islamic fundamentalists as intolerant, narrow-minded, and biased.

In the study, Ensari and Miller (2002, Study 1) had Muslim secularists in Istanbul play the role of an interviewer and test administrator. The participant's task was to interview and give a 10-item cognitive ability task to a female confederate, who posed either as a typical or an atypical Islamic fundamentalist. When the confederate posed as a typical Islamic fundamentalist, she wore a scarf, a black shirt, and a dark blue coat with long sleeves, and carried an Islamic newspaper when she entered the laboratory. When she introduced herself, she stated that she is an Islamic person. (Although most people in Turkey are Muslims, the term Islamic is uniformly understood to mean Islamic fundamentalists.) She further stated that she lived with her family, read the religious newspaper, liked to watch the religious television channel, and voted for the Islamic political party.

When the confederate posed as an atypical Islamic fundamentalist, she wore a blue t-shirt and a black skirt, with no scarf and no coat. She carried a secularist newspaper when she entered the laboratory. She also introduced herself as an Islamic person. However, when she described her preference for newspaper, television channel, and political party, it became obvious to the participant that she was not a typical Islamic person. She also mentioned that she lived alone, which is not common among female Islamic fundamentalists.

Another important manipulation in this study is whether the confederate disclosed information about herself. In the self-disclosure condition, during the interview, the confederate described where she came from, how many siblings she had, what she liked to do after graduation, how she liked to spend her free time, as well as two good and two bad things about herself. In the no self-disclosure condition, she talked mostly about the university (e.g., when it was built, how to get parking permit on campus), and four popular student clubs in the university.

Next, the participant administered the cognitive ability task to the confederate. The confederate always gave 8 correct answers out of 10. Finally, the participant was asked to evaluate the qualifications of four freshmen applicants (two secularists and two Islamic fundamentalists) who applied to transfer from one department to another, based on some filler information unrelated to religiosity (e.g., major, high school attended, year in school).

Will contact with an "Islamic person" be able to change a secularist's negative attitude toward other Islamic undergraduates? The results show that it will when the "Islamic person" is a typical member of Islamic fun-damentalists *and* when she disclosed information about herself. In this condition, the participants rated the two Islamic applicants favorably, and more so than in the three remaining experimental conditions. Apparently, meeting and interacting with a typical out-group member who is willing to open up in communication may change one's negative attitudes toward an out-group. Based on this study and an additional study conducted in California on liberals' attitudes toward conservatives, the investigators conclude that intercultural bias can be reduced through intercultural con-tact, provided that the following conditions are present. First, the contact occurs under a cooperative atmosphere. Second, the cultural identity of the interaction partner remains salient throughout the interaction. Third, the interaction partner is seen to be a typical member of his or her cultural group. Fourth, self-disclosure occurs during the interaction. When these conditions are met, intercultural contact reduces negative bias toward the out-group (Ensari & Miller, 2002).

Psychological Costs of Intercultural Contacts

The meeting of two cultures never occurs in a social vacuum. When an individual meets another culture, the meeting place is often situated in a rich social–historical context, where the dimensions of social comparison and social dominance may be highly salient. For the disadvantaged cul-tural group, contact with the advantaged group may bring psychological costs. Again, we use the experiences of African Americans in the United States to illustrate our points, because this is one of the most researched underprivileged groups in social psychology.

Rejection Sensitivity

This is how Ian, an African American informant in a focus group study (Mendoza-Denton, Downey, Purdie, Davis, & Pietrzak, 2002) described his experiences in the New York subway:

> Every day, I wear a suit and tie. I get on the train. I always have *The New York Times*, and a cup of coffee too. But you know what? Every day, I am the last person people sit next to on the train! Especially white women. Do you know that one day I got off the train and I hap-pened to be walking behind this woman and she clutched her bag, started walking faster, and kept turning around, as if I was following her! Like I wanted to take her purse … I'm so used to this happening

that even when a woman might be in a rush to get to work, and maybe she didn't even see me, I think she's scared and running away from me. Your mind starts to play tricks on you like that, after a while.

Despite the legal protection of the rights to equal opportunities, recent studies revealed that prejudice toward black people persists, albeit in very subtle forms, in North America (Kunda, Davies, Adams, & Spencer, 2002; Payne, 2001). For example, Payne (2001, Experiment 2) had white undergraduates make speeded judgments of whether a figure presented on a computer screen was a hand tool or a handgun. These students were more likely to misperceive a hand tool as a handgun when the presentation of the target figure was preceded by a brief presentation of the face of a black man than when it was preceded by a brief presentation of a white face. Although these discriminatory practices are often very subtle, some African Americans are particularly sensitive to these cues, and may interpret them as signals of themselves being excluded from the mainstream society. Mendoza-Denton et al. (2002) refer to this kind of sensitivity as race-based rejection sensitivity.

In one study, Mendoza-Denton et al. (2002, Study 2) had European American, Asian American and African American students explain some hypothetical events. Two examples of these events are: "Imagine that you are in class one day, and the professor asks a particularly difficult question. A few people, including yourself, raise their hands to answer the question," and "Imagine that you are in a pharmacy, trying to pick out a few items. While you're looking at the different brands, you notice one of the store clerks glancing your way." European American undergraduates rarely used race to explain these events. Asian American undergraduates did so to some extent, but African American undergraduates did so relatively frequently.

Mendoza-Denton et al. (2002, Study 1) have also constructed a measure to assess individual differences in race-based rejection sensitivity. For each hypothetical situation they use to assess race-based attribution, they have the respondents indicate how concerned or anxious they would be that they would be rejected because of their race, and the likelihood that they would be rejected because of their race. This measure predicts African Americans' academic performance, interpersonal relationship, and subjective well-being. For example, African American undergraduates with higher levels of race-based rejection sensitivity report higher levels of rejection, lower sense of belonging in the university, and lower levels of well-being and positivity toward peers and professors. In addition, African American undergraduates with relatively high race-based rejection sensitivity show no improvement in well-being over a 3-week period, and they display a decline in grade point average (GPA) over five semesters. In contrast, African American undergraduates with relatively low levels of race-based rejection sensitivity show consistent improvement in well-being over a 3-week period and a slight increase in GPA over five semesters (Mendoza-Denton et al., Study 3).

Meet the Researcher: Rodolfo Mendoza-Denton

"To me, there is nothing as magical—or humbling—as travel. All of one's convictions—from what foods can constitute breakfast to what constitutes appropriate behavior at a social gathering—are brought into question by travel. The sheer enormity of a whole country doing things differently from you forces you to consider that perhaps 'truth' is relative. This is why it always makes me sad to see people being so judgmental of, even punitive towards, others who violate cultural norms. Little wonder, then, that I became drawn to cultural psychology, the central tenet of which is that culture and person make each other up. I do research and teach students within this framework, hoping that those who are impacted by my work will be able to accept that their version of 'true and indisputable' is not the only version, and that they will be glad, not shocked, when somebody offers them something unexpected for breakfast."

Rodolfo Mendoza-Denton was born and raised in Mexico City. He pursued a Ph.D. in social psychology at Columbia University and became an Assistant Professor at the University of California, Berkeley in 2002.

Stereotype Threat

When two persons meet, the possibility of social comparison emerges: Who is better in a given domain? The meeting of two cultures may bring up a similar social comparison question: Which culture is better in a given domain? A performance difference between two cultural groups might have originated from culture-biased test materials, and unequal opportunities to develop the abilities the tests assess. This difference may be reified, exaggerated, and crystallized into cultural stereotypes. Negative stereotypes of African Americans' intellectual aptitude may have followed such a developmental path (Gould, 1981).

Unfortunately, for African Americans, once the negative stereotype about their group's intellectual ability is crystallized, some may unwittingly display behavior that will reinforce the stereotype. When taking an intellectual test, they may feel threatened by the negative reputation of their group, and fear that they may end up confirming the stereotype. Paradoxically, the threat of confirming a negative group stereotype would hurt their performance in the test, and they end up confirming the group stereotype against their will. Research has shown that this debilitating effect may occur as long as African Americans are aware of their group's reputation and when they value intellectual ability. It would occur even when the test-takers do not believe in the stereotype, and take the test in the absence of European Americans. This phenomenon has been referred to as stereotype threat (Steele, 1997).

Although stereotype threat is a general threat posed by negative reputations about one's own group, it has been applied to understand cultural differences in standardized test performance in the United States. Taking a standardized test (such as the Scholastic Aptitude Test (SAT)) is a situation that could call out the reputation of one's group in intellectual performance. When this happens, individuals in a negatively reputed group would feel the burden of their group's reputation on their back when they respond to the test items. They value intellectual abilities, and want to do well in the test. At the same time, their group's reputation also poses a threat, making them doubt their abilities and fear that they may confirm the group's negative stereotype.

In a series of studies, Steele and Aronson (1995) had African and European American students complete a Graduate Record Examination (GRE) type test of verbal ability. The investigators also obtained the participants' SAT scores, which were used to project the research participants' performance in the GRE-type verbal ability test. The major research question was whether stereotype threat would hurt African American students' performance on the verbal test, so that they would not be able to attain the level of performance projected from their SAT scores.

Participants in these experiments were randomly assigned to the diagnostic or the nondiagnostic condition. Before working on the verbal ability test, participants in the diagnostic condition learned that the test was indicative of their strengths and weaknesses in reading and verbal reasoning abilities. For African American students in this condition, the negative reputation of their group on verbal abilities might pose a stereotype threat. In the nondiagnostic condition, participants learned that the study concerned psychological factors related to verbal reasoning, and no reference was made to verbal abilities. Therefore, African American students in this condition should not experience stereotype threat. European Americans do not have a negative reputation on verbal abilities, and they should not be affected by the diagnosticity manipulation.

The results confirm the prediction that stereotype threat could impair performance of members of a negatively stigmatized group. In these experiments, when the test was not diagnostic of verbal ability, African and European Americans were able to reach their projected performance to the same extent. However, when the test was "diagnostic" of verbal abilities, African American students were significantly less able to attain their projected performance than were European American students. Whereas European American students' performance was not affected by the diagnosticity manipulation, making the test diagnostic of verbal abilities significantly depressed African Americans' performance (Steele & Aronson, 1995; Studies 1 and 2).

An additional study (Steele & Aronson, 1995, Study 4) showed that even when the participants were not told that the test was diagnostic of verbal ability, making African American students aware of their ethnocultural identity could also pose a stereotype threat. The design of this study was identical to the two studies described above, except that ethnic identity manipulation replaced the diagnosticity manipulation. All participants were told that the study concerned psychological factors related to verbal reasoning. To make ethnicity salient (ethnicity salient condition), half of the participants were asked to indicate their ethnicity in a brief personal information questionnaire prior to taking the test, and half were not (ethnicity nonsalient condition).

When ethnocultural identity was not salient, African and European Americans were equally capable of reaching their projected performance. However, when ethnocultural identity was salient, African Americans were less able to reach their projected performance, compared to their European American counterparts. In short, the findings from these studies confirm that the existence of a stereotype that reflects negatively on one's group (*vis-à-vis* a comparison group) may pose a stereotype threat in situations where one is at risk of confirming it as a self-characterization. African American students are aware of their group's negative reputation on reading and verbal abilities. When they enter and interpret a situation as one where an African American's verbal abilities are being assessed, they may experience a stereotype threat and debilitate. Chronic exposure to ability impugning stereotypes, repeated activation of stereotype threat, and the decreased performance and its associated consequences could be psychologically torturous. As a long-term defense against the psychological pain invoked by stereotype threat, some African Americans may choose to psychologically and behaviorally disengage from the threatened domain (see Steele, 1997). When they decide that intellectual ability is not what they care about, they are less bothered by their group's negative reputation and their own "inferiority" in intellectual ability.

These findings also raise the issue of whether standardized tests such as the SATs and GREs are culture-fair. If African and European Americans' performance on a GRE-type test can be differentially affected by whether or not the test taker is asked to indicate their ethnicity, similar tests of intellectual abilities may not be culture-fair. However, it is important to point out that in the stereotype threat studies reviewed above, the major performance measure is the participants' actual performance relative to their projected performance. In these studies, based on SAT scores, the researchers estimated how well each participant would perform in the experimental task: Those with higher SAT scores were expected to perform better in the experimental task. The effect of stereotype threat on performance is measured by the extent to which the participants would perform above or below the projected performance in the experimental task. When African Americans experience stereotype threat, they would likely perform below the level of performance projected from their SAT scores. However, even in the stereotype threat condition, African American students' relative performance on the experimental task may still correspond closely to the relative level of performance projected from their SAT scores. In other words, in spite of the effect of stereotype threat, SAT scores could still be highly predictive of actual performance in an experimental task. If this is indeed the case, standardized test scores (like SATs) may still be the best available, albeit not perfectly culture-fair, predictors of an individual's performance in a verbal ability test. However, because the investigators did not report the relationship of SAT scores and participants' performance in the experimental tasks, it is impossible to assess the validity of standardized tests.

Controlling Mechanisms

What are the controlling mechanisms for stereotype threat; what is needed to turn it on? It can be argued that African Americans are vulnerable to stereotype threat in the intellectual domain, because they have a history of being stigmatized in this domain, and have internalized the feelings of inferiority. Similarly, women are vulnerable to stereotype threat in the domain of mathematics, because they too have a history of being stigmatized in mathematics and have internalized the feelings of inferiority. However, Aronson (Aronson, Lustina, Good, & Keough, 1999) contends that both a history of stigmatization and internalized feelings of inferiority are not necessary for an individual to experience stereotype threat. To provide evidence for his contention, he selected Caucasian men who scored 610 (out of 800) or above on the mathematics section of SAT. The selected participants also indicated that mathematics was important to them. These participants were selected because they were unlikely to have a chronic history of stigmatization and internalized inferiority feelings in the domain of mathematics. Therefore, if it can be shown that this group could also be led to experience stereotype threat, then history of stigmatization and internalized inferiority feelings are not necessary for the activation of stereotype threat.

The participants were randomly assigned to the stereotype condition and the control condition. All participants were given 20 min to complete 18 questions derived from the GRE mathematics subject test. To activate stereotype threat, prior to taking the mathematics test, participants in the stereotype condition were asked to skim over national newspapers and prominent journal articles that emphasized a "growing gap in academic performance between Asian and white students." They were also told that the study was specifically concerned with understanding why Asians appeared to outperform other students on tests of math ability. This manipulation was intended to make the participants feel targeted by a stereotype relevant to their mathematical ability. Participants in the control condition did not read any articles or hear any mention of Asian–White ability differences prior to completing the mathematics test.

The results revealed that male white students who were good at mathematics might also be vulnerable to stereotype threat. Performance was significantly lower in the stereotype condition than in the control condition, suggesting that a chronic history of stigmatization and internalized feelings of inferiority are not necessary for the activation of stereotype threat.

In a subsequent study, Aronson (Aronson et al., 1999, Study 2) replicated these findings with another sample of male white students with high SAT-Quantitative scores. In addition, he found that stereotype threat in the domain of mathematics occurred only among participants who strongly identified with mathematical ability. When the participants did not see mathematics to be very important to the self, they did not under-perform subsequent to learning about Asians' superiority in mathematics over whites. Taken together, it appears that mere awareness of one's group's negative reputation in an identified domain is sufficient to turn on stereotype threat.

Mediating Mechanisms

The next question is: What mediates the effect of stereotype threat? Steele (1997) posits that stereotype threat activates the cognition that one is taking a test in an identified domain as a member of one's group. Because one's group has a negative reputation in the domain, one fears that one would confirm the negative stereotype and incorporate it into one's self-characterization. According to this position, group identity and self-doubt should mediate the effect of stereotype threat.

Steele and Aronson (1995, Study 3) provided some evidence for this position. In this study, African and European American students were recruited to either take a diagnostic test of verbal abilities or participate in a study about the psychological factors of verbal reasoning. After the participants had reviewed some sample items in the test, they took a word completion task. The task consisted of 80 word fragments with missing letters specified as blank spaces (e.g., L A ___ ___). Some of these word fragments had one possible solution as a word reflecting race or African Americans [e.g., ___ ___ C E (RACE), MI ___ ___ ___ ___ ___ ___ (MINORITY), CO ___ ___ ___ (COLOR)], and some had one possible solution as a word reflecting self-doubts [e.g., LO ___ ___ ___ (LOSER), SHA ___ ___ (SHAME), W ___ ___ K (WEAK)]. If ethnic identity and self-doubt were cognitively accessible, participants would more likely complete these word fragments with words related to race and self-doubt than words unrelated to these ideas. For example, for CO___ ___ ___, they would more likely complete it with COLOR than with COAST. For SHA ___ ___, they would more likely complete it with SHAME than with SHAPE.

When the diagnosticity of the test was not emphasized, African Americans and European Americans did not differ in the likelihood of listing words related to race or self-doubt. However, when the test was depicted as a diagnostic test of verbal abilities, African Americans were much more likely to list words related to race, and self-doubt.

An additional study (Blascovich, Spencer, Quinn, & Steele, 2001) showed that when African American students took a "test of intelligence" developed by a European American professor, they showed increased arterial blood pressure (relative to their baseline level) 10 min into experiment, and their blood pressure remained high throughout the experimental session. This did not result from African American students' habitual physiological responses to taking tests, because another group of African American students who took the same test presented to them as a culture-fair test developed by an African American professor did not display these physiological responses. European American students did not display increased arterial blood pressure regardless of whether the test was presented as a test developed by an European American professor or an African American professor. Apparently, stereotype threat is a stressful experience.

Fearing that one would likely confirm one's group's negative reputation in the intellectual domain, individuals under stereotype threat may reduce their motivation to perform and elicit a disruptive reduction in cognitive effort (Croizet, Despres, Gauzins, Huguet, Leyens, & Moet, 2004). Metabolic demands generated by brain activity during mental effort would result in peripheral cardiovascular reactions (Kramer & Weber,

2000), causing interval fluctuations between consecutive heartbeats. Thus, heart-rate variability is a sensitive measure of the amount of cognitive effort committed to meet cognitive processing demands (Jorna, 1992). One study (Croizet et al., 2004) showed that when stereotype threat was activated, performance in the stereotyped group was poorer than that in the nonstereotyped group. In addition, heart-rate variability was lower in the stereotyped group than in the nonstereotyped group, indicating a lower level of cognitive effort in the stereotyped group. Mediation analysis indicated that reduction in cognitive effort was one reason why performance was lower under stereotype threat.

In short, the effect of stereotype threat on performance seems to be mediated by attention to one's cultural group membership, self-doubt, stress reactions, and reduction in mental effort.

Maintaining the Status Quo: Majority Group's Reactions to Group Stereotypes

Thus far, we have focused on the negatively stereotyped group's responses to their group's negative reputation. However, there is another side of the story—how do members of the positively stereotyped group respond to their group's positive reputation?

Danso and Esses (2001) used a personality measure to assess the levels of social dominance in a group of European Canadian participants. According to social dominance theory (e.g., Pratto, 1999; Sidanius & Pratto, 1999), in social contexts in which groups have unequal power, some ideologies would emerge to justify and maintain group hierarchy. Moreover, some individuals adhere more strongly to these ideologies than others. Because the stereotype of European Canadians' superiority over black people in the intellectual domain is widely distributed in Canada, some European Canadians may believe that they are entitled to such a position of superiority. These individuals are said to have a strong social dominance orientation.

For some European Canadians, being in a situation in which a black experimenter administers a test of intellectual ability to them may constitute a threat to white superiority. In response to the threat, they may increase their effort to maintain the perception of white intellectual superiority. This was what Danso and Esses (2001) found in their study: European Canadians who adhere strongly to the social dominance orientation did better in a test of mathematical ability when tested by a black experimenter than by a Caucasian experimenter. However, among European Canadians with weak social dominance orientation, the ethnic identity of the experimenter had no effect on their performance.

Dominance-seeking members of a positively reputed group may try to outperform others when the situation confers an opportunity to enhance their status (Josephs, Newman, Brown, & Beer, 2003). In one study, the participants were all male undergraduates, and they were preselected as being highly identified with mathematics. There is consistent evidence across a wide variety of animal species that behaviors intended to achieve, maintain, and enhance status (i.e., dominant and power-seeking behaviors) are observed primarily among high testosterone individuals (e.g., Mazur & Booth, 1998). Thus, to identify dominant individuals, the participants' levels of testosterone were evaluated through analyzing the enzyme immunoassays of salivary samples collected from the participants. After saliva collection, participants were told that they would be taking a test of mathematical reasoning abilities. At this point, the participants were randomly assigned to one of two experimental conditions. In the status enhancement potential condition, participants were told that the test would identify only those who were "exceptional" in math ability compared to everyone else. In the no status enhancement potential condition, participants were told that the test would identify only those "weak" in mathematics ability compared to everyone else. Next, all participants were given 20 min to solve 20 questions drawn from the quantitative section of the GRE.

The results showed that high testosterone males performed better on the GRE questions than low testosterone males only when they learned that the test provided an opportunity for status enhancement. When the test could only identify individuals with weak mathematics abilities and hence had no status enhancement potential, high and low testosterone males did not differ in their performance. In short, in an identified domain where one's group has a more favorable reputation than other groups, individuals with a strong dominance orientation may be particularly motivated to do well in a test, when the test-taking situation offers an opportunity for status enhancement. The increased motivation may in turn lead to better performance, again confirming the prevailing stereotypes.

In sum, when social comparison and social dominance are made salient, intercultural contact will evoke a set of psychological processes that maintain the hierarchical rankings of the positively reputed groups over the negatively reputed groups in valued domains. Such psychological processes may lead to performance impairment as well as feelings of inferiority in the negatively reputed groups. Accordingly, although intercultural contact may confer psychological benefits in some situations, it may also bring psychological costs to the underprivileged groups in the society.

Conclusion

In an article on multicultural education, Maehr and Yamaguchi (2001) made the following remarks:

> A standard programmatic answer to managing cultural diversity often has involved emphasizing the value of differentness. For example, in the United States, certain months have been designated to celebrate the country's diversity ... Such celebrations serve to highlight the differences among American students by their ethnic background. Further, these distinctions may only succeed in making not only differentness, but also disadvantageness, an issue for the child—especially so in school and classroom contexts, where social comparisons, competition and focus on being the smartest and the best is the order of the day.

Josephs et al. (2003) point out that most performance-based stereotypes are explicit or implicit statements of comparison between two or more groups (e.g., African Americans have poor intellectual abilities compared to European Americans; women possess poor math ability compared to men). Therefore, there is connection between situations capable of confirming a performance stereotype and situations involving the gain or loss of status. Maehr and Yamaguchi's comments highlight how the focus on competitiveness in American society fuels social comparisons, making the historically disadvantaged group liable to rejection sensitivity and stereotype threat.

As discussed in the first part of the current chapter, intercultural contact could confer important psychological benefits. In an increasingly global environment, intercultural contact may contribute to the accumulation of social capital or to the development of networks, mutual understandings, and shared knowledge that facilitate cooperation within and among groups. However, when social comparison and dominance are highlighted, intercultural contact could create a burden for the disadvantaged groups. A major challenge for educators and social capital developers is how they can construct a model of cultural competence that recognizes cultural differences without promoting cultural stereotypes at the same time, and a model that will protect cultural minorities from the harmful effects of stereotype threat while simultaneously empowering cultural minorities.

Globalization and Multicultural Identities

11

Tsunami and Globalization

It was 6:29 on the Boxing Day morning of 2004 when the massive under-sea earthquake happened off Sumatra. The earthquake was over 9 in magnitude on the Richter scale. At 9:51, another earthquake hit the Great Nicobar Island, over 7 in magnitude. The undersea quakes sent off killing waves, claiming over 100,000 lives.

The tsunami drew the world's attention to the indigenous tribes in the Andaman and Nicobar Islands, when the killing waves brutally hit their homeland and drove them closer to the verge of extinction. These tribes have successfully shielded themselves from other civilizations. The Andaman's Sentinelese, estimated to have a population of 100, live on the North Sentinel Island, 64 km southwest of Port Blair, India. Their ancestors were thought to be Burmese nomads who were swept away to the Andamans by the sea, and settled there. The Sentinelese have their own language, which has no script, and is unintelligible even to other tribes on the islands. For subsistence, they hunt for wild boars, sea turtles, and fish. Both men and women wear nothing except a waist belt of bark (for men only) and some leaf ornaments around the head, neck, and arms. The Sentinelese are among the most isolated communities in the world; they have almost no interaction with other tribes and would use bows and iron-tipped arrows to drive away outsiders.

On the Little Andaman Island lives the Onge tribe, with a population of around 100 before the tsunami. The Onge are foragers, and speak their own language, which again has no script. The Shompen reside on the Great Nicobar Island and numbered around 280 before the earthquakes. Shompen is a semi-nomadic tribe. Its major economic activities include fishing, foraging, and hunting. Its members feed on turtle, snakes, lizards, and crocodiles. Interaction with outsiders without permission from the head of the tribe is strictly prohibited.

Over the years, the tribes on the Andaman and Nicobar islands have been able to preserve their indigenous lifestyles. Because their homeland is very close to the epicenter of the quake, the world's attention was directed to them. However, for precisely the same reason, the fate of these tribes has become uncertain; they are at great risk of extinction because of the tsunami and the calamities that followed this natural disaster.

The tsunami also revealed the scale of globalization that has taken place in South Asia. On December 30, 2004, the *Times of India* adopted the title "Wave of Globalization takes pain beyond Asia" for its front-page story. According to the story:

> Sunday's tsunami spread a ring of destruction through nearly a dozen countries. Those are the places most directly affected, and on a calamitous scale. But the disaster has rippled far beyond Asia, making it truly a tragedy felt across the globe.
>
> Among the tens of thousands of people missing or dead, thousands are believed to have come from outside the region, including many who were spending their holidays at Thai, Malaysian, and Indonesian resorts. Reported deaths now cover at least 40 nationalities, reaching from South Africa to South Korea, with surprising concentrations of people still unaccounted for from European countries.

Indeed, the disaster has taken the lives of British actor Richard Attenborough's daughter and granddaughter, almost claimed the lives of Olympic skier Ingemar Stenmark and Czech model Petra Nemcova, and injured Hong Kong actor Jet Li. In the news article mentioned above, the reporter made the following remarks:

> The disaster's reach is an unsettling reminder that globalization has brought the world closer together in unexpected ways so that people now share the pain as well as profit from far-flung places. Even for people who have never left home, otherwise abstract calamities in distant lands now frequently have a familiar face.

Indeed, the new millennium has started off in the direction of increased global connectivity and intercultural migration. Globalization has made it increasingly difficult for indigenous tribes like the Andamanian tribes to remain "uncontaminated" by the outside world. At the same time, the increased speed of globalization has raised some interesting questions: Is the world becoming a global village? Will all regional differences be resolved through multilateral cultural hegemony? To people living in multicultural societies, the increased intercultural connectivity has also offered them rich multicultural experiences, as well as several different cultural perspectives to define the self. Many of these individuals may feel the need to construct a multicultural identity: What does it mean to be a multicultural individual? What does it mean to have a multicultural self?

It is beyond the scope of the current chapter to provide a comprehensive and thorough analysis of these issues. In fact, research on them from a social psychological perspective is almost nonexistent. Due to the dearth of social psychological research data, to offer an intelligible account of some of these issues, we rely extensively on findings from the cognate disciplines (e.g., consumer research, cultural and ethnographic studies, political sociology). The current chapter aims to use some illustrative examples to highlight both the complexity and the significance of these issues, as well as the urgent need to conduct systematic social psychological research on them.

Migration and Globalization

As mentioned, the multinational casualties of the undersea earthquakes in South Asia revealed the extent of population movement across national borders. Migration is a major component of population movement. According to the World Bank Group (2004), in 1985–1990, the annual rate of growth of the world's migrant population was 2.6%. The growth rate decelerated in the early 1990s due to immigration restrictions imposed by high-income countries, and accelerated again starting from 1997. First World countries are the major receiving countries of international migrants, whereas Third World countries are the major sending countries. Over 60% of the world migrants moved from developing countries to developed countries. Some major destination countries are the United States, Germany, Australia, Canada, and the United Kingdom. Countries with the highest foreign or foreign-born population in the total population are Luxembourg, Australia, Switzerland, Canada, the United States, Austria, and Germany. In 2000, 10.4% of the total US population (compared to 7.9% in 1990) and 12.4% of the total US labor force (compared to 9.4% in 1990) were foreign born. Many migrants are *temporary* international workers (e.g., Filipino domestic helpers in Hong Kong) who move from one country to another for employment. Business travel and tourism are two other major components of population movements.

Migration influences the ethnic composition of both the sending and receiving countries. For example, the United States receives approximately 97 million international travelers by air alone annually (Figure 11.1). Similarly, Canada has a population of about 31 million people, but has close to 50 million entries by nonresident travelers annually (Richmond, 2002).

Globalization involves movement of people across the globe, as well as the spread of the global economy to regional economies around the world. As noted in Chapter 10, multinational corporations employ workers and export their commodities and services to consumers in many developing countries. From the perspective of economics of international trade, investment of multinational corporations in a developing country brings jobs and

income to the country. For example, when Nokia establishes its business in Brazil, it provides jobs for workers there, brings tax revenue for the local government, makes mobile communication available to the local people at lower costs, and provides training and advancement for local workers and managers.

Yet, opposition to corporate globalization has been growing for several years. Most activists of various antiglobalization movements are not against

FIGURE 11.1. Monument to the Immigrant, New Orleans, Louisiana: "Drago and Klara Cvitanovich immigrated from Croatia in June, 1964, with a vision that only hard work and perseverance could make happen. What they gave to their sons and others is an example for generations to follow."

greater economic interdependency and cooperation between nations via global trade. What really concerns antiglobalization activists is that globalization is often driven by the narrow economic interests of large multinational corporations at the expense of the interests of the developing countries and the less privileged groups in developed countries. The antiglobalization demonstration that took place in Seattle during the World Trade Organization (WTO) Ministerial Conference, November 29–December 3, 1999 revealed the widespread concerns about possible abuse of multinational corporate power. Well-known multinational corporations such as Nike sneakers, Gap jeans, Starbucks coffee, McDonalds, and Shell Oil have been accused of union-busting, sweatshop working conditions, and child labor practices on a global scale. The litany of castigation includes paying low wages, offering minimal health benefits, depleting old-growth and rain forests, using unsafe pesticides, bio-engineering agriculture crops, violating animal rights, and colluding with violent and repressive regimes.

The social economic implications of globalization have received increasing attention not only in public discourse but also in social science research. At the societal level, as globalization proceeds, previously isolated economies are integrated into the world economy via international trade and investment. Some developing countries have benefited from this process. The most globalized developing countries (e.g., China and some other Asian countries) enjoyed the highest GNP per capita growth, while most developing countries that failed to participate in globalization processes face negative income growth rates. The 10 countries and regions that have enjoyed the highest average rate of growth in income between 1980 and 2003 are China, Singapore, South Korea, Vietnam, Taiwan, Oman, Malaysia, Thailand, India, and Indonesia, with an average GDP growth rate of 5.3–9.5%. However, there is also evidence that the gap between the richest and poorest countries, and that between the richest and poorest groups of individuals in many nations (including the most industrialized states such as the United States and Western European countries), have increased (Alderson & Nielsen, 2002). For instance, 12% of the world's population resides in North America and Western Europe and accounts for 60% of the world's private consumption spending. In contrast, one-third of the world's population lives in South Asia or sub-Saharan Africa and accounts for only 3.2% of the world's private consumption spending (Worldwatch Institute, 2004). China is the most globalized developing country, with the highest average annual rate of growth in income among the developing countries. However, in 2001, 16.6% of China's total population earned less than US$ 1 per day; 11.0% were undernourished (World Development Indicators Database, 2004). In 2004, 2.8 billion people in the world survived on US\$ 2 per day, and 825 million were undernourished. Within an industrialized country, the problem of income inequality has been aggravated by direct investment outflow, import of cheaper consumer goods, and to a lesser extent inflow of international labor through migration (Alderson & Nielsen, 2002).

Psychologically, with the rapid growth of global linkages and global consciousness, social life is organized on a global scale. As Robertson (1992, p. 8) noted, globalization involves "the compression of the world and the intensification of consciousness of the world as a whole." The rapid speed of air transportation, and the instantaneous electronic transfer of information and capital have led to what Anthony Giddens (1985) refers to as time–space distanciation, or the experiential compression of time and space. A postmodern, global culture is often characterized as one "of virtuality in the global flows which transcend time and space" (Castells, 1998, p. 350). The constraints that bounded different knowledge traditions to a confined space have disintegrated. Consequently, contemporary culture travelers would no longer be surprised at coexistence of different cultural traditions in the same space. For example, a culture traveler may find a CNBC headquarters right next to a Hindu temple in Mumbai, India, or a KFC Restaurant and a Haagen-Dazs ice-cream house in Shanghai's heritage culture reservation area. In China, popular magazines are filled with commercial messages promoting individualism and modern lifestyles to the younger generation (Zhang & Shavitt, 2003).

The demographic changes and meeting of different cultures in the same space accompanying globalization have important implications for the coordination of knowledge and negotiation of identities in global cities. To begin, globalization requires integration of local economies into the global market, which is grounded in the capitalist logic. A defining feature of the capitalist logic is instrumental rationality, a kind of rationality defined in terms of efficiency and feasibility of achieving goals via calculative and strategic use of means (Weber, 1904/1958). Instrumental rationality flourished in Europe during the Enlightenment Period when a coalescence of individualistic ideas became popular. These ideas include religious individualism (the emphasis on the individual's personal relationship with God, and the belief that salvation is contingent on personal faith and needs no intermediaries), economic individualism (the belief that individual performance determines the reward one deserves), political individualism (the beliefs that individual rights are protected by law, and that political systems are set up to satisfy individual needs), methodological individualism (the belief that all social phenomena should be understood as resulting from the psychological processes of individuals), and psychological individualism (the belief in the value of the individual, self-actualization, individual uniqueness and individual identity; Ho & Chiu, 1994). These ideas are major elements in the mainstream knowledge tradition in most industrialized countries, consisting of the United States and most Western European countries. The question is: will globalization ultimately lead to homogenization of cultures via *global hegemony*?

Will Globalization Lead to Homogenization of Cultures?

At first glance, the global hegemony project is destined to succeed. Western nations, representatives of the global culture, are generally perceived to be more economically advanced than non-Western nations. Developing countries that aspire to become an industrialized nation may treat the Western economic powers as reference nations not only in the domain of economic development, but also in the realm of cultural restructuring. The global culture has been characterized as new, modern, scientific, and results-oriented. It privileges consumerism, individualism, competition, and efficiency (Pilkington & Johnson, 2003). These values may be seen as values that separate advanced societies from economically backward traditional economies. Thus, the global culture may become the reference culture for some developing countries, which seek to emulate Western economic powers by embracing global values. As a consequence, global culture exerts its hegemonic influence on some local cultures via voluntary submission to the global culture (van Strien, 1997).

In addition, the capitalist logic in the global market emphasizes the use of scientific knowledge and technology to achieve controllable and predictable results. To navigate the global market smoothly, instead of relying on traditional knowledge and experience, one needs scientific and professional knowledge in business administration. Not surprisingly, globalization in many developing countries is often accompanied by a vast demand for MBA programs. For example, according to the US and Foreign Commercial Service and the US Department of State (2004), China's rapid entry into global markets since 1990 was accompanied by a rapidly increasing demand for MBA and EMBA education. In 1991, the Chinese government began to authorize Chinese universities to offer MBA programs. By 2004, 87 universities in China were permitted to offer MBA education, and the number of MBA and EMBA programs had increased from a nonexistent base in 1990 to 150–200 in 2004. Approximately 10,000 students graduated from MBA programs in 2004, compared to 86 in 1991. China estimates that by 2006, the annual demand for MBA graduates will increase to 37,500. The most common MBA programs in China are domestic MBA programs that rely exclusively on local faculty to provide business education. However, the programs that enjoy higher prestige are usually foreign-partnered programs. These programs, which have the strongest appeal to middle and senior level professionals, are characterized by selective admissions criteria, with English proficiency often a requirement, and a blend of local and foreign faculty. In short, as a result of globalization, in the economic domain, traditional practices are often gradually replaced by management principles widely practiced in the global economies.

Furthermore, globalization has brought rapid change in consumption patterns, and the spread of global "brand-name" goods. An expanding consumerist culture with its attending global marketing strategies such as global advertising tends to exploit similar basic material desires and create similar lifestyles (Parameswaran, 2002). Globalization has led to the spread of the consumer class from the developed nations to the developing nations. The consumer class consists of users of televisions, telephones, and the Internet, along with the culture and ideals these products transmit (Worldwatch Institute, 2004). An individual in the consumer class has the consumption pattern, lifestyle, and culture that became fashionable in Europe, North America, and Japan in the 20th century. As incomes rise, more people can afford a multitude of consumer items associated with a modern lifestyle and greater prosperity (e.g., mobile phone, personal computer, Internet connection, television, and multimedia entertainment system). In 2002, 1.12 billion households (three-quarters of humanity) owned at least one television set. There were 1.1 billion fixed phone lines, another 1.1 billion mobile phones, and 600 million Internet users. With globalization, the consumer class has spread to the developing countries. In 2002, China and India had a combined consumer class of 362 million people, more than all of Western Europe (although China and India's large consumer class constituted only 16% of the region's population, whereas 89% of Europeans belonged to the consumer class). In China, some 11,000 more cars emerged onto the roads every day in 2003 (Worldwatch Institute, 2004). According to the World Development Indicators Database (2004), in 2002, 32.8% of the total population in China had fixed line and/or mobile phones (compared to 0.4% in 1995), and 2.8% had personal computers (compared to 0.2% in 1995).

To appreciate how extensively globalization has changed local food cultures in globalized developing countries, one can pay a brief visit to the supermarkets in these countries, and observe how soft drinks like Coca-Cola, Pepsi, Sprite, and Seven-Up fill the shelves there. According to the 2003 Zenith Report on Global Soft Drinks, in 2002, the United States was still the world's biggest soft drinks market, with 24% of the global market share. The runners-up were two globalized developing countries: Mexico and China. Interestingly, the five countries with the fastest growing soft drinks consumption from 1997 to 2002 were exclusively from the emerging regions of Asia, East Europe and the Middle East. The number of McDonald's restaurants in developing countries increased from 448 in 1991 to 1824 in 1996. For example, in East Asia, Southeast Asia, and the Pacific Region, the number of McDonald's restaurants increased from 236 in 1991 to 898 in 1996. In Latin America and the Caribbean, the increase during the same period was from 212 to 837. Additionally, globalization may also lead to homogenization of culture within a country. For example, in the United States, there are over 14,000 freestanding coffee houses, and Starbucks owns about 30% of the total (Daniels, 2003). Starbucks, with its Europe-inspired modern decor, upscale, corporate ambience, and international product offerings, has acquired the status of a cultural icon (Holt, 2002). The global success of global brands such as McDonald's and Starbucks has led some writers to predict an inevitable colonization of world cultures by international corporate brands (Falk, 1999). George Ritzer (1993), for example, has described the projected corporate colonization of local cultures as "McDonaldization of society."

There is some evidence that globalization may lead to the demise of local cultures. As noted, globalization involves the continuing transformation of the society via science and technology (Fischer, 1999). Penetration of science and technology education, which supports and is in turn supported by instrumental rationality, is a good indicator of the extent of globalization in a country. In a comparative study of 20 nations that differ widely in the extent of globalization (e.g., from Sweden to Romania, Brazil, Mexico, and Thailand), Tzeng and Henderson (1999) reported that the best country-level predictor of the level of globalization is the country's level of involvement in science education. Countries with more mature global economies have greater educational expenditures per capita, a greater number of university professors per capita, a higher percentage of the adult population with college level education, and a greater number of students attending institutions of higher learning abroad. In addition, in countries with more mature global economies, people identify more strongly with the value of scientific education.

The above finding illustrates that globalization is associated with greater emphasis on higher learning and scientific education. However, this does not imply that globalization has erosive effects on local cultures, unless one assumes that scientific education is incompatible with local cultures. The validity of this assumption is highly questionable.

Other studies have sought to link exposure to the global culture, directly via working in global industries such as tourism or indirectly through participation in higher education institutions, to the demise of indigenous knowledge traditions. For example, in one study, participants from Kenya and the United States generated 20 statements to describe themselves. Among pastoral nomads in Kenya, only 18% of their spontaneous self-descriptions referenced personal attributes. The remaining 82% referenced memberships in social categories. By comparison, the percentage of self-descriptions that referenced personal attributes was 42% for hotel workers and university staff in Kenya, 83% for university students in Kenya, and 87% for American undergraduates (Ma & Schoeneman, 1997).

However, findings from this kind of comparative studies are difficult to interpret. For example, in the study conducted in Kenya, college students and employees in hotels and universities might belong to a self-selected sample with a strong preference for the global culture or a cosmopolitan (vs. tribal) identity. Thus, their American-like responses to the self-description test could be expressions of their self-chosen identity rather than indentations caused by globalization's erosive effects.

In short, although some people believe that globalization would lead to the demise of local cultures and homogenization of world cultures, there is little evidence for this belief. In fact, as we will see in the next section, globalization does not have an overriding influence on local cultures. Instead, local cultures may react to the force of the global market in various ways. The dynamic interaction of the global and the local has received a lot of attention in the social science literature.

Globalization and Cultural Diversity

Pluralization

Some writers disagree that globalization will inevitably result in homogenization of culture. Lal (2000) makes a distinction between the material and the cosmological beliefs in a culture. Material beliefs pertain to ways of making a living or beliefs about the material world, particularly the economy. By contrast, cosmological beliefs define the purpose and meaning of life and an individual's relationship to others. Lal believes that although the material beliefs in the global culture will gain popularity as a country is integrated into the global market, cosmological beliefs in local cultures are relatively resistant to the influence of globalization (Figure 11.2).

Consistent with this hypothesis, based on detailed analyses of longitudinal survey data from 65 societies, Inglehart and Baker (2000) found that economic development is accompanied by increased adherence to values that emphasize secularism, rationality, and self-expression, which may reflect increased reliance on science, instrumental rationality, and

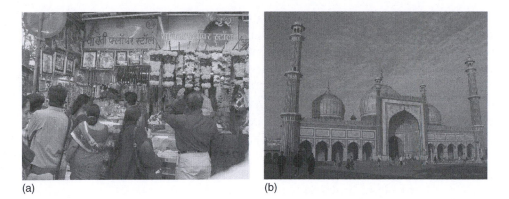

(a)   (b)

FIGURE 11.2. Some cultural practices, particularly those related to cosmological or religious beliefs, tend to persist in spite of globalization. In India, despite extensive globalization, Hinduism and Islamism remain widespread: (a) Hindus buying religious offerings in Mumbai, and (b) the Jama Mosque in Delhi.

individualism for guiding economic activities. However, the broad knowledge tradition (e.g., Protestantism, Confucianism) that defines personhood and sociality in a society leaves an imprint on values, which endures despite the erosive effects of globalization.

According to these findings, globalization does not always result in the demise of local cultures. With globalization, new values, beliefs, and practices associated with the global culture may gain popularity in the economic sphere (e.g., in work settings and the marketplace). Meanwhile, local cultural traditions may retain their authority in other domains of life (e.g., the family and interpersonal domains). Thus, instead of homogenizing culture, globalization may lead to pluralization of cultures via the meeting of global and local cultures in one locality.

Glocalization

Because the spread of the global culture may provoke resistance and reactions from local cultures, globalization has been characterized as a process that generates contradictory spaces (Sassen, 1998). Despite the global success of Starbucks Coffee, it is condemned for propagating "a soul-numbing aesthetic homogeneity and sanitized versions of creative arts" (Thompson & Arsel, 2004, p. 634). One outcome of the contestation of global and local culture is the adaptation of global norms or practices to local traditions, a process that is often referred to as glocalization (Robertson, 1995). There are many examples of glocalization in developing countries. Three such examples are glocalization of practices in the shopping mall, of international brands, and of the functions of global consumer products.

The contestation of global and local cultures is most intense in the marketplace, where the globalized capital seeks complete domination (Parameswaran, 2002). The shopping mall is an outpost of the globalized economy. The global integration of the consumer market has changed people's shopping behavior. Before, people shopped at the corner store or the market. Now supermarkets and malls dominate. Because many malls are planned and built by no more than 10 transnational architectural firms, malls throughout the world share common features of aesthetics, architecture and design. For this reason, the shopping mall is also an architectural symbol of globalization. However, even in the shopping mall, which has been assumed to be an archetypical globalized space, aspects of the local culture are co-opted into the world of consumption (Salcedo, 2003). For example, in the Philippines' Megamall, there is a church constructed for Catholic masses. In Saudi Arabia, there is a mall where foreign women perform the sales work and men are prohibited to enter.

Santana (2003) has analyzed the success story of MTV Asia, which richly illustrates the phenomenon of glocalization. MTV is an American brand name that has rapidly infiltrated the global market. However, as MTV enters Southeast Asian countries, Indonesia's Padi and Singapore's Stefanie Sun are also featured in MTV Asia's programs. Although these Asian singers' faces are not familiar to an average American, their voices have reshaped MTV's global image.

MTV's Asian programming began in 1992 when MTV Japan was launched, and quickly became a phenomenal success after MTV Asia was introduced in 1995. MTV Asia is more than a simple carbon copy of its Western divisions. Instead, it has addressed the region's distinct local tastes by consistently increasing the number of programs featuring Asian music. In 2003, local programs constituted up to 80% of MTV Asia's programming.

As MTV entered the new millennium, three new subdivisions— MTV Philippines, MTV Thailand, and MTV Indonesia—were established. The creation of specialized channels in different countries that meet the needs of the target local audiences reflects MTV's commitment to its goal of localizing MTV's global image. When a survey showed that 95% of Thai teenagers preferred local to foreign music, MTV Thailand was created. Frank Brown, President of MTV Asia, offered a prelude to the establishment of these three highly successful subdivisions at the C21 World Marketing Conference in 2000. He said, "It's very important that what we're going to market in each country fits with the local culture."

In some instances, instead of extinguishing local music, MTV revitalizes it. For example, before MTV aired the program MTV Salam Dangdut,

dangdut had long been unpopular among young people in Indonesia. When MTV aired this program, local audiences began to appreciate this traditional Indonesian music, and young people hailed it as cool. In other instances, MTV Asia has provided some local, previously obscure, musicians with the publicity and venues to achieve mass popularity. Their burgeoning popularity has, in turn, helped the domestic music industry to flourish.

MTV Asia does more than turn the global brand of MTV local; it has also helped to turn local music global. MTV has increased the popularity of many Asian performers outside their own country. Shows like MTV Asia Awards have provided Asian singers with opportunities to perform in front of the world. Some MTV Asia shows have brought a lot of Western media attention to Asian singers such as Padi from Indonesia and Jay Chou from Taiwan. In short, MTV is a global brand that has turned local and is helping local music turn global.

A recent ethnographic study (Yoon, 2003) has revealed how the mobile phone, a global technology, is used to further local cultural goals in South Korea. Koreans value *cheong*, which is an expression of affective and attached relationships between people closely related to one another. Koreans emphasize strong attachment to members of the extended family. Once a person is accepted as a member of the *cheong* network, he or she is treated as family. *Cheong* requires sharing of affection or attachment with other members in the network through face-to-face interactions.

In South Korea, globalization is perceived as having the potential of destroying *cheong*. Particularly because the use of mobile phones permits young people to bypass traditional face-to-face communication, there is concern that mobile phones may replace traditional means of communication with an individualized indirect mode of communication, leading to separation of young Koreans from family-oriented social relations. However, as shown in Yoon's (2003) study, the consumption of new personal communication technology, instead of destroying local cultural tradition, plays a crucial role in reinventing and strengthening the local tradition by maintaining local sociality of *cheong* without face-to-face interaction.

For instance, in South Korea, young people often purchase a mobile phone in order to access peer networks or avoid being excluded from peer communication. Some use their mobile phones to connect primarily with current school friends or old friends who are now enrolled in another school. Others use them to develop newly acquired friendships. Interestingly, young South Koreans describe technologically mediated communications not grounded in face-to-face interaction, such as text messaging, as "pretending," "not real" and "childish." As Yoon (2003, p. 332) noted, "Young Koreans appropriate the mobile phone as useful technology when it is based on a face-to-face relationship; in contrast, mobile communication for young people may be felt to be restrictive and boring when it is dissociated from such direct interaction. For this reason, it can be argued that mobile communication articulates face-to-face friendships, but does not negate or move beyond them."

The popular use of mobile phones in South Korea is also accompanied by development of consensus concerning the etiquette of mobile phone use. For example, young South Koreans consider it impolite to receive phone calls during class time. Meanwhile, mobile phones also make it easier for parents to monitor and control their children's behaviors. As one informant in the Yoon (2003) study said in an interview, "My mum has often sent me messages whenever she feels bored at home, since I showed her how to use text messaging. … Actually, I have just got a message from my mum. She asked me to buy something on my way home. So, she now wants to make sure I've done it by sending a text message." In short, the popularity of mobile phones does not result in erosion of traditional sociality. In this example, parents use mobile phones to engage their children in communication even when face-to-face interactions are not possible. As Yoon (2003, p. 341) concluded from these observations, "young people reworked traditional and local sociality by practicing strategies of reappropriating global technology." The examples described in this section illustrate how local cultures and the forces of globalization interpenetrate and shape each other, producing heterogeneity as global brands and products acquire a variety of localized meanings (D. Miller, 1998).

Internal Differentiation

Globalization may also promote internal differentiation of culture. The meeting of global and local cultures may inspire construction of new cultural modes and lifestyles. For example, in India, globalization has challenged the traditional notion of the female gender and inspired alternative conceptions of womanhood (Figure 11.3). In Hindu patriarchal beliefs, the female gender is essential and primordial (Mahalingam, 2003). In one study, when asked to imagine that a man's brain was transplanted to a woman's head (figurally, the house of mind), and vice versa, most American participants believed that a brain transplant would change the gender behaviors of both a man and a woman. Most Indian participants also believed that transplanting a woman's brain to a man's head would change the man's behavior. In other words, they believe that gender is in the mind of the individuals. By contrast, Indian men, particularly

FIGURE 11.3. Globalization affords alternative construction of gender in India, promoting internal differentiation of gender in the country.

Brahmin males, believed that transplanting a man's brain to a woman's head would not change the woman's behaviors. To Brahmin men, a woman's body biologically predisposes her to behave in a feminine manner, so she would exhibit feminine qualities, and even the most radical medical intervention could not alter this biological predisposition (Mahalingam & Rodriguez, 2003).

However, globalization has brought new educational and employment opportunities to women in India, and hence reduced their reliance on their husbands and fathers. In addition, as shown in an in-depth ethnographic study conducted in West Bengal, India (Ganguly-Scrase, 2003), in promoting a consumerist ideology, the mass media have created a new consuming subject, a glamorous "liberated" woman that epitomizes independent mobility through shopping. In televised advertisements, this consuming subject will appear in the form of a glamorous woman dressed up in Westernized high-fashion, who drives a sports car and shops in a modern mall enjoyably, all by herself. Using images of this new consuming subject, younger women in Bengal construct new models of womanhood that stand in opposition to the traditional patriarchal gender norms and challenge the gender ideologies in Bengali culture.

In summary, although there have been some concerns that globalization might undermine cultural diversity, there are also reasons to expect that despite extensive globalization, the processes of pluralization, glocalization, and internal differentiation will foster cultural diversity in developing countries.

Migration and Management of Multicultural Identities

Recall that migration is a major facet of globalization. As people move from their home country to a new country, they acquire new cultural experiences. At the same time, they also acquire multiple cultural identities and need to face the issue of managing multiple cultural identities (Arnett, 2002; Hong, Wan, No, & Chiu, in press).

Individuals with multiple cultural identities may experience intrapersonal conflict as well as conflicting demands across different cultural contexts. For some, these cultural identities have a lot of overlap and are compatible with each other. For others, these identities carry conflicting expectations (Roccas & Brewer, 2002). For example, during the US–Iraq War, some Iraqi immigrants in the US might believe that the War would benefit Iraq by bringing American style democracy to their heritage country, and hence would not feel any conflict between their American and Iraqi identities. However, other Iraqi immigrants might feel that being an American and being an Iraqi called for different attitudes toward the War (e.g., supporting the American troops vs. denouncing invasion of their heritage country). As this example illustrates, depending on how multiple identities are represented, there may be little or intense identity conflict. When one feels that one cannot meet the expectations from two cultural identities simultaneously, one is likely to experience intrapersonal identity conflict. In contrast, when two cultural identities are represented as compatible, bicultural individuals may experience little internal identity conflict.

Even when there is little internal conflict *within* multiculturals, there may be differing demands and expectations placed on members of each cultural group—to be culturally authentic, to be loyal to the group, speak the language, and follow the norms, along with numerous others. A response from a US immigrant from Taiwan in an in-depth interview

(Hong et al., 2006) illustrates the conflicting external demands a bicultural individual may experience:

> Um … well since I live in both places [Taiwan & the US] and like every year I go back to Taiwan to visit I find myself changing within the two cultures. It's like I go back to Taiwan they sometimes get scared of me because I'm too open and stuff. So I try to be more and more like um like fit into their definition um but when I come back I sometimes feel myself a little bit overwhelmed like oh everybody's so open but then after like a month I get used to it. And then I go back to Taiwan again and then they're not used to me again so it's like a cycle kind of …."

The conflicting demands and expectations from different cultural groups necessitate management of situation-appropriate responses.

Successful management of multicultural identities involves resolution of conflicts arising from these manifold internal and external demands (Hong et al., in press). This requires both overt and conscious flexibility (Birman, 1998; Phinney & Devich-Navarro, 1997), along with more subtle adaptability to the cultural requirements of the situation (see Chapter 10). It also demands increased proficiency in choosing among identity options to emphasize the desirable aspects of the self in context (Sprott, 1994; White, 1990).

Migrants have at their disposal numerous means of managing multiple cultural identities. However, the scope of management strategies that can be effectively deployed is often limited, depending on prescribed social policies within a society (e.g., Berry, 2001), attitudes toward multiculturalism held by the majority or dominant group (e.g., LaFromboise, Coleman, & Gerton, 1993; Montreuil & Bourhis, 2001), and available personal resources (e.g., Camilleri & Malewska-Peyre, 1997). For example, the option of retaining one's heritage cultural identity is more available in a host society that values multiculturalism than in one that emphasizes assimilation. Likewise, assimilation is an unlikely option when entries into the majority group are restricted, and when personal resources are very limited.

Within these constraints, individuals may adopt a variety of strategies to negotiate their multiple identities. Engagement in multicultural identity negotiation may yield overt behaviors in tune with changing cultural environments. Meanwhile, management processes may also generate internal ambivalence regarding identity loyalties and cultural affiliation.

Development of Multicultural Identity

Every multicultural identity may have a unique developmental history and a distinct developmental trajectory, depending on individuals' prior experiences and current goals, as well as specific features in the multicultural context. In addition, as the multicultural context changes, individuals' experiences and goals also change, and the multicultural identity is updated (Hong et al., in press).

As individuals acquire knowledge and practices of a new culture, knowledge and practices of the heritage culture are not displaced from memory. Instead, they are retained. Moreover, several cultural identities can co-exist within any given individual without adverse psychological consequences (e.g., S. Lee, Sobal, & Frongillo, 2003; Ryder, Alden, & Paulhus, 2000; Tsai, Ying, & Lee, 2000).

Furthermore, individuals may strategically evoke cultural identities to enhance their consonance with changing environments. As Padilla and Perez (2003) point out, in adapting to a new cultural context, newcomers may adapt identity strategies flexibly to the changing multicultural context. For instance, whether newcomers are motivated to acculturate to the mainstream culture depends on the cultural and racial diversity of the place of settlement, how the dominant groups evaluate the newcomers' identities, or the extant relations among dominant and nondominant groups prior to their arrival.

Strategies of Multicultural Identity Negotiation

Research has identified three broad categories of identity negotiation strategies: integration, alternation, or synergy. Preference for identity negotiation strategies may change over the life course, and any given individual may synchronously use all or a subset of these strategies.

The strategy of *integration* involves blending of two or more identities into one coherent identity (LaFromboise et al., 1993; Sprott, 1994). Through integration, elements from two or more cultures fuse into a unitary (multicultural) identity. As such, the development of an integrated multicultural identity can be viewed as an additive process in that new cultural identities are "added to" existing cultural identities. One study (Lau-Gesk, 2003; Experiment 1) illustrates the additive nature of integration. The participants, who were monocultural East Asians, monocultural European Americans, or Asian Americans, evaluated the persuasive appeal of either an individually focused advertisement or an interpersonally focused advertisement for a brand of coffee. The individually focused advertisement includes messages such as "Make yourself proud," and "Do it for you, and nobody else but you," whereas the interpersonally focused advertisement contains messages such as "Make your friends and family proud," and "Do it for them, and nobody else but them." Monocultural East Asians liked the interpersonally focused advertisement more than they did the individually focused one, and European Americans showed the opposite pattern. Interestingly, Asian Americans liked the interpersonally focused advertisement as much as the monocultural East Asians did, and the individually focused advertisement as much as the monocultural European Americans did.

Moreover, certain aspects of the situation may call out knowledge of the self associated with one culture more than knowledge of the self associated with another culture. For example, in one study, Chinese Americans completed sentences that began with "I as an American ..." or "I as Chinese." The completed sentences referenced human rights (which are highly valued in American culture) much more frequently when the sentences started with "I being an American" than when it started with "I being a Chinese." Likewise, the completed sentences mentioned duties and obligations (which are heavily emphasized in Chinese culture) much more frequently when the sentences started with "I being a Chinese" than "I being an American" (Hong et al., 2001). Individuals with an integrated multicultural identity are often described as having highly developed identities in each culture, which are utilized in culturally appropriate ways in different contexts (e.g., Oyserman, 1993; Oyserman, Sakamoto, & Lauffer, 1998; Suinn, Ahuna, & Khoo, 1992; Yamada & Singelis, 1999).

The strategy of *alternation* involves switching back and forth among cultural identities depending on the fit of the identity with the immediate context. As mentioned in Chapter 8, Ross et al. (2002) showed that bilingual–bicultural Chinese Canadians are more likely to access independent self-construal when responding in English than in Chinese. Other evidence also indicates that bicultural individuals may shift cultural interpretive frames based on available cultural cues (Hong et al., 1997, 2000, 2003; Wong & Hong, 2005).

The strategy of *synergy* involves the development of a new identity that cannot be reduced to the sum of its constituent identities (Anthias, 2001; Benet-Martinez et al., 2002). An example of synergy in the domain of language is creolization, in which a new grammar is constructed out of the continued interaction of groups speaking two or more distinct languages. The concept of a synergistic multicultural identity is analogous to that of bilingualism. As Grosjean (1989) puts it, the bilingual must be approached as a person with a "unique and specific linguistic configuration ... and not the sum of two monolinguals" (p. 6). Furthermore, the synergistic effects of cultures on identities do not entail a loss of competency in the original cultures.

Meet the Researcher: Verónica Benet-Martínez

*"How much is the parrot?" a woman asked. "Wow, ma'am," uttered the owner, "this is a very expensive parrot, because he speaks both Spanish and English." "Oh really? Can you get him to speak in both languages?" "Sure you can. Look, it's quite simple: If you pull the left leg he speaks English." And he pulled the parrot's left leg. "**Good morning,**" said the bird. "And if you pull the right leg like this, he speaks Spanish." And the parrot said: "**Buenos Dias!**" At which point the woman asked: "What happens if you pull both of his legs, will he speak Tex-Mex?" "Noooo," answered the parrot. "I will fall on my ass !!"*

(*Mexican American folk tale*)

Verónica Benet-Martínez was born and raised in Barcelona in a bilingual home, where she and her siblings spoke Catalan to their father and Castilian to their mother, a very common situation in bilingual Catalunya. She pursued a Ph.D. in social-personality at the UC Davis, and later was a postdoctoral researcher at UC Berkeley. She is now a Professor at UC Riverside.

Compartmentalization of Cultural Identities

Instead of integrating multiple cultural identities into an integrated or synergistic identity, some multicultural individuals may compartmentalize their cultural identities. They experience their cultural identities as in opposition, keep these identities separate, and feel conflicted between these identities (Benet-Martinez et al., 2002). In the case of first-generation Asian immigrants in North America, some may feel that they are just an Asian living in America. They are fearful of losing identification with their heritage culture, and of assimilating into the mainstream culture. Oftentimes, they have little motivation to improve their proficiency in English. Among second-generation Asian Americans, some may feel that they are mostly an American, and feel being caught between two cultures. They tend not to be proficient in their heritage language and are not eager to improve their skills in this language (Young & Gardner, 1990).

Asian Americans who compartmentalize their cultural identities may identify primarily with their heritage culture or the mainstream American culture, but not both. This idea was tested in an experiment (Lau-Gesk, 2003; Experiment 2), in which Asian Americans were presented with an advertisement for a facial cream product. The advertisement contained either an individually focused persuasive message ("Your face. As individual as your fingerprint?"), an interpersonally focused message ("Your face. A reflection of your family?"), or a dual focused message with both an individually focused and an interpersonally focused appeal ("Your face. A reflection of your family? As individual as your fingerprint?"). Compared to Asian Americans with a blended bicultural identity, those with compartmentalized identities liked a single-focused message (the individually focused message or the interpersonally focused message) more and the dual-focused message less. This finding suggests that bicultural individuals find an advertisement more appealing when it contains messages that are congruent with their bicultural identity: Bicultural individuals with a blended identity prefer messages that contain ideas from both cultures; bicultural individuals with compartmentalized identities do not like messages that contain seemingly conflicting ideas from the two cultures.

Meet the Researcher: Loraine Lau-Gesk

"Cross cultural experimental researchers have only recently begun to investigate the psychological underpinnings of multiculturalism and to accept the possibility of individuals having access to and being equally influenced by multiple cultures. I feel it is indeed an exciting time for people working in this area, with so many questions left unanswered, existing theories challenged, and new theories awaiting discovery."

Loraine was born in New York and raised in Southern California, where multiculturalism abounds. A Chinese American with a first generation father and second generation mother and whose husband is Caucasian, Loraine is particularly interested in understanding the psychology underlying different types of multiculturals such as truly blended individuals whose parents are of distinct cultural backgrounds, those with first or second generation parents of the same cultural background and those who themselves are first generation immigrants. She received her Ph.D. at UCLA, and is now an Assistant Professor of Marketing at University of California at Irvine.

Identity Ambivalence, Marginalization and Alienation

How migrants manage their cultural identities may result in different levels of intrapersonal identity conflict. In addition, acculturation stress may arise when migrants' ethnocultural identity becomes very salient and evokes exclusion or rejection by dominant cultural groups. Sometimes, victimization ensues when exclusion is justified and explained in terms of the minorities' lack of knowledge of the mainstream culture or fluency in the language of the dominant groups (Kanno, 2003; Pang, 2000).

Many minority group members in the United States are sensitive to both the differentness and the disadvantageousness of their ethnic–cultural tradition (see Chapter 10). Here is how a Vietnamese American informant in an ethnographic study expressed her frustration:

> I have been here 18 years and if somebody had been to Vietnam and spoke the language would think they knew that country well … Americans still think of me as a foreigner (Sparrow, 2000; p. 188).

With the awareness of their differentness and disadvantageousness, some minority group members have sought to fit in the mainstream culture by developing a secondary cultural identity, as revealed in the report of another informant in the same ethnographic study:

> As a result of all these differences and having been forced to adapt to this new culture, I have developed another cultural identity which is capable of surviving in this new environment …. This identity functions like a second personality that appears when it is necessary to adopt a culturally appropriate behavior in the new culture (Sparrow, 2000, p. 192).

The same themes of ethnocultural discrimination, the desire to preserve the heritage cultural tradition, consciousness of the benefits of biculturalism, and motivation for bicultural identity development also emerged in an ethnographic study of a Chinese community in Chicago (Lu, 2001).

Multicultural minorities may also experience identity ambivalence when they are approached with intimacy and familiarity in one context and responded to with fear and distance by the same individuals in another context (Zaharna, 1989). Additionally, identity ambivalence and alienation may result from intragroup conflicts among newly arrived and established cultural groups who settle within the same geographical area. Niemann, Romero, Arredondo, and Rodriguez (1999) found that US Mexicans perceived more rejection and discrimination from

Chicanas/Chicanos (US born Mexican Americans) than from Anglo Americans. Similarly, Japanese Peruvians and Japanese Brazilians who traveled to Japan as migrant workers during the late 1980s and throughout the 1990s were treated as Peruvians/Brazilians by the Japanese, but as Japanese in their respective countries of Peru and Brazil (Takenaka, 1999; Tsuda, 2003).

Japanese migration to Brazil began at the beginning of the 20th century, when the Brazilian government decided that Japanese workers were technologically minded enough to work in the expanding coffee plantations in Brazil. Encounters with the ethnically and culturally different Brazilians had heightened the salience of the imported workers' Japanese identity.

In the 1930s, Japan became a global imperial power. This development fuelled an anti-Japanese movement in Brazil. The tide of anti-Japanese sentiment rose as Japan entered World War II. In response to their negative minority status, some Japanese in Brazil adopted the majority cultural patterns in exchange for better acceptance into the majority society. As a result, a synthetic bicultural identity known as Japanese Brazilian emerged and gained popularity among the Brazil-born Japanese.

After World War II, Japan rapidly rose to the top of the global order to become the second largest economy in the world. Consequently, the hierarchical relationship between Brazil and Japan on the global scale was reversed. As Japan rose in global prominence and prestige, Japanese Brazilians started to embrace their Japanese cultural heritage and dissociate themselves from the undesirable aspects of Brazil's Third World culture, resulting in a reaffirmation of the Japanese identity after decades of attempts to assimilate to Brazilian culture.

When the Brazilian economy crumbled in the 1980s, some Japanese Brazilians, attracted by the abundance of job opportunities in Japan, migrated to Japan. In Japan, the Japanese Brazilians were seen to have been Brazilianized, and were treated as "foreigners" in their "homeland." As a result, they were socially and culturally marginalized (Tsuda, 2001). In short, as the previous examples illustrate, feelings of exclusion by the established group increase the likelihood that migrants will develop ambivalent or marginal identities.

Theoretical Implications of the Developmental Perspective

The development of multicultural identity is an adaptive response to changing circumstances, through alignment of cultural identities with prior experiences, and current goals. This developmental perspective to multicultural identities has two major advantages. First, many writers have focused on the hypothesized negative consequences of identity shifts. Terms such as "culture shock," "acculturation stress," and "identity confusion" are illustrative of the negative slant with which multicultural identity management has been addressed. From the developmental perspective, these seemingly negative experiences grow out from the awareness of cultural differences, and of the intercultural relations in the broader multicultural context. In this sense, management of multicultural identities represents a deliberate effort to retain or reformulate the current identity in light of new cultural experiences (Hong et al., in press). Identity shift *per se* does not cause these "negative experiences." Instead, they surface only at certain transitional stages of multicultural identity development, and are symptomatic of the intergroup relations in the broader multicultural context.

Second, a developmental perspective demands attention to identify and analyze the processes that mediate the construction and management of multicultural identity. Recent studies have captured a few snapshots of these processes. Coming in contact with different cultural traditions increases self-awareness of one's own cultural embeddedness (Sussman, 2000; Zaharna, 1989). With this heightened awareness, individuals are prone to identify, compare, and choose from the cultural identity options that are currently available (Camilleri & Malewska-Peyre, 1997; Verkuyten & de Wolf, 2002). With prolonged contact, individuals may develop adjustment repertoires, which, in turn, lead to sustained identity shifts or the internalization of new cultural identities.

Once multiple identities are internalized, individuals will discriminatively access the complex knowledge associated with each cultural identity in response to changing contexts, while concurrently acquiring new cultural knowledge from their new cultural experiences. As individuals gain greater access to multicultural life experiences, different identity management strategies, which were initially conscious and effortful mental control, may be practiced at a relatively automatic or nonconscious level. Development of such expertise in managing multicultural identities may be facilitated in the societies that encourage and provide sociopolitical support for multiculturalism (Berry, 2001). In these societies, individuals can readily access many different ways of negotiating multicultural identities.

Colonization and Identity Negotiation

Identity negotiation is a historically constituted process. As noted in this and the previous chapter, processes such as globalization and racial tensions are integral parts of the context of identity negotiation in almost every country. Two other major constituent parts are colonization and postcolonization. By the time of World War I, the European powers had come to rule over 85% of the rest of the globe. The world order has been reconstituted in response to the aftermath of the world wars, the civil and ethnic wars following them, and the collapse of the Communist Bloc. Many former colonies have established national independence. However, the impact of colonization on cultural identity negotiation can still be felt in some post- and neo-colonial regions.

For example, Réunion is an island in the Indian Ocean. When the Portuguese discovered it in 1513, the island was uninhabited. From the 17th to the 19th century, French immigration supplemented by Africans, Chinese, Malays, and Malabar Indians gave the island its ethnic mix. Many plantation workers, of whom many were slaves, spoke different languages. Gradually, Creole, a linguistic intermediary that could be easily understood by all, surfaced and was used for daily communication among the plantation workers. Creole also cemented the relations between different ethnic components in the slave society, and the Creole identity gradually evolved as a common identity built around the Creole language. The Creole identity bound together the heterogeneous cultures on the island. Today, creolization has become a term used in cultural discourse to refer to the process whereby a human group attempts "to create a new local culture from the whole range of cultural resources available to the different components that together constitute a creolized society" (Medea, 2002, p. 127).

In 1946, Réunion became a French department, and officially entered the neo-colonial era. Since then, the French government has implemented a series of assimilation policies, emphasizing French culture and denying the worth of the Réunionese people's language, values, and culture. In addition, as Réunion was gradually globalized, its economy was dominated by the service sector with its consequent focus on consumption, international finance, banks, and multinational corporations.

These changes have rejuvenated the identity negotiation process on the island. For the first 30 years of Réunion's existence as a department, there were attempts to creolize the Western influence imposed on the islanders. In the early 1980s, there were conscious cultural movements to assert a distinctive Creole identity (Medea, 2002). In the foreseeable future, the contestation of the global French culture and the local Creole culture will add new pages to this oceanic island's social history.

In a multicultural environment, cultural clashes may lead to adoption of separatist strategies in identity management, while countries in the wake of severe racial antagonism may seek to replace exclusionist identities with an inclusive one. South Africa's social history is a case in point.

In 1652, Dutch merchant Jan van Riebeeck landed at the Cape of Good Hope. Subsequently, European migrants started to settle in South Africa. In 1795, South Africa was annexed to the United Kingdom, and the colonial government attempted to enforce the separation of white and black settlement areas. In 1910 the South African Union, a "democratic" state, was founded, in which only the white population were granted the right to vote. As the separatist Afrikaner identity strengthened, in the 1940s, the Afrikaner National Party was able to gain a strong majority. In 1948, the apartheid laws were enacted to maintain white domination and enforce racial separation. These laws and other apartheid laws passed subsequently institutionalized territorial separation and police repression.

The separation policies started to evoke strong reactions in the 1970s. In 1976, thousands of pupils demonstrated against Afrikaans as a compulsory school subject. After a brutal suppression of the uprising, the unrest spread over the whole country. In 1989, the South African government openly admitted the failure of apartheid policies, and opened the door to the first general election in April 1994.

In 1994, South Africa was a desolate state in the wake of apartheid. It faced the challenge of finding a cultural identity that would promise unity and reconciliation after several centuries of cultural clashes and racial tension. Against this historical backdrop, South Africans rediscovered the Biblical symbol of the rainbow to represent peaceful harmonization of different racial and cultural traditions. In 1994, Archbishop Desmond Tutu proclaimed proudly in a televised thanksgiving service: "We are the rainbow people of God. We are free—all of us, black and white together!"

The rainbow people identity is an identity defined by a peaceful union of diverse cultural and racial traditions. As an inclusive identity as well as a political symbol consciously crafted to achieve a political purpose, it has received initial strong support in the new country. In 1994, 65% of South Africans favored the rainbow people identity. However, the percentage of supporters dropped to 48% in 1999. In 1996, 17% of South Africans considered the rainbow people identity a source of national pride. Again, the percentage dropped to 11% in 1999 (Dickow & Moller, 2002). The waning appeal of the rainbow people identity casts doubt on the efficacy of using an inclusive identity to manage diverse cultural groups in a multicultural nation.

Conclusion

In this chapter, we describe some social psychological consequences of globalization, migration, and colonization. The research examples reviewed in this chapter illustrate the historical constitution of cultural identity. Each country or group has its unique social and political history, and has followed a distinctive course of cultural identity development. In addition, identity negotiation may change course in response to the changing power relations in the society. The research examples reviewed in this chapter also illustrate the multiplicity of cultural traditions represented in the mind of individuals in a globalized world, and the socio-political dimensions that underlie negotiations of multicultural identities. All these suggest that a complete analysis of multicultural psychology demands attention to a critical analysis of the embeddedness of individual psychology in a rich historical and political multicultural context. Despite its success in mapping cultural differences in cognition and behaviors, cultural psychology has barely set foot on this intellectual territory. Most of the evidence reviewed in the current chapter is drawn from research in our cognate disciplines. This may be the intellectual territory where theories of cultural psychology will meet their final challenges.

Scientific Study of Cultural Processes

12

▶ ## *Contents at a Glance*

Studying Culture in Coffee Shops

Psychologists interested in cultures are used to the practice of distributing surveys or psychological tests to comparable samples from societies with markedly different models of selfhood and sociality. Research adopting this strategy has revealed striking cultural differences in human cognitions, motivation, affect, and behaviors. These findings call for a cultural perspective to understanding how culture shapes psychology. Indeed, Segall, Lonner, and Berry (1998) sanctify cross-cultural research as a scholarly discipline that has led to "the flowering of culture in behavioral research."

The contribution of comparative studies of cultures cannot be overstated. However, these studies, which typically focus on identifying relatively stable, culture-characteristic psychological meanings, suffer a major limitation: They often fail to capture the dynamic nature of cultural processes (Hong & Chiu, 2001). In this concluding chapter, by highlighting some conceptual and methodological limitations of the dominant cross-cultural approach to studying culture, we call researchers' attention to the study of culture as a host of dynamic social psychological processes. We also seek to outline a few methodological approaches to studying cultural processes, and suggest a few future research directions.

Skeptical of the usefulness of comparative studies for describing dynamic cultural processes like those described in the previous chapter, some researchers have relied on interpretive case studies. One such study (Thompson & Arsel, 2004) was conducted in six local coffee shops in Chicago. Some of them were decorated with countercultural symbols and bohemian atmospherics, whereas others exhibited a more polished, bourgeois ambience. These coffee shops embodied oppositional local cultural meanings in stark contrast to the global cultural meanings that Starbucks Coffee represents.

To understand consumers' anticorporate sentiments (see Chapter 11), the investigators interviewed regular patrons of these local coffee shops, and undertook extensive participant observations. These rich observations furnish the research report with animated accounts of how café *flaneurs* and oppositional localists respond to the homogenization impact of international corporate brands on Chicago's local cultures.

The urban *flaneur* seeks pleasure and artistic inspiration through people watching. They immerse themselves in a leisurely fashion in the continual buzz of conversations and motion of the crowd, more often as voyeuristic observers than as active participants. The dynamic space at local coffee shops invigorates the urban *flaneur* with brief glimpses into the life of other people, and the stimulating artistic décor, music, and visual art offer a stream of inspirations. Café *flaneurs* view Starbucks as a conservative, unauthentic cultural space catering for bland corporate clientele.

Contrariwise, the oppositional localist denounces Starbucks for crowding out all the local coffee shops, resulting in homogenization of local cultures. One informant in the study (Thompson & Arsel, 2004, p. 636) said:

> Like I feel, especially in Chicago, our theory was the reason we weren't able to find a really good coffee shop there is because a Starbucks is on almost every corner. Starbucks is awful. There is even a *Simpsons* episode where Bart Simpson walks into the mall, and then you see a Starbucks and you see next door, "Coming Soon–Starbucks." Then he leaves and you see the whole mall from the inside, and it's wall-to-wall Starbucks. It's funny, but in a way it's true.

Oppositional localists view local coffee shops, particularly bohemian coffee shops that exude an alternative, antiestablishment aura, as outposts for like-minded activists to challenge prevailing corporate power structures, and to defy the alienating forces of commercialization. In short, the study described above and many other interpretive case studies animate the contestation of cultural meanings in a globalized society.

Interpretive case analyses provide detailed narrations of how individuals enact cultural meanings in specific contexts. However, this method, like all other research methods, also has its limitations. First, not all cultural processes are accessible to conscious reflection. Second, informants' accounts of psychological processes are susceptible to various perceptual and memory distortions (Nisbett & Wilson, 1977). Finally, the generality of observations from specific cases is limited. It is difficult to induce from these observations basic social psychological principles that mediate cultural processes. The glocalization experiences in Chicago may be very different from those in other globalized cities.

In Chapter 2, we describe the global and the focal approaches to studying cultures. Researchers adopting the global approach generally favor cross-cultural comparisons, whereas those adopting the focal approach generally favor ethnographic or interpretive case studies. We conclude in Chapter 2 that both approaches and their preferred research methods can provide valuable insights into the relationship of culture and psychology. However, to capture the dynamic nature of cultural processes, social psychologists need to supplement these two descriptive approaches with other research tools. In the previous chapters, we review research that relies on a broader range of research methods, such as experimental simulation and culture priming. In the current chapter, we provide a more systematic introduction to these tools.

Beyond Description of Cultural Differences

The validity of cross-cultural comparisons is predicated on the assumption that cultures are comparable. Typically, in cross-cultural comparisons, research participants from two or more target cultures respond to the same psychological measure, which may range from a value survey to responses to hypothetical situations, and performance on a certain cognitive task. Cultures are comparable only when three requirements are met. First, the psychological construct under investigation has the same meaning in the target cultures. Second, the responses of the research participants from the target cultures are equally indicative of the underlying construct. Finally, the research participants in the differing cultural samples are recruited from comparable populations.

Comparability of Cultures

Construct Equivalence

Construct equivalence of a measure is established when the psychological construct being measured has the same meaning in the target cultures. Cross-cultural findings are difficult to interpret when a measure does not possess construct equivalence. For example, research has revealed greater adherence to the value of self-reliance among Chinese than among European American undergraduates (Triandis et al., 1990). This finding seems to suggest that relative to American culture, Chinese culture is a more individualist culture. However, this conclusion is warranted only when self-reliance means the same thing in both Chinese and European American cultures. For most European Americans, the underlying motive of self-reliance is to assert one's independence from the group. Contrariwise, to many Chinese, self-reliance is driven by a concern for the collective. In an interdependent system, the group has the responsibility to take care of those who fail to support themselves. Accordingly, individuals would avoid imposing a burden on the group by adhering to the value of self-reliance.

Cross-cultural psychologists have devised a variety of techniques to protect the cross-construct equivalence of a psychological measure (van de Vijver & Leung, 1997). For example, to ensure that the construct being measured has the same meaning in the target cultures, researchers can examine the construct's correlations with other theoretically meaningful constructs in each culture. Cross-cultural equivalence is established when the construct being measured has the same pattern of theoretically meaningful correlations with measures of other constructs in each target culture. For example, some researchers hypothesize that the self-enhancement motivation, which is prevalent in North American culture, is absent in Japanese culture (Heine et al., 1999; see Chapter 8). To test this hypothesis, it is important to establish the construct equivalence of the self-enhancement measure in Japanese and North American cultures. For example, conceptually, self-enhancement is positively related to self-esteem (Brown, 1988). Therefore, the measure used to assess the relative tendency to self-enhance should correlate positively with self-esteem in both Japanese and North American cultures. Research using measures that meet this criterion found that Japanese also self-enhance, and hence rejected the strong assertion that the self-enhancement motive is absent in Japanese culture (Kobayashi & Brown, 2003; Kurman, 2003).

Oftentimes, the same psychological process may have different manifestations in different cultural contexts. This presents another challenge to the construct validity of a psychological measure. For example, in North American culture, self-enhancement often takes the form of asserting and exaggerating one's positive personal qualities. In Japanese societies, the same motive is often expressed in the form of asserting and exaggerating one's socially approved interpersonal qualities (Kurman, 2001; see Chapter 8). In Chapter 6, we also review cultural differences in cognitive dissonance. For North Americans, cognitive dissonance arises from the need to rationalize personal choices to the self. For Japanese, cognitive dissonance arises from the need to rationalize choices for the significant others (Fein et al., 2003).

The foregoing analysis has important implications for psychological studies of culture. Research on cultural differences should not be restricted to studying how cultures differ in the relative prevalence of certain psychological phenomena. Other equally important issues include how cultures differ in the way the meaning of a psychological construct is constructed, and how universal processes may take on different behavioral expressions and social psychological functions in different cultural contexts.

Measurement Equivalence

Aside from construct equivalence, measurement equivalence is another requirement for valid cross-cultural comparisons. For example, when a respondent rates the self as highly assertive on a bipolar scale that ranges from "highly submissive" to "highly assertive," does this rating have the same meaning independent of the respondent's cultural membership?

Researchers often use the technique of back-translation to establish measurement equivalence of an item. As an illustration, consider a hypothetical research example in which North Americans and South Koreans are compared on their level of self-esteem. Most established measures of self-esteem were developed by American researchers and written in English. To establish these measures' measurement equivalence when they are exported to South Korean culture, an English–Korean bilingual translates the English measures into Korean. Then, another English–Korean bilingual back-translates the Korean version into English. Discrepancies in translation are then identified and corrected by comparing the original English version with the back-translated version. Although back-translation is a useful technique to ensure a measure's translation equivalence, it often fails to capture subtle differences in the nuances of the same item in different languages or cultures. In the self-assertion example, "highly assertive" carries a positive connotation in North American culture. However, being highly assertive is not considered to be a socially desirable trait in some East Asian cultures.

Research has also revealed systematic cultural differences in respondents' response styles. For example, compared to Americans, Chinese are less likely to give extreme responses (using the extreme end points on a rating scale) and more likely to check the mid-point on a rating scale (C. Chen et al., 1995). Socially desirable responding poses another threat to the validity of a measure. However, cultures differ in what constitutes socially desirable responses. A typical socially desirable response in European American culture projects the self-image of a superhuman (e.g., "I am in complete control of my fate"). Contrariwise, a typical socially desirable response in East Asian cultures projects the self-image of a super-nice person (e.g., "I have never dropped litter on the street") (Lalwani et al., in press; see Chapter 4).

Other studies have shown that participants in different cultures may use different referent groups and hence different standards when they respond to a rating scale item (Heine, Lehman, Peng, & Greenholtz, 2002). For example, when asked how much they value an individualist value, respondents tend to compare themselves to their peers in the same culture. Thus, Japanese would rate themselves as individualists when they perceive themselves to be more individualist than other Japanese. Similarly, European Americans would rate themselves as individualists when they consider themselves more individualist than other European Americans. Because the level of individualism Japanese attribute to their peers may differ from that European Americans attribute to their peers, responses from the two cultural samples cannot be directly compared.

The problems reviewed above are particularly relevant in studies that rely primarily on participants' subjective self-reports. However, issues related to measurement equivalence also present problems to studies that compare cultures on "objective" performance measures. For example, participants from different cultures may differ in how familiar they are with the format and contents of the performance measures. In addition, as discussed in Chapter 10, because of their distinctive cultural experiences, participants may react differently to the same test situation. For example, African Americans may experience stereotype threat when their verbal and quantitative skills are assessed with standardized tests, particularly when their ethnic identity is salient in the test environment (Steele, 1997).

Sampling Equivalence

The validity of cross-cultural comparisons also rests on the assumption that comparable samples are drawn from the target cultures. A widely used practice in cross-cultural studies is to compare college students from different national samples. Aside from convenience, there are some advantages of using college students in cross-cultural comparisons. For example, college student samples from different countries have comparable levels of educational attainment. Moreover, relative to the general public, college students may be more familiar with the intellectual tradition in their culture. However, relying exclusively on college student samples also has severe methodological shortcomings. In most countries, university education is a highly Westernized institution (Figure 12.1). College students in the non-Western world are socialized into university culture. Consequently, they may have very different cultural experiences from other people in their country. For example, they would likely have relatively extensive exposure to Western cultural traditions, and feel the need to negotiate a multicultural identity that incorporates the global cultural tradition with the local ones (see Chapter 11). Additionally, university education may be differently accessible to the general population. In some countries, university education is available to a large proportion of the population. In others, it is a privilege of a highly selective elitist class. In short, findings based on comparisons of college students from just a few cultures need to be interpreted with caution. These issues can be addressed if the researchers can recruit representative samples from a large number of nations.

Conclusion

Many studies have revealed striking cultural differences in a wide range of psychological phenomena. However, due to the methodological issues

FIGURE 12.1. University is a Western institution; universities in many countries are modeled on Western universities. This campus scene depicted in this picture looks like the Main Quad at the University of Illinois at Urbana-Champaign. In fact, this picture was taken at Tsinghua University in China. The founding fathers of Tsinghua University borrowed the architectural blueprint from the University of Illinois when they designed the campus for Tsinghua University.

reviewed above, researchers should exercise interpretive caution when they draw inferences regarding cultural differences from these findings. In addition, when national cultures are compared, it is important to recognize that aside from dominant cultural traditions, countries also differ in political stability, level of affluence, and many other factors that might influence their citizens' attitudes and behaviors. These extraneous variables need to be assessed and statistically controlled. Confidence in the validity of cross-cultural comparison can be greatly enhanced if the same finding is replicated with different samples and different research methods.

Interpretive Ambiguity of Quasi-Experimental Data

Cross-cultural data illustrate *how* cultures differ, but are not informative of *why* cultures differ. In cross-cultural comparison, researchers use participants from different cultural groups as proxies for cultures (Lehman et al., 2004). Studies that compare natural groups are referred to as quasi-experiments. Unlike true experiments, in quasi-experiments, participants are not randomly assigned to an experimental condition (Cook & Campbell, 1986). Like gender and age groups, participants from different cultures are natural groups. As such, cross-cultural studies are quasi-experiments. Because research participants are not randomly assigned to a culture, it is not legitimate to infer from the cultural differences observed in comparative studies that culture *causes* these differences. As an illustration of this point, consider the following set of arguments:

> Premise I: Individualism is more widely distributed in European American culture than in Japanese culture, whereas collectivism is more widely distributed in Japanese culture.

> Premise II: Idiocentrists (individuals who subscribe to individualism) prefer direct communication in negotiation and allocentrists (individuals who subscribe to collectivism) prefer indirect communication.

> Inference: Compared to Japanese, European Americans should prefer direct communication more and indirect communication less.

In this set of arguments, the inference follows logically from the two premises, and has received some empirical support (Ohbuchi et al., 1999; see Chapter 7).

In Chapters 2 and 8, we review evidence that casts doubt on Premise I: European Americans are not more individualist or less collectivist than

Japanese in all life domains. Even if this were indeed the case, it would be premature to conclude that the observed cultural difference in communication *arises from* the differing distributions of individualism and collectivism in European American and Japanese cultures, because the American and Japanese samples also differ on many dimensions other than individualism and collectivism. It is possible that the observed difference arises from relative prevalence of individualism and collectivism, but it is also possible that it arises from other systematic differences between the two cultural samples.

Mediation Analysis and Its Limitations

Some investigators have applied mediation analysis to address this interpretive issue. Mediation analysis is a statistical technique for evaluating whether an observed difference between two or more groups is mediated by a hypothesized construct. In the example of cultural difference in direct versus indirect communication, the difference between European Americans and Japanese is hypothesized to run through the cultural variable of individualism–collectivism. This mediation hypothesis is illustrated in Figure 12.2.

To test this mediation hypothesis, the investigator would have the participant report how important individualist and collectivist values are to them, in addition to completing the communication style assessment. To show that cultural difference in communication style runs through individualism–collectivism, the following criteria need to be met. First, the expected cultural group difference in communication is observed: Compared to Japanese, European Americans prefer direct communication more and indirect communication less. Second, the two cultural groups differ in individualism–collectivism in the expected direction: Compared to Japanese, European Americans value individualism more and collectivism less. Third, individualism–collectivism is systematically related to communication style: Individualism (vs. collectivism) is positively related to preference for direct communication and negatively related to preference for indirect communication. Finally, after the effect of individualism–collectivism has been

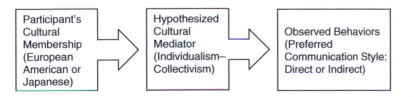

FIGURE 12.2. Illustration of a mediation hypothesis.

controlled for statistically, the difference between European Americans and Japanese in communication style disappears. Meeting the last criterion is particularly important for the mediation hypothesis; it shows that cultural membership of the participants has no independent influence on communication styles aside from its impact via individualism and collectivism (Baron & Kenny, 1986).

Mediation analysis can help clarify whether an observed behavioral difference between two or more cultural groups runs through the hypothesized cultural construct. However, it has a strong underlying assumption: cultural differences in behaviors are mediated by internalized values or beliefs. In the above example, individuals in an individualist (collectivist) culture internalize individualist (collectivist) values. Moreover, the internalized values provide guidelines for social behaviors.

Not everybody internalizes the dominant cultural values in their society (Ryan & Deci, 2000; Wrong, 1961). In every society, some individuals are idiocentrics, and some are allocentrics (Triandis et al., 1985; see Chapter 2 for individual differences in adherence to cultural values within culture). Internalization of dominant cultural values is particularly weak among individuals who do not identify with their culture (Jetten et al., 2002; see Chapter 4).

More importantly, not all behaviors are mediated by internalized beliefs and values. An important insight from social psychology is that in many circumstances, how individuals represent the situational norm has an inordinate amount of authority over behaviors (Latane, 1981). For example, whether a victim in an emergency situation will receive help from a bystander depends not on the bystander's personal attitude, but on how the bystander represents the perceived situational norm. The bystander will observe how other bystanders behave and use others' behavior to evaluate whether offering help is a situation-appropriate response. If others do not offer help, the bystander may view helping as a situation-inappropriate response, and hence withhold the altruistic act (Latane & Darley, 1968). In the realm of culture and behavior, there is ample evidence that culture-characteristic behaviors arise not only from internalized beliefs or values, but also from representations of shared norms in the society (Chapters 7 and 8). For these reasons, the utility of mediation analysis in identifying specific cultural mediators of behaviors is limited. Consistent with this idea, contemporary assessments of the research evidence have found little evidence that internalized values (such as individualism and collectivism) mediate cultural differences in normative behaviors such as reward allocation and conflict mediation (R. Chiu & Kosinski, 1994; K. Leung, 1987; Weldon & Jehn, 1995).

Explaining Cultures

The Role of Process Analysis in Scientific Study of Culture

> every science passes through a phase in which it considered its basic subject matter to be some sort of substance or structure. Fire was identified with phlogiston; heat with caloric; and life with vital fluid. Every science has passed beyond that phase, recognizing its subject matter as being some sort of process: combustion in the case of fire; random thermal motion in case of heat; and certain kinds of far from thermodynamic equilibrium in the case of life (Bickhard, 2003, p. 122).

Similar historical shift is occurring in the social psychology of culture. The focus in social psychology of culture is still on some sort of substance or structure: How do cultures differ? What are the deep structures of cultures? However, there is increasing recognition that to explain culture, we need to understand cultural processes. Bickhard (2003) submits that causality resides in process, not substances. Particle physics has sought to locate causality in the fundamental particles, and treat higher-level causal regularities as emergents from the causal dance of the particles within whatever configuration they have with each other. As such, all higher-level phenomena are causally epiphenomenal, and therefore lack causal efficacy. More importantly, in particle physics, higher-level phenomena emerge when particles engage in organization. However, particles do not themselves have organization.

Counterparts of the metaphysical assumptions in particle physics can be found in some theories in social psychology of culture. Two examples are the dynamic social impact theory (Latane, 1996) and the connectionist model (Y. Kashima et al., 2000) of cultural emergence introduced in Chapter 9. In these theories, culture is a higher-order emergent that does not possess causal efficacy. Instead, the causality of all cultural phenomena is resident in the lowest level of fundamental substances. From the perspective of cultural evolution, the lowest level of fundamental substances is memes (Dawkins, 1976, see Chapter 4). In addition, memes do not themselves have organization; cultural phenomena emerge when memes engage in self-organization (see Chapter 9 for principles of self-organization).

A paradigmatic shift in physics occurred when physicists began to recognize that there are no particles. What appear as particle interactions are actually quantized oscillatory processes. Unlike particles, which are supposed to take on some irreducible forms, quantum fields are organized processes. In quantum physics, all causal power is resident in process organizations, and new organizations of process give rise to higher-level phenomena (Bickhard, 2003).

Extending this view to social psychology of culture, explaining culture involves identification of basic principles that give rise to organized cultural processes. In this book, we adopt a knowledge perspective to culture, which places a strong emphasis on organized cultural processes. From the knowledge perspective, culture consists of a collection of loosely organized shared knowledge constantly being created, maintained, reproduced, and transformed by a collection of interconnected individuals (Chapter 1). Cultural differences in behavior are understood not with reference to differing deep structures in different cultures, but in terms of specific knowledge structures (Chapters 5–7). Each knowledge structure has a specified range of applicability. Thus, instead of focusing on global cultural differences, our analysis focuses on the social psychological consequences when specific knowledge structures are activated in concrete situations. Accordingly, the effects of culture are expected to be domain- and context-specific (J. Chen et al., in press; Matsumoto, 1989; Chapter 8). Additionally, cultural meanings are created, maintained, reproduced, and transformed for adaptive purposes. Thus, explaining cultural processes demands attention to culture's evolutionary, social, and psychological functions (Chapter 4). As the social–political context evolves, cultural knowledge in the society will be redistributed, and its shared meanings will be renegotiated (Chapters 9 and 11). In the previous chapters, we have described research that used a variety of empirical methods for probing cultural processes. Next, we briefly describe how some of these methods can be applied to study specific cultural processes.

Methods for Studying Cultural Processes

Extraction of Normative Meanings

A good starting point for analyzing cultural processes is to extract normative meanings from people's cultural experiences. When it comes to extraction of normative meanings, there is no substitute for cultural submersion and keen observations. Interpretive case analysis and ethnographic studies like the anti-Starbucks study described at the start of this chapter offer rich insights into the normative anti-corporate sentiments in different groups of local coffee shop patrons in Chicago. Analyzing recurrent themes in everyday conservations is another useful means for identifying shared ideas (Heider, 1958). The comparative analysis of recurrent themes in collaborative personal storytelling described in Chapter 9 is a good example of how discursive analysis generates important insights on the differing socialization emphases in the United States and Taiwan (P. Miller et al., 1997). Alternatively, researchers can look for recurrent themes in external carriers of culture (see Chapter 9). They may search for dominant themes in the way physical space is organized in shared environments (Miyamoto et al., 2006), in recurring interpersonal events (Kitayama et al., 1997; Morling et al., 2002), and in the mass media (Zhang & Shavitt, 2003).

Assessment of Distribution of Normative Meanings

Once normative meanings are identified, their distributions in the cultural group can be assessed. Two characteristics distinguish cultural knowledge from personal knowledge. First, cultural knowledge is distributed knowledge; it is possessed by a sizable proportion of individuals belonging to the culture. Second, individuals in the culture expect others in the culture to share this knowledge; they know many others in the culture possess this knowledge (Ho & Chiu, 1998). We refer to the first characteristic as *population distribution* and the second as *intersubjective consensus* (C. Wan et al., 2004). Representative sample surveys and psychological testing are useful tools for assessing population distribution of cultural meanings. Percentages of participants who subscribe to a certain cultural idea or display its characteristic behavior indicate how widely distributed the idea is in the population. Researchers can assess intersubjective consensus by having participants estimate how widely distributed a certain cultural idea is in their culture. The extent of agreement in the participants' estimations indicates the extent of intersubjective consensus (C. Wan et al., 2004). Additionally, researchers can assess distribution of a cultural idea by evaluating the extent to which the idea is dispersed in the mass media (e.g., F. Lee et al., 1996; H. Kim & Markus, 1999; T. Menon et al., 1999) and instituted in the society's family, educational, social, and political legal practices (e.g., Cohen, 1996).

Identifying a Cultural Idea's Range of Applicability

As mentioned, every cultural idea has its range of applicability; it impacts behaviors in a specified set of domains and contexts. For example, the belief that a person's personality can be changed is more widely distributed in South Korea than in the United States (Norenzayan et al., 2002), and this belief impacts causal attribution only when the perceiver is aware of the situational constraints on behavior. Accordingly, South Koreans and European Americans should differ in the tendency to explain behaviors in terms of dispositional attributions only when situational constraints are salient (I. Choi & Nisbett, 1998). Similarly, many Chinese believe that the group is a primary agent of action. However, Chinese perceivers display a greater tendency to explain ambiguous behaviors in terms of group dispositions only when the contrast between individual and group agency is made salient in the situation (Hong et al., 2003). The motivation to maintain interpersonal harmony is relatively strong in Chinese culture. However, only when in-group members are involved in social interactions does this motivation influence Chinese people's cooperative and conflict management behavior (K. Leung, 1988; Wong & Hong, 2005). In short, researchers can determine a cultural idea's range of applicability by identifying the boundary conditions of the idea's influence. When a cultural idea's range of applicability is fully specified, researchers can make more precise predictions of when a cultural idea will impact behaviors in concrete situations and when it will not.

Establishing a Cultural Idea's Causal Impact

An important insight from the knowledge perspective to culture is that a cultural idea is a knowledge structure that can be independently activated in the presence of pertinent situational cues. Thus, as long as a cultural idea is available to an individual, the presence of pertinent situational cues can call out the idea, even when it has a relatively low level of chronic accessibility (Hong et al., 2000, Chapter 8). Accordingly, researchers can experimentally activate a certain cultural idea and observe its subsequent psychological consequences. Because in these culture-priming studies, participants are randomly assigned to the experimental or control conditions, researchers can more confidently infer culture's causal impact from the data.

Another insight from the knowledge perspective is that cultural knowledge falls into different categories. Furthermore, different categories of cultural knowledge are differentially sensitive to the cueing of different types of culture primes. For example, procedural knowledge (knowledge of how to perform a cognitive production, such as attention and categorization) is learned through repeated applications of a learned routine. As noted in Chapter 5, environmental affordance plays an important role in the acquisition of culture-characteristic procedural knowledge. Thus, culture-typical features of the environment are effective primes of culture-characteristic procedural knowledge. Individuals, independently of their own cultural background, when randomly assigned to familiarize themselves with the characteristic physical layout of a certain culture, become more proficient in the cognitive productions associated with the culture (Miyamoto et al., 2006; see Chapter 5).

Declarative knowledge consists of representations of the self, other people, social groups, events, and norms. Conceiving of the self as an independent entity versus the nexus in a network of social relations is associated with different self-processes (Markus & Kitayama, 1991). In Chapter 6, we review a few experimental procedures that are devised to enhance the momentary accessibility of the independent or interdependent self-construal. Findings from these studies generally show that irrespective of the participants' cultural background, activating the independent (interdependent) self shifts self-processes in the direction of the activated self-construal. For example, the independent self-construal is widely distributed in Western cultures. Despite this, Westerners primed with an interdependent self-construal increase their adherence to collectivist values (Gardner et al., 1999) and the tendency to mimic others' behaviors (van Baaren et al., 2003). Direct activation of other person representations (representations of others and groups) is expected to produce analogous effects.

As mentioned in Chapter 7, an event representation has a script-like structure, and represents how one event is transformed into another. When a frame in the script is activated, the frames following it will be activated as well. For example, a man who has internalized the culture of honor script may respond aggressively to a provocative remark, because the remark calls out subsequent frames in the well-rehearsed script: "Interpret the remark as an attack on his honor," "Feel infuriated and seek retaliation," "Use or threaten the use of violence to coerce submission from the perpetrator as a means to restore honor," and "Feel proud for standing up against an attack on honor regardless of the outcome" (Cohen et al., 1996).

Finally, norm representations are activated when one's connectedness or obligations to the group are made salient, or when there is a heightened motivation to enforce group norms. For example, individuals increase adherence to cultural norms when their cultural identification is activated (Jetten et al., 2002). Following cultural norms in decision-making becomes more likely when decision-makers need to explain their decisions to in-group members (Briley et al., 2000). The effect of cultural norms is particularly pronounced when the individuals' concerns about social desirability and maintenance of the social–moral order are activated (Tetlock, 2002).

In short, culture may influence behaviors through several different routes (e.g., experiences with the physical environment, internalized self-construal, and representations of shared norms). In addition, different priming procedures should be followed when examining different types of cultural influence.

Identifying the Social Psychological Functions of Culture

Cultural ideas are adaptive responses to recurring problems in the environment and in collective living. In Chapter 4, we identify several psychological functions of culture. To examine the social psychological functions of culture, researchers can experimentally induce the need to perform the hypothesized function. The tendency to rely on cultural ideas as behavioral guides should increase when the need to perform the hypothesized function is induced. Two psychological functions of culture are provision of epistemic security in the face of informational uncertainty and management of existential anxiety. Adopting this approach, research has shown that the likelihood of following cultural guides in forming judgment and adherence to prevailing cultural norms increase considerably when the need to attain epistemic security or to reduce existential anxiety is induced (C. Chiu et al., 2000; Halloran & Kashima, 2004; E. Kashima et al., 2004).

A similar approach can be adopted to identify the social psychological functions of a specific cultural idea. For example, as mentioned in Chapter 7, collective responsibility assignment in Japan and China may serve a social control function. By holding the collective accountable for its individual members' action, the collective is motivated to monitor the behaviors of its members and stop them before they commit undesirable behaviors (Bell & Tetlock, 1989; C. Chiu & Hong, 1992). To test this idea, researchers can activate the goal of enforcing social control in an experiment. If collective responsibility functions to enforce social control in Chinese societies, Chinese participants should attribute greater collective responsibility of an individual's wrongdoing to the group in response to this goal manipulation.

New Research Directions

Thus far, we have introduced some relatively widely used empirical approaches to studying cultural processes. Aside from these approaches, some researchers have taken social psychological study of cultural processes into new directions and developed new research techniques.

Experimental Simulation of Cultural Evolution

Culture is an evolutionary process; culture is constantly being reproduced and re-made. To capture the dynamic processes involved in the reproduction and transformation of cultures, some researchers have sought to simulate how cultural ideas are reproduced through interpersonal communication (see Chapter 9). Some exemplary works have used experimental simulation techniques such as serial reproduction (Y. Kashima, 2002b; Lyons & Kashima, 2001, 2003), and simulation of dynamic social impact (Latane & Bourgeois, 1996; Latane & L'Herrou, 1996). Other researchers have created experimental conditions to simulate different kinds of institutional constraints on the development of cultural patterns (Suzuki & Yamagishi, 2004).

Developmental Analysis

Culture consists of a set of learned habits (Triandis, 2004). An important goal in social psychology of culture is to understand how individuals are socialized into their culture. Developmental studies, despite their apparent theoretical significance, are rare in the extant literature. In Chapter 5, we describe J. Miller's (1984) study in which social explanations of Indians and Americans were compared. In this study, participants were recruited from different age groups. This study illustrates how culture-characteristic patterns of social explanations emerge, and how they crystallize with age.

Cultural Cognitive Neuroscience

Recent advances in cognitive neuroscience have enabled researchers to pick up neuroanatomical traces of cognitive processes with sophisticated brain imaging techniques, such as functional magnetic resonance imaging (fMRI). Taking advantage of these technological advancements, some researchers have begun to measure association of culture and cognition at the neuroanatomical level. For example, Zhu (Qi & Zhu, 2002; H. Yang & Zhu, 2004; Zhu & Zhang, 2002) has discovered systematic differences between Chinese and Westerners in referential encoding and recognition memory.

The self-referential encoding effect is a classical finding in memory research. In a self-referential encoding study, on each trial, a personality adjective is presented on the computer screen. In one condition, the participants are required to judge whether the adjective describes the self; they are led to encode the adjective with reference to the self. In other conditions, the judgment target is changed to the participant's mother or a public figure. In these conditions, the adjective is encoded with reference to the mother or a public figure. Later, the participants are given a surprise recognition test; the adjectives the participants have seen before are mixed with new adjectives and then they are asked to identify the old adjectives. When Western participants are tested in this experiment, recognition accuracy tends to be higher if the adjectives were encoded with reference to the self than with reference to the mother or a public figure (Klein & Kihlstrom, 1986).

Zhu and his colleagues (Qi & Zhu, 2002; K. Yang & Zhu, 2004; Zhu & Zhang, 2002) found that Chinese participants also showed superior memory performance on the same task when the adjectives were encoded with reference to the self than with reference to a public figure. However, interestingly, Chinese participants also displayed superior recognition when the adjectives were encoded with reference to the mother than with reference to a public figure. The size of the self-referential encoding effect was comparable to that of the mother-referential encoding effect. Additionally, the mother-referential encoding effect was significant when Chinese students in Beijing were primed with Chinese cultural icons prior to performing the encoding task, and disappeared entirely when they were primed with American cultural icons (Zhu & Huo, 2001). These data demonstrate how culture shapes memory processes, and the findings are consistent with those reviewed in Chapter 6. Chinese position the self and the mother in the same social psychological space and the public figure in a different one. Contrariwise, Americans position the self and others (including the mother) in different social psychological spaces.

The self-referential encoding effect is potentially localizable to the medial prefrontal cortex (MPFC) (Craik, Moroz, Moscovitch, Stuss, Winocur, Tulving, & Kapur, 1999; Kelley, Macrae, Wyland, Caglar, Inati, & Heatherton, 2002). To pick up the neuroanatomical traces of cultural differences in self- and mother-referential processing, Zhu used fMRI to take Chinese and Western participants' brain images during the encoding phase of the experiment. For Western participants, enhanced MPFC activities were detected in the self-referenced condition compared to the public figure-referenced condition. However, no additional MPFC activities were found in the mother-referenced condition compared to the public figure-referenced condition. Chinese participants also showed enhanced MPFC activities in the self-referenced condition compared to the stranger-referenced condition. Additionally, they showed increased excitation in the MPFC in the mother-referenced condition compared to the public figure-referenced condition. In short, Chinese participants exhibited similar brain activities when they encoded self- and mother-related information, whereas Western participants showed different patterns of brain activities when they encoded these two kinds of information.

Zhu's research program offers convergent evidence of the association of culture and social information processing. It also demonstrates the utility of applying multiple methods (cross-cultural comparison, culture priming, and neuroanatomy) to study dynamic cultural differences.

Meet the Researcher: Ying Zhu

"How did I start to connect culture, self, and the brain in my research? I have followed the work of F. Craik (an influential memory researcher) since he published the first PET study of self-referential encoding in 1999. In the same year, a friend introduced Hazel Markus's paper on culture and self to me. Putting these two research traditions together, I discovered the mother-referential effect on recognition memory among Chinese in our behavioral studies. Encouraged by Conway's comments on this work, I began to search for evidence of cultural constitution of the self in the brain. Social psychologists have found cultural differences in perception, attention, categorization, causal attribution, thinking style, and self-processes. If you can find a paradigm to study these differences in a neuroimaging study, you may discover intriguing connections between culture and the brain."

Ying Zhu is Professor of Psychology at Peking University, China.

Psychic Unity and Cultural Relativity

> It is universally acknowledged that there is a great uniformity among the actions of men [*sic*], in all nations and ages, and that human nature still remains the same, in its principles and operations (Hume, 1784/1894, p. 358).

Comparative studies of cultures have uncovered striking cultural differences in basic psychological processes. These discoveries seem to have shattered Hume's hopes for psychic unity. They also raise a fundamental question: Do we need multiple local systems of psychology to understand the psychological processes of different cultural groups? If so, what is the prospect for universal principles of psychology?

On the one hand, through social interactions, social meanings are constructed collaboratively, which in turn color the way social experiences are interpreted (Lau et al., 2001). Inevitably, all interpretations of social experiences in a cultural community are imbued with shared cultural meanings. Accordingly, the notion of culture-free social meaning is a conceptual impossibility, and the prospect for psychic unity seems to be rather dim.

On the other hand, the capability for creating and cumulating culture is the result of a long history of cognitive and biological evolution. Humans in all cultures are biologically endowed with a host of cognitive abilities, including the abilities to represent others' behaviors as intended actions, reflect on their past experiences, predict future events, encode their experiences in memory, and externalize memories in external memory devices (Chapter 3). These abilities enable people in all cultural communities to store, transmit, and refine knowledge passed down from their ancestors. The common biological endowments the human species inherits lay a *universal* biological–cognitive foundation, on which different cultural communities put up their own house of consciousness. In short, research scientists may discover, amid pronounced cultural variations in behaviors, psychic unity in a cognitive architecture common to humankind, whose design constrains the plasticity of basic cognitive operations in knowledge creation and application (see S. Li, 2003).

There are two lessons social psychology of culture can learn from mainstream social and personality psychology. First, social psychological research has discovered striking situational variations in behaviors. However, few social psychologists believe that we need a different set of basic principles to explain behaviors in every particular situation. Instead, most social psychologists share the optimism that research will identify a finite set of basic principles that will account for situational variations of behaviors. A challenge for social psychology of culture is to identify a manageable set of basic principles that can explain behavioral variations across cultures.

Second, researchers can acknowledge the cultural relativity of meanings without accepting the notion of incommensurability. As personality psychologist George Kelly (1955) pointed out, when two persons employ similar constructs to grasp their experience, they would go through similar psychological processes. However, people do not need to go through similar psychological processes in order to understand each other. As long as a person can cognitively represent the construction processes of another person, social understanding is attainable. Social psychology of culture can borrow a lesson from Kelly's personal construct theory. Invariably, people look through a cultural lens when they construct reality. However, with increased global connectivity, a cultural group has access to many cultural lenses, and people can and do see the world through different cultural lenses (Chapter 10). In our view, the ability to construct reality from different cultural perspectives allows people with diverse cultural backgrounds to understand each other.

On the issue of whether we need to supplant mainstream social psychology with multiple local systems of psychology, we concur with Joan Miller (1997) that social psychology of culture "should be grounded on findings from recent mainstream psychological research" and "an appropriate level of analysis needs to be chosen to avoid proliferation of theories that may have limited explanatory force" (p. 116).

What is Social about Social Psychology of Culture?

In Chapter 1, we raise the question of what is social about social psychology of culture. Through decades of research, social psychologists have provided many illustrations of the reciprocal influence of culture and psychology. Few social psychologists would disagree that the ways we interact with the physical and social environment consciously or subconsciously influence the ways we represent reality. Few would disagree that culture is a product of collaborative action. People are active agents; they do not passively receive the influence of culture. Instead, they create it, use it as tools to attain valued goals, reproduce it, and refine it.

Despite this, few would disagree that social psychology of culture has remained a relatively socially indifferent discipline. Indeed, the discipline has been preoccupied with how cultures differ in certain social psychological phenomena (Lehman et al., 2004). Most recent research has focused on how Easterners differ from European Americans in well-established phenomena in American social psychology (e.g., self-enhancement, the fundamental attribution error, cognitive dissonance, social comparison).

Some studies (e.g., Steele, 1997; Chapter 10) seek to address how cultural minorities in the United States manage their personal and collective self-esteem. However, the interactions of culture and social power have largely escaped social psychologists' attention. Few studies have examined developing countries' psychological responses to the hegemonic influence of the global culture, or to unequal distributions of power and privileges in intercultural contexts. Systematic studies on the psychological consequences of culture change in developing countries are rare (see Chapters 10 and 11). Increased global connectivity has turned many societies into multicultural societies. Yet the social psychological implications of multiculturality are largely unexplored (see Chapter 9).

For social psychology of culture, the challenge ahead is to construct communicable theories that are socially and culturally relevant to the increasingly globalized world. A shift from cultural differences to cultural processes is a good starting point for this challenging project. We wish to close with an optimistic prediction: With another decade of research, social psychology of culture will shed new light on the dynamic nature of people's cultural experiences *in vivo*, and will be ready to engage in dialogues on important global issues.

References

Aaker, J., Benet-Martinez, V., & Garolera, J. (2001). Consumption symbols as carriers of culture: A study of Japanese and Spanish brand personality. *Journal of Personality and Social Psychology, 81*, 492–508.

Aaker, J., & Schmitt, B. (2001). Culture-dependent assimilation and differentiation of the self: Preferences for consumption symbols in the United States and China. *Journal of Cross-Cultural Psychology, 32*, 561–576.

Adair, W. L., Okumura, T., & Brett, J. M. (2001). Negotiation behavior when cultures collide: The United States and Japan. *Journal of Applied Psychology, 86*, 371–385.

Ajzen, I., & Fishbein, M. (1980). *Understanding attitudes and predicting social behavior.* Englewood Cliffs, NJ: Prentice-Hall.

Akimoto, S. A., & Sanbonmatsu, D. M. (1999). Differences in self-effacing behavior between European and Japanese Americans: Effect on competence evaluation. *Journal of Cross-Cultural Psychology, 30*, 159–177.

Alderson, A. S., & Nielsen, F. (2002). Globalization and the great u-turn: Income inequality trends in 16 OECD countries. *American Journal of Sociology, 107*, 1244–1299.

Allport, G. W. (1954). *The nature of prejudice.* Cambridge, MA: Addison-Wesley.

Anthias, F. (2001). New hybridities, old concepts: The limits of "culture." *Ethnic & Racial Studies, 24*, 619–641.

Ape culture hints at earlier evolution. (2003, January 2). Retrieved December 27, 2003, from http://news.bbc.co.uk/1/hi/sci/tech/2622101.stm

Appadurai, A. (1996). *Modernity at large: Cultural dimensions of globalization.* Minneapolis, MN: University of Minnesota Press.

Arnett, J. J. (2002). The psychology of globalization. *American Psychologist, 57*, 774–783.

Aronson, J., Lustina, M. J., Good, C., & Keough, K. (1999). When white men can't do math: Necessary and sufficient factors in stereotype threat. *Journal of Experimental Social Psychology, 35*, 29–46.

Au, T. (1983). Chinese and English counterfactuals: The Sapir–Whorf hypothesis revisited. *Cognition, 15*, 155–187.

Au, T. (1984). Counterfactuals: In reply to Alfred Bloom. *Cognition, 17*, 289–302.

Austin, J. L. (1962). *How to do things with words.* Cambridge, MA: Harvard University Press.

Bandura, A. (2001). Social cognitive theory: An agentic perspective. *Annual review of psychology* (Vol. 52, pp. 1–26). Palo Alto: Annual Reviews, Inc.

Bandura, A. (2002). Social cognitive theory in cultural context. *Applied Psychology: An International Review, 51*, 269–290.

Bargh, J. A., Chen, M., & Burrows, L. (1996). Automaticity of social behavior: Direct effects of trait construct and stereotype activation on action. *Journal of Personality and Social Psychology, 71*, 230–244.

Barnard, F. M. (1968). Culture and civilization in modern times. In P. P. Winter (Ed.), *Dictionary of the history of ideas: Studies of selected pivotal ideas* (Vol. 1, pp. 613–620). New York: Charles Scribner's Sons.

Baron, J., & Miller, J. G. (2000). Limiting the scope of moral obligations to help: A cross-cultural investigation. *Journal of Cross-Cultural Psychology, 31,* 703–725.

Baron, R. M., & Kenny, D. A. (1986). The moderator–mediator variable distinction in social psychological research: Conceptual, strategic, and statistical considerations. *Journal of Personality and Social Psychology, 51,* 1173–1182.

Barth, F. (2002). An anthropology of knowledge. *Current Anthropology, 43,* 1–18.

Baumeister, R. (1991). *Escaping the self: Alcoholism, spirituality, masochism, and other flights from the burden of selfhood.* New York: Basic Books.

Baumeister, R., Zhang, L., & Vohs, K. D. (2004). Gossip as cultural learning. *Review of General Psychology, 8,* 111–121.

Becker, E. (1973). *The denial of death.* New York: Free Press.

Bell, N. E., & Tetlock, P. E. (1989). The intuitive politician and the assignment of blame in organizations. In R. A. Ciacalone & P. Rosenfeld (Eds.), *Impression management in the organization* (pp. 105–123). Hillsdale, NJ: Lawrence Erlbaum Associates, Inc.

Bempechat, J., & Drago-Severson, E. (1999). Cross-national differences in academic achievement: Beyond etic conceptions of children's understandings. *Review of Educational Research, 69,* 287–314.

Benet-Martinez, V., Leu, J., Lee, F., & Morris, M. W. (2002). Negotiating biculturalism: Cultural frame switching in biculturals with oppositional versus compatible cultural identities. *Journal of Cross-Cultural Psychology, 33,* 492–516.

Berlin, B., & Kay, P. (1969). *Basic color terms: Their universality and evolution.* Berkeley, CA: University of California Press.

Berry, J. W. (2001). A psychology of immigration. *Journal of Social Issues, 57,* 615–631.

Bickhard, M. H. (2003). Part II: Applications of process-based theories: Process and emergence: Normative function and representation. *Axiomathes, 14,* 121–155.

Biehl, M., Matsumoto, D., Ekman, P., & Hearn, V. (1997). Matsumoto and Ekman's Japanese and Caucasian facial expressions of emotion (JACFEE): Reliability data and cross-national differences. *Journal of Nonverbal Behavior, 21,* 3–21.

Birman, D. (1998). Biculturalism and perceived competence of Latino immigrant adolescents. *American Journal of Community Psychology, 26,* 335–354.

Blascovich, J., Spencer, S. J., Quinn, D., & Steele, C. (2001). African Americans and high blood pressure: The role of stereotype threat. *Psychological Science, 12,* 225–229.

Blinco, P. M. (1992). A cross-cultural study of task persistence of young children in Japan and the United States. *Journal of Cross-Cultural Psychology, 23,* 407–415.

Bochner, S. (1994). Cross-cultural differences in the self-concept. A test of Hofstede's individualism/collectivism dimension. *Journal of Cross-Cultural Psychology, 25,* 273–283.

Bond, M. H., & Cheung, M.-k. (1984). Experimenter's language choice and ethnic affirmation by Chinese trilinguals in Hong Kong. *International Journal of Intercultural Relations, 8,* 347–356.

Bond, M. H., & Cheung, T.-S. (1983). College students' spontaneous self-concept: The effect of culture among respondents in Hong Kong, Japan, and the United States. *Journal of Cross-Cultural Psychology, 14,* 153–171.

Bond, M. H., Leung, K., & Wan, K.-c. (1978). The social impact of self-effacing attributions: The Chinese case. *Journal of Social Psychology, 118,* 157–166.

Bond, M. H., Wan, K.-c., Leung, K., & Giacalone, R. A. (1985). How are responses to verbal insult related to cultural collectivism and power distance? *Journal of Cross-Cultural Psychology, 16,* 111–127.

Boone, J. L., & Smith, E. A. (1998). Is it evolution yet? A critique of evolutionary archaeology. *Current Anthropology, 39,* S141–S157.

Braine, L. G. (1968). Asymmetries of pattern perception observed in Israelis. *Neuropsychologia, 6,* 73–88.

Brauer, M., Judd, C. M., & Jacquelin, V. (2001). The communication of social stereotypes: The effects of group discussion and information distribution on stereotypic appraisals. *Journal of Personality and Social Psychology, 81,* 463–475.

Braumann, C. (1999). Writing for culture: Why a successful concept should not be discarded. *Current Anthropology, 40,* S1–S27.

Brenneis, D. (2002). Some cases for culture. *Human Development, 45,* 264–269.

Brewer, M. B. (1991). The social self: On being the same and different at the same time. *Personality and Social Psychology Bulletin, 17,* 475–482.

Briley, D. A., Morris, M. W., & Simonson, I. (2000). Reasons as carriers of culture: Dynamic versus dispositional models of cultural influence on decision-making. *Journal of Consumer Research, 27,* 157–178.

Briley, D. A., & Wyer, R. S. Jr. (2002). The effect of group membership salience on the avoidance of negative outcomes: Implications for social and consumer decisions. *Journal of Consumer Research, 29,* 400–415.

Brockner, J., & Chen, Y.-r. (1996). The moderating roles of self-esteem and self-construal in reaction to a threat to the self: Evidence from the People's Republic of China and the United States. *Journal of Personality and Social Psychology, 71,* 603–615.

Brown, J. D. (1988). *The self.* New York: McGraw-Hill.

Brown, L. T., & Anthony, R. G. (1990). Continuing the search for social intelligence. *Personality and Individual Differences, 11,* 463–470.

Bruner, J. (1990). *Act of meaning.* Cambridge, MA: Harvard University Press.

Bugental, D. B. (2000). Acquisition of the algorithms of social life: A domain-based approach. *Psychological Bulletin, 126,* 187–219.

Burchell, S. C. (1966). *Age of progress.* New York: Time-Life Books.

Burnstein, E., Crandall, C., & Kitayama, S. (1994). Some neo-Darwinian rules for altruism: Weighing cues for inclusive fitness as a function of the biological importance of the decision. *Journal of Personality and Social Psychology, 67,* 773–789.

Cader, M. (1994). *Saturday night live: The first twenty years.* Boston: Cader Books.

Camilleri, C., & Malewska-Peyre, H. (1997). Socialization and identity strategies. In J. W. Berry, P. R. Dasen, & T. S. Saraswathi (Eds.), *Handbook of cross-cultural psychology, Vol. 2: Basic processes and human development* (2nd ed., pp. 41–67). Boston, MA: Allyn & Bacon.

Campbell, D. T. (1965). Variation and selective retention in socio-cultural evolution. In J. R. Barringer, G. Blanksten, & R. Mack (Eds.), *Social change in developing areas* (pp. 19–49). Cambridge, MA: Schenkman.

Carlson, R. (1984). What's social about social psychology? Where's the person in personality research? *Journal of Personality and Social Psychology, 47,* 1304–1309.

Carnevale, P. J. (1995). Property, culture, and negotiation. In R. Kramer & D. M. Messick (Eds.), *Negotiation as a social process* (pp. 309–323). Newbury Park, CA: Sage.

Carroll, J. B., & Casagrande, J. B. (1958). The function of language classification in behavior. In E. E. Maccoby, T. R. Newcomb, & E. L. Hartley (Eds.), *Readings in social psychology* (3rd ed.). New York: Holt, Rinehart & Winston.

Castano, E., Yzerbyt, V., Paladino, M., & Sacchi, S. (2002). I belong, therefore, I exist: Ingroup identification, ingroup entitativity, and ingroup bias. *Personality and Social Psychology Bulletin, 28,* 135–143.

Castelli, U., Arcuri, L., & Zogmaister, C. (2003). Perceiving ingroup members who use stereotypes: Implicit conformity and similarity. *European Journal of Social Psychology, 33,* 163–175.

Castells, M. (1998). *The end of millennium.* Oxford, UK: Blackwell.

Chan, H. M., Chan, K. M., Cheung, T. S., King, A. Y. C., Chiu, C.-y., & Yang, C. F. (2001). How Confucian are Chinese today? Construction of an ideal type and its application to three Chinese communities. *Sociological Research, 92,* 33–48.

Chang, E. C., Asakawa, K., & Sanna, L. J. (2001). Cultural variations on optimistic and pessimistic bias: Do Easterners really expect the worst and Westerners really expect the best when predicting future life events? *Journal of Personality and Social Psychology, 81,* 476–491.

Chao, M. M. (2005, January). *Is adherence to cultural knowledge tradition always associated with close-mindedness? A case for motivated cultural cognition.* Paper presented at the Society for Personality and Social Psychology Conference, New Orleans, LA.

Chen, C., Lee, S.-y., & Stevenson, H. W. (1995). Response style and cross-cultural comparisons of rating scales among East Asian and North American students. *Psychological Science, 6,* 170–175.

Chen, C., & Stevenson, H. W. (1995). Motivation and mathematics achievement: A comparative study of Asian-American, Caucasian-American, and East Asian high school students. *Child Development, 66,* 1215–1234.

Chen, J., Chiu, C.-y., Roese, N. J., Tam, K.-p., & Lau, I. Y.-m. (in press). Culture and counterfactuals: On the importance of life events. *Journal of Cross-Cultural Psychology.*

Chen, Z. X., Tsui, A. S., & Farh, J.-l. (2002). Loyalty to supervisor vs. organizational commitment: Relationships to employee performance in China. *Journal of Occupational and Organizational Psychology, 75,* 339–356.

Cheng, B.-c., Shieh, P.-y., & Chou, L.-f. (2002). The principal's leadership, leader–member exchange quality, and the teacher's extra-role behavior: The effects of transformational and paternalistic leadership. *Studies on Indigenous Psychology, 17,* 105–161.

Cheng, C., Chiu, C.-y., Hong, Y.-y., & Cheung, J. S. (2001). Discriminative facility and its role in the perceived quality of interactional experiences. *Journal of Personality, 69,* 765–786.

Cheng, C., Lee, S.-L., & Chiu, C.-y. (1999). Dialectic thinking in daily life. *Hong Kong Journal of Social Sciences, 15,* 1–26.

Cheung, T.-S., Chan, H.-M., Chan, K.-M., King, A. Y.-K., Chiu, C., & Yang, C.-F. (2003). On Zhongyong rationality: The Confucian doctrine of the mean as a missing link between instrumental rationality and communicative rationality. *Asian Journal of Social Science, 31,* 107–127.

Chirkov, V. L., Kim, Y., Ryan, R. M., & Kaplan, U. (2003). Differentiating autonomy from individualism and independence: A self-determination theory perspective on internalization of cultural orientations and well-being. *Journal of Personality and Social Psychology, 84,* 97–110.

Chirkov, V. L., & Ryan, R. M. (2001). Parent and teacher autonomy-support in Russian and U.S. adolescents: Common effects on well-being and academic motivation. *Journal of Cross-Cultural Psychology, 32,* 618–635.

Chiu, C.-y. (1990a). Normative expectations of social behavior, and concern for members among the collective in Chinese culture. *Journal of Psychology, 124,* 103–111.

Chiu, C.-y. (1990b). Distributive justice among Hong Kong Chinese college students. *Journal of Social Psychology, 130,* 649–656.

Chiu, C.-y. (1991a). Role expectation as the principal criterion used in justice judgment among Hong Kong college students. *Journal of Psychology, 125,* 557–565.

Chiu, C.-y. (1991b). Hierarchical social relations and justice judgment among Hong Kong Chinese college students. *Journal of Social Psychology, 131,* 885–887.

Chiu, C.-y. (1991c). Responses to injustice in Chinese popular sayings and among Hong Kong college students. *Journal of Social Psychology, 131,* 655–665.

Chiu, C.-y. (2001). Assessment of Zhong-yong (dialectic) thinking: Preliminary findings from a cross-regional study. *Hong Kong Journal of Social Sciences, 18*, 33–55.

Chiu, C.-y., & Chen, J. (2004). Symbols and interactions: Application of the CCC model to culture, language, and social identity. In S.-h. Ng, C. Candlin, & C.-y. Chiu (Eds.), *Language matters: Communication, culture, and social identity.* Hong Kong: City University of Hong Kong Press.

Chiu, C.-y., Dweck, C. S., Tong, J. Y.-y., & Fu, J. H.-y. (1997a). Implicit theories and conceptions of morality. *Journal of Personality and Social Psychology, 73*, 923–940.

Chiu, C.-y., & Hong, Y.-y. (1992). The effect of intentionality and validation on collective responsibility attribution among Hong Kong Chinese. *Journal of Psychology, 126*, 291–300.

Chiu, C.-y., & Hong, Y.-y. (1997). Justice from a Chinese perspective. In H. S. R. Kao & D. Sinha (Eds.), *Asian perspectives on psychology* (pp. 164–184). Thousand Oaks, CA: Sage.

Chiu, C.-y., & Hong, Y. (2005). Cultural competence: Dynamic processes. In A. Elliot & C. S. Dweck (Eds.), *Handbook of motivation and competence* (pp. 489–505). New York: Guilford.

Chiu, C.-y., Hong, Y.-y., & Dweck, C. S. (1997b). Lay dispositionism and implicit theories of personality. *Journal of Personality and Social Psychology, 73*, 19–30.

Chiu, C.-y., Hong, Y.-y., Mischel, W., & Shoda, Y. (1995). Discriminative facility in social competence. *Social Cognition, 13*, 49–70.

Chiu, C.-y., Krauss, R. M., & Lau, I. (1998). Some cognitive consequences of communication. In S. R. Fussell & R. J. Kreuz (Eds.), *Social and cognitive approaches to interpersonal communication* (pp. 259–276). Mahwah, NJ: Lawrence Erlbaum Associates, Inc.

Chiu, C.-y., Krauss, R. M., & Lee, S. (1999). Communication and social cognition: A post-Whorfian approach. In T. Sugiman, M. Karasawa, J. Liu, & C. Ward (Eds.), *Progress in Asian social psychology* (Vol. 2, pp. 127–143). Map-ku, Korea: Kyoyook-Kwahak-Sa.

Chiu, C.-y., Leung, A. K.-y., & Kwan, L. (in press). Language, cognition and culture: The Whorfian hypothesis and beyond. In S. Kitayama & D. Cohen (Eds.), *Handbook of cultural psychology.* New York: Guilford.

Chiu, C.-y., Morris, M. W., Hong, Y.-y., & Menon, T. (2000). Motivated cultural cognition: The impact of implicit cultural theories on dispositional attribution varies as a function of need for closure. *Journal of Personality and Social Psychology, 78*, 247–259.

Chiu, C.-y., Tsang, S. C., & Yang, C. F. (1988). The role of "face" situation and attitudinal antecedents in Chinese consumer complaint behavior. *Journal of Social Psychology, 128*, 173–180.

Chiu, R. K., & Kosinski, F. A. (1994). Is Chinese conflict-handling behavior influenced by Chinese values? *Social Behavior & Personality, 22*, 81–90.

Choi, I., & Choi, Y. (2002). Culture and self-concept flexibility. *Personality and Social Psychology Bulletin, 28*, 1508–1517.

Choi, I., Dalal, R., Kim-Prieto, C., & Park, H. (2003). Culture and judgment of causal relevance. *Journal of Personality and Social Psychology, 84*, 46–59.

Choi, I., & Nisbett, R. E. (1998). Situational salience and cultural differences in the correspondence bias and actor–observer bias. *Personality and Social Psychology Bulletin, 24*, 949–960.

Choi, I., & Nisbett, R. E. (2000). Cultural psychology of surprise: Holistic theories and recognition of contradiction. *Journal of Personality and Social Psychology, 79*, 890–905.

Choi, S.-C., Kim, U., & Choi, S.-H. (1993). Indigenous analysis of collective representations: A Korean perspective. In U. Kim & J. W. Berry (Eds.), *Indigenous psychologies: Research and experience in cultural context* (pp. 193–210). Newbury Park, CA: Sage.

Chopra, T. (2000). *The holy cow and other Indian stories.* New Delhi: Prakash Book Depot.

Chu, D. L. (1975). *Essays on the history of the Chinese legal system.* Taipei: Zhiwen.

Chu, J.-l., & Yang, K.-s. (1976). The effects of relative performance and individual modernity on distributive behavior among Chinese college students. *Bulletin of Institute of Ethnology, Academia Sinica, 41,* 79–95.

Clark, H. H., & Carlson, T. B. (1982). Speech acts and hearers' beliefs. In N. V. Smith (Ed.), *Mutual knowledge* (pp. 1–59). New York: Academic Press.

Clark, H. H., & Marshall, C. E. (1981). Definite reference and mutual knowledge. In A. K. Joshi, I. Sag, & B. Webber (Eds.), *Elements of discourse understanding* (pp. 10–63). Cambridge, UK: Cambridge University Press.

Clark, H. H., & Murphy, G. L. (1982). Audience design in meaning and reference. In J.-F. L. Ny & W. Kintsch (Eds.), *Language and comprehension* (pp. 287–296). New York: North Holland.

Clark, H. H., Schreuder, R., & Buttrick, S. (1983). Common ground and the understanding of demonstrative reference. *Journal of Verbal Learning and Verbal Behavior, 22,* 245–258.

Clarke, M., Losoff, A., McCracken, M. D., & Rood, D. (1984). Linguistic relativity and sex/gender studies: Epistemological and methodological considerations. *Language Learning, 34,* 47–67.

Clarke, M., Losoff, A., McCracken, M. D., & Still, J. (1981). Gender perception in Arabic and English. *Language Learning, 31,* 159–169.

Cohen, D. (1996). Law, social policy, and violence: The impact of regional cultures. *Journal of Personality and Social Psychology, 70,* 961–978.

Cohen, D. (1998). Culture, self-organization, and patterns of violence. *Journal of Personality and Social Psychology, 75,* 408–419.

Cohen, D. (2001). Cultural variation: Considerations and implications. *Psychological Bulletin, 127,* 451–471.

Cohen, D., & Gunz, A. (2002). As seen by the other … Perspectives on the self in the memories and emotional perceptions of Easterners and Westerners. *Psychological Science, 13,* 55–59.

Cohen, D., & Nisbett, R. E. (1994). Self-protection and the culture of honor: Explaining southern violence. *Personality and Social Psychology Bulletin, 20,* 551–567.

Cohen, D., & Nisbett, R. E. (1997). Field experiments examining the culture of honor: The role of institutions in perpetuating norms about violence. *Personality and Social Psychology Bulletin, 23,* 1188–1199.

Cohen, D., Nisbett, R. E., Bowdle, B. F., & Schwarz, N. (1996). Insult, aggression, and the Southern culture of honor: An "experimental ethnography." *Journal of Personality and Social Psychology, 70,* 945–960.

Conniff, R. (2003). Rethinking primate aggression. *Smithsonian, 14,* 60–67.

Cook, T. D., & Campbell, D. T. (1986). The causal assumptions of quasi-experimental practice: The origins of quasi-experimental practice. *Synthese (Historical Archive), 68,* 141–180.

Cousins, S. D. (1989). Culture and self-perception in Japan and the United States. *Journal of Personality and Social Psychology, 56,* 124–131.

Craik, F. I. M., Moroz, T. M., Moscovitch, M., Stuss, D. T., Winocur, G., Tulving, E., & Kapur, S. (1999). In search of the self: A positron emission tomography study. *Psychological Science, 10,* 26–34.

Croizet, J.-C., Despres, G., Gauzins, M.-E., Huguet, P., Leyens, K.-P., & Moet, A. (2004). Stereotype threat undermines intellectual performance by triggering a disruptive mental load. *Personality and Social Psychology Bulletin, 30,* 721–731.

Cunningham, P. B., Foster, S. L., & Henggeler, S. W. (2002). The elusive concept of cultural competence. *Children's Services: Social Policy, Research and Practice, 5,* 231–243.

D'Andrade, R. (1987). A folk model of the mind. In D. Holland & N. Quinn (Eds.), *Cultural models in language and thought* (pp. 112–148). Cambridge, UK: Cambridge University Press.

D'Andrade, R. (2002). Cultural Darwinism and language. *American Anthropologist, 104,* 223–232.

Daniels, C. (2003). Mr. Coffee. *Fortune,* April 14, pp. 139–141.

Danso, H. A., & Esses, V. M. (2001). Black experimenters and the intellectual test performance of White participants: The tables are turned. *Journal of Experimental Social Psychology, 37,* 158–165.

Das, G. (2001). *India unbound.* New York: A.A. Knopf.

Davidoff, J. (2001). Language and perceptual categorization. *Trends in Cognitive Sciences, 5,* 382–387.

Davis, M. H., & Stephan, W. G. (1980). Attributions for exam performance. *Journal of Applied Psychology, 10,* 235–248.

Dawkins, R. (1976). *The selfish gene.* Oxford: Oxford University Press.

Dawkins, R. (1996). *The blind watchmaker: Why the evidence of evolution reveals a universe without design.* New York: W.W. Norton & Company.

Derlega, V. J., Cukur, C. S., Kuang, J. C. Y., & Forsyth, D. R. (2002). Interdependent construal of self and the endorsement of conflict resolution strategies in interpersonal, intergroup, and international disputes. *Journal of Cross-Cultural Psychology, 33,* 610–625.

De Sonneville, L. M. J., Verschoor, C. A., Njiokiktjien, C., Op het Veld, V., Toorenaar, N., & Vranken, M. (2002). Facial identity and facial emotions: Speed, accuracy, and processing strategies in children and adults. *Journal of Clinical and Experimental Neuropsychology, 24,* 200-213.

de Waal, F. B. M. (1999). Cultural primatology comes of age. *Nature, 399,* 635–636.

Dickow, H., & Moller, V. (2002). South Africa's "rainbow people", national pride and optimism: A trend study. *Social Indicators Research, 59,* 175–202.

Diener, E., & Diener, M. (1995). Cross-cultural correlates of life satisfaction and self-esteem. *Journal of Personality and Social Psychology, 68,* 653–663.

Dijksterhuis, A., Spears, R., & Lepinasse, V. (2001). Reflecting and deflecting stereotypes: Assimilation and contrast in impression formation and automatic behavior. *Journal of Experimental Social Psychology, 37,* 286–299.

Dijksterhuis, A., Spears, R., Postmes, T., Stapel, D., Koomen, W., van Knippenberg, A., & Scheepers, D. (1998). Seeing one thing and doing another: Contrast effects in automatic behavior. *Journal of Personality and Social Psychology, 75,* 862–871.

DiMaggio, D. (1997). Culture cognition. *Annual Review of Sociology, 23,* 263–287.

Dirks, N. B. (2001). *Castes of mind: Colonialism and the making of modern India.* Princeton, NJ: Princeton University Press.

Doi, L. T. (1956). Japanese language as an expression of Japanese psychology. *Western Speech, 20,* 90–96.

Donald, M. (1993). Precis of "Origins of the modern mind: Three stages in the evolution of culture and cognition." *Behavioral and Brain Sciences, 16,* 737–791.

Dunbar, R. I. M. (2004). Gossip in evolutionary perspective. *Review of General Psychology, 8,* 100–110.

Dunbar, R. I. M., Duncan, N. D. C., & Marriott, A. (1997). Human conversational behavior. *Human Nature, 8,* 231–246.

Dweck, C. S., Chiu, C.-y., & Hong, Y.-y. (1995). Implicit theories and their role in judgments and reactions: A world from two perspectives. *Psychological Inquiry, 6,* 267–285.

Dweck, C. S., Hong, Y.-y., & Chiu, C.-y. (1993). Implicit theories: Individual differences in the likelihood and meaning of dispositional inference. Special Issue: On inferring personal dispositions from behavior. *Personality and Social Psychology Bulletin, 19,* 644–656.

Earle, M. J. (1969). A cross-cultural and cross-language comparison of dogmatism scores. *Journal of Social Psychology, 79*, 19–24.

Eaton, M. J., & Dembo, M. H. (2001). Differences in the motivational beliefs of Asian American and non-Asian students. *Journal of Educational Psychology, 89*, 433–440.

Eid, M., & Diener, E. (2001). Norms for experiencing emotions in different cultures: Inter- and intranational differences. *Journal of Personality and Social Psychology, 81*, 869–885.

Ekman, P. (1972). Universals and cultural differences in facial expressions of emotions. In J. Cole (Ed.), *Nebraska symposium on motivation, 1971* (Vol. 19, pp. 207–282). Lincoln, NE: University of Nebraska Press.

Ekman, P. (1994). Strong evidence for universals in facial expressions: A reply to Russell's mistaken critique. *Psychological Bulletin, 115*, 268–287.

Elfenbein, H. A., & Ambady, N. (2003). When familiarity breeds accuracy: Cultural exposure and facial emotion recognition. *Journal of Personality and Social Psychology, 85*, 276–290.

Elfenbein, H. A., & Nalini, A. (2002). On the universality and cultural specificity of emotion recognition: A meta-analysis. *Psychological Bulletin, 128*, 203–235.

Elliot, A. J., Chirkov, V. I., Kim, Y., & Sheldon, K. M. (2001). A cross-cultural analysis of avoidance (relative to approach) personal goals. *Psychological Science, 12*, 505–510.

Engebretson, D., & Fullmer, D. (1970). Cross-cultural differences in territoriality: Interaction distances of native Japanese, Hawaii Japanese, and American Caucasians. *Journal of Cross-Cultural Psychology, 1*, 261–269.

Ensari, N., & Miller, N. (2002). The out-group must not be so bad after all: The effects of disclosure, typicality, and salience on intergroup bias. *Journal of Personality and Social Psychology, 83*, 313–329.

Ervin, S. M. (1962). The connotations of gender. *Word, 18*, 249–261.

Ervin-Tripp, S. (1964). An analysis of the interaction of language, topic, and listener. *American Anthropologist, 66*, 86–102.

Falk, R. (1999). *Predatory globalization*. Cambridge: Polity Press.

Fallshore, M., & Schooler, J. W. (1995). The verbal vulnerability of perceptual expertise. *Journal of Experimental Psychology: Learning, Memory, and Cognition, 21*, 1608–1623.

Farh, J.-l., & Cheng, B.-s. (2000). A cultural analysis of paternalistic leadership in Chinese organizations. In J. T. Li, A. S. Tsui, & E. Weldon (Eds.), *Management and organizations in the Chinese context* (pp. 84–127). London: Macmillan.

Fein, S., Hoshino-Browne, E., Davies, P. G., & Spencer, S. J. (2003). Self-image maintenance goals and sociocultural norms in motivated social perception. In S. J. Spencer, S. Fein, M. P. Zanna, & J. Olson (Eds.), *Motivated social perception: The Ontario symposium* (Vol. 9, pp. 21–44). Mahwah, NJ: Lawrence Erlbaum Associates, Inc.

Fincham, F. D., & Jaspars, J. M. (1979). Attribution of responsibility: From man the scientist to man as lawyer. In L. Berkowitz (Ed.), *Advances in experimental social psychology* (Vol. 13, pp. 81–183). San Diego: Academic Press.

Fincham, F. D., & Schultz, T. R. (1981). Intervening causation and the mitigation of responsibility for harm. *British Journal of Social Psychology, 20*, 113–120.

Fischer, M. M. J. (1999). Emergent forms of life: Anthropologies of late or postmodernities. *Annual Review of Anthropology, 28*, 455–478.

Fiske, A. P. (2000). Complementarity theory: Why human social capacities evolved to require cultural complements? *Personality and Social Psychology Review, 4*, 76–94.

Fiske, A. P. (2002). Using individualism–collectivism to compare cultures – a critique of the validity and measurement of the constructs: Comments on Oyserman et al. (2002). *Psychological Bulletin, 128*, 78–88.

Florian, V., & Mikulincer, M. (1998). Terror management in childhood: Does death concep-tualization moderate the effects of mortality salience on similar and different others? *Journal of Personality and Social Psychology, 24,* 1104–1112.

Fong, C. P. S., & Wyer, R. S. Jr. (2003). Cultural, social, and emotional determinants of deci-sions under uncertainty. *Organizational Behavior and Human Decision Processes, 90,* 304–322.

Ford, M. E., & Tisak, M. S. (1983). A further search for social intelligence. *Journal of Educational Psychology, 75,* 196–206.

Fox, R. (1970). The cultural animal. *Encounter, 35,* 31–42.

Fox, R. (1989). *The search for society: Quest for a biosocial science and morality.* New Brunswick, NJ: Rutgers University Press.

Freeman, R. D. (1980). Visual acuity is better for letters in rows than in columns. *Nature, 286,* 62–64.

Fremantle, A. (1965). *Age of faith.* New York: Time-Life Books.

Friedman, J. (1994). *Cultural identity and global process.* London: Sage.

Fu, H.-y., & Chiu, C.-y. (2004). *Studying cultures from a shorter distance: Change and mainte-nance of cultural values in multicultural environment.* Unpublished manuscript.

Fu, H.-y., Morris, M. W., Lee, S.-l., & Chiu, C.-y. (2002, August). *Why do individuals follow cul-tural norms: Need for closure, script-based expectancies, and conflict resolution choices.* Paper presented at the Academy of Management, Division of Conflict Management, Denver, CO.

Furby, L. (1986). Psychology and justice. In R. L. Cohen (Ed.), *Justice: Views from the social sciences* (pp. 153–203). New York: Plenum.

Fussell, S. R., & Krauss, R. M. (1989a). The effects of intended audience on message pro-duction and comprehension: Reference in a common ground framework. *Journal of Experimental Social Psychology, 25,* 203–219.

Fussell, S. R., & Krauss, R. M. (1989b). Understanding friends and strangers: The effects of audience design on message comprehension. *European Journal of Social Psychology, 19,* 509–525.

Fussell, S. R., & Krauss, R. M. (1991). Accuracy and bias in estimates of others' knowledge. *European Journal of Social Psychology, 21,* 445–454.

Fussell, S. R., & Krauss, R. M. (1992). Coordination of knowledge in communication: Effects of speakers' assumptions about others' knowledge. *Journal of Personality and Social Psychology, 62,* 378–391.

Fwu, B.-j., & Wang, H.-h. (2002). The social status of teachers in Taiwan. *Comparative Education, 38,* 211–224.

Gabora, L. (1997). The origin and evolution of culture and creativity. *Journal of Memetics: Evolutionary Models of Information Transmissions, 1.* http://jomemit.cfpm.org/vol1/gabora_1.htm

Gabunia, L., Vekua, A., Lordkipanidze, D., Swisher, C. C., Ferring, R., Justus, A., Nioradze, M., Tvalchrelidze, M., Anton, S. C., Bosinski, G., Joris, O., de Lumley, M. A., Majsuradze, G., & Mouskhelishvili, A. (2000). Earliest Pleistocene hominid cranial remains from Dmanisi, Republic of Georgia: Taxonomy, geological setting, and age. *Science, 288,* 1019–1025.

Gaertner, S. L., Dovidio, J. F., Anastasio, P. A., Bachman, B. A., & Rust, M. C. (1993). The common ingroup identity model: Recategorization and the reduction of intergroup bias. *European Review of Social Psychology, 4,* 1–26.

Gaertner, S. L., Dovidio, J. F., Nier, J. A., Ward, C. W., & Banker, B. S. (1999). Across cultural divides: The value of a superordinate identity. In D. A. Prentice & D. T. Miller (Eds.),

Cultural divides: Understanding and overcoming group conflict (pp. 173–212). New York: Russell Sage Foundation.

Gaertner, S. L., Rust, M. C., Dovidio, J. F., Bachman, B. A., & Anastasio, P. A. (1994). The contact hypothesis: The role of a common ingroup identity on reducing intergroup bias. *Small Group Research*, 25, 224–249.

Galef, B. (1992). The question of animal culture. *Human Nature*, 3, 157–178.

Ganguly-Scrase, R. (2003). Paradoxes of globalization, liberalization, and gender equality: The worldviews of the lower middle class in West Bengal, India. *Gender & Society*, 17, 544–566.

Gardner, W. L., Gabriel, S., & Lee, A. (1999). "I" value freedom, but "we" value relationships: Self-construal priming mirrors cultural differences in judgment. *Psychological Science*, 10, 321–326.

Geertz, C. (1973). *The interpretation of culture.* New York: Basic Books.

Gelfand, M. J., Higgins, M., Nishii, L. H., Rava, J. L., Dominquez, A., Murakami, F., Yamaguchi, S., & Toyama, M. (2002). Culture and egocentric perceptions of fairness in conflict and negotiation. *Journal of Applied Psychology*, 87, 833–845.

Gelfand, M. J., Nishii, L. H., Holcombe, K. M., Dyer, M., Ohbuchi, K.-l., & Fukuno, M. (2001). Cultural influences on cognitive representations of conflict: Interpretations of conflict episodes in the United States and Japan. *Journal of Applied Psychology*, 86, 1059–1074.

Gelfand, M. J., & Realo, A. (1999). Individualism–collectivism and accountability in intergroup negotiations. *Journal of Applied Psychology*, 84, 721–736.

Gelfand, M. J., Spurlock, D., Sniezek, J. A., & Shao, L. (2000). Culture and social prediction: The role of information in enhancing confidence in social predictions in the United States and China. *Journal of Cross-Cultural Psychology*, 31, 498–516.

Gergen, K. J., Gulerce, A., Lock, A., & Misra, G. (1996). Psychological science in cultural context. *American Psychologist*, 51, 496–503.

Gervey, B.M., Chiu, C.-y., Hong, Y., & Dweck, C. S. (1999). Implicit theories: The impact of person information on decision-making. *Personality and Social Psychology Bulletin*, 25, 17–27.

Giddens, A. (1985). *The nation state and violence.* Cambridge: Polity Press.

Gilbert, D. (1989). Thinking lightly about others: Automatic components in the social inference process. In J. S. Uleman & J. A. Bargh (Eds.), *Unintended thought: Limits of awareness, intention, and control* (pp. 189–212). New York: Guilford Press.

Gilbert, D., Krull, D., & Pelham, B. (1988). Of thoughts unspoken: Social inference and the self-regulation of behavior. *Journal of Personality and Social Psychology*, 55, 685–694.

Gilbert, D., Pelham, B., & Krull, D. (1988). On cognitive busyness: When person perceivers meet persons perceived. *Journal of Personality and Social Psychology*, 54, 733–740.

Gjerde, P. F., & Onishi, M. (2000). Selves, cultures, and nations: The psychological imagination of the Japanese in the era of globalization. *Human Development*, 43, 216–226.

Goodall, J. (1988). *In the shadow of man.* Boston: Houghton Mifflin.

Goodenough, W. H. (1961). Comment on cultural evolution. *Daedalus*, 90, 521–528.

Gould, S. J. (1981). *The mismeasure of man.* New York: Norton.

Grant, H., & Dweck, C. S. (2001). Cross-cultural response to failure: Considering outcome attributions with different goals. In F. Salili, C.-y. Chiu, & Y.-y. Hong (Eds.), *Student motivation: The culture and context of learning* (pp. 203–219). New York: Kluwer Academic/Plenum.

Greenberg, J., Pyszczynski, T., Solomon, S., Rosenblatt, A., Veeder, M., Kirkland, S., & Lyon, D. (1990). Evidence for terror management theory II: The effects of mortality salience on reactions to those who threaten and bolster the cultural worldview. *Journal of Personality and Social Psychology, 58*, 308–318.

Greenberg, J., Pyszczynski, T., Solomon, S., Simon, L., & Breus, M. (1994). Role of consciousness and accessibility of death-related thoughts in mortality salience effects. *Journal of Personality and Social Psychology, 67*, 627–637.

Greenberg, J., Simon, L., Harmon-Jones, E., Solomon, S., Pyszczynski, T., & Lyon, D. (1995). Testing alternative explanations for mortality salience effects: Terror management, value accessibility, or worrisome thoughts? *European Journal of Social Psychology, 25*, 417–433.

Greenberg, J., Solomon, S., & Pyszczynski, T. (1997). Terror management theory of self-esteem and cultural worldview: Empirical assessments and conceptual refinements. In P. M. Zanna (Ed.), *Advances in experimental social psychology* (Vol. 29, pp. 61–141). San Diego, CA: Academic Press.

Greenfield, P. M. (2000). Three approaches to the psychology of culture: Where do they come from? Where can they go? *Asian Journal of Social Psychology, 3*, 223–240.

Grosjean, F. (1989). Neurolinguists, beware! The bilingual is not two monolinguals in one person. *Brain & Language, 36*, 3–15.

Gudykunst, W. B., Schmidt, K. L., Nishida, T., Bond, M. H., Leung, K., Wang, G., & Baraclough, R. A. (1992). The influence of individualism–collectivism, self-monitoring, and predicted-outcome value on communication in ingroup and outgroup relationships. *Journal of Cross-Cultural Psychology, 23*, 196–213.

Guimond, S., & Palmer, D. L. (1985). The political socialization of commerce and social science students: Epistemic authority and attitude change. *Journal of Applied Social Psychology, 26*, 1985–2013.

Gutierres, S. E., Kenrick, D. T., & Partch, J. J. (1999). Beauty, dominance, and the mating game: Contrast effects in self-assessment reflect gender differences in mate selections. *Personality and Social Psychology Bulletin, 25*, 1126–1135.

Haberstroh, S., Oyserman, D., Schwarz, N., Kuehnen, U., & Ji, L. (2002). Is the interdependent self more sensitive to question context than the independent self? Self-construal and the observation of conversational norms. *Journal of Experimental Social Psychology, 38*, 323–329.

Hall, E. T. (1966). *The hidden dimension*. Garden City, NY: Doubleday.

Hall, E. T. (1990). *Understanding cultural differences*. Yarmouth, ME: Intercultural Press.

Hallahan, M., Lee, F., & Herzog, T. (1997). It's not just whether you win or lose, it's also where you play the game: A naturalistic, cross-cultural examination of the positivity bias. *Journal of Cross-Cultural Psychology, 28*, 768–778.

Halloran, M. J., & Kashima, E. S. (2004). Social identity and worldview validation: The effects of ingroup identity primes and mortality salience on value endorsement. *Personality and Social Psychology Bulletin, 30*, 915–925.

Hampton, J. A. (1997). Emergent attributes in combined concepts. In T. B. Ward, S. M. Smith, & J. Vaid (Eds.), *Creative thought: An investigation of conceptual structures and processes* (pp. 83–110). Washington, DC: American Psychological Association.

Han, S.-P., & Shavitt, S. (1994). Persuasion and culture: Advertising appeals in individualistic and collectivistic societies. *Journal of Experimental Social Psychology, 30*, 326–350.

Hansen, N. D., Pepitone-Arreola-Rockwell, F., & Greene, A. F. (2000). Multicultural competence: Criteria and case examples. *Professional Psychology – Research and Practice, 31*, 652–660.

Harmon-Jones, E., Simon, L., Pyszczynski, T., Solomon, S., & McGregor, H. (1997). Terror management theory and self-esteem: Evidence that increased self-esteem reduces mortality salience effects. *Journal of Personality and Social Psychology, 72*, 24–36.

Harris, M. (1964). *The nature of cultural things*. New York: Random House.

Hattori, R., & Maeda, E. (2000, January). The Japanese employment system (summary). *Bank of Japan Monthly Bulletin*. http://www.boj.or.jp/en/ronbun/00/ron0001a.htm

Headland, T. N., & Bailey, R. C. (Eds.) (1991). Special issue on "human foragers in tropical rain forests." *Human Ecology, 19*, 115–285.

Heath, C. (1996). Do people prefer to pass along good or bad news? Valence and relevance as predictors of transmission propensity. *Organizational Behavior and Human Decision Processes, 68*, 79–94.

Heath, C., Bell, C., & Sternberg, E. (2001). Emotional selection in memes: The case of urban legends. *Journal of Personality and Social Psychology, 81*, 1028–1041.

Heaven, P. C. L. (1999). Group identities and human values. *Journal of Social Psychology, 139*, 590–595.

Heaven, P. C. L., Stones, C., Simbayi, L., & Le Roux, A. (2000). Human values and social identities among samples of white and black South Africans. *International Journal of Psychology, 35*, 67–72.

Heider, E. R., & Olivier, D. C. (1972). The structure of the color space in naming and memory for two languages. *Cognitive Psychology, 3*, 337–354.

Heider, F. (1958). *The psychology of interpersonal relations*. New York: Wiley.

Heine, S. J. (2003). An exploration of cultural variation in self-enhancing and self-improving motivations. In V. Murphy-Berman & J. J. Berman (Eds.), *Cross-cultural differences in perspectives on the self, Nebraska symposium on motivation* (Vol. 49, pp. 102–128). Lincoln, NE: University of Nebraska Press.

Heine, S. J., Kitayama, S., Lehman, D. R., Takata, T., Ide, E., Leung, C., & Matsumoto, H. (2001). Divergent consequences of success and failure in Japan and North America: An investigation of self-improving motivations and malleable selves. *Journal of Personality and Social Psychology, 81*, 599–615.

Heine, S. J., & Lehman, D. R. (1995). Cultural variation in unrealistic optimism: Does the West feel more invulnerable than the East? *Journal of Personality and Social Psychology, 68*, 595–607.

Heine, S. J., & Lehman, D. R. (1997). Culture, dissonance, and self-affirmation. *Personality and Social Psychology Bulletin, 23*, 389–400.

Heine, S. J., & Lehman, D. R. (1999). Culture, self-discrepancies, and self satisfaction. *Personality and Social Psychology Bulletin, 25*, 915–925.

Heine, S. J., Lehman, D. R., Markus, H., & Kitayama, S. (1999). Is there a universal need for positive self-regard? *Psychological Review, 106*, 766–794.

Heine, S. J., Lehman, D. R., Peng, K., & Greenholtz, J. (2002). What's wrong with cross-cultural comparisons of subjective Likert scales? The reference-group effect. *Journal of Personality and Social Psychology, 82*, 903–918.

Heine, S. J., & Renshaw, K. (2002). Interjudge agreement, self-enhancement, and liking: Cross-cultural divergences. *Personality and Social Psychological Bulletin, 28*, 442–451.

Hernandez, M., & Iyengar, S. S. (2001). What drives whom? A cultural perspective on human agency. *Social Cognition, 19*, 269–294.

Hess, R. D., Chih-Mei, C., & McDevitt, T. M. (1987). Cultural variations in family beliefs about children's performance in mathematics: Comparisons among People's Republic of China, Chinese-Americans, and Caucasian-American families. *Journal of Educational Psychology, 79*, 179–188.

Hetts, J. J., Sakuma, M., & Pelham, B. W. (1999). Two roads to positive self-regard: Implicit and explicit self-evaluation and culture. *Journal of Experimental Social Psychology, 35*, 512–559.

Hewes, G. W. (1973). Primate communication and the gestural origins of language. *Current Anthropology, 14*, 5–24.

Heylighen, F., & Campbell, D. T. (1995). Selection of organization at the social level: Obstacles and facilitators of metasystem transitions. *World Futures: The Journal of General Evolution, 45*, 181–212.

Higgins, E. T. (1996). Knowledge activation: Accessibility, applicability and salience. In E. T. Higgins & A. E. Kruglanski (Eds.), *Social psychology: Handbook of basic principles* (pp. 133–168). New York: Guilford.

Higgins, E. T., & Brendl, C. M. (1995). Accessibility and applicability: Some "activation rules" influencing judgment. *Journal of Experimental Social Psychology, 31*, 218–243.

Higgins, E. T., Friedman, R. S., Harlow, R. E., Idson, L. C., Ayduk, O. N., & Taylor, A. (2001). Achievement orientations from subjective histories of success: Promotion pride versus prevention pride. *European Journal of Social Psychology, 31*, 3–23.

Higgins, E. T., King, G. A., & Mavin, G. H. (1982). Individual construct accessibility and subjective impressions and recall. *Journal of Personality and Social Psychology, 43*, 3547.

Higgins, E. T., & McCann, C. D. (1984). Social encoding and subsequent attitudes, impressions and memory: 'Context-driven' and motivational aspects of processing. *Journal of Personality and Social Psychology, 47*, 26–39.

Higgins, E. T., McCann, C. D., & Fondacaro, R. (1982). The "communication game": Goal-directed encoding and cognitive consequences. *Social Cognition, 1*, 21–37.

Ho, D. Y. F. (1976). On the concept of face. *American Journal of Sociology, 81*, 867–884.

Ho, D. Y. F. (1987). Fatherhood in Chinese culture. In M. E. Lamb (Ed.), *The father's role: Cross-cultural perspectives* (pp. 227–245). Hillsdale, NJ: Lawrence Erlbaum Associates, Inc.

Ho, D. Y. F. (1988). Asian psychology: A dialogue on indigenization and beyond. In A. C. Paranijpe, D. Y. F. Ho, & W. R. Rieter (Eds.), *Asian contribution to psychology* (pp. 63–71). New York: Praeger.

Ho, D. Y. F. (1994). Filial piety, authoritarian moralism, and cognitive conservatism in Chinese societies. *Genetic, Social, and General Psychology Monographs, 120*, 347–365.

Ho, D. Y. F. (1996). Filial piety and its psychological consequences. In M. H. Bond (Ed.), *The handbook of Chinese psychology* (pp. 155–165). Hong Kong: Oxford University Press.

Ho, D. Y. F. (1998). Indigenous psychologies: Asian perspectives. *Journal of Cross-Cultural Psychology, 29*, 88–103.

Ho, D. Y. F., Chau, A. W. L., Chiu, C.-y., & Peng, S. Q. (2003). Ideological orientation and political transition in Hong Kong: Confidence in the future. *Political Psychology, 24*, 403–413.

Ho, D. Y. F., & Chiu, C.-y. (1994). Component ideas of individualism, collectivism, and social organization: An application in the study of Chinese culture. In U. Kim, H. C. Triandis, C. Kagitcibasi, G. Choi, & G. Yoon (Eds.), *Individualism and collectivism: Theory, method and applications* (pp. 137–156). Thousand Oaks, CA: Sage.

Ho, D. Y. F., & Chiu, C.-y. (1998). Collective representations as a metaconstruct: An analysis based on methodological relationism. *Culture and Psychology, 4*, 349–369.

Ho, D. Y. F., & Kang, T. K. (1984). Intergenerational comparisons of child-rearing attitudes and practices in Hong Kong. *Developmental Psychology, 20*, 1004–1016.

Ho, D. Y. F., Peng, S.-q., & Chan, S.-f. F. (2001). Authority and learning in Confucian-heritage education: A relational methodological analysis. In C.-y. Chiu, F. Salili, & Y.-y. Hong (Eds.), *Multiple competencies and self-regulated learning* (pp. 29–47). Greenwich, CT: Information Age Publishing.

Hoffman, C., Lau, I., & Johnson, D. R. (1986). The linguistic relativity of person cognition: An English–Chinese comparison. *Journal of Personality and Social Psychology, 51*, 1097–1105.

Hofstede, G. H. (1980). *Culture's consequences: International differences in work-related values.* Beverly Hills, CA: Sage.

Hofstede, G. H. (1991). *Culture and organizations: Software of the mind.* London: McGraw-Hill.

Hofstede, G. H. (2001). *Culture's consequences: Comparing values, behaviors, institutions, and organizations across nations.* Thousand Oaks, CA: Sage.

Hogan, R. T., & Emler, N. P. (1978). The biases in contemporary social psychology. *Social Research, 45,* 478–534.

Hogg, M. A. (2004). Social identity, self-categorization, and communication in small groups. In S.-h. Ng, C. N. Candlin, & C.-y. Chiu (Eds.), *Language matters: Communication, culture, and identity* (pp. 221–243). Hong Kong: City University of Hong Kong Press.

Hogg, M. A., & Abrams, D. (1988). *Social identifications: A social psychology of intergroup relations and group processes.* London: Routledge.

Hogg, M. A., & Mullin, B.-A. (1999). Joining groups to reduce uncertainty: Subjective uncertainty reduction and group identification. In D. Abrams & M. A. Hogg (Eds.), *Social identification and social cognition* (pp. 249–279). Oxford, UK: Blackwell.

Holt, D. B. (2002). How to build an iconic brand? *Market Leader, 21* (Summer), 35–42.

Hong, Y.-y., Benet-Martinez, V., Chiu, C.-y., & Morris, M. W. (2003). Boundaries of cultural influence: Construct activation as a mechanism for cultural differences in social perception. *Journal of Cross-Cultural Psychology, 34,* 453–464.

Hong, Y.-y., & Chiu, C.-y. (2001). Toward a paradigm shift: From cross-cultural differences in social-cognition to social-cognitive mediation of cultural differences. *Social Cognition, 19,* 181–196.

Hong, Y.-y., Chiu, C.-y., & Dweck, C. S. (1995). Implicit theories and self-confidence in achievement. In M. Kernis (Ed.), *Efficacy, agency and self-esteem* (pp. 197–216). New York: Plenum.

Hong, Y.-y., Chiu, C.-y., Dweck, C. S., & Sacks, R. (1997a). Implicit theories and evaluative processes in person cognition. *Journal of Experimental Social Psychology, 33,* 296–323.

Hong, Y.-y., Chiu, C.-y., & Kung, T. M. (1997b). Bringing culture out in front: Effects of cultural meaning system activation on social cognition. In K. Leung, Y. Kashima, U. Kim, & S. Yamaguchi (Eds.), *Progress in Asian social psychology* (Vol. 1, pp. 135–146). Singapore: Wiley.

Hong, Y.-y., Chiu, C.-y., Yeung, G., & Tong, Y. (1999). Effects of self-categorization on intergroup perceptions: The case of Hong Kong facing 1997. *International Journal of Intercultural Relations, 23,* 257–279.

Hong, Y.-y., Ip, G., Chiu, C.-y., Morris, M. W., & Menon, T. (2001). Cultural identity and dynamic construction of the self: Collective duties and individual rights in Chinese and American cultures. *Social Cognition, 19,* 251–269.

Hong, Y.-y., Morris, M. W., Chiu, C.-y., & Benet-Martinez, V. (2000). Multicultural minds: A dynamic constructivist approach to culture and cognition. *American Psychologist, 55,* 709–720.

Hong, Y.-y., Roisman, G. I., & Chen, J. (2006). A model of cultural attachment: A new approach for studying bicultural experience. In M. H. Bornstein & L. Cote (Eds.), *Acculturation and parent child relationships: Measurement and development* (pp. 135–170). Hillsdale, NJ: Lawrence Erlbaum Associates, Inc.

Hong, Y.-y., Wan, C., No, S., & Chiu, C.-y. (in press). Multicultural identities. In S. Kitayama & D. Cohen (Eds.), *Handbook of cultural psychology.* New York: Guilford.

Hoosain, R. (1986). Language, orthography and cognitive processes: Chinese perspectives for the Sapir–Whorf hypothesis. *International Journal of Behavioral Development, 9,* 507–525.

Hsieh, T. T.-y., Shybut, J., & Lotsof, E. J. (1969). Internal versus external control and ethnic group membership: A cross-cultural comparison. *Journal of Consulting and Clinical Psychology, 33,* 122–124.

Hsu, F. L. K. (1981). *Americans and Chinese: Passages to differences* (3rd ed.). Honolulu, HI: University of Hawaii Press.

Huang, L., & Harris, M. B. (1973). Conformity in Chinese and Americans: A field experiment. *Journal of Cross-Cultural Psychology, 4,* 427–434.

Hui, C. H., & Triandis, H. C. (1986). Individualism–collectivism: A study of cross-cultural researchers. *Journal of Cross-Cultural Psychology, 17,* 225–248.

Hui, C. H., Triandis, H. C., & Yee, C. (1991). Cultural differences in reward allocation: Is collectivism the explanation? *British Journal of Social Psychology, 30,* 145–157.

Hume, D. (1784/1894). *Essays literary, moral and political.* London: Routledge.

Hwang, K.-k. (1999). Filial piety and loyalty: Two types of social identification in Confucianism. *Asian Journal of Social Psychology, 2,* 163–183.

Hwang, K.-k. (2000). Chinese relationalism: Theoretical construction and methodological considerations. *Journal of the Theory of Social Behavior, 30,* 154–178.

Hwang, K.-k. (2001). The deep structure of Confucianism: A social psychological approach. *Asian Philosophy, 11,* 179–204.

Inglehart, R. (1997). *Modernization and post-modernization: Cultural, economic, and political change in 43 societies.* Princeton, NJ: Princeton University Press.

Inglehart, R., & Baker, W. E. (2000). Modernization, cultural change, and the persistence of traditional values. *American Sociological Review, 65,* 19–51.

Ip, G. W.-m., & Bond, M. H. (1995). Culture, values, and the spontaneous self-concept. *Asian Journal of Psychology, 1,* 29–35.

Ip, G. W.-m., Chen, J., & Chiu, C.-y. (2004). *Need for cognitive closure moderates cross-cultural difference in socially desirable responding.* Unpublished manuscript. University of Illinois, Urbana-Champaign.

Ip, G. W.-m., Chen, J., & Chiu, C.-y. (in press). The relationship of promotion focus, need for cognitive closure, and categorical accessibility in American and Hong Kong Chinese university students. *Journal of Creative Behavior.*

Ishii, K., Reyes, J. A., & Kitayama, S. (2003). Spontaneous attention to word content versus emotional tone: Differences among three cultures. *Psychological Science, 14,* 39–46.

Iyengar, S. S., & DeVoe, S. E. (2003). Rethinking the value of choice: Cultural mediators of intrinsic motivation. In V. Murphy-Berman & J. J. Berman (Eds.), *Cross-cultural differences in perspectives on the self* (pp. 129–174). Lincoln, NE: University of Nebraska Press.

Iyengar, S. S., & Lepper, M. R. (1999). Rethinking the value of choice: A cultural perspective on intrinsic motivation. *Journal of Personality and Social Psychology, 76,* 349–366.

Izard, C. E. (1971). *The face of emotion.* New York: Appleton-Century-Crofts.

Jackson, T. (2002). The management of people across cultures: Valuing people differently. *Human Resource Management, 41,* 455–475.

Jahoda, G. (1979). A cross-cultural perspective on experimental social psychology. *Personality and Social Psychology Bulletin, 5,* 142–148.

James, W. (1950/1890). *The principles of psychology.* New York: Dover.

Jellen, H. U., & Urban, K. (1989). Assessing creative potential worldwide: The first cross-cultural application of the Test for Creative Thinking – Drawing Production (TCT–DP). *Gifted Educational International, 6,* 78–86.

Jetten, J., Postmes, T., & Mcauliffe, B. (2002). "We're all individuals": Group norms of individualism and collectivism, levels of identification and identity threat. *European Journal of Social Psychology, 32,* 189–207.

Ji, L.-j., Nisbett, R. E., & Su, Y. (2001). Culture, change, and prediction. *Psychological Science*, *12*, 450–456.

Ji, L.-j., Peng, K., & Nisbett, R. E. (2000). Culture, control, and perception of relationships in the environment. *Journal of Personality and Social Psychology*, *78*, 943–955.

Ji, L.-j., Zhang, Z., & Nisbett, R. E. (2004). Is it culture or is it language? Examination of language effects in cross-cultural research on categorization. *Journal of Personality and Social Psychology*, *87*, 57–65.

Jorna, P. (1992). Spectral analysis of heart rate and psychological state: A review of its validity as workload index. *Biological Psychology*, *34*, 237–257.

Josephs, R. A., Newman, M. L., Brown, T. R. P., & Beer, J. M. (2003). Status, testosterone, and human intellectual performance: Stereotype threat as status concern. *Psychological Science*, *14*, 158–163.

Ju, T. Z. (1981). *Chinese law and Chinese society*. Peking: Chunghua.

Kameda, T., & Diasuke, N. (2002). Cost-benefit analysis of social/cultural learning in a nonstationary uncertain environment: An evolutionary simulation and an experiment with human subjects. *Evolution and Behavior*, *25*, 373–393.

Kameda, T., Takezawa, M., & Hastie, R. (2003). The logic of social sharing: An evolutionary game analysis of adaptive norm development. *Personality and Social Psychology Review*, *7*, 2–19.

Kanagawa, C., Cross, S. E., & Markus, H. R. (2001). "Who am I?" The cultural psychology of the conceptual self. *Personality and Social Psychology Bulletin*, *27*, 90–103.

Kanno, Y. (2003). *Negotiating bilingual and bicultural identities: Japanese returnees betwixt two worlds*. Mahwah, NJ: Lawrence Erlbaum Associates, Inc.

Kanouse, D. E., Gumpert, P., & Canavan-Gumpert, D. (1981). The semantics of praise. In J. H. Harvey, W. Ickes, & R. F. Kidd (Eds.), *New directions in attribution research* (Vol. 3, pp. 97–115). Hillsdale, NJ: Lawrence Erlbaum Associates, Inc.

Kashima, E. S., Halloran, M. J., Yuki, M., & Kashima, Y. (2004). The effects of personal and collective mortality salience on individualism: Comparing Australians and Japanese with higher and lower self-esteem. *Journal of Experimental Social Psychology*, *40*, 384–392.

Kashima, E. S., & Kashima, Y. (1998). Culture and language: The case of cultural dimensions and personal pronoun use. *Journal of Cross-Cultural Psychology*, *29*, 461–486.

Kashima, Y. (1999). Culture, groups, and coordination problems. *Psychologische Beitrage*, *41*, 237–251.

Kashima, Y. (2000a). Conceptions of culture and person for psychology. *Journal of Cross-Cultural Psychology*, *31*, 14–32.

Kashima, Y. (2000b). Maintaining cultural stereotypes in the serial reproduction of narratives. *Personality and Social Psychology Bulletin*, *26*, 594–604.

Kashima, Y., & Foddy, M. (2002). Time and self: The historical construction of the self. In Y. Kashima, M. Foddy, & M. J. Platow (Eds.), *Self and identity: Personal, social and symbolic* (pp. 181–206). Mahwah, NJ: Lawrence Erlbaum Associates, Inc.

Kashima, Y., & Kashima, E. (2003). Individualism, GNP, climate, and pronoun drop: Is individualism determined by affluence and climate, or does language use play a role? *Journal of Cross-Cultural Psychology*, *34*, 125–134.

Kashima, Y., Kashima, E., & Aldridge, J. (2001). Towards cultural dynamics of self-conceptions. In C. Sedikides & M. B. Brewer (Eds.), *Individual self, relational self, and collective self: Partners, opponents, and strangers* (pp. 277–298). Philadelphia, PA: Psychology Press.

Kashima, Y., Kashima, E., Chiu, C.-y., Farsides, T., Gelfand, M., Hong, Y.-y., Kim, U., Strack, F., Worth, L., Yuki, M., & Yzerbyt, V. (2005). Culture, essentialism, and agency: Are individuals universally believed to be more real entities than groups? *European Journal of Social Psychology, 35,* 147–169.

Kashima, Y., Woolcock, J., & Kashima, E. (2000). Group impressions as dynamic configurations: The tensor product model of group impression formation and change. *Psychological Review, 107,* 914–942.

Kashima, Y., Yamaguchi, S., Kim, U., Choi, S.-c., Gelfand, M. J., & Yuki, M. (1995). Culture, gender, and self: A perspective from individualism–collectivism research. *Journal of Personality and Social Psychology, 69,* 925–937.

Kawai, M. (1965). Newly acquired precultural behavior of the natural troop of Japanese monkeys on Konsima Islet. *Primates, 6,* 1–30.

Kawamura, S. (1959). The process of subcultural propagation among Japanese macaques. *Primates, 2,* 43–60.

Kay, P., & Kempton, W. (1984). What is the Sapir-Whorf hypothesis? *American Anthropologist, 86,* 65–79.

Kay, P., & McDaniel, C. K. (1978). The linguistic significance of the meanings of basic color terms. *Language, 54,* 610–646.

Keesing, R. M. (1974). Theories of culture. *Annual Review of Anthropology, 3,* 73–97.

Kelley, W. M., Macrae, C. N., Wyland, C. L., Caglar, S., Inati, S., & Heatherton, T. F. (2002). Finding the self? An event-related fMRI study. *Journal of Cognitive Neuroscience, 14,* 785–794.

Kelly, G. (1955). *A theory of personality: The psychology of personal constructs.* New York: Norton.

Kenrick, D. T., Groth, G. E., Trost, M. R., & Sadalla, E. K. (1993). Integrating evolutionary and social exchange perspectives on relationships: Effects of gender, self-appraisal, and involvement level on mate selection criteria. *Journal of Personality and Social Psychology, 64,* 951–969.

Kenrick, D. T., & Keefe, R. C. (1992). Age preferences in mates reflect sex differences in human reproductive strategies. *Behavioral and Brain Sciences, 15,* 75–133.

Kenrick, D. T., Li, M., & Butner, J. (2003). Dynamical evolutionary psychology: Individual decision rules and emergent social norms. *Psychological Review, 110,* 3–28.

Kenrick, D. T., Maner, J. K., Butner, J., Li, N. P., Becker, D. V., & Schaller, M. (2002). Dynamical evolutionary psychology: Mapping the domains of the new interactionist paradigm. *Personality and Social Psychology Review, 6,* 347–356.

Kenrick, D. T., Neuberg, S. L., Zierk, K. L., & Krones, J. M. (1994). Evolution and social cognition: Contrast effects as a function of sex, dominance, and physical attractiveness. *Personality and Social Psychology Bulletin, 20,* 210–217.

Kim, H. S. (2002). We talk, therefore we think? A cultural analysis of the effect of talking on thinking. *Journal of Personality and Social Psychology, 83,* 828–842.

Kim, H. S., & Drolet, A. (2003). Choice and self-expression: A cultural analysis of variety-seeking. *Journal of Personality and Social Psychology, 85,* 373–382.

Kim, H. S., & Markus, H. R. (1999). Deviance or uniqueness, harmony or conformity? A cultural analysis. *Journal of Personality and Social Psychology, 77,* 785–800.

Kim, J., Kim, M.-s., Kam, K. Y., & Shin, H.-c. (2003). Influence of self-construals on the perception of different self-presentation styles in Korea. *Asian Journal of Social Psychology, 6,* 89–101.

Kim, U., Park, S., & Park, D. (2000). The challenge of cross-cultural psychology: The role of the indigenous psychologies. *Journal of Cross-Cultural Psychology, 31,* 63–75.

Kitayama, S. (2002). Culture and basic psychological processes – toward a system view of culture: Comment on Oyserman et al. (2002). *Psychological Bulletin, 128,* 89–96.

Kitayama, S., Duffy, S., Kawamura, T., & Larsen, J. T. (2003). Perceiving an object and its context in different cultures: A cultural look at new look. *Psychological Science, 14*, 201–206.

Kitayama, S., & Ishii, K. (2002). Word and voice: Spontaneous attention to emotional utterances in two languages. *Cognition and Emotion, 16*, 29–59.

Kitayama, S., & Karasawa, M. (1997). Implicit self-esteem in Japan: Name letters and birthday numbers. *Personality and Social Psychology Bulletin, 23*, 736–742.

Kitayama, S., & Markus, H. R. (1999). Yin and yang of the Japanese self: The cultural psychology of personality coherence. In D. Cervone & Y. Shoda (Eds.), *The coherence of personality: Social cognitive bases of personality consistency, variability, and organization* (pp. 242–302). New York: Guilford Press.

Kitayama, S., Markus, H. R., Matsumoto, H., & Norasakkunkit, V. (1997). Individual and collective processes of self-esteem management: Self-enhancement in the United States and self-depreciation in Japan. *Journal of Personality and Social Psychology, 72*, 1245–1267.

Kitayama, S., Takagi, H., & Matsumoto, H. (1995). Causal attribution of success and failure: Cultural psychology of the Japanese self. *Japanese Psychological Review, 38*, 247–280.

Kitayama, S., & Uchida, Y. (2003). Explicit self-criticism and implicit self-regard: Evaluating self and friend in two cultures. *Journal of Experimental Social Psychology, 39*, 476–482.

Kittler, A. F., Parker, J. G., & La Greca, A. M. (2002). Developmental and gender differences in preadolescents' judgments of the veracity of gossip. *Merrill-Palmer Quarterly, 48*, 105–132.

Klein, S. B., & Kihlstrom, J. F. (1986). Elaboration, organization, and the self-reference effect in memory. *Journal of Experimental Psychology: General, 115*, 26–38.

Kluckhohn, C. (1954). Culture and behavior. In G. Lindzey (Ed.), *Handbook of social psychology* (Vol. 2, pp. 921–976). Cambridge, MA: Addison-Wesley.

Knowles, E. D., Morris, M. W., Chiu, C.-y., & Hong, Y.-y. (2001). Culture and process of person perception: Evidence for automaticity among East Asians in correcting for situational influences on behavior. *Personality and Social Psychology Bulletin, 27*, 1344–1356.

Kobayashi, C., & Brown, J. D. (2003). Self-esteem and self-enhancement in Japan and America. *Journal of Cross-Cultural Psychology, 34*, 567–580.

Kobayashi, C., & Greenwald, A. G. (2003). Implicit–explicit differences in self-enhancement for Americans and Japanese. *Journal of Cross-Cultural Psychology, 34*, 522–541.

Kosic, A., Kruglanski, A. W., Pierro, A., & Mannetti, L. (2004). The social cognition of immigrants' acculturation: Effects of the need for closure and the reference group at entry. *Journal of Personality and Social Psychology, 86*, 796–813.

Kramer, A. F., & Weber, T. (2000). Applications of psychophysiology to human factors. In J. T. Cacioppo, L. G. Tassinary, & G. G. Berntson (Eds.), *Handbook of psychophysiology* (2nd ed., pp. 794–814). Cambridge, UK: Cambridge University Press.

Krauss, R. M., & Chiu, C.-y. (1998). Language and social psychology. In D. Gilbert, S. Fiske-Emory, & G. Lindzey (Eds.), *Handbook of social psychology* (4th ed., Vol. 2, pp. 41–88). New York: Guilford.

Krauss, R. M., & Fussell, S. R. (1991). Perspective-taking in communication: Representations of others' knowledge in reference. *Social Cognition, 9*, 2–24.

Krauss, R. M., & Fussell, S. R. (1996). Social psychological models of interpersonal communication. In E. T. Higgins & A. Kruglanski (Eds.), *Social psychology: Basic principles* (pp. 655–701). New York: Guilford Press.

Krauss, R. M., Fussell, S. R., & Chen, Y. (1995). Coordination of perspective in dialogue: Intrapersonal and interpersonal processes. In I. Markova, C. G. Graumann, & K. Foppa (Eds.), *Mutualities in dialogue* (pp. 124–145). Cambridge, UK: Cambridge University Press.

Krauss, R. M., & Glucksberg, S. (1977). Social and nonsocial speech. *Scientific American, 236*, 100–105.

Krauss, R. M., Vivekananthan, P. S., & Weinheimer, S. (1968). "Inner speech" and "external speech". *Journal of Personality and Social Psychology, 9*, 295–300.

Kroeber, A. L., & Kluckhohn, C. (1952). *Culture: A critical review of concepts and definitions.* Cambridge, MA: Harvard University Press.

Kronenfeld, D. B., Armstrong, J. D., & Wilmoth, S. (1985). Exploring the internal structure of linguistic categories: An extensionist semantic view. In J. W. D. Dougherty (Ed.), *Directions in cognitive anthropology* (pp. 81–119). Urbana, IL: University of Illinois Press.

Kruglanski, A. W., Shah, J. Y., Pierro, A., & Mannetti, L. (2002). When similarity breeds content: Need for closure and the allure of homogeneous and self-resembling groups. *Journal of Personality and Social Psychology, 83*, 648–662.

Kruglanski, A. W., & Webster, D. M. (1996). Motivated closing of the mind: "Seizing" and "freezing." *Psychological Review, 103*, 263–283.

Kruglanski, A. W., Webster, D. M., & Klem, A. (1993). Motivated resistance and openness to persuasion in the presence or absence of prior information. *Journal of Personality and Social Psychology, 65*, 861–876.

Kudo, E., & Numazaki, M. (2003). Explicit and direct self-serving bias in Japan: Reexamination of self-serving bias for success and failure. *Journal of Cross-Cultural Psychology, 34*, 511–521.

Küehnen, U., & Oyserman, D. (2002). Thinking about the self influences thinking in general: Cognitive consequences of silent self-concept. *Journal of Experimental Social Psychology, 38*, 492–499.

Kunda, Z., Davies, P. G., Adams, B. D., & Spencer, S. J. (2002). The dynamic time course of stereotype activation: Activation, dissipation, and resurrection. *Journal of Personality and Social Psychology, 82*, 283–299.

Kurman, J. (2001). Self-enhancement: Is it restricted to individualistic cultures? *Personality and Social Psychology Bulletin, 27*, 1705–1716.

Kurman, J. (2003). Why is self-enhancement low in certain collectivist cultures? An investigation of two competing explanations. *Journal of Cross-Cultural Psychology, 34*, 496–510.

Kurman, J., & Sriram, N. (1997). Self-enhancement, generality of self-evaluation, and affectivity in Israel and Singapore. *Journal of Cross-Cultural Psychology, 28*, 421–441.

Kurman, J., & Sriram, N. (2002). Interrelationships among vertical and horizontal collectivism, modesty, and self-enhancement. *Journal of Cross-Cultural Psychology, 33*, 71–86.

Kwan, V. S. Y., Bond, M. H., & Singelis, T. M. (1997). Pancultural explanations for life satisfaction: Adding relationship harmony to self-esteem. *Journal of Personality and Social Psychology, 73*, 1038–1051.

LaFramboise, T., Coleman, H. L., & Gerton, J. (1993). Psychological impact of biculturalism: Evidence and theory. *Psychological Bulletin, 114*, 395–412.

Lal, D. (2000). Does modernization require westernization? *The Independent Review, 5*, 5–24.

Lalwani, A., Shavitt, S., & Johnson, T. (in press). What is the relation between cultural orientation and socially desirable responding? *Journal of Personality and Social Psychology.*

Lam, S.-F., Lau, I. Y., Chiu, C.-y., Hong, Y.-y., & Peng, S.-Q. (1999). Differential emphases on modernity and Confucian values in social categorization: The case of Hong Kong adolescents in political transition. *International Journal of Intercultural Relations, 23*, 237–256.

Landau, M. J., Johns, M., Greenberg, J., Pyszczynski, T., Martens, A., Goldberg, J. L., & Solomon, S. (2004). A function of form: Terror management and structuring of social world. *Journal of Personality and Social Psychology, 87*, 190–210.

Latane, B. (1981). The psychology of social impact. *American Psychologist, 36*, 343–356.

Latane, B. (1996). Dynamic social impact: The creation of culture by communication. *Journal of Communication, 46*, 13–25.

Latane, B., & Bourgeois, M. J. (1996). Experimental evidence for dynamic social impact: The emergence of subcultures in electronic groups. *Journal of Communication, 46*, 35–47.

Latane, B., & Darley, J. (1968). Group inhibition of bystander intervention in emergencies. *Journal of Personality and Social Psychology, 10*, 215–221.

Latane, B., & L'Herrou, T. (1996). Spatial clustering in the conformity game: Dynamic social impact in electronic groups. *Journal of Personality and Social Psychology, 70*, 1218–1230.

Lau, I. Y.-M., Chiu, C.-y., & Hong, Y.-y. (2001a). I know what you know: Assumptions about others' knowledge and their effects on message construction. *Social Cognition, 19*, 587–600.

Lau, I. Y.-m., Chiu, C.-y., & Lee, S.-l. (2001b). Communication and shared reality: Implications for the psychological foundations of culture. *Social Cognition, 19*, 350–371.

Lau-Gesk, L. G. (2003). Activating culture through persuasion appeals: An examination of the bicultural consumer. *Journal of Consumer Psychology, 13*, 301–315.

Lawson, C. W., & Saltmarshe, D. K. (2002). The psychology of economic transformation: The impact of the market on social institutions, status and values in a northern Albanian village. *Journal of Economic Psychology, 23*, 487–500.

Lebra, T. S. (1976). *Japanese patterns of behavior*. Honolulu, HI: The University Press of Hawaii.

Lee, A. Y., Aaker, J. L., & Gardner, W. L. (2000). The pleasure and pains of distinct self-construals: The role of interdependence in regulatory focus. *Journal of Personality and Social Psychology, 78*, 1122–1134.

Lee, F., Hallahan, M., & Herzog, T. (1996). Explaining real-life events: How culture and domain shape attributions. *Personality and Social Psychology Bulletin, 22*, 732–741.

Lee, S., Sobal, J., & Frongillo, E. A. (2003). Comparison of models of acculturation: The case of Korean Americans. *Journal of Cross-Cultural Psychology, 34*, 282–296.

Lee, S.-l. (2002). *Communication and shared representation: The role of knowledge estimation*. Unpublished doctoral dissertation, University of Hong Kong.

Lee, S.-l., Chiu, C.-y., & Chan, T.-k. (2005). Some boundary conditions of the expressor culture effect in emotion recognition: Evidence from Hong Kong Chinese perceivers. *Asian Journal of Social Psychology, 8*, 224–243.

Lehman, A., & Bernsten, M. (2003). Evolution and the structure of health and disease: A unifying theory of biology and culture with medical implications. Retrieved December 30, 2003, from http://www.serpentfd.org/index.html

Lehman, D., Chiu, C.-y., & Schaller, M. (2004). Culture and psychology. *Annual Review of Psychology, 55*, 689–714.

LeResche, D. (1992). Comparison of the American mediation process with a Korean-American harmony restoration process. Special issue: Diversity: Some implications for mediation. *Mediation Quarterly, 9*, 323–339.

Leung, K. (1987). Some determinants of reactions to procedural models for conflict resolution: A cross-national study. *Journal of Personality and Social Psychology, 53*, 898–908.

Leung, K. (1988). Some determinants of conflict avoidance. *Journal of Cross-Cultural Psychology, 19*, 125–136.

Leung, K., & Bond, M. H. (1982). How Chinese and Americans reward task-related contributions: A preliminary study. *Psychologia, 25*, 32–39.

Leung, K., & Bond, M. H. (1984). The impact of cultural collectivism on reward allocation. *Journal of Personality and Social Psychology, 47*, 793–804.

Leung, K., & Bond, M. H. (2004). Social axioms: A model for social beliefs in multicultural perspective. In M. P. Zanna (Ed.), *Advances in experimental social psychology* (Vol. 36, pp. 119–197). New York: Academic Press.

Leung, K., Bond, M. H., Reimel de Carrasquel, S., Munoz, C., Hernandez, M., Murakami, F., Yamaguchi, S., Bierbrauer, G., & Singelis, T. M. (2002). Social axioms: The search for universal dimensions of general beliefs about how the world functions. *Journal of Cross-Cultural Psychology, 33*, 286–302.

Leung, K., & Park, H.-j. (1986). Effects of interactional goal on choice of allocation rule: A cross-national study. *Organizational Behavior and Decision-Making, 37*, 111–120.

Leung, K.-y. (2005, February). *Multicultural experiences and creative conceptual expansion.* Paper presented at the Annual Meeting of the Society for Personality and Social Psychology, New Orleans, LA.

Leung, K.-y. A., Chiu, C.-y., & Hong, Y.-y. (2004, January). *Bicultural individuals accommodate their interaction strategies to the projected distribution of promotion- and prevention-focused regulatory focus in interaction partner's cultural group.* Paper presented at the 5th Annual Meeting of the Society for Personality and Social Psychology, Austin, TX.

Levelt, W. J. (1989). *Speaking: From intentions to articulation.* Cambridge, MA: MIT Press.

Li, J.-L., & Yeh, S.-l. (2003). Do "Chinese and Americans see opposite apparent motion in a Chinese character"? Tse and Cavanagh (2000) replicated and revised. *Visual Cognition, 10*, 537–547.

Li, N. P., Bailey, J. M., Kenrick, D. T., & Linsenmeier, J. A. (2002). The necessities and luxuries of mate preferences: Testing the tradeoffs. *Journal of Personality and Social Psychology, 82*, 947–955.

Li, Q., & Hong, Y.-y. (2001). Intergroup perceptual accuracy predicts real-life intergroup interactions. *Group Processes & Intergroup Relations, 4*, 341–354.

Li, S. (2003). Biocultural orchestration of developmental plasticity across levels: The interplay of biology and culture in shaping the mind and behavior across the life span. *Psychological Bulletin, 129*, 171–194.

Lillard, A. (1998). Ethnogpsychologies: Cultural variations in theories of mind. *Psychological Bulletin, 123*, 3–32.

Lindahl, L., & Odelstad, J. (2000). An algebraic analysis of normative systems. *Ratio Juris, 13*, 261–278.

Liu, L. G. (1985). Reasoning counterfactually in Chinese: Are there any obstacles? *Cognition, 21*, 239–270.

Lockwood, P., Marshall, T. C., & Sadler, P. (2005). Promoting success or preventing failure: Cultural differences in motivation by positive and negative role models. *Personality and Social Psychology Bulletin, 31*, 379–392.

Lowell, A. L. (1934). *At war with academic traditions in America.* Cambridge, MA: Harvard University Press.

Lu, X. (2001). Bicultural identity development and Chinese community formation: An ethnographic study of Chinese schools in Chicago. *The Howard Journal of Communications, 12*, 203–220.

Lynch, A. (1996). *Thought contagion: How belief spreads through society.* New York: Basic Books.

Lyons, A., & Kashima, Y. (2001). The reproduction of culture: Communication processes tend to maintain cultural stereotypes. *Social Cognition, 19*, 372–394.

Lyons, A., & Kashima, Y. (2003). How are stereotypes maintained through communication? The influence of stereotype sharedness. *Personality and Social Psychology Bulletin, 85*, 989–1005.

Ma, V., & Schoeneman, T. J. (1997). Individualism versus collectivism: A comparison of Kenyan and American self-concepts. *Basic and Applied Social Psychology, 19*, 261–273.

Maehr, M. L., & Yamaguchi, R. (2001). Cultural diversity, student motivation and achievement. In F. Salili, C.-y. Chiu, & Y.-y. Hong (Eds.), *Student motivation: The culture and context of learning* (pp. 123–148). New York: Kluwer Academic/Plenum.

Mahalingam, R. (2003). Essentialism, culture, and beliefs about gender among the Aravanis of Tamil Nadu, India. *Sex Roles, 49,* 489–496.

Mahalingam, R., & Rodriguez, J. (2003). Essentialism, power and cultural psychology of gender. *Journal of Cognition and Culture, 3,* 157–174.

Malt, B. C., Sloman, S. A., Gennari, S., Shi, M., & Wang, Y. (1999). Knowing versus naming: Similarity and the linguistic categorization of artifacts. *Journal of Memory and Language, 40,* 230–262.

Marin, G., Triandis, H. C., Betancourt, H., & Kashima, Y. (1983). Ethnic affirmation versus social desirability: Explaining discrepancies in bilinguals' responses to a questionnaire. *Journal of Cross-Cultural Psychology, 14,* 173–186.

Markus, H. R., & Kitayama, S. (1991). Culture and self: Implications for cognition, emotion, and motivation. *Psychological Review, 98,* 224–253.

Markus, H. R., & Kitayama, S. (1994). A collective fear of the collective: Implications for selves and theories of selves. *Personality and Social Psychology Bulletin, 20,* 568–579.

Markus, H. R., & Kitayama, S. (2003a). Culture, self, and the reality of the social. *Psychological Inquiry, 14,* 277–283.

Markus, H. R., & Kitayama, S. (2003b). Models of agency: Sociocultural diversity in the construction of action. In V. Murphy-Berman & J. J. Berman (Eds.), *Cross-cultural differences in perspectives on the self* (pp. 1–57). Lincoln, NE: University of Nebraska Press.

Martinez, I., & Shatz, M. (1996). Linguistic influences on categorization in preschool children: A cross-linguistic study. *Journal of Child Language, 23,* 529–545.

Masuda, T., Ellsworth, P. C., Mesquita, B., Leu, J., Tanida, S., & van de Veerdonk, E. (2004). *A face on the crowd or a crowd on a face.* Manuscript submitted for publication.

Masuda, T., & Kitayama, S. (2004). Perceived-induced constraint and attitude attribution in Japan and in the US: A case for cultural dependence of the correspondence bias. *Journal of Experimental Social Psychology, 40,* 409–416.

Masuda, T., & Nisbett, R. E. (2001). Attending holistically versus analytically: Comparing the context sensitivity of Japanese and Americans. *Journal of Personality and Social Psychology, 81,* 922–934.

Masuda, T., & Nisbett, R. E. (2004). *Culture and change blindness.* Manuscript submitted for publication.

Matsumoto, D. (1989). Cultural influences on the perception of emotion. *Journal of Cross-Cultural Psychology, 20,* 92–105.

Matsumoto, D. (1992). American–Japanese cultural differences in the recognition of universal facial expressions. *Journal of Cross-Cultural Psychology, 23,* 72–84.

Matsumoto, D. (2001). Culture and emotion. In D. Matsumoto (Ed.), *The handbook of culture and psychology* (pp. 171–194). New York: Oxford University Press.

Matsumoto, D., Consolacion, T., Yamada, H., Suzuki, R., Franklin, B., Paul, S., Ray, R., & Uchida, H. (2002). American–Japanese cultural differences in judgments of emotional expressions of different intensities. *Cognition & Emotion, 16,* 721–747.

Matsumoto, D., & Ekman, P. (1989). American–Japanese cultural differences in intensity ratings of facial expressions of emotion. *Motivation and Emotion, 13,* 143–157.

Matsumoto, D., Kasri, F., & Kooken, K. (1999). American–Japanese cultural differences in judgments of expression intensity and subjective experience. *Cognition & Emotion, 13,* 201–218.

Mazur, A., & Booth, A. (1998). Testosterone and dominance in men. *Behavioral and Brain Sciences, 21,* 353–397.

McCann, C. D., Higgins, E. T., & Fondacaro, R. A. (1991). Primacy and recency in communication and self-persuasion: How successive audiences and multiple encodings influence subsequent judgments. *Social Cognition, 9,* 47–66.

McGregor, H., Liberman, J., Greenberg, J., Solomon, S., Arndt, J., Simon, L., & Pyszczynski, T. (1998). Terror management and aggression: Evidence that mortality salience motivates aggression against worldview-threatening others. *Journal of Personality and Social Psychology*, *74*, 590–605.

Mead, G. H. (1934/1962). *Mind, self, and society: From the standpoint of a social behaviorist*. Chicago, IL: University of Chicago Press.

Meade, R. D., & Barnard, W. A. (1973). Conformity and anticonformity among American and Chinese. *Journal of Social Psychology*, *89*, 15–24.

Meade, R. D., & Whittaker, J. O. (1967). A cross-cultural study of authoritarianism. *Journal of Social Psychology*, *72*, 2–7.

Medea, L. (2002). Creolisation and globalization in a neo-colonial context: The case of Reunion. *Social Identities*, *8*, 125–141.

Medin, D. L., & Atran, S. (2004). The native mind: Biological categorization and reasoning in development and across cultures. *Psychological Review*, *111*, 960–983.

Meggers, B. J. (1971). *Amazonia: Man and nature in a counterfeit paradise*. Chicago: Aldine.

Mendoza-Denton, R., Downey, G., Purdie, V. J., Davis, A., & Pietrzak, J. (2002). Sensitivity to status-based rejection: Implications for African American students' college experience. *Journal of Personality and Social Psychology*, *83*, 896–918.

Menon, T., & Morris, M. W. (2001). Social structure in North American and Chinese cultures: Reciprocal influence between objective and subjective structures. *Journal of Psychology in Chinese Societies*, *2*, 27–50.

Menon, T., Morris, M. W., Chiu, C.-y., & Hong, Y.-y. (1999). Culture and the construal of agency: Attribution to individual versus group dispositions. *Journal of Personality and Social Psychology*, *76*, 701–717.

Menon, U., & Shweder, R. A. (1994). Kali's tongue: Cultural psychology and the power of shame in Orissa, India. In S. Kitayama & H. Markus (Eds.), *Emotion and culture* (pp. 141–185). Washington, DC: American Psychological Association.

Middlemist, R. D., Knowles, E. S., & Matter, C. F. (1976). Personal space invasions in the lavatory: Suggestive evidence for arousal. *Journal of Personality and Social Psychology*, *33*, 541–546.

Miller, D. (1998). Coca-Cola: A sweet black drink from Trinidad. In D. Miller (Ed.), *Material culture: Why some things matter* (pp. 169–187). Chicago: University of Chicago Press.

Miller, D. T., & Ross, M. (1975). Self-serving biases in the attribution of causality: Fact or fiction? *Psychological Bulletin*, *82*, 213–225.

Miller, J. G. (1984). Culture and the development of everyday social explanation. *Journal of Personality and Social Psychology*, *46*, 961–978.

Miller, J. G. (1997). Theoretical issues in cultural psychology. In J. W. Berry, Y. Poortinga, & J. Pandey (Eds.), *Handbook of cross-cultural psychology: Vol. 1: Theoretical and methodological perspectives* (2nd ed., pp. 85–128). Boston, MA: Allyn & Bacon.

Miller, J. G. (2003). Culture and agency: Implications for psychological theories of motivation and social development. In V. Murphy-Berman & J. J. Berman (Eds.), *Cultural differences in perspectives on the self* (pp. 59–99). Lincoln, NE: University of Nebraska Press.

Miller, J. G., & Bersoff, D. M. (1992). Culture and moral judgment: How are conflicts between justice and interpersonal responsibilities resolved? *Journal of Personality and Social Psychology*, *62*, 541–554.

Miller, J. G., & Bersoff, D. M. (1994). Cultural influences on the moral status of reciprocity and the discounting of endogenous motivation. *Personality and Social Psychology Bulletin*, *20*, 592–602.

Miller, J. G., & Bersoff, D. M. (1998). The role of liking in perceptions of moral responsibility to help: A cultural perspective. *Journal of Experimental Social Psychology*, *34*, 443–469.

Miller, P. J., Fung, H., & Mintz, J. (1996). Self-construction through narrative practices: A Chinese and American comparison of early socialization. *Ethos*, *24*, 1–44.

Miller, P., Wiley, A. R., Fung, H., & Liang, C.-h. (1997). Personal storytelling as a medium of socialization in Chinese and American families. *Child Development*, *68*, 557–568.

Miyamoto, Y., & Kitayama, S. (2002). Cultural variation in correspondence bias: The critical role of attitude diagnosticity of socially constrained behavior. *Journal of Personality and Social Psychology*, *83*, 1239–1248.

Miyamoto, Y., Nisbett, R. E., & Masuda, T. (2006). Culture and the physical environment: Holistic versus analytic perceptual affordances. *Psychological Science*, *17*, 113–119.

Montreuil, A., & Bourhis, R. Y. (2001). Majority acculturation orientations toward "valued" and "devalued" immigrants. *Journal of Cross-Cultural Psychology*, *32*, 698–719.

Moon, V. (2001). *Growing up untouchable in India: A Dalit autobiography.* Lanham, MD: Rowman & Littlefield Publishers.

Morling, B., Kitayama, S., & Miyamoto, Y. (2002). Cultural practices emphasize influence in the United States and adjustment in Japan. *Personality and Social Psychology Bulletin*, *28*, 311–323.

Morris, M. W., Leung, K., Ames, D., & Lickel, B. (1999). Incorporating perspectives from inside and outside: Synergy between emic and etic research on culture and justice. *Academy of Management Review*, *24*, 781–796.

Morris, M. W., & Peng, K. (1994). Culture and cause: American and Chinese attributions for social and physical events. *Journal of Personality and Social Psychology*, *67*, 949–971.

Moscovici, S. (1988). Notes towards a description of social representations. *European Journal of Social Psychology*, *18*, 211–250.

Muramoto, Y. (2003). An indirect self-enhancement in relationship among Japanese. *Journal of Cross-Cultural Psychology*, *34*, 552–566.

Nemeth, C., & Kwan, J. (1985). Originality of word associations as a function of majority versus minority influence. *Social Psychology Quarterly*, *48*, 277–282.

Ng, S. H., & Bradac, J. (1993). *Power in language: Verbal communication and social influence.* Newbury Park, CA: Sage.

Niemann, Y. F., Romero, A. J., Arredondo, J., & Rodriguez, V. (1999). What does it mean to be "Mexican"? Social construction of an ethnic identity. *Hispanic Journal of Behavioral Sciences*, *21*, 47–60.

Nisbett, R. E. (1993). Violence and U. S. regional culture. *American Psychologist*, *48*, 441–449.

Nisbett, R. E. (2003). *The geography of thought: How Asians and westerners think differently.* New York: Free Press.

Nisbett, R. E., & Cohen, D. (1996). *Culture of honor: The psychology of violence in the South.* Boulder, CO: Westview.

Nisbett, R. E., Peng, K., Choi, I., & Norenzayan, A. (2001). Culture and systems of thought: Holistic versus analytic cognition. *Psychological Review*, *108*, 291–310.

Nisbett, R. E., & Wilson, T. D. (1977). Telling more than we can know: Verbal reports on mental processes. *Psychological Review*, *84*, 231–259.

Nishida, T. (1985). *A study of the history of Chinese criminal laws.* Peking: Peking University Press.

Niu, W., & Sternberg, R. J. (2002). Contemporary studies on the concept of creativity: The East and the West. *Journal of Creative Behavior*, *36*, 269–288.

Norenzayan, A., Choi, I., & Nisbett, R. E. (2002a). Cultural similarities and differences in social inference: Evidence from behavioral predictions and lay theories of behavior. *Personality and Social Psychology Bulletin*, *28*, 109–120.

Norenzayan, A., Smith, E. E., Kim, B. J., & Nisbett, R. E. (2002b). Cultural preferences for formal versus intuitive reasoning. *Cognitive Science*, *26*, 653–684.

Northrup, M. (2000). Multicultural Cinderella stories. *Book Links*, *9*, 1–4. http://www. ala.org/ ContentGroups/Book_Links/Multicultural_Cinderella_Stories.htm

Offermann, L. R., & Phan, L. U. (2002). Culturally intelligent leadership for a diverse world. In R. E. Riggio, S. E. Murphy, and & F. Pirazollo (Eds.), *Multiple intelligences and leadership. LEA's organization and management series* (pp. 187–214). Mahwah, NJ: Lawrence Erlbaum Associates, Inc.

Ohbuchi, K.-i., Fukushima, O., & Tedeschi, J. T. (1999). Cultural values in conflict management: Goal orientation, goal attainment, and tactical decision. *Journal of Cross-Cultural Psychology*, *30*, 51–71.

Oishi, S., & Diener, E. (2001). Goals, culture, and subjective well-being. *Personality and Social Psychology Bulletin*, *27*, 1674–1682.

Oishi, S., & Diener, E. (2003). Culture and well-being: The cycle of action, evaluation and decision. *Personality and Social Psychology Bulletin*, *29*, 939–949.

Oishi, S., Wyer, R. S. Jr., & Colcombe, S. J. (2000). Cultural variation in the use of current life satisfaction to predict the future. *Journal of Personality and Social Psychology*, *78*, 434–445.

O'Neil, D. (2001–2004). Patterns of subsistence: Classification of cultures based on sources and techniques of acquiring food and other necessities. Retrieved May 8, 2005, from http://anthro.palomar.edu/subsistence/default.htm

Oyserman, D. (1993). The lens of personhood: Viewing the self and others in a multicultural society. *Journal of Personality and Social Psychology*, *65*, 993–1009.

Oyserman, D., Coon, H. M., & Kemmelmeier, M. (2002). Rethinking individualism and collectivism: Evaluation of theoretical assumptions and meta-analyses. *Psychological Bulletin*, *128*, 3–72.

Oyserman, D., Sakamoto, I., & Lauffer, A. (1998). Cultural accommodation: Hybridity and the framing of social obligation. *Journal of Personality and Social Psychology*, *74*, 1606–1618.

Padilla, A. M., & Perez, W. (2003). Acculturation, social identity, and social cognition: A new perspective. *Hispanic Journal of Behavioral Sciences*, *25*, 35–55.

Pang, C. L. (2000). *Negotiating identity in contemporary Japan: The case of Kikokushijo.* London: Kegan Paul.

Parameswaran, R. (2002). Local culture in global media: Excavating colonial and material discourses in *National Geographic. Communication Theory*, *12*, 287–315.

Parish, S. (1991). The sacred mind: Newar cultural representations of mental life and the production of moral consciousness. *Ethos*, *19*, 313–351.

Parker, I. (1989). *The crisis in modern social psychology – and how to end it.* London: Routledge.

Parr, L. A., & de Waal, F. B. M. (1999). Visual kin recognition in chimpanzees. *Nature*, *399*, 647–648.

Paulhus, D. (1984). Two component models of socially desirable responding. *Journal of Personality and Social Psychology*, *46*, 598–609.

Payne, B. K. (2001). Prejudice and perception: The role of automatic and controlled processes in misperceiving a weapon. *Journal of Personality and Social Psychology*, *81*, 181–192.

Peng, K., & Nisbett, R. E. (1999). Culture, dialectics, and reasoning about contradiction. *American Psychologist*, *54*, 741–754.

Phinney, J. S., & Devich-Navarro, M. (1997). Variations in bicultural identification among African American and Mexican American adolescents. *Journal of Research on Adolescence*, *7*, 3–32.

Pickett, C. L., Bonner, B. L., & Coleman, J. M. (2002). Motivated self-stereotyping: Heightened assimilation and differentiation needs result in increased levels of positive and negative self-stereotyping. *Journal of Personality and Social Psychology*, *82*, 543–562.

Pickett, C. L., & Brewer, M. B. (2001). Assimilation and differentiation needs as motivational determinants of perceived ingroup and outgroup homogeneity. *Journal of Experimental Social Psychology*, 37, 341–348.

Pilkington, H., & Johnson, R. (2003). Relations of identity and power in global/local context. *Cultural Studies*, 6, 259–283.

Poortinga, Y. H. (2003). Coherence of culture and generalizability of data: Two questionable assumptions in cross-cultural psychology. In V. Murphy-Berman and J. J. Berman (Eds.), *Cross-cultural differences in perspectives on the self. Nebraska symposium on motivation* (Vol. 49, pp. 257–305). Lincoln, NE: University of Nebraska Press.

Popper, K. R. (1966). *The open society and its enemies: Vol 2. The high tide of prophecy: Hegel, Marx, and the aftermath* (5th ed.). London: Routledge.

Pratto, F. (1999). The puzzle of continuing inequality: Piecing together psychological, social, and cultural forces in social dominance theory. In M. P. Zanna (Ed.), *Advances in experimental social psychology* (Vol. 31, pp. 191–263). San Diego: Academic Press.

Pyszczynski, T., Greenberg, T., & Solomon, S. (1999). A dual-process model of defense against conscious and unconscious death-related thoughts: An extension of terror management theory. *Psychological Review*, 106, 835–845.

Pyszczynski, T., Greenberg, J., & Solomon, S. (2000). Proximal and distal defense: A new perspective on unconscious motivation. *Current Directions in Psychological Science*, 9, 156–160.

Qi, J., & Zhu, Y. (2002). Self-reference effect of Chinese college students. *Psychological Science*, 25, 275–278.

Reynolds, V. (1976). *The biology of human action*. Reading, UK: W. H. Freeman & Company.

Rhee, E., Uleman, J. S., Lee, H. K., & Roman, R. J. (1995). Spontaneous self-descriptions and ethnic identities in individualistic and collectivistic cultures. *Journal of Personality and Social Psychology*, 69, 142–152.

Richmond, A. H. (2002). Globalization: Implications for immigrants and refugees. *Ethnic and Racial Studies*, 25, 707–727.

Ritzer, G. (1993). *The McDonaldization of society*. Thousand Oaks, CA: Sage.

Roberson, D., Davidoff, J., & Shapiro, L. (2002). Squaring the circle: The cultural relativity of good shape. *Journal of Cognition and Culture*, 2, 29–51.

Roberson, D., Davies, I., & Davidoff, J. (2000). Color categories are not universal: Replications and new evidence from a stone-age culture. *Journal of Experimental Psychology: General*, 129, 369–398.

Robertson, R. (1992). *Globalization: Social theory and global culture*. London: Sage.

Robertson, R. (1995). Globalization: Time–space and homogeneity–heterogeneity. In M. Featherstone, S. Lash, & R. Robertson (Eds.), *Global modernities* (pp. 25–44). London: Sage.

Roccas, S., & Brewer, M. (2002). Social identity complexity. *Personality and Social Psychology Review*, 6, 88–106.

Rohner, R. P. (1984). Toward a conception culture for cross-cultural psychology. *Journal of Cross-Cultural Psychology*, 15, 111–138.

Ronen, S., & Shenkar, O. (1985). Clustering countries on attitudinal dimensions: A review and synthesis. *Academy of Management Review*, 10, 435–454.

Rosch, E. H. (1973). On the internal structure of perceptual and semantic categories. In T. E. Moore (Ed.), *Cognitive development and the acquisition of language* (pp. 254–279). New York: Academic Press.

Ross, M., Xun, W. Q. E., & Wilson, A. E. (2002). Language and the bicultural self. *Personality and Social Psychology Bulletin*, 28, 1040–1050.

Rothbaum, F., & Tsang, B. Y.-P. (1998). Lovesongs in the United States and China on the nature of romantic love. *Journal of Cross-Cultural Psychology, 29*, 306–319.

Rothbaum, F., & Xu, X. (1995). The theme of giving back to parents in Chinese and American songs. *Journal of Cross-Cultural Psychology, 26*, 698–713.

Rubin, D. C., & Kontis, T. C. (1983). A schema for common cents. *Memory and Cognition, 11*, 335–341.

Rubinstein, D. (2004). Language games and natural reactions. *Journal for the Theory of Social Behavior, 34*, 55–71.

Rudowicz, E., Lok, D., & Kitto, J. (1995). Use of the Torrance tests of creative thinking in an exploratory study of creativity in Hong Kong primary school children: A cross-cultural comparison. *International Journal of Psychology, 30*, 417–430.

Ryan, R. M., & Deci, E. L. (2000). Self-determination theory and the facilitation of intrinsic motivation, social development, and well-being. *American Psychologist, 55*, 68–78.

Ryder, A. G., Alden, L. E., & Paulhus, D. L. (2000). Is acculturation unidimensional or bidimensional? A head-to-head comparison in the prediction of personality, self-identity, and adjustment. *Journal of Personality and Social Psychology, 79*, 49–65.

Said, E. W. (1991). *Orientalism*. London: Penguin Books.

Salcedo, R. (2003). When the global meets the local at the mall. *American Behavioral Scientist, 46*, 1084–1103.

Salili, F. (1995). Explaining Chinese students' motivation and achievement. In M. L. Maehr & P. R. Pintrich (Eds.), *Advances in motivation and achievement* (Vol. 9, pp. 73–118). Greenwich, CT: JAI Press.

Salili, F., Chiu, C.-y., & Lai, S. (2001). The influence of culture and context on students' motivational orientation and performance. In F. Salili, C.-y. Chiu, & Y.-y. Hong (Eds.), *Student motivation: The culture and context of learning* (pp. 221–247). New York: Kluwer Academic/Plenum.

Sampson, E. E. (1977). Psychology and the American ideal. *Journal of Personality and Social Psychology, 35*, 767–782.

Sampson, E. E. (1978). Scientific paradigms and social values: Wanted – a scientific revolution. *Journal of Personality and Social Psychology, 36*, 1332–1343.

Sanchez-Burks, J., Lee, F., Choi, I., Nisbett, R., Zhao, S., & Koo, J. (2003). Conversing across cultures: East–West communication styles in work and nonwork contexts. *Journal of Personality and Social Psychology, 85*, 363–372.

Santana, K. (2003, August 12). MTV goes to Asia. *Yale Global*. Retrieved April 2, 2005, from http://www.globalpolicy.org/globaliz/cultural/2003/0812mtv.htm

Sassen, S. (1998). *Globalization and its discontents: Essays on the new mobility of people and money*. New York: The New Press.

Schaller, M., & Crandall, C. S. (2004). *The psychological foundation of culture*. Mahwah, NJ: Lawrence Erlbaum Associates, Inc.

Scherer, K. R., & Wallbott, H. G. (1994). Evidence of universality and cultural variation of differential emotion response patterning. *Journal of Personality and Social Psychology, 66*, 310–328.

Schimmack, U., Radhakrishnan, P., Oishi, S., Dzokoto, V., & Ahadi, S. (2002). Culture, personality, and subjective well-being: Integrating process models of life satisfaction. *Journal of Personality and Social Psychology, 82*, 582–593.

Schneider, D. (1968). *American kinship: A cultural account*. Englewood Cliffs, NJ: Prentice-Hall.

Schooler, J. W., & Engstler-Schooler, T. Y. (1990). Visual overshadowing of visual memories: Some things are better left unsaid. *Cognitive Psychology, 22*, 36–71.

Schwartz, S. H. (1992). Universals in the content and structure of values: Theoretical advances and empirical tests in 20 countries. In M. Zanna (Ed.), *Advances in experimental social psychology* (Vol. 25, pp. 1–66). New York: Academic Press.

Schwartz, S. H. (1994). Beyond individualism and collectivism: New cultural dimensions of values. In U. Kim, H. C. Triandis, C. Kagitcibasi, S.-C. Choi, & G. Yoon (Eds.), *Individualism and collectivism: Theory, method and applications* (pp. 85–122). Newbury Park, CA: Sage.

Schwartz, S. H., & Bilsky, W. (1987). Toward a universal psychological structure of human values. *Journal of Personality and Social Psychology, 53,* 550–562.

Schwimmer, B. (1995–2003). Kinship and social organization, an interactive tutorial. Retrieved December 22, 2003, from http://www.umanitoba.ca/faculties/arts/anthropology/kintitle.html

Searle, J. R. (1975). A taxonomy of illocutionary acts. In K. Gunderson (Ed.), *Language, mind, and knowledge* (pp. 125–139). Minneapolis, MN: University of Minnesota Press.

Sechrist, G. B., & Stangor, C. (2001). Perceived consensus influences intergroup behavior and stereotype accessibility. *Journal of Personality and Social Psychology, 80,* 645–654.

Sedikides, C., Gaertner, L., & Toguchi, Y. (2003). Pancultural self-enhancement. *Journal of Personality and Social Psychology, 84,* 60–79.

Segall, M. H., Lonner, W. J., & Berry, J. W. (1998). Cross-cultural psychology as a scholarly discipline: On the flowering of culture in behavioral research. *American Psychologist, 53,* 1101–1110.

Seligman, M. E. P. (1995). *The optimistic child.* Boston, MA: Houghton Mifflin.

Sera, M. D., Berge, D., & del Castillio Pintado, J. (1994). Grammatical and conceptual forces in the attribution of gender by English and Spanish speakers. *Child Development, 68,* 820–831.

Sera, M. D., Elieff, C., Forbes, J., Burch, M. C., Rodriguez, W., & Dubois, D. P. (2002). When language affects cognition and when it does not: An analysis of grammatical gender and classification. *Journal of Experimental Psychology: General, 131,* 377–397.

Sethi, S., Lepper, M. R., & Ross, L. (1999). Independence from whom? Interdependence with whom? Cultural perspectives on ingroups versus outgroups. In D. Miller & D. Prentice (Eds.), *Cultural divides.* New York: Sage.

Sham, M. (2002). Issues in the study of indigenous psychologies: Historical perspectives, cultural interdependence and institutional regulations. *Asian Journal of Social Psychology, 5,* 79–91.

Shatz, M., Diesendruck, G., Martinez-Beck, I., & Akar, D. (2003). The influence of language and socioeconomic status on children's understanding of false belief. *Developmental Psychology, 39,* 717–729.

Shore, B. (1996). *Culture in mind: Cognition, culture, and the problem of meaning.* New York: Oxford University Press.

Shore, B. (2002). Taking culture seriously. *Human development, 45,* 226–228.

Schubert, T. W., & Hafner, M. (2003). Contrast from social stereotypes in automatic behavior. *Journal of Experimental Social Psychology, 39,* 577–584.

Schultz, T. R., Schleifer, M., & Altman, I. (1981). Judgments of causation, responsibility, and punishment in case of harm-doing. *Canadian Journal of Behavioral Science, 13,* 238–253.

Shweder, R. A., & Miller, J. G. (1985). The social construction of the person: How is it possible? In K. Kenneth & K. E. Davis (Eds.), *The social construction of the person* (pp. 41–69). New York: Springer.

Sidanius, J., & Pratto, F. (1999). *Social dominance: An intergroup theory of social hierarchy and oppression.* New York: Cambridge University Press.

Simonton, D. K. (1975). Sociocultural context of individual creativity: A transhistorical time-series analysis. *Journal of Personality and Social Psychology, 32*, 1119–1133.

Simonton, D. K. (1997). Foreign influence and national development: The impact of open milieus on Japanese civilization. *Journal of Personality and Social Psychology, 72*, 86–94.

Simonton, D. K. (2000). Creativity: Cognitive, personal, developmental, and social aspects. *American Psychologist, 55*, 151–158.

Sinaceur, M., Heath, C., & Cole, S. (in press). Emotional and deliberative reactions to a public crisis: Mad Cow Disease in France. *Psychological Science.*

Singh, D. (1993). Adaptive significance of female physical attractiveness: Role of waist-to-hip ratio. *Journal of Personality and Social Psychology, 65*, 293–307.

Singh, P. N., Huang, S. C., & Thompson, G. G. (1962). A comparative study of selected attitudes, values, and personality characteristics of American, Chinese, and Indian students. *Journal of Social Psychology, 57*, 123–132.

Solomon, S., Greenberg, J., & Pyszczynski, T. (1991). A terror management theory of social behavior: The psychological functions of self-esteem and cultural worldview. In L. Berkowitz (Ed.), *Advances in experimental social psychology* (Vol. 24, pp. 93–159). San Diego, CA: Academic Press.

Sparrow, L. M. (2000). Beyond multicultural man: Complexities of identity. *International Journal of Intercultural Relations, 24*, 173–201.

Spears, R., Gordijn, E., Dijksterhuis, A., & Stapel, D. A. (2004). Reaction in action: Intergroup contrast in automatic behavior. *Personality and Social Psychology Bulletin, 30*, 605–616.

Sperber, D. (1996). *Explaining culture: A naturalistic approach.* Cambridge, MA: Blackwell.

Sprott, J. E. (1994). "Symbolic ethnicity" and Alaska natives of mixed ancestry living in Anchorage: Enduring group or a sign of impending assimilation? *Human Organization, 53*, 311–322.

Steele, C. (1997). A threat in the air: How stereotypes shape intellectual identity and performance. *American Psychologist, 52*, 613–629.

Steele, C. M., & Aronson, J. (1995). Stereotype threat and the intellectual test performance of African Americans. *Journal of Personality and Social Psychology, 69*, 797–811.

Sternberg, R. J., & Smith, C. (1985). Social intelligence and decoding skills in nonverbal intelligence. *Social Cognition, 3*, 168–192.

Stewart, S. M., Bond, M. H., Deeds, O., & Chung, S. F. (1999). Intergenerational patterns of values and autonomy expectations in cultures of relatedness and separateness. *Journal of Cross-Cultural Psychology, 30*, 575–593.

Su, S. K., Chiu, C.-y., Hong, Y.-y., Leung, K., Peng, K., & Morris, M. W. (1999). Self organization and social organization: American and Chinese constructions. In T. R. Tyler, R. Kramer, & O. John (Eds.), *The psychology of the social self* (pp. 193–222). Mahwah, NJ: Lawrence Erlbaum Associates, Inc.

Sue, D. W., Bingham, R. P., Porche-Burke, L., & Vasquez, M. (1999). The diversification of psychology: A multicultural revolution. *American Psychologist, 54*, 1061–1069.

Suh, E. M. (1999). *Self and the use of emotion information: Joining culture, personality, and situational influence.* Unpublished manuscript.

Suh, E. M. (2002). Culture, identity consistency, and subjective well-being. *Journal of Personality and Social Psychology, 83*, 1378–1391.

Suh, E. M., Diener, E., Oishi, S., & Triandis, H. C. (1998). The shifting basis of life satisfaction judgments across cultures: Emotions versus norms. *Journal of Personality and Social Psychology, 74*, 482–493.

Suinn, R. M., Ahuna, C., & Khoo, G. (1992). The Suinn–Lew Asian Self-Identity Acculturation Scale: Concurrent and factorial validation. *Educational and Psychological Measurement, 52*, 1041–1046.

Sundberg, N. D., Rohila, P. K., & Tyler, L. E. (1970). Values of Indian and American adolescents. *Journal of Personality and Social Psychology, 16*, 374–397.

Sussman, N. M. (2000). The dynamic nature of cultural identity throughout cultural transitions: Why home is not so sweet. *Personality and Social Psychology Review, 4*, 355–373.

Sussman, N. N., & Rosenfeld, H. M. (1982). Influence of culture, language, and sex on conversational distance. *Journal of Personality and Social Psychology, 42*, 66–74.

Suter, R. (2001, December 11). How culture defines role of leadership: Korea–Switzerland comparison. *The Korea Herald*.

Suzuki, N., & Yamagishi, T. (2004, July). *Socio-institutional basis of holistic cognition*. Poster presented at the Mind, Culture and Evolution Conference, Vancouver, Canada.

Tafarodi, R. W., Lang, J. M., & Smith, A. J. (1999). Self-esteem and the cultural trade-off: Evidence for the role of individualism–collectivism. *Journal of Cross-Cultural Psychology, 30*, 620–640.

Tafarodi, R. W., & Swann, W. B. Jr. (1996). Individualism–collectivism and global self-esteem: Evidence for a cultural trade-off. *Journal of Cross-Cultural Psychology, 27*, 651–672.

Taifel, H., & Turner, J. C. (1979). The social identity theory of intergroup behavior. In W. G. Austin & S. Worchel (Eds.), *Psychology of intergroup relations* (pp. 94–109). Chicago: Nelson-Hall.

Takano, Y., & Osaka, E. (1999). An unsupported common view: Comparing Japan and the U.S. on individualism/collectivism. *Asian Journal of Social Psychology, 2*, 311–341.

Takata, T. (2003). Self-enhancement and self-criticism in Japanese culture: An experimental analysis. *Journal of Cross-Cultural Psychology, 34*, 542–551.

Takenaka, A. (1999). Transnational community and its ethnic consequences: The return migration and the transformation of ethnicity of Japanese Peruvians. *American Behavioral Scientist, 42*, 1459–1474.

Tao, V., & Hong, Y.-y. (2000). A meaning system approach to Chinese students' achievement goals. *Journal of Psychology in the Chinese Societies, 1*, 13–38.

Tetlock, P. E. (2002). Deviant functionalist metaphors for judgment and choice: The intuitive politician, theologian, and prosecutor. *Psychological Review, 109*, 451–471.

Thompson, C. J., & Arsel, Z. (2004). The Starbucks brandscape and consumers' (anticorporate) experiences of glocalization. *Journal of Consumer Research, 2004*, 632–642.

Thorndike, E. L. (1920). Intelligence and its uses. *Harper's Magazine, 140*, 227–235.

Tobin, J. J., Wu, D. Y. H., & Davidson, D. H. (1989). *Preschool in three cultures: Japan, China and the United States*. New Haven, CT: Yale University Press.

Tomasello, M. (1996). Do apes age? In C. Heyes & B. Galef (Eds.), *Social learning in animals: The roots of culture* (pp. 319–346). New York: Academic Press.

Tomasello, M. (1999). The human adaptation for culture. *Annual Review of Anthropology, 28*, 509–529.

Tomasello, M. (2001). Cultural transmission: A view from chimpanzees and human infants. *Journal of Cross-Cultural Psychology, 32*, 135–146.

Tong, Y., & Chiu, C.-y. (2002). Implicit theories and evaluation-based organization of impressions: An application of the memory search paradigm. *Personality and Social Psychology Bulletin, 28*, 1518–1527.

Tong, Y., Hong, Y.-y., Lee, S., & Chiu, C.-y. (1999). Language as a carrier of social identity. *International Journal of Intercultural Relations, 23*, 281–296.

Trafimow, D., Silverman, E. S., Fan, R. M.-t., & Law, J. S. F. (1997). The effects of language and priming on the relative accessibility of the private self and the collective self. *Journal of Cross-Cultural Psychology, 28*, 107–123.

Trafimow, D., Triandis, H. C., & Goto, S. G. (1991). Some tests of the distinction between the private self and the collective self. *Journal of Personality and Social Psychology, 60,* 649–655.

Triandis, H. C. (1964). Cultural influences upon cognitive processes. In L. Berkowitz (Ed.), *Advances in experimental social psychology* (Vol. 1, pp. 1–48). New York: Academic Press.

Triandis, H. C. (1980). Introduction to handbook of cross-cultural psychology. In H. C. Triandis & W. W. Lambert (Eds.), *Handbook of cross-cultural psychology* (Vol. 1, pp. 1–14). Boston, MA: Allyn & Bacon.

Triandis, H. C. (1989). The self and social behavior in differing cultural contexts. *Psychological Review, 96,* 506–520.

Triandis, H. C. (1990). Cross-cultural studies of individualism and collectivism. In J. Berman (Ed.), *Nebraska symposium on motivation 1989* (pp. 44–133). Lincoln, NE: University of Nebraska Press.

Triandis, H. C. (1994). *Culture and social behavior.* New York: McGraw-Hill.

Triandis, H. C. (1995). *Individualism and collectivism.* Boulder, CO: Westview Press.

Triandis, H. C. (1996). The psychological measurement of cultural syndromes. *American Psychologist, 51,* 407–415.

Triandis, H. C. (2000). Dialectics between cultural and cross-cultural psychology. *Asian Journal of Social Psychology, 3,* 185–197.

Triandis, H. C. (2004). Dimensions of culture beyond Hofstede. In H. Vinken, J. Soeters, & P. Ester (Eds.), *Comparing cultures: Dimensions of culture in a comparative perspective.* Leiden, The Netherlands: Brill Publishers.

Triandis, H. C., Bontempo, R., Villareal, M. J., & Asai, M. L. (1988). Individualism and collectivism: Cross-cultural perspective on self–group relationships. *Journal of Personality and Social Psychology, 54,* 323–338.

Triandis, H. C., Lambert, W. W., Berry, J. W., Lonner, W. J., Heron, A., Brislin, R., & Draguns, J. (Eds.) (1980–1981). *Handbook of cross-cultural psychology* (6 Vols.). Boston, MA: Allyn & Bacon.

Triandis, H. C., Leung, K., Villareal, M. J., & Clack, F. U. (1985). Allocentric and idiocentric tendencies: Convergent and discriminant validation. *Journal of Research in Personality, 19,* 395–415.

Triandis, H. C., McCusker, C., & Hui, C.-h. (1990). Multimethod probes of individualism and collectivism. *Journal of Personality and Social Psychology, 59,* 1006–1020.

Tsai, J. L., Ying, Y., & Lee, P. A. (2000). The meaning of "being Chinese" and "being American": Variation among Chinese American young adults. *Journal of Cross-Cultural Psychology, 31,* 302–332.

Tse, P., & Cavanagh, P. (2000). Chinese and Americans see opposite apparent motion in a Chinese character. *Cognition, 74,* B27–B32.

Tsuda, T. (2001). When identities become modern: Japanese emigration to Brazil and the global contextualization of identity. *Ethnic and Racial Studies, 24,* 412–432.

Tsuda, T. (2003). *Strangers in the ethnic homeland: Japanese Brazilian return migration in transnational perspective.* New York: Columbia University Press.

Turban, E., & Aronson, J. (1988). *Decision support systems and intelligent systems.* Upper Saddle River, NJ: Prentice-Hall.

Turner, J. C., Hogg, M. A., Oakes, P. J., Reicher, S. D., & Wetherell, M. S. (1987). *Rediscovering the social group: A self-categorization theory.* Oxford, UK: Blackwell.

Turner, J. C., Oakes, P. J., Haslam, S. A., & McGarty, C. (1994). Self and collective: Cognition and social context. *Personality and Social Psychology Bulletin, 20,* 454–463.

Tzeng, O. C. S., & Henderson, M. M. (1999). Objective and subjective cultural relationships related to industrial modernization and social progress. *International Journal of Intercultural Relations, 23,* 411–445.

U. S. & Foreign Commercial Service & U. S. Department of State. (2004). Promising market for MBA and EMBA education in East China. Retrieved April 2, 2005, from http://strategis.ic.gc.ca/epic/internet/inimr-ri.nsf/en/gr127226e.html

Uskul, A. K., Hynie, M., & Lalonde, R. N. (2004). Interdependence as a mediator between culture and interpersonal closeness for Euro-Canadians and Turks. *Journal of Cross-cultural Psychology, 35*, 174–191.

Van Baaren, R. B., Maddux, W. W., Chartrand, T., de Bouter, C., & van Knippenberg, A. (2003). It takes two to mimic: Behavioral consequences of self-construals. *Journal of Personality and Social Psychology, 84*, 1093–1102.

Vandello, J. A., & Cohen, D. (1999). Patterns of individualism and collectivism across the United States. *Journal of Personality and Social Psychology, 77*, 279–292.

Vandello, J. A., & Cohen, D. (2003). Male honor and female infidelity: Implicit cultural scripts that perpetuate domestic violence. *Journal of Personality and Social Psychology, 84*, 997–1010.

Van de Vijver, F., & Leung, K. (1997). *Methods and data analysis for cross-cultural research.* Thousand Oaks, CA: Sage.

van Schaik, C. P., Ancrenaz, M., Borgen, G., Galdikas, B., Knott, C. D., Singleton, I., Suzuki, A., Utami, S. S., & Merrill, M. (2003). Orangutan cultures and the evolution of material culture. *Science, 299*, 102–105.

van Strien, P. J. (1997). The American "colonization" of northwest European social psychology after World War II. *Journal of the History of the Behavioral Sciences, 33*, 349–363.

Vekua, A., Lordkipanidze, D., Rightmire, G. P., Agusti, J., Ferring, R., Majsuradze, G., Mouskhelishvili, A., Nioradze, M., de Leon, M. P., Tappen, M., Tvalchrelidze, M., & Zollikofer, C. (2002). A new skull of early homo from Dmanisi, Georgia. *Science, 297*, 85–89.

Verkuyten, M., & de Wolf, A. (2002). Being, feeling and doing: Discourses and ethnic self-definitions among minority group members. *Culture and Psychology, 8*, 371–399.

Verkuyten, M., & Pouliasi, K. (2002). Biculturalism among older children: Cultural frame switching, attributions, self-identification, and attitudes. *Journal of Cross-Cultural Psychology, 33*, 596–609.

Visalberghi, E., & Fragaszy, D. M. (1990). Food washing behavior in tufted capuchin monkeys, *Cebus apella*, and crabeating macaques, *Nacaca fascicularis*. *Animal Behavior, 40*, 829–836.

Vygotsky, L. S. (1978). *Mind in society: The development of higher psychological processes.* Cambridge, MA: Harvard University Press.

Wagar, B., & Cohen, D. (2003). Culture, memory, and the self: An analysis of the personal and collective self in long-term memory. *Journal of Experimental Social Psychology, 39*, 468–475.

Walton, M. (2003, January 2). Study Reveals Complex Orangutan Culture. Retrieved December 27, 2003, from http://www.cnn.com/2003/TECH/science/01/02/coolsc.orangutans

Wan, C., Chiu, C.-y., Peng, S., & Tam, K.-p. (2004a). *Measuring cultures through intersubjective norms: Implications for differentiation of multiple identities.* Manuscript submitted for publication.

Wan, C., Chiu, C.-y., Tam, K.-p., Lee, S.-l., Lau, I., & Peng, S. (2004b). *Consensus on consensus: The role of intersubjective value consensus in cultural identification.* Manuscript submitted for publication.

Wan, W. W.-n., & Chiu, C.-y. (2002). Effects of novel conceptual combination on creativity. *Journal of Creative Behavior, 36*, 227–240.

Wang, Q. (2001). Culture effects on adults' earliest childhood recollection and self-description: Implications for the relation between memory and the self. *Journal of Personality and Social Psychology, 81*, 220–233.

Wang, Q. (2004). The emergence of cultural self-constructs: Autobiographical memory and self-description in European American and Chinese children. *Developmental Psychology, 40*, 3–15.

Wang, Y., Wiley, A., & Chiu, C.-y. (in press). Independence-supportive praise versus interdependence promoting praise. *International Journal of Behavioral Development.*

Ward, T. B. (1994). Structured imagination: The role of conceptual structure in exemplar generation. *Cognitive Psychology, 27*, 1–40.

Ward, T. B., Patterson, M. J., Sifonis, C. M., Dodds, R. A., & Saunders, K. N. (2002). The role of graded category structure in imaginative thought. *Memory and Cognition, 30*, 199–216.

Watson, O. M. (1970). *Proxemic behavior: A cross-cultural study.* The Hague: Mouton.

Weber, M. (1904/1958). *The Protestant ethic and the spirit of capitalism.* (T. Parsons, Trans.). New York: Charles Scribner's Sons. (Reprint)

Webster, D. M., & Kruglanski, A. W. (1994). Individual differences in need for cognitive closure. *Journal of Personality and Social Psychology, 67*, 1049–1062.

Weisz, J. R., Rothbaum, F. M., & Blackburn, T. C. (1984). Standing out and standing in: The psychology of control in America and Japan. *American Psychologist, 39*, 955–969.

Weldon, E., & Jehn, K. A. (1995). Examining cross-cultural differences in conflict management behavior: A strategy for future research. *International Journal of Conflict Management, 6*, 387–403.

White, K., & Lehman, D. R. (2005). Culture and social comparison seeking: The role of self-motives. *Personality and Social Psychology Bulletin, 31*, 232–242.

White, M. (1990). *Ethnic options: Choosing identities in America.* Berkeley, CA: University of California Press.

Whiten, A., Goodall, J., McGrew, W. C., Nishida, T., Reynolds, V., Sugiyama, Y., Tutin, C. E. G., Wrangham, R. W., & Boesch, C. (1999). Cultures in chimpanzees. *Nature, 399*, 682–685.

Whorf, B. L. (1956). *Language, thought, and reality: Selected writings of Benjamin Lee Whorf.* New York: Wiley.

Wilkes-Gibbs, D., & Kim, P. H. (1991). *Discourse influences on memory for visual forms.* Paper presented at the 1991 meeting of the Psychonomic Society, San Francisco, CA.

Wong, K. (2003, November). Stranger in a new land. *Scientific American, 289*, 74–83.

Wong, R. Y., & Hong, Y. (2005). Dynamic influences of culture on cooperation in the prisoner's dilemma. *Psychological Science, 16*, 429–434.

World Bank Group. (2004). *Beyond economic growth: An introduction to sustainable development* (2nd ed.). Retrieved April 2, 2005, from http://www.worldbank.org/depweb/beyond/beyond.htm

World Development Indicators Database. (2004). *China country profile.* Retrieved April 2, 2005, from http://devdata.worldbank.org/external/CPProfile.asp?SelectedCountry=CHN&CCODE=CHN&CNAME=China&PTYPE=CP

Worldwatch Institute. (2004, January 7). *State of the world 2004: Consumption by the numbers.* Retrieved April 2, 2005, from http://www.worldwatch.org/press/news/2004/01/07/

Wrong, D. H. (1961). The oversocialized conception of man in modern sociology. *American Sociological Review, 26*, 183–193.

Wyer, R. S. Jr. (2004). *Social comprehension and judgment: The role of situated models, narratives, and implicit theories.* Mahwah, NJ: Lawrence Erlbaum Associates, Inc.

Yamada, A., & Singelis, T. M. (1999). Biculturalism and self-construal. *International Journal of Intercultural Relations, 23,* 697–709.

Yamagishi, T., & Takahashi, N. (1994). Evolution of norms without metanorms. In U. Shulz, W. Albers, & U. Mueller (Eds.), *Social dilemmas and cooperation* (pp. 311–326). Berlin, Germany: Springer.

Yang, C. F., & Hui, C. H. (1986). Equal distribution of reward and feeling of unfairness. *Chinese Journal of Psychology, 28,* 61–71.

Yang, H., & Zhu, Y. (2004). The self and retrieval-induced forgetting, *Acta Psychologica Sinica, 36,* 154–159.

Yang, K. S. (2000). Monocultural and cross-cultural indigenous approaches: The royal road to the development of a balanced global psychology. *Asian Journal of Social Psychology, 3,* 241–263.

Yang, K. S. (2003). Beyond Maslow's culture-bound linear theory: A preliminary statement of the double-Y model of basic human needs. In V. Murphy-Berman & J. J. Berman (Eds.), *Cultural differences in perspectives on the self* (pp. 175–255). Lincoln, NE: University of Nebraska Press.

Yang, K. S., & Bond, M. H. (1980). Ethnic affirmation by Chinese bilinguals. *Journal of Cross-Cultural Psychology, 11,* 411–425.

Yang, K. S., & Ho, D. Y. F. (1988). The role of yuan in Chinese social life: A conceptual and empirical analysis. In A. C. Paranjpe, D. Y. F. Ho, & R. W. Rieber (Eds.), *Asian contributions to psychology* (pp. 263–281). New York: Praeger.

Yeh, K.-h. (1997). Changes in the Taiwan people's concept of filial piety. In L. Y. Chang, Y. H. Liu, & F. C. Wang (Eds.), *Taiwanese society in 1990s* (pp. 171–214). Taipei: Academia Sinica.

Yeh, K.-h. (2002). Is living with elderly parents still a filial obligation for Chinese people? *Journal of Psychology in Chinese Societies, 3,* 61–84.

Yeh, K.-h. (2003). The beneficial and harmful effects of filial piety: An integrative analysis. In K.-s. Yang, K.-k. Hwang, P. B. Pederson, & I. Daibo (Eds.), *Progress in Asian social psychology: Conceptual and empirical contributions* (pp. 67–82). New York: Praeger.

Yeh, K.-h., & Bedford, O. (2003). A test of the dual filial piety model. *Asian Journal of Social Psychology, 6,* 215–228.

Yoon, K. (2003). Retraditionalizing the mobile: Young people's sociality and mobile phone. *Cultural Studies, 6,* 327–343.

Young, M. Y., & Gardner, R. C. (1990). Modes of acculturation and second language proficiency. *Canadian Journal of Behavioral Science, 22,* 59–71.

Young, S. B. (1981). The concept of justice in pre-imperial China. In R. W. Wilson, S. L. Greenblat, & A. A. Wilson (Eds.), *Moral behavior in Chinese society* (pp. 38–71). New York: Praeger.

Yu, A.-b., & Yang, K.-s. (1994). The nature of achievement motivation in collectivist societies. In U. Kim, H. C. Triandis, C. Kagitcibasi, G. Choi, & G. Yoon (Eds.), *Individualism and collectivism: Theory, method and applications* (pp. 239–266). Thousand Oaks, CA: Sage.

Yue, X., & Ng, S. H. (1999). Filial obligations and expectations in China: Current views from young and old people in Beijing. *Asian Journal of Social Psychology, 2,* 215–226.

Yuki, M. (2003). Intergroup comparison versus intragroup relationships: A cross-cultural examination of social identity theory in North American and East Asian cultural contexts. *Social Psychology Quarterly, 66,* 166–183.

Yuki, M., Maddux, W. W., Brewer, M. B., & Takemura, K. (2005). Cross-cultural differences in relationship- and group-based trust. *Social and Personality Bulletin, 31,* 48–62.

Zaharna, R. S. (1989). Self-shock: The double-binding challenge of identity. *International Journal of Intercultural Relations, 13,* 501–525.

Zemba, Y., Young, M. J., & Morris, M. W. (2003). *Intuitive logics for blaming executives for organizational harms: How Japanese differ from Americans.* Unpublished manuscript.

Zenith International (2003, December 12). Soft drinks set to become world's leading beverage sector. Retrieved April 2, 2005, from http://www. zenithinternational.com/pr/pr.cfm? ContentID=103

Zhang, J. (1984). Preliminary research on the characteristics of the feudal judicial system of China. *Theses of Law of China, 1,* 245–266.

Zhang, J., & Shavitt, S. (2003). Cultural values in advertisements to the Chinese X-generation. *Journal of Advertising, 32,* 23–33.

Zhu, Y., & Huo, Y. (2001, August). *Effects of cultural meaning system activation on memory by self.* Paper presented at the International Conference of Cognitive Science. Beijing, China.

Zhu, Y., & Zhang, L. (2002). An experimental study on the self-reference effect. *Science in China (Series C), 45,* 121–128.

Author Index

Subject Index